Ecumenism and History

Studies in Honour of John H.Y. Briggs

Professor John H.Y. Briggs, MA, FSA, FRHistS

(Photograph courtesy of *The Baptist Times*)

Ecumenism and History

Studies in Honour of John H.Y. Briggs

Edited by

Anthony R. Cross

Foreword by Georges Lemopoulos

paternoster
press

Copyright © Anthony R. Cross and the Contributors 2002

First published 2002 by Paternoster Press

Paternoster Press is an imprint of Paternoster Publishing
P.O. Box 300, Carlisle, Cumbria, CA3 0QS, U.K.
and P.O. Box 1047, Waynesboro, GA 30830–2047, U.S.A

08 07 06 05 04 03 02   8 7 6 5 4 3 2

The right of Anthony R. Cross to be identified as the Editor of this Work
has been asserted by him in accordance with the Copyright, Designs
and Patents Act 1988

*All rights reserved. No part of this publication may be reproduced, stored in a retrieval system, or transmitted in any form by any means, electronic, mechanical, photocopying, recording or otherwise, without the prior permission of the publisher or a license permitting restricted copying. In the UK such licenses are issued by the Copyright Licensing Agency,
90 Tottenham Court Road, London W1P 9HE.*

British Library Cataloguing in Publication Data
A catalogue record for this book is available from the British Library

ISBN 1-84227-135-0

Typeset by A.R. Cross
Printed and bound in Great Britain
for Paternoster Publishing
by Nottingham Alpha Graphics

Contributors

David Bebbington is Professor of History at the University of Stirling, Scotland.

William H. Brackney is Professor of Religion and Chair of the Department of Religion, Baylor University, Texas, USA. He is also Director of the Program in Baptist Studies.

Clyde Binfield is Professor Associate in History, University of Sheffield, Sheffield, England.

Faith Bowers is Sub-Editor of the *Baptist Quarterly* and a member of Bloomsbury Central Baptist Church, London, England.

Keith W. Clements is General Secretary of the Conference of European Churches, Geneva, Switzerland.

Anthony R. Cross is an Editorial Consultant for Paternoster Press, Carlisle, England.

Paul S. Fiddes is Principal of Regent's Park College, University of Oxford, England, and University Research Lecturer in Theology.

Brian Haymes is Minister of Bloomsbury Central Baptist Church, London, England.

David J. Jeremy is Professor in the Centre for Business History, Manchester Metropolitan University, Manchester, England.

Georges Lemopoulos is Deputy General Secretary of the World Council of Churches, Geneva, Switzerland.

Herbert B. McGonigle is Principal of the Nazarene Theological College, Didsbury, Manchester, England, and the Senior Lecturer in Historical Theology and Wesley Studies.

John E. Morgan-Wynne was Tutor in New Testament, Regent's Park College, Oxford 1965–87, Principal, Bristol Baptist College 1987–93, and Minister of Ilkley Baptist Church, Ilkley, England, 1994–2002.

Richard V. Pierard is Professor of History, Emeritus, Indiana State University, and Scholar in Residence and Adjunct Professor, Gordon College, Wenham, Massachusetts, USA. In 2002 he was Visiting Professor, University of Otago, New Zealand.

Ian M. Randall is Director of Baptist and Anabaptist Studies, International Baptist Theological Seminary, Prague, Czech Republic, and Lecturer in Church History, Spurgeon's College, London, England.

Marjorie Reeves is Honorary Fellow, St Anne's and St Hugh's Colleges, Oxford, England.

Keith Robbins is Vice-Chancellor of the University of Wales, Lampeter, Wales.

Brian Stanley is Henry Martyn Lecturer in Mission Studies in the Cambridge Theological Federation and Fellow of St Edmund's College, University of Cambridge, England.

Haddon Willmer is Emeritus Professor of Theology at the University of Leeds, England, and Research Tutor at the Oxford Centre for Mission Studies.

Contents

Foreword..xi
Georges Lemopoulos

Introduction..xxi

John H.Y. Briggs MA, FSA, FRHistS: An Appreciation 1
Faith Bowers

PART ONE: ECUMENISM AND HISTORY

Chapter 1
Baptism, Christology and the Creeds in the Early Church:
Implications for Ecumenical Dialogue..23
Anthony R. Cross

Chapter 2
John Wesley — Exemplar of the Catholic Spirit 50
Herbert B. McGonigle

Chapter 3
Worlds of Ambiguity: The YMCA, the YWCA, the WSCF
and Mission, Nationalism, Ecumenism and the Explosion
of Empire...69
J.C.G. Binfield

Chapter 4
Edinburgh 1910 and the *Oikoumene* 89
Brian Stanley

Chapter 5
The Christian World Communions: Denominational Ecumenism
on a Global Scale 106
Richard V. Pierard

Chapter 6
Church and Salvation: A Comparative Study of Free Church and
Orthodox Thinking..120
Paul S. Fiddes

Chapter 7
Disciples and Baptists: A Study in Comparative Polities..................149
William H. Brackney

Chapter 8
Making Too Little and Too Much of Baptism? 175
Brian Haymes

PART TWO: HISTORY

Chapter 9
Pure Clay and Time's Mud: Biography as History........................193
Keith W. Clements

Chapter 10
Writing Local Church History...208
Haddon Willmer

Chapter 11
Attitudes towards Erring Brothers and Sisters in Early Christianity
as Reflected in the New Testament...225
John E. Morgan-Wynne

Chapter 12
The Sociology of Hymns in Western Christianity 254
Marjorie Reeves

Chapter 13
The Democratization of British Christianity: The Baptist Case
1770–1870..265
D.W. Bebbington

Chapter 14
'Every Apostolic Church a Mission Society': European Baptist
Origins and Identity...281
Ian M. Randall

Chapter 15
Business Men as Preachers among Methodists in the Early
Twentieth Century..302
David J. Jeremy

Chapter 16
Britain, World History, Christianity and the Millennium..................326
Keith G. Robbins

Select Publications of John H.Y. Briggs..343

Index..351

Foreword

Georges Lemopoulos

It is a real pleasure and a privilege for me to contribute a Foreword to this volume in honour of John Briggs, the distinguished church historian, the committed ecumenist, the friend and companion.

I understand the aim of the present collection of essays to be an expression of gratitude for what John Briggs, his life and his work, mean to many of us. Indeed, the collection attempts to confirm that the imprints left by this learned scholar and devout ecumenist are palpable in a considerable number of fields. It also attests to the fact that the wide circle of those who value the person—a person of faith and commitment to his faith, a person of openness and sincere dedication to dialogue, a person with precious advice and a generous smile in all circumstances—transcends geographical, cultural, and confessional borders.

Devoted to academic life, the church, and the ecumenical movement, John Briggs is treasured by his colleagues and friends for more than one reason. One would honour the professor who taught for many years with passion for his subject and love for his students. Another would commend the lay person who faithfully served his community as a dedicated church worker. Yet another would praise the leading British Baptist who helped his church, as well as other churches in his country and his continent, to see ways forward in responding to their common calling.

Having met John Briggs and worked with him for more than a decade mainly in the circles of the World Council of Churches (WCC), I will offer here a few personal reflections in an attempt to depict the historian of the ecumenical movement, the evangelical, the bridge-builder, and the man of the institution. These attributes—only a few among many others—characterize the person. At the same time, they exceed the limits of a simple personal characteristic, of a mere personal contribution or achievement, and point clearly to broad areas of particular importance for churches' life and witness today. They rather represent an exciting blend of history, ecumenism, and personal commitment!

The Historian

John Briggs' name will soon appear as one of the three editors of the third volume of the *History of the Ecumenical Movement*. This volume will cover the last part of the twentieth century, namely the years from the fourth assembly of the WCC in Uppsala (1968) to the eighth assembly in Harare (1998).

It is generally admitted by historians of the ecumenical movement that while the first half of the century could be seen as the period of the genesis and formation of the WCC (1910–48), the subsequent years (1948–68) could be considered as the period of consolidation and expansion of the fellowship of churches on their way towards *koinonia* in faith, life and witness. A few facts speak for themselves: the number of WCC member churches has doubled since the first assembly in Amsterdam (1948); nearly two-thirds of member churches come now from the South making the council more truly a world body; new ecumenical organizations at local, national, and regional levels have created a worldwide ecumenical network of which the WCC is an integral part.

This being the case, after an era of successive achievements and justified euphoria, the last quarter of the twentieth century has constituted a period during which the fellowship of churches has been profoundly tested. Unfortunately this has also been a period during which many tensions have been revealed in the relationship between the churches and the world, as well as between churches themselves.

It was during this period that the growing pollution of the environment, the population explosion, the world monetary crisis, the world food crisis also affecting other commodities, the widening gap between rich and poor within and between nations, have converged to create a situation which threaten the very future of the international community. It was also during this period that the economic system which had dominated the world for the past two hundred years began breaking down, while the ideological system which has dominated part of the world for several decades has come to an end. It was during this period that the joy over the liberation from all sorts of oppression was succeeded by the pain which the growing waves of violence had caused in the lives of individuals, communities, churches and peoples.

In many cases, churches have simply followed or imitated the world. Their relationships reflected very often and to a large degree the antagonisms and tensions prevailing in the secular world of nations. Therefore, severe tests were posed to the intention of the churches—and of the WCC, as a fellowship of churches—to witness credibly to the gospel of reconciliation in the midst of a tragically divided world.

Foreword

In other cases, churches have courageously raised their voices and opposed acts of injustice. They refused to accept images of the others as enemies. They brought hope into the lives of people and renewal in the lives of entire communities. They built bridges across political, ideological or religious divides. Obviously, this situation created confusion in the minds of simple people, as it did for the task of historians. How to analyze and report such a complex, often controversial, situation? How to assess the successive 'crises' that, towards the end of the twentieth century, marked the ecumenical movement as a whole and the WCC as a fellowship of churches? Because, when churches committed themselves to stand against racism, there has been an almost unprecedented controversy dividing Christians and churches; when churches wanted to respond to challenges raised by ethical issues, the danger of new doctrinal divisions and new confessional confrontations have surfaced again; when churches wanted to celebrate together the fall of the Berlin Wall and the end of the Cold War, they soon discovered that their respective reading of history was radically different and that their expectations for the future were conflicting rather than like-minded. The controversies which have arisen over positions the WCC had taken on social, political and ethical issues made it clear that the WCC was a fellowship of churches with frequently conflicting interests, commitments and loyalties.

John Briggs, the historian, has been among those who faced these ecumenical controversies and historical dilemmas head on and with open eyes, deploying all his skills and resources in order to understand and interpret the facts in their full reality. John Briggs, the ecumenist, committed himself to remain with those who struggled to be free to discover and attempt new ways of overcoming all obstacles through co-operation rather than in confrontation. Surely this happened because John Briggs, the man of faith, did not seek his own security in evading the issues and pursuing his own personal interests by refusing to be involved, by retreating into a world of self-indulgence or of religious escape.

This was John Briggs' response indicating a way of faith, hope and love. A response openly and courageously shared with fellow evangelicals and Orthodox friends. A response that tried to do justice to people in North and South, in East and West, as they have struggled to witness to their faith. A response always grounded on the centrality of our common faith in Jesus Christ, the common Lord and Saviour.

John Briggs would constantly join all those who insisted that the essence of good news is that God was reconciling the world unto himself and has now called us to a ministry of reconciliation: a ministry that pertains both to reconciliation between God and humans, as well as to reconciliation between individuals and groups alienated from each other.

The essence of our common calling consists in looking at the gospel as the good news of the possibility of a new beginning.

The Evangelical

Evangelicalism and *ecumenism* have often been presented as two competing and mutually exclusive movements. Contrary to popular belief, however, a large number of evangelical and pentecostal churches are members of the WCC. Yet, in recent years, there has been a growing awareness that the WCC cannot and should not limit its perception and its efforts for relations with evangelicals exclusively to its own constituency. International evangelical organizations (most of which are based in the Northern hemisphere and represent Western culture), non-Western mission movements (most of which have evangelical roots and continue to grow fast), as well as churches and groups born on the fringes of the mainline churches, constitute a reality which has to be taken seriously into consideration.

Indeed, no church today, and no ecumenical organization, can declare their ecumenical commitment to constitute an exclusive asset. During the last few decades, nearly all churches have become active in the ecumenical field. The scope of ecumenical relations and of ecumenical co-operation has widened. New centres of ecumenical initiatives have developed and new forms of ecumenical collaboration have emerged. It is within this wider ecumenical context that the WCC found itself involved in a new set of relationships and confronted with new realities and new questions.

As an instrument of the world-wide ecumenical movement, the WCC openly and repeatedly affirmed that the ecumenical movement cannot and should not be seen as standing over against the reality of the evangelical movement. As a matter of fact, the ecumenical movement and its institutions cannot and definitely should not ignore the reality of evangelicalism in North America, pentecostalism in Latin America, or the independent churches in Africa. It has gradually become a widely shared conviction that the WCC would cut itself off from the source of ecumenical vitality, especially in the South, if it did not work on a broader scale of relationships. Therefore, WCC–evangelical relations have come to mean a rather elaborate task embracing at least three different types of activities: (a) working with those evangelicals and constituencies in WCC member churches whose voices are very often not sufficiently heard in proportion to their presence in their own churches and in the ecumenical movement; (b) seeking new ways of dialogue and co-operation with evangelical, pentecostal and independent churches and movements that are outside the membership of the WCC, but could somehow be related to it in the future; (c) interacting with more established evangelical movements and organizations—such as the Lausanne Committee and the World Evangelical Fellowship—taking seriously into consideration the fact that their fundamental concerns are also part of the ecumenical movement and the churches which participate in it.

All these were then studied in the light of the nature and work of the WCC in general and included in a policy statement, coming fifty years after the founding of the WCC. A careful study of the policy statement entitled 'Towards a Common Understanding and Vision of the World Council of Churches' would reveal to the reader clear signals in the sense that the fellowship of the council's member churches was ready to recognize its own part of responsibility and do its best in order to heal the situation in the area of relationship with evangelical churches and communities: 'The fellowship of the WCC is limited by the absence of other churches which, for various reasons, have not sought membership. For example, unjustifiable barriers have arisen between the WCC and some *Evangelical and Pentecostal churches* because of tendencies on both sides to caricature or remain indifferent to each other. Some of these barriers have begun to break down through the development of ongoing contacts...'[1] It is widely admitted, however, that barriers do not break down by themselves, and that developing contacts usually need tremendous human investment. Even policy statements have their drafters, or those who amend them.

Here again, we find John Briggs. With other friends he struggled to be a genuine ambassador voicing the concerns of what he believed to be two ecumenical partners and definitely not two enemy camps! In a period deeply influenced by the Cold War mentality, admitting and presenting confrontation as the only possible way, he raised his voice together with those of some friends, arguing for exactly the opposite: cooperation is possible and necessary, a common response to the common calling is imperative. John Briggs, the historian, argued several times that in church history, which certainly transcends our own and limited historical experience, *evangelicalism* and *ecumenism* represent two distinct and complementary streams. John Briggs, the man of dialogue, actively participated in a series of encounters between evangelicals and Orthodox, showing once again that there are alternatives to confrontation, and that the tensions between two historical, theological and ecclesiological traditions can be turned into a constructive power and energy. In addition to all these, John Briggs, the ecumenist, became instrumental in helping

---

1 'Towards a Common Understanding and Vision of the World Council of Churches', in *Assembly Workbook: Harare 1998* (Geneva: WCC Publications, 1998), pp. 95-116. Quotation from section 4.12, italics original. See also http://www.wcc-coe.org/wcc/who/cuv-e.html.

the WCC to study, screen and assess applications from many local communities and churches, including evangelical, pentecostal, and African independent churches.

The Bridge-Builder

Orthodox churches have participated in the contemporary ecumenical movement since its very inception. The Ecumenical Patriarchate of Constantinople had invited 'All Churches of Christ' to form a 'League of Churches', following the model of the 'League of Nations'. Orthodox churches have been among the founding members of the WCC. Yet, there has always been a certain tension in their relationship both to the WCC as an institution and to Protestant churches who were their partners within the fellowship of churches. Relations have gradually deteriorated and in April 1998, an inter-Orthodox meeting was convened by the Ecumenical Patriarchate in Thessaloniki, Greece. This meeting came as a response of the Eastern Orthodox Churches to the request of the Moscow Patriarchate and the Church of Serbia, as well as to the withdrawal of the Georgian Orthodox Church from the membership of the WCC (1997).

The meeting attempted an initial evaluation of the situation. In a positive spirit, it stated that participants in the meeting were 'unanimous in their understanding of the necessity for continuing their participation in various forms of inter-Christian activities'. In a rather critical spirit, it expressed concern about 'certain developments within some Protestant members of the Council that are reflected in the debates of the WCC', lack of progress in theological discussions and the perception that the present structure of the WCC makes Orthodox participation increasingly difficult. In a challenging spirit, the meeting urged that a commission be created to discuss 'acceptable forms of Orthodox participation in the ecumenical movement and the radical restructuring of the WCC'.

Then followed the withdrawal of the Bulgarian Orthodox Church from the WCC (1998). Obviously, some Orthodox churches were experiencing internal tensions, due in large part to groups who stand against the ecumenical movement. The critical attitude of the Orthodox, however, was also due to a sharpened perception by Orthodox churches of problems related to the structures of the WCC and to the way the council functions.

All this happened before the assembly in Harare. In view of this increasing Orthodox 'malaise' and critique, the WCC initiated a process of intensive consultation with its Orthodox and other member churches. This process culminated in the decision of the assembly to create a Special Commission on Orthodox participation in the World Council of Churches. According to the assembly resolution, the commission was

Foreword

established 'to study and analyze the whole spectrum of questions related to Orthodox participation in the WCC, recognizing that many of these concerns are of importance to other member churches as well'. The commission was given the mandate 'to devote a period of at least three years to studying the full range of issues related to participation of Orthodox Churches in the WCC, and to present proposals about changes in structure, working style and ethos to the Central Committee for decision'.[2]

John Briggs' recognized commitment to the ecumenical movement, his theological and ecclesiological positions sharpened through dialogue, as well as the relations of trust and friendship he had developed throughout the years with Orthodox and Protestant sisters and brothers from East and West, from North and South, constituted once again an important capital, a precious instrument, a source of decisive contributions. He was unanimously proposed to the membership of the newly created Special Commission for his sensitivity to all sides, his objectivity in the search for solutions to the benefit of all parties concerned, and his integrity.

Again the many talents of the person have been particularly appreciated. The issues at stake constituted an extremely complex equation involving many unknown parameters: the sources of tension were both theological and ecclesiological, historical and cultural, ecumenical and political, spiritual and institutional. The commission's agenda—and by extension an important portion of the ecumenical agenda as a whole—included fundamental issues such as the ecclesiological meaning of being in fellowship with one another, as well as the ecclesiological and spiritual potential of praying with one another. It also included matters of a more institutional character, and yet extremely important for almost all ecumenical organizations at various levels, such as decision-making processes, and the meaning of membership in ecumenical organizations.

The Man of the Institution

Very early in the reflection process that led the WCC to its policy statement 'Towards a Common Understanding and Vision of the World Council of Churches', the critical dilemma surfaced as to whether the WCC should primarily be seen as a 'fellowship of churches' or as a simple ecumenical structure, an ecumenical 'institution'. The reflection process concluded with an unequivocal statement that, being primarily a

---

2 'Special Commission on Orthodox participation in the World Council of Churches', in Diane Kessler (ed.), *Together on the Way: Official Report of the Eighth Assembly of the World Council of Churches* (Geneva: WCC Publications, 1999), p. 152.

'fellowship of churches', the WCC should be seen as 'more than a mere functional association of churches set up to organize activities in areas of common interest'.[3] To put it another way, the essence of the council is not primarily what the churches *do* together, but rather what the churches *are* together. The essence of the council is the relationship of the member churches to one another, not their relationship to the structure of the council.

As important as this statement may be, it leaves open a number of key questions about the character and nature of the institution, the unavoidable 'structure' of the WCC. Hence the additional source of tension as to how the WCC should be considered as an institution having its own life, its own mechanisms of decision-making, its own instruments of communication.

John Briggs has been one of those who showed the way. He did so not so much through academic exercises and writings, but rather through a living example. He literally served both with equal dedication and enthusiasm.

While the theologian eloquently advocated for the primacy of the fellowship over the institution, the historian knew by experience that an institution at the service of the fellowship is imperative, that the institutional structure can serve to build up fellowship, that the institutional framework can provide the space for continuing conversation about and experience of the nature of the fellowship. While the theologian offered his reflections on the ecclesiological understanding of the fellowship and the meaning of membership, the committed friend served the governing bodies, struggled with budgets, accounting systems and audits. While the experienced academic has actively participated in particularly sensitive discussions on the future of the Ecumenical Institute of Bossey—in fact on ecumenical formation in general and on the future of the ecumenical movement in particular— what I call 'the man of the institution' invested with equal passion, time and energy to face institutional problems ranging from staff management to staff pensions!

Thus John Briggs has become the friend and colleague valued by both his fellow members in the governing bodies and the Geneva-based staff community. He has been the one who cheered people on to the appointed goals, encouraged them in times of difficulty, celebrated with them when something was accomplished.

---

3 'Towards a Common Understanding and Vision', section 3.2.

A Word to Conclude

What John Briggs shared with many others during his long-standing commitment to his church, to his profession and to the ecumenical movement is a form of celebration: a celebration of shared faith, a celebration of life, a celebration of hope. For all these, his many friends thank God with joy and gratitude.

Introduction

The essays in this volume are presented in honour of John H.Y. Briggs by a group of his friends, colleagues and former research students. In his many and various roles—scholar, professor, mentor, author, editor, Baptist, Free Churchman and ecumenist—he has played an active role in the life of the church and British higher education spanning five decades. As a Baptist he has served his denomination in the local churches in which he and his wife, Joyce, have been in membership; the Baptist Union through various of its committees; the Baptist Historical Society, not least as editor of the *Baptist Quarterly* since 1985; but also through the Baptist World Alliance, for instance as Chairman of its Heritage Commission. As a Free Churchman he has been Principal of the Free Church Westhill College, now University of Birmingham, Westhill, and Convenor of the Free Churches Group, which in 2001 became part of Churches Together in England. As an ecumenist he has served the British Council of Churches; the World Council of Churches, particularly notable as a member of the Executive and Central Committees; and in his participation in discussions between Evangelicals and the Orthodox Church which have led to a greater understanding between these two traditions. As an historian and educationalist he has lectured at the University of Keele, University of Birmingham, Westhill, and is now Senior Research Fellow in Ecclesiastical History and Director of the Centre for Baptist History and Heritage at Regent's Park College, Oxford. Testimony to his prominence as a scholar is reflected in his being elected a Fellow of the Royal Historical Society in 1975 and Fellow of the Society of Antiquaries a year later. His many publications, religious and secular, reflect his interests in local history, particularly in and around the Potteries, but also in Victorian history, as well as his many Baptist, Free Church and ecumenical writings.

It seemed fitting, then, that a volume in Professor Briggs' honour should explore the themes of ecumenism and history which typify his own work. The book falls into two parts: Part 1 consists of studies in ecumenism and history, while Part 2 is made up of essays on a range of historical subjects. In both parts a broadly chronological order has been followed but there are a number of contributions which are more thematic in nature. It will quickly become clear that the arrangement is to some degree arbitrary, but this order was felt to provide a reasonable structure to the book.

The editor particularly wishes to thank the contributors for their willingness to share in this project, to those who have helped in the locating of information and material, to Jeremy Mudditt for all his help and encouragement, and to Paternoster Press for publishing this Festschrift.

John H.Y. Briggs, MA FSA FRHistS: An Appreciation

Faith Bowers

Early Life

John Henry York Briggs was born into a Baptist family in London in 1938, the youngest of three brothers. York was the maiden name of his maternal grandmother who had grown up in the Moulton church in Northamptonshire but had come to London as a young servant girl. The Briggs' worshipped at Upton Baptist Chapel, Lambeth, a church founded in 1785 but later overshadowed by Spurgeon's Metropolitan Tabernacle. John's grandfather, father and aunt served as Upton deacons. Like many good Baptists at the dawn of the twentieth century, John's grandfather, Henry James Briggs, a scientific instrument maker, was a political activist and early trades unionist. John's father, Archibald Tevendale Briggs, a linotype engineer, was also a keen trades unionist, losing his job at one firm as a result, and then working on newspaper machines. The family's religion demanded active and principled participation in the world. In private the boys' father sometimes admitted that it was not always easy for a working man who twice experienced periods of unemployment to serve on the diaconate alongside company directors who had inherited wealth and status, but he was able to maintain good relationships with them.

Upton Chapel was bombed early in the war and the Baptists moved in with the larger Christ Church Congregational Church. Although exempt from conscription, Upton's minister chose to join up and they had a temporary pastor, trained for missionary service but unable to proceed to India. When the churches eventually combined, Christ Church members and most from Upton wanted to keep the missionary pastor, but the Briggs family held on principle to Upton's prior commitment to the minister on military service. This unresolved disagreement caused them to leave. Living in Herne Hill, they joined Chatsworth Baptist Church, West Norwood. Meanwhile Mrs Briggs was evacuated with the younger boys, David and John, first to Cray's Pond, near Goring, and then to Stoney Stratford. Peter, some years older, remained at school in Dulwich and was living with the missionary minister at the time of the split, adding to the determination needed for their father's stand.

John almost did not survive Cray's Pond. Once when the whole family were there they went for a walk, with little David pushing baby John strapped in the pram. Suddenly they heard and saw one of the new bombers, the first four-engined Stirlings which had been kept a secret, out on a practice flight from RAF Benson. They all gazed up at this monster aircraft. David stepped backwards, tripped on the raised edge of the pond and toppled backwards, taking John with him. Peter has a vivid memory of the horror of the upturned pram with both little boys submerged beneath.

John followed his brothers to Dulwich College and distinguished himself there, becoming a prefect, though never a sportsman. While at school, John joined the Crusaders. The local leader, known as 'the Colonel', had a strong influence on the boys. John maintained his association with the Crusaders over the years. His national service was in the Royal Air Force, where he was almost an estate agent, arranging for service personnel to be housed in civilian property. Eric Ives says he became a Station Adjutant and chuckles at John already finding his niche—organizing people!

Like John, Haddon Willmer arrived in Cambridge in 1958, both fresh from the RAF, but John sporting his officer's greatcoat. Both read History, John at Christ's College, Willmer at Emmanuel. He remembers John as 'predominantly a Robert Hall Society person, who also went to CICCU [Cambridge Inter-Collegiate Christian Union]', whereas Willmer himself was more active in the Christian Union but also went to the Baptist students' Robert Hall Society. John worshipped at the St Andrew's Street Baptist Church, 'the more respectable place', whereas Willmer preferred Zion and the 'quirky humorous way' of Raymond Brown, later to become Principal of Spurgeon's College. Both shared in Baptist student missions at Ilford and Wisbech. When President of the Robert Hall Society, John asked Willmer to be study secretary. They undertook a series on 'The Church' and judged inadequate the notes Arthur Jestice (minister of St Andrew's Street 1958–78) had written.

> Probably it was I who disliked them, since I am that kind of censorious person, and was already on the way to trying to be a theologian. Anyway, John let me go ahead and Arthur was very gracious in not noticing how drastically we had revised/ reversed the tenor of his notes. Our student escapades together were very serious and earnest. Years later, John said he had found those notes again and thought they weren't bad... John seemed to me then, as he does still, to be a person at home in world and church. I got a sense from him—I don't think we have ever talked about it—that he had grown up in the Baptist tradition, in home and church and was stable in his roots, and able to blossom in the wider world. I was by contrast on skids. I had been through at least seven churches on the independent evangelical fringes of the Baptist denomination by the time I left home for the RAF, and in Cambridge, as I became a theologian, I thought sometimes about being Anglican or Roman

Catholic, and mostly wrestled with the plausibility of being an atheist or at least a Bible reader weary with all the churches. That I have settled down and stayed a Baptist and been a member of one Baptist church for thirty-five years has roots in Cambridge, with John and Raymond Brown having significant effects.

At Cambridge, a sign of things to come, John took part in activities of both the Christian Union and the Student Christian Movement, those opposite poles of Christian student life. With firm roots in the Baptist society this was possible, as I was finding in London. Peter says this was also in keeping with the family's approach, where basically conservative religion was tempered by unusual open-mindedness; he remembers their father buying and reading all the SCM books. John proceeded to Exeter for postgraduate studies, transferring to the William Knibb Society for Baptist students there. He was President of the Baptist Students' Federation 1961–62. It was at the annual conferences of BSF that I first encountered John.

Home Life

John met his future wife, Joyce, at the Sixth World Youth Conference of the Baptist World Alliance in Beirut in July 1963. Her father, a draper in Leamington Spa, had been a Strict Baptist and John treasures his father-in-law's bedside copy of *Gadsby's Hymns*. Clyde Binfield has heard John compare his more 'liberal' Baptist background which anguished over drink with his wife's upbringing, stricter but with no hang-up over alcohol. John evidently came to terms with this: his Keele colleague, Andor Gomme, says he and his wife 'were a little puzzled that so prominent a member of the Baptist church should be such a bonviveur— but pleased at the same time, since one always ate and drank well at their house. John's choice of wines was to be relied on.'

At first John was warden of a hall of residence and they lived on the campus, then bought a house nearby. Binfield observes that John 'was rare among Keele colleagues in actually living in Stoke-on-Trent where he had sussed out a quite splendid, rather Italianate nineteenth-century villa in an unlikely enclave, which evolved exactly as an established don's house should—full of interesting things in interesting juxtaposition.' Peter Briggs was amused at that description, remembering the 'ghastly place' as they bought it. The interesting things included antique furniture and a collection of Staffordshire figurines, especially of C.H. Spurgeon. I never visited their home, but mutual friends described the sense there of stepping back into the Victorian era. Joyce is a keen gardener, sometimes with John as 'labourer'. They went in for 'decently sized' dogs and Meg Soper remembers the amusement of visiting students when John announced, 'I'll just go and discipline the dog'—surely an unequal combat! Andor Gomme and Peter Egginton both mention meeting John and Joyce enjoying musical events in Birmingham. Binfield reflected on shared interests in stately home and garden crawls, and the Buxton Festival: 'In practice, joint outings were more often mutually promised than achieved, but enjoyed vicariously' when staying at each other's homes for stints of external examining. John is often away from home but when he moved to Birmingham ahead of Joyce, who had to sell the house in Stoke, he took to ringing me in the evening, the length and chattiness of his calls during those months making me aware that he was missing his wife's presence.

John and Joyce have three sons. When moving to Birmingham, John chuckled at how usefully they had reared their family—with Jeremy an estate agent and Justin a solicitor. Marcus is the computer expert. Some years ago John arranged for his son to instruct him in word-processing during the long vacation. To judge from his competence by the next term, teaching skills had been inherited.

In the early seventies Doreen Rosman, then in the final year of doctoral studies, lodged with the Briggs. She remembers John as a tease, and sometimes 'wonderfully off-hand': 'on one occasion when I had agreed to stay at home with a sick child he hurried out saying, "You can change the baby's nappy, can't you?" I never knew if he was simply anxious to avoid doing a messy job himself or if indeed he knew that I had never changed a nappy in my life!' They 'entertained in style but in a warm and relaxed way'. John enjoys cooking and is, according to his former secretary, Carolyn Busfield, an excellent, thrifty shopper who gets good value for money.

Historian versus Administrator

Eric Ives first met John as a postgraduate at the earliest Inter-Varsity Fellowship Christianity and History Conferences. In the late 1950s John helped him with some Inter-Schools Christian Fellowship courses for sixth-formers in the Easter holidays, relating their studies to the Christian faith and giving them a more mature exposure to Christianity. Academic sessions were relevant to 'A' levels, while the evenings had multi-media presentations, raising Christian issues. These conferences, 'quite avant-garde and challenging', served their time well.

In the first post-Robbins round of jobs as higher education expanded, John and Clyde Binfield applied for the same post at Keele. It went to John. Keele offered Binfield a post in European history instead, but he went to Sheffield. John remained at Keele from 1965 until his 'first retirement' in 1997. They kept in touch, sharing interests 'in Victorian studies, British History with an integrated ecclesiastical, political, social and cultural aspect, local history, and *mutatis mutandis*, Baptist/ Congregational history'. They had similar interests in denominational and ecumenical matters, a similar theological viewpoint, and 'perhaps, too, a similar obstinate, inherited loyalty and affection for the traditions in which we had been formed'. John's doctoral studies were not completed: he describes himself as 'a kingmaker rather than a king'. His students achieved doctorates but his multiple activities have meant that he has always found it easier to research a contained topic for a short paper than to work through a prolonged study.

According to David Bebbington, John was 'originally recruited to promote Victorian studies, which was then a novel vogue, and he suited that role well. Later his teaching widened, even encompassing a course on the Reformation. He enjoyed co-operating with other departments at Keele.' Bebbington, while still a schoolboy, heard John give a paper at the Baptist Historical Society Summer School at Spurgeon's College in 1968, and was 'mightily impressed by the verve and wit with which it was delivered. It made me want to go and do likewise.' Later they met at the IVF Historians' Study Group. David remembers John speaking at Cambridge during a mission in 1974 on a Christian's approach to history.

Professor Andor Gomme, John's colleague for over thirty years, describes how

> Together with Walter Simon, then Professor of History, John and I designed and founded the post-graduate course in Victorian Studies, which opened its doors in 1967. Simon soon withdrew from active participation and from then on the two of us ran the course together, with considerable additional help from other colleagues. The course was designed fundamentally as a cross- or inter-disciplinary one, and it was a principle of all the seminars that tutors from different disciplines would always be present. From the start we attempted to include the study not only of the literature and social history of the Victorian period but also the history of ideas (including important developments in science) and of the arts. In this way we hoped to do something towards fulfilling at higher-degree level the inter-disciplinary ambitions on which Keele was founded. For a dozen years or so, because I was John's academic senior, I was technically Supervisor of the course, but the administration was largely in his hands with the extremely capable assistance of Carolyn Busfield, for many years secretary of the History Department. When I stepped down from this position John formally took over. We had initially a tough fight to get a two-year post-graduate course (three years for part-timers) accepted by the university authorities; but hard arguing about the amount of material which it was desirable to include won the day. We subsequently had further fights to have the title changed from MA to MLitt, in order to distinguish the course from one-year MAs, and eventually to allow the introduction of a PhD, including coursework.

> John was always an engaging colleague to work with—bluff and good-humoured, and a cheerful presence especially on the field-trips to important Victorian sites

which were built in to the course from the start. Another feature, which was sadly kept up rather fitfully, was an annual dinner, sometimes at a nearby restaurant at which a special Victorian dinner was prepared, but alternatively at either the Briggses' house in the Villas at Stoke (a suitably Victorian venue) or at ours here. John's bonhomie on such occasions very much set the tone of the evening. Twice or thrice, excursions to a Victorian music hall at Crewe theatre were occasions of much hilarity.

Meg Soper, one of the first Victorian Studies' students, found the course 'an enriching experience', with excellent and convivial tutors. She remembers John teaching social, economic and religious history, always good humoured and well prepared.

Watching from Stirling, Bebbington saw John as 'enormously active at Keele'. He was reputed to be as active on university committees as any member of the university. Willmer, visiting Keele to preach in the 1970s, found John making 'a remarkable contribution for a relatively junior member of staff'. Ives mentioned his heavy involvement in 'the upper echelons of Keele administration'. John served as Head of the History Department for many years, Chairman of the Board of Humanities, Adviser to the Vice-Chancellor, and on many University bodies and committees. The competitive pressures on academics used not to be so great as in recent years and John enjoyed the administrative work. Carolyn Busfield found him quite demanding—she felt he had learned in the RAF to expect things to be ready for him—but he worked hard himself and it was a joy to work with someone of such equable temperament, never ruffled or short-tempered. She observes that John was unusual in having a wide circle of friends beyond the academic world, and enjoyed helping with his book on Newcastle-under-Lyme and the ceramic industry, which was very well received in the local community. This came out of his interest in the Workers Education Association.

Ives sternly considers that John spent too much time on administration to the detriment of his academic research: 'that is why he has never cut much ice as an historian'. Had he been in Ives's department, he would have been 'taken in hand academically' and not allowed to take on so much else! With a laugh Ives admits that this would have been to waste John's outstanding and rarer gifts as an effective manager: 'His big contribution is that he makes things work!' Meanwhile his academic papers appear in 'all manner of odd places', because he often writes for special occasions, making it hard for the bibliographer to track his work down.

Binfield, whose own interests are so similar, is more generous to John as an historian:

In a sense he has been both underestimated and taken for granted by his colleagues. He belongs to that line of peculiarly *Free Church* scholars whose publications have never hit the stratosphere, in part because their interests are not seen as sexy by the rest of the world, but in larger part because (a) their interests are so easily focused on a dense, locally autonomous world, and (b) their understanding of our sensitivity to the world is largely reflected in their *formation* in it: they are trained to be activists—in their local church and in its wider concerns. What makes them good historians also makes them useful citizens—and John has been a useful citizen par excellence:... the chapel at Keele University, the world of Robert Denholm House [i.e. the Sunday School Union/National Council for Christian Education], Regent's Park College, the Baptist World Alliance, the World Council of Churches. All that helps to explain the call of Westhill. It is immensely time-consuming, genuinely exhilarating; it constantly feeds insights to a perceptive mind; it creates unlikely but rewarding networks—all of it an utter mystery to most of his academic colleagues, assuming they are aware of it. It is actually on a world scale—but to colleagues it is as odd as anything, for what can be smaller or more side-lineable than Baptists (or URC or Methodists...)?

Save for the workaholic (and I would judge that John is too naturally gregarious *and* responsible to be a workaholic), all this means that the GREAT BOOKS are pushed into an ever receding future. Nonetheless, John's publications, when *coldly* assessed, are considerable and their range is in fact impressive...the work that is required for the *Baptist Quarterly*...the composition of a quarterly is a relentless task—the good editor needs to get inside the skin of his/her contributors (and frequently to rewrite their work without them realizing it); and the nature of the *Quarterly* makes the Editorial a particular responsibility.

A significant paper on 'She-preachers, Widows and Other Women: The Feminine Dimension in Baptist Life Since 1600', was written for a *Baptist Quarterly* issue focused on women (vol. 31.7 [July, 1986], pp. 337-52). John became editor of the journal late in 1985, inheriting some material, so this was the first issue on which he stamped his editorship. He researched his paper with enthusiasm but, as articles flowed in from women contributors, he doubted there was room for his. John had made it clear when he took over that I was his assistant, not just the typesetter, so I persuaded him to let me prune it to fit, without losing much content, rather than hold it over. It enhanced the focused issue, even though I sacrificed John's distinctive style. He accepted this graciously, the foundation of our partnership in editing. Having worked closely with him since 1985, editing the writings of others and ourselves, I know how good John is at churning out short papers on a specific topic and of a contained length. These he produces rapidly, as when I nag him for yet another editorial, yet they are thoughtful and well-written.

Settling to write a sustained book is another matter. His longest—and long promised—work, *The English Baptists of the Nineteenth Century* (1994) only materialized when we found a way of working that recognized this. John effectively wrote a series of essays and sent me them to type. His handwriting, never the clearest, was often adversely affected by movements of train or plane, but I could make informed guesses at the illegible and highlighted these for him to check. Gradually the parts came together into a fine book. A disadvantage of this peripatetic writing was that he drafted without reference works to hand, so the final stage required a concentrated effort at base. Evening after evening John would work through a section and, late at night, dictate footnotes to me on the telephone. Anxious to meet the final deadline, we accepted this as necessary. John was taken aback one night to be greeted by my son: 'Can't you leave my mother in peace on Mothers' Day?' John was contrite—but dictated the day's notes nonetheless. I treasure the inscription in my copy of that book, 'Without your help, this would not have been.'

Much of John's publishing activity has been collaborative. Bebbington observes that some of John's greatest achievements have been in collective scholarship. 'He was the driving force behind the *Lion Handbook of Christian History*, which has proved an international bestseller. Likewise he played a big part in the *Blackwell Dictionary of Evangelical Biography*, editing the Baptist contributions as well as submitting many himself.' He has done his share on the new *Dictionary of National Biography* and a variety of other reference works. Again the contribution of short articles and encouraging and editing other writers suits John's gifts.

The Lion book, *Christianity: A World Faith* ((1985), with the second edition, *A Quiet Revolution* (1989), was a visionary work conceived by John—'John at his best', judges Peter Briggs with some pride, having himself worked for the church in Africa. It begins with the statement that 'This book was the brainchild of John Briggs, who was responsible for the original idea and the basic outline.' Over sixty distinguished contributors from six continents tell 'the extraordinary story of a faith followed by one in three people worldwide', now that the faith 'once dominated by Westerners has taken off into Africa, Asia, Latin America' and reveals 'the astonishing variety and vitality of contemporary Christianity'.

The Teacher

The teaching aspect of academia clearly appeals to John. He has taught undergraduates and extra-mural local history students, as well as supervising many postgraduates, internal and external. In his last years at Keele, he reckoned he was supervising as many postgraduates as anyone in the country. Within the Baptist Historical Society I felt odd, taking a research degree through London rather than Keele. John was also in demand as an external examiner. Binfield found him 'immensely, indeed deceptively, useful—his standards were clear, but at once realistic *and* kindly'. Willmer observed: 'John is a sharp but sensible understanding examiner, with no need to prove himself by playing the inquisitorial torturer.' When John hears of someone failing to obtain a doctorate, his reaction is revealing. 'Who was the supervisor?' he sternly demands. His students were not allowed to submit until he was confident of success, even if, revising yet again, they found him a hard taskmaster.

Binfield suspected that Keele only realized what the university owed him after he retired.

> He was a prime mover in his department and faculty: an excellent dean, head of department, etc.; a man to know and have on one's side in University politics (and a man to shoot tigers with). His achievements were those that really give a department its reputation among students and prospective students, even if the world of Research Achievement Exercises might be less impressed (quite wrongly). John was a prime mover in Keele's MA in Victorian Studies (one of the earlier ones in that sort of field) and his interests in ecclesiastical and local history made him invaluable in getting a steady stream of postgraduate students (I have enjoyed acting as external examiner for several of them). These students are the backbone of what now has to be called an arts department's 'research culture'—but few recognize that, because they do not bring in the full-time fees for the Arts and Humanities Research Board and so on!

In his editing I see something of what has made John a good postgraduate supervisor. He is annoyed when fellow academics offer slipshod pieces, and laments that increasingly he has had to teach postgraduates how to write coherently and how to reference their work. What have their earlier teachers been about? By contrast, he has time for the amateur who has unearthed something of interest, even if it comes poorly packaged, buried beneath a mass of words or mythology. Simple rejection would be easier than helping them develop their research more effectively. This calls for John's incisive evaluation and his kindness.

Doreen Rosman was taught by John as an undergraduate and postgraduate. After consulting two former fellow students, she wrote:

> When asked what she remembered about John, one immediately replied, 'the bow tie and expansive gestures'. He taught us in the late 1960s and we recall him as a lively and enthusiastic teacher. At that time it was rumoured that students were scared of him but we were not conscious of that ourselves. I suspect that the source of the rumour lay in John's expectations of his students: he wanted them to engage with the subjects they were studying and sometimes adopted a provocative approach to prompt reactions or response. His style invited vigorous debate and he disliked student passivity: a girl who told him that she did not have any questions about the subjects we had been studying received very short shrift.

On the other hand he went out of his way to help those of us who showed interest in what we were doing. In order to cater for the range of interest within a special subject class of which I was a member he sub-divided the group and offered a choice of two topics each week. This enabled us to study aspects of the subject that particularly attracted us but substantially increased his own workload. He was both generous and trusting: a friend and I recall being allowed to use his books in his office when he was not there in the evenings. Behind his slightly abrasive manner there was a genuine interest in and concern about the people he was teaching.

My friend recollects that as a referee he went way beyond the call of duty, consulting with a colleague how best to present her case and helping her with interview technique. At the time she had very little self-confidence but not withstanding his reputation she never felt threatened by John. On the contrary she recalls how much he encouraged her.

After I graduated he became my research supervisor and although I was unsure of myself and what I was doing John never lost faith in me...

John spent most of his working life at Keele and whole-heartedly embraced the distinctive ethos of the place. The impetus for a University College of North Staffordshire came from people involved in adult education in the area and John helped keep this tradition alive. He was always supportive of adult education and played an active part in making local people aware of their own history. Another fundamental characteristic of Keele was its commitment to interdisciplinary study: in the early years all students shared in a common 'foundation year' programme comprising arts, sciences and social sciences and were then required to study joint honours degrees. Some members of staff who came to Keele from more traditional universities resented the obligation to participate in foundation year activities and wanted merely to concentrate on their own subjects. By contrast John embraced the opportunities which Keele offered for collaboration across disciplines...

Keele has always been one of the smallest British universities and in the early days in particular it consciously maintained a strong community spirit. When I went there in 1966 all students were guaranteed four years accommodation on campus and many members of staff lived in staff houses in the university grounds. John gave himself whole-heartedly to community life and served for a while as a warden in one of the halls of residence. Much of his community activity was focused on the ecumenical University Chapel in which he played a leading role for many years. He combined deep commitment to his own Baptist principles with a readiness to work alongside and worship with people from very different traditions.

Baptist Life

John has always been a Baptist activist, in his local church, the wider denominational world and ecumenical circles. His brother Peter suspects that he gave up some career opportunities to be free to work for Baptists, but that would accord with inherited principles. David Russell, former General Secretary of the Baptist Union of Great Britain, offered this assessment:

> John is a Church historian of no mean merit, recording and interpreting with accuracy and insight the events of the past, not least as these reflect the life of our Baptist communion during the twentieth century. At the same time he is an active 'churchman', deeply involved in the 'living tradition' which finds expression not only in his own Baptist denomination, but also and perhaps particularly in the world-wide Church.
>
> His contribution to Baptist affairs has not been limited to written records; it has involved him in the life of the local church, the theological colleges and the Baptist Union where he has played a prominent part over the years in not a few of its Committees and Commissions. Even more impressive is the part he has played in the life of the World-Church through the World Council of Churches as a member of its Central Committee where he has continued the long and highly-valued ministry of Dr E.A. Payne in earlier days and in so doing has enhanced the name of Baptists as worthy participants in the ecumenical movement.
>
> His ebullient personality, his sound judgment, his profound sense of history and its relevance for the days in which we are now living have greatly enhanced the life of the Christian Church at its local, national and global levels.

Dr Russell often shared a room with John on their travels and enjoyed John's kindly care of an older colleague apt to mislay things.

On leaving Keele's ecumenical community for Birmingham, John joined Highgate, a small inner-city Baptist church. At Keele he was a very acceptable preacher around the local churches and still finds time to preach in Birmingham. Binfield observes that John 'preaches well: he has that increasingly rare ability to lead worship in a way that allows his congregation to feel *confident* in what he is doing'. For Doreen Rosman, 'one of John's endearing characteristics is his personal engagement with whatever he takes on. I heard him preach to tiny village congregations, giving himself as fully to them as to much larger gatherings.' Siôr Coleman, a chaplain in South Birmingham Mental Health Trust, was delighted to find John could communicate well with the small congregation of people with very severe learning disabilities at Monyhull Hospital's chapel. When Haddon Willmer was President of the Yorkshire Baptist Association he particularly wanted John to address the Yorkshire Assembly. On that occasion he delivered 'an utterance too weighty and comprehensive for the audience I'm afraid, but I was grateful for it'. Basil Amey remembers him as an effective conference speaker for the Baptist Men's Movement.

The denomination has two prominent laymen, both academics, with similar names: John Biggs says confusion began at Cambridge, not helped by both belonging 'to that diminishing number who are likely to be seen wearing a bow tie'. When Briggs became active in the World Council of Churches, Biggs was often asked about conditions in El Salvador or East Timor. Doubtless the historian was sometimes expected to be an authority on ecological concerns.

John Briggs has served on the Council of the Baptist Union of Great Britain for over thirty years. With his skills in adult education, he was a key figure in the introduction of the Christian Training Programme, a distance learning programme with a process of continuous assessment used primarily in the training of lay pastors and preachers. From 1974–81 he chaired the Mission Main Committee. In 1989 he became chairman of the Advisory Committee on Church Relations, assisting the General Secretary in ecumenical matters. As ecumenical developments made increasing demands, this committee could not cope adequately with all the business, so John helped create the Faith and Unity Executive, with feeder committees dealing with doctrine and worship, church relations, local ecumenical activities, and international relations. He moderated this executive through the first formative years, 1992–96. He has served on Union committees dealing with scholarships, international relations, students in higher education, the new headquarters, Baptist House, general purposes, the Agenda Committee, and the Staffing Sub-committee. He has represented Baptists on the Council of Churches for Britain and Ireland. When in 1994 the Government allowed certain denominations to monitor alterations to listed buildings, John became a member of the Baptist Listed Buildings Advisory Committee. He has long served on the Baptist Historical Society's committee. As with other involvements, he cannot attend every meeting but is an asset when present, generally available for consultation, and a long-serving editor of the Society's journal, the *Baptist Quarterly*.

In June 1974 John was elected to the Council of Regent's Park College, in Oxford, attending his first meeting that October. In 1985 he joined the Executive Committee and chaired both Council and Executive Committee, 1987–2001. Eric Ives, also on the governing body, says John was 'very active there, a very competent manager of college affairs...and the governors are 'not push-overs!' He 'was instrumental in shifting the college constitution to make Council an advisory body with a Management Committee which meets more frequently'. John resigned as chairman of both bodies from 31 August 2001, to become, from 1 September, Senior Research Fellow in Church History, a part-time post appropriate to semi-retirement.

While serving the Baptist family of churches at home and representing them ecumenically, John has given sterling service internationally within the Baptist World Alliance. He served on the Academic and Theological Education Workgroup 1985–90, and the Executive Committee of Study

John H.Y. Briggs, MA, FSA, FRHistS 13

and Research 1991-95, when he was also on the Resolutions Committee, which met at times when others at council meetings were relaxing or in bed. As they framed public declarations on shared concerns in terms acceptable to those from East, West, North and South, John's interpersonal and editorial skills came into play. He was 'a great colleague' on that committee, recalls Keith Jones, now Rector of the International Baptist Theological Seminary in Prague, 'good at jollying us along and finding a form of words to keep all sides happy'. He was in at the beginning of the BWA Heritage Commission—I remember him reporting its creation to the Baptist Historical Society with delight. He chaired this Commission 1990-95, and continued as a supportive Vice-Chairman through the next quinquennium. He was also an active participant in the BWA-sponsored Summit on Baptists against Racism, held at Ebenezer Baptist Church, Atlanta, Georgia, in January 1999.

My own first appearance on the BWA scene was at Montreal in 1990, appointed to a workgroup which proved far from happy. As commission meetings were open, that first evening I slipped into the Heritage Commission, joining a row of historians' wives at the side. When John appeared he summoned me to the table, commending me warmly to his fellows, and I was swiftly added to the commission's membership, affording me many happy hours at that and subsequent meetings. As I found my way into the BWA scene, John supplied helpful guidance, usually tossed out casually. Most memorable was his advice on iron rations for travellers: take two packets of digestive biscuits and at the first opportunity buy a bunch of bananas in their natural protective wrapping. With these in reserve, you know you can survive strange meals at erratic times.

Dr Eljee Bentley, an American archivist, met John through the BWA in Amman, Jordan, in 1987. She too made friends within the Heritage Commission, making her want to return in subsequent years. Soon after John became chairman she was appointed secretary. 'In some BWA commissions/committees the chair rarely consults the officers, but that was not John's way. He worked with the officers and with the group. The Heritage Commission had begun as a group endeavor and under John's style of leadership, the group became a family.' She knew few BWA people, whereas John 'knew everybody', and she often joined him for meals, finding she was always welcome to 'be part of whatever group he was with'. In 1994 the council met in Uppsala in an unexpected heatwave. The day of the opening dinner, the Heritage Commission had visited the Stockholm seminary and John and Eljee returned together, hot and crumpled but too late to change to fresh and formal clothes. She was keenly aware of this, but he, undaunted, led her to join Tomas Mackey and Raul Scialabba, prominent Argentine Baptists, both immaculately dressed, but, of course, friends of John's. John was comfortable, so she relaxed and enjoyed the evening.

At the 1995 BWA Congress in Buenos Aires, each commission had to run workshops and mount a booth in the exhibition hall, a new venture. Heritage members brought assorted materials from which we created the display. Bentley describes how

> We had to plan with little knowledge of the venue or participants and with great trepidation. The commission events at the Seoul Congress had been chaotic. John got quite a few of us involved, and it went well. The exhibit booth, about which we had had great foreboding, turned out to be what we all liked best about the Congress. We had so many visitors, so many people interested in Baptist history. And we—working together—had fun! The booth became our 'home' in Buenos Aires. And it wasn't because the booth was a comfortable place: we had to wear layer after layer of clothing in that unheated hall. The booth was home, because that was where our 'family' was.

Somewhat reluctantly Bentley succeeded John in the Commission chair:

> John said, 'I'll help you'. He did. He gave me suggestions as to whom to ask to present papers. He didn't push his suggestions. He made them at my request. And he was there as I chaired my first meetings. He was there in Hong Kong when I got myself (and the commission and the BWA) in the middle of a South African standoff. His presence gave me courage.

In fact, they handled that South African clash in a way that moved beyond the combative stances of both parties and helped us understand and have some sympathy with both. I remember it as a time when the past informed the present and may have contributed to improved relations.

After leaving Keele, John could attend less, but still sent helpful suggestions to Bentley: 'And I knew his support was behind me. That meant more than I can say.' She had only one complaint: John 'does not always communicate promptly. After we both got email, he did better. But before email, I would get worried. He'd said he'd let me know, but when? I need not have worried. John may not be prompt, but he is dependable. If John says he will do something, he will do it.'

With Don Black, John represented British Baptists when the Baptist Union of Nicaragua celebrated its fiftieth anniversary. Both spoke at the opening Assembly. Nicaraguan Baptists wanted these visitors to understand why they were collaborating with the Castro government for the people's good in town and country. They showed their work there and sent their visitors to El Salvador, to see the contrast with a country dominated by American money. In Nicaragua they saw horrific evidence of torture under the earlier regime. Don was amazed at John's apparent lack of emotion, but guessed that his calm manner had to be a protective device.

Ecumenical Life

John holds to the principles which distinguish Baptists, but works gladly with Christians from other traditions. John was one of the two English representatives on the Central Committee of the World Council of Churches from 1983 to 1998, and on the Executive Committee 1991–98. The Central Committee is a body of some 150 members, and the Executive Committee about forty strong. The other English member of the Central Committee, the Rt Revd Barry Rogerson, Bishop of Bristol, describes John 'as assiduous, listening and willing to fight for what he believes is right'. John served on the Staffing and Nominations Committee of the Executive which determines who works in Geneva and on the various commissions and boards, and he moderated the Audit Committee, keeping the finances in order. On behalf of the WCC, to build relations or in connection with membership applications, John visited churches in Argentina, East Timor and the three Baltic countries after the political changes in Eastern Europe. He was quite extensively involved with East Timor in the context of WCC International Affairs.

Although no longer on the Central Committee, John continues to serve the WCC as a member of the Special Committee on Orthodox Relations, set up in 1999 to explore how the Orthodox might be helped to remain in the WCC and the implications of this for others. This committee, half Orthodox, half other, is central to the future of the WCC. He is also on the Study Group on Membership set up by the Executive Committee in 2001; this again has serious implications, not least for the way the Orthodox view the WCC. He is co-editor of Volume 3 of the *The History of the Ecumenical Movement*.

Birmingham

Keele retired John earlier than he had expected so he was delighted with the invitation to become Principal of Westhill College of Higher Education in 1997, by far the largest of the eight autonomous colleges in the Selly Oak Federation. As the only united Free Churches' college in the country, Westhill had always lived precariously with its church identity. The main work for over seventy years had been primary teacher training. Alongside this were courses for youth and community workers, a department of church education and the regional Religious Education Centre. Degree courses, validated by the University of Birmingham, were only one aspect of the work. Eventually Westhill was accredited by the University, resulting in significant changes in the early 1990s. The college began to move into research, and abandoned primary teacher training in favour of a BA course in general humanities. The college retained a Postgraduate Certificate of Education programme and offered some MEd degrees. Nevertheless, Westhill could not survive alone. There was an abortive attempt to 'journey together' with the Roman Catholic Newman College. Financial problems loomed, Principal Jack Priestley retired in poor health, and twelve of the fifty staff left. It was clear that Westhill College had to join the university.

At this stage Eric Ives, Pro-Vice-Chancellor of Birmingham University, Professor of History, and Chairman of the Governors of Westhill, headhunted John, the man 'who makes things work'. He became Principal to supervise a five-year 'Strategic Alliance', a rationalizing process. The university made John a Professor and Pro-Vice-Chancellor as he cleared a path through the various legal and financial complexities. Binfield reflected, somewhat irreverently, that Westhill knew what it was about in appointing John:

> All the skills acquired on Baptist and Ecumenical jaunts, mingled with the Realpolitik of Keele, would be exactly what Westhill would need. Status-wise it adds the perfect, possibly ambiguous, flourish to a career—on the one hand, at last a Professor...and a Pro-Vice-Chancellor (i.e. wheeler dealer with ceremonial knobs on), but, Westhill...isn't that some rum Dissenting outfit from Selly Oak? Not quite the real thing? But it is, for a convinced Free Churchman, very much the real thing. It brings John's career together in a very satisfying, indeed elegant, way.

Presiding over this merger was no sinecure. Eric Ives knew he had found the right man, who 'did a very good job for Westhill'. The university absorbed the college as the 'University of Birmingham, Westhill', a faculty under a professor, with courses in continuing education and research projects. Meanwhile the Selly Oak Federation was split up. The university now has a Selly Oak Campus and a Westhill Campus. A Joint Consultative Group replaced the separate governing body. The Free Churches still provide trustees to the Westhill Foundation: assorted trusts complicate the university's intention of buying the land and buildings. By Christmas 2000 the university was satisfied that John had completed the task for which he was appointed, and the Westhill trustees decreed that he should retire at the end of that academic year in July 2001.

New Opportunities

On 7 March 2001 John preached at the closing service of the Free Church Council. As Moderator, he is steering the Free Churches Group into collaborative partnership with Churches Together in England—yet another body that this forward-looking historian is helping to steer into a new phase of life for the twenty-first century.

Still not ready to retire, John was delighted with the Regent's Park College appointment as Senior Research Fellow. He told the Baptist Historical Society committee that it would be good to have research students again. Hearing this, Eric Ives laughed: 'How typical of John! At this stage he should be settling at last to his own research!'

In addition John is now formally registered with the University of Wales and with the Czech Ministry of Education as one of the adjunct teaching staff of the International Baptist Theological Seminary in Prague as Visiting Lecturer in Baptist History.

A Useful Career

When asked to contribute the biographical article to this Festschrift I was delighted, but it has proved surprisingly challenging. Outlining John's career was straightforward, though supplying dates, like a good historian, was harder. The standard reference books had not caught up with this Pro-Vice-Chancellor. I turned to those who knew him, only to find that most liked John but did not *know* him well. Behind the genial manner, John protects his space. A mutual friend tells me that Joyce, whom I have not met, is even more private, yet they have a reputation for warm hospitality. Doreen Rosman observed, 'your comment that for all his ebullient friendliness John is a rather private person struck me as exactly right'. Keith Jones 'always enjoyed his company', and found him a 'good companion in the usual Baptist gossip', yet never knew him well. Haddon Willmer reflects on the nature of his old friend:

> Over the years, John and I have stayed in touch, and feel good friends, sure of each other, but never intimate. As you say, he is a private person, not closed or defensive, but simply relating to others through action, institution, impersonal means. He is none the less for that. The world and church needs such people and should value them—one only has to reflect on the agony and confusion caused in the churches by all the leaders and preachers who use their supposedly ministerial positions to project their personalities and build their empires, to see that people like John are invaluable...
>
> John is a person I would trust with all sorts of things, personally, if I had to, but I cannot pretend to know him at all deeply. Whether if we were near neighbours, we would ever get beneath the skin I cannot guess. He is not driven or disturbed by great worries or by dreams; perhaps that is why he has remained a historian who has never embarked in any little theological boat on the wild sea.

Doreen Rosman perceives that John's kindness can 'lift the skin' a little: 'John doesn't talk much about emotions but I know he can respond to individual need with sympathy and sensitivity. I wonder whether he reveals his feelings on important matters more easily on paper than face to face.' She remembers perceptive and affirming letters when bereaved and when considering a career change.

Another former Victorian Studies student mentions John's kindness. David Rothwell was Head of History at Rutland Sixth Form College, 1971–75, where he founded a History Society which sometimes had visiting lecturers.

> I asked John if he would be prepared to travel from Keele to Rutland, give a talk to this tiny and insignificant group, and in reward only receive his travel expenses. This John most happily agreed to do. His talk was well delivered, and John behaved with charm and courtesy to the entire group. I must confess that this particular kindness is one that I cherish.

For myself, I value a relationship in which I can admit to ignorance without feeling embarrassed. If John mentions something I probably ought to know about but do not, I ask—and have learned much from John's readiness to pause and give a clear, concise explanation. Just occasionally he admits to sharing my ignorance. Our relationship may not be intimate, but it is comfortable. He must often have been tired from travel or long hours when I have rung to chivvy him for yet another editorial, but I cannot remember him ever seeming irritable. His is an equable temperament, calm, dependable, good-humoured, and sometimes humorous. Doreen Rosman added a postscript to her letter:

> I've just found a letter from John written in 1988 which contains what I see as characteristic humour. In response to my first word-processed Christmas letter John wrote: 'I thought I ought to show equal prowess... The fascinating thing, especially for a Methodist, is the theological implications of the technology—that I whose technique is so imperfect can produce something that is perfect helps me to understand a hitherto very difficult Wesleyan emphasis. And as for redemption, even this letter contains a host of redeemed sins that you cannot detect, plus the ones that have eluded my eye!...
>
> What intrigues me about your letter is which parts are standardised and which not; again you see theologically significant—did Moses really have a word-processor, or whoever pseudopigraphed his work, happily cutting and pasting J, D, E and P!

In gathering these reflections, I struggled to reconcile the public personality with the private man. I felt that the picture emerging was not fair to my colleague, yet it was hard to pinpoint what was missing. Our mutual friend, Eljee Bentley, helped here. Probably Eljee and I both respond to something in John because we too get satisfaction from background work that enables others. She wrote:

> I like John, admire him immensely, and know that he is what made me want to become active in the commission and in the Baptist World Alliance. Yet I cannot

say why. What is it about John that I like so much? I am unable to give you any well-thought explanation of my feelings nor pithy description of John. I cannot recall any special incidents of particular interest... I came to respect his knowledge, his integrity, his willingness to do his part. But more impressive is his humility. He does not push himself. He allows others to do what they can, then offers help if it is needed. He never displays his cleverness. He is kind. He is comfortable with who he is and makes others comfortable in his presence. He likes to laugh.

There, surely, is the key to John's personality. The world is puzzled by an able man who has no need to blow his own trumpet but contentedly plays the accompaniment that holds things together: so John remains something of an enigma to many. It must say something about the security of the family, wartime disruptions notwithstanding, and the assurance of the faith in which he was nurtured. His elder brother judges that John's ability to accept the people he meets 'at their face value' is also part of their Nonconformist heritage, which would neither patronize nor kowtow to others. John is comfortable with himself as he is. He does not need to prove himself. As Willmer realized long ago, John is 'at home in world and church'. Perhaps this has made him a disappointing academic, not sufficiently interested in personal success to promote his own career, but it makes him a teacher who encourages others to achieve, an examiner with no need to 'play the inquisitorial torturer', a kindly editor helping writers give of their best, yet a struggling author himself, because his own work rarely seems the most important call on his time. It makes him an effective administrator and negotiator, not concerned to enhance his own reputation but eager to build structures that work and to ease inter-personal relationships, whether in the government of universities or the reconciling of different religious cultures.

Many will not understand such rare playing down of self. Some are not altogether comfortable with John, perhaps because he is comfortable with himself, which is hardly fashionable in individualistic contemporary culture. Many Victorians, in that period beloved of John, were more concerned with a person's *usefulness* in society. John's life has been—and continues to be—eminently useful.

ACKNOWLEDGEMENTS

In compiling this biographical article I acknowledge with gratitude contributions received, mostly in May–July 2001, by post, email, telephone or conversations face to face. These include substantial letters from Professor David Bebbington (1 June 2000), Professor Clyde Binfield (29 May 2000), Professor Andor Gomme, Dr Doreen Rosman and Dr Haddon Willmer, and shorter contributions from the Revd Dr David Russell, the Rt Revd Barry Rogerson, Mr David Rothwell, Dr John Biggs, Professor David Vincent and the Revd Keith Jones. I had extended telephone conversations with Mr Peter Briggs, Professor Eric Ives, the Revd David Tennant, the Revd Ruth Bottoms, Mrs Meg Soper, Mrs Carolyn Busfield and the Revd Peter Egginton. I talked with the Revd Don Black, the Revd Basil Amey and Dr Mary Tanner. The Revd Simon Oxley supplied information on the WCC, Fiona Floate on Regent's Park College, Sylvia Holmes on the Baptist Union and Ruby Burke on the BWA.

PART ONE

ECUMENISM AND HISTORY

CHAPTER 1

Baptism, Christology and the Creeds in the Early Church: Implications for Ecumenical Dialogue

Anthony R. Cross

Introduction

A major feature of the ecumenical movement's search for unity has been its focus, conducted largely through its Faith and Order Commission and its regional commissions and local expressions, on three key issues: baptism, eucharist and ministry.[1] This process is best known for the publication in 1982 of the Lima Text, *Baptism, Eucharist and Ministry* (*BEM*).[2] However, this should in no way be regarded as the culmination of the process, rather it is a significant milestone in an on-going work.[3] Within this larger framework of the ecumenical movement, Professor John Briggs has played an important part over many years, as a Baptist, Free Churchman and committed ecumenist.[4]

In pursuit of the goal of Christian unity numerous conferences, committees, reports and publications have striven for greater

---

1   On the modern ecumenical movement see, e.g., R. Rouse and S.C. Neill (eds.), *A History of the Ecumenical Movement 1517–1948* (Geneva: World Council of Churches, 3rd edn, 1986), particularly chs 8–15; H.E. Fey (ed.), *The Ecumenical Advance: A History of the Ecumenical Movement 1948–1968* (Geneva: World Council of Churches, 2nd edn, 1986); L. Vischer (ed.), *A Documentary History of the Faith and Order Movement 1927–1963* (St Louis, MO: Bethany Press, 1963); and G. Gassmann (ed.), *Documentary History of Faith and Order 1963–1993* (Faith and Order Paper, 159; Geneva: World Council of Churches, 1993).

2   *Baptism, Eucharist and Ministry* (Faith and Order Paper, 111; Geneva: World Council of Churches, 1982).

3   See M. Thurian (ed.), *Churches Respond to BEM: Official Responses to the 'Baptism, Eucharist and Ministry' Text* (6 vols; Faith and Order Papers, 129, 132, 135, 137, 143 and 144; Geneva: World Council of Churches, 1986–88).

4   See Faith Bowers' biographical sketch in the present volume.

understanding and closer co-operation. In Faith and Order's theological discussions there has been a methodological shift from comparative studies to those seeking convergence on vital theological issues.[5] But it must be admitted that while there have been significant advances in interchurch relations directly attributable to the ecumenical movement, there continue to be major obstacles, which often comprise a combination of theological and practical issues. A key problem continues to be the mutual recognition of one anothers' understanding of what it is to be a church: in short, mutual recognition of the churchly nature of the various Christian traditions. This is much less of a problem for those denominations which have a 'Church' ecclesiology—the Roman Catholic Church, Orthodox Church, Anglican/Episcopalian Church, Lutheran Church and Methodist Church, for instance—but it is a major problem for those 'denominations' whose ecclesiologies are radically different. There is a problem here for Baptists whose ecclesiology does not lead them to form the Baptist Church: rather, local Baptist churches join together in associations of churches who covenant to walk together in the work of the kingdom.[6] Baptist ecclesiology begins with the local Baptist church, and their regional, national and international bodies are associations and unions of churches. This was one of the reasons why the Southern Baptist Convention declined to join the World Council of Churches.[7]

This is not to say that Baptists are not an ecclesial community as some have defined it, it is simply a different way of being the church: an ecclesiology which other 'Churches' struggle to understand. Other traditions for whom this is problematic are the Society of Friends and Salvation Army, neither of whom practise the sacraments of baptism and communion. What is more, neither they nor the Brethren have a ministry as understood by others. Further, many Pentecostal and restorationist traditions do not understand themselves to be denominations as such, rather they see themselves as movements of the Spirit. But I and many

---

5   Vischer (ed.), *A Documentary History*, pp. 85-86, reports the statement of the Third Faith and Order Conference held in Lund, Sweden, in 1952: 'we can make no real advance towards unity if we only compare our several conceptions of the nature of the Church... We need, therefore, to penetrate behind our divisions to a deeper and richer understanding of the mystery of the God-given union of Christ with his Church.'

6   See P.S. Fiddes, '"Walking Together": The Place of Covenant Theology in Baptist Life Yesterday and Today', in W.H. Brackney, P.S. Fiddes and J.H.Y. Briggs (eds.), *Pilgrim Pathways: Essays in Baptist History in Honour of B.R. White* (Macon, GA: Mercer University Press, 1999), pp. 47-74.

7   See R.G. Torbet, *A History of the Baptists* (Valley Forge, PA: Judson Press, 3rd edn, 1973), p. 445: '[the Southern Baptist Convention] claimed that membership in the World Council would threaten the autonomy of free churches and might jeopardize the witness of Baptists to believer's baptism and a regenerate church.'

others wish to argue that all these traditions are genuine Christian communities, denominations, in the truest New Testament sense of being churches, and what binds them together as such is not an ecclesiology, nor an understanding of baptism, eucharist or ministry, but the fact that they are an expression of the corporate life in the triune God.

A major development in ecumenical discussions occured at the third Faith and Order Conference held in Lund, Sweden, in 1952. Previous discussion had revolved around the comparative study of theological differences, but this changed to the search for theological convergence. The conference is also notable for what is known as the 'Lund Principle'. This is, in fact, a question which was put to all participating churches, and asked whether they 'should not act together in all matters except those in which deep differences of conviction compel them to act separately?'[8] Over the fifty years since Lund there have been considerable developments in theological convergence,[9] but there continue to be major differences between the participating traditions on ecclesiology, baptism, eucharist and ministry. It needs also to be recognized that while many within these traditions are committed and prepared to participate in theological studies whose purpose is to find greater degrees of theological convergence on these and other issues, there are nevertheless many who remain unconvinced and outside such ecumenical dialogue.

The most recent illustration of such a major stumbling-block is the declaration of the Roman Catholic Church's attitude to other denominations as expressed by Cardinal Joseph Ratzinger in the Congregation for the Doctrine of the Faith's *Dominus Iesus* issued in 2000 and ratified by the Pope.[10] But before it can be discussed, it must be set in the context of the major turning point in the Roman Catholic Church's attitude towards other denominations which was signalled by Vatican II's 'Decree on Ecumenism' (1964). In contrast to centuries of tradition which declared there to be no salvation outside of the Roman Catholic Church, the decree took a new approach, focusing 'more on a

---

8 Vischer (ed.), *A Documentary History*, p. 86. See also W.M.S. West, 'Lund Principle', in N. Lossky *et al.* (eds.), *Dictionary of the Ecumenical Movement* (Geneva: WCC Publications, 1991), pp. 633-34.

9 Among the many documents, see, e.g., M. Thurian and G. Wainwright, *Baptism and Eucharist: Ecumenical Covergence in Celebration* (Faith and Order Paper, 117; Geneva: World Council of Churches/Grand Rapids: Eerdmans, 1983).

10 J. Ratzinger, *Dominus Iesus: On the Unicity and Salvific Universality of Jesus Christ and the Church* (Congregation for the Doctrine of the Faith, 2000), downloaded from the Vatican website, 18 October 2000. For a recent study of the post-Vatican II Roman Catholic Church's interpretation of *extra ecclesiam nulla salus* ('no salvation outside the church'), in which 'the church' has traditionally been understood as the Roman Catholic Church, see F.A. Sullivan, *Salvation Outside the Church? Tracing the History of the Catholic Response* (New York/Mahwah, NJ: Paulist Press, 1992).

"pilgrim" Church moving towards Christ than on a movement of "return" to the Roman Catholic Church'. As such, it went 'beyond the assertion that the Catholic Church is the true Church to assert that Jesus, in His Spirit, is at work in the Churches and Communities beyond the visible borders of the Catholic Church', asserting that 'believers in Christ who are baptized are truly reborn and truly our brothers and that God uses their worship to sanctify and save them'.[11] The decree is also noteworthy for its use of the term 'ecclesial community' to convey the sense

> that the more a Church has of the *essential structures* of the Catholic Church, the more it approaches the ideal of the Church. On this institutional scale of measurement, some are more properly called Churches than others, and the Decree regards Eastern Churches as practically sister Churches of the Roman Catholic Church. (Cf. Art. 14, par. 1 and par. 2). Another reason, of course, for the expression 'ecclesial Communities' and the word 'Communities' throughout the Decree is that some Christian bodies do not wish to be called 'Church.'[12]

It is precisely these 'essential structures' which continue to prove problematic in ecumenical discussions as they involve major differences in theological principles on ecclesiology, baptism, eucharist and ministry, and over which there continues to be mutual misunderstanding.[13] Clearly Baptist bodies do not constitute a 'Church' in this sense, but are unions of churches. But while there was much to debate and many issues still to

---

11 W.M. Abbott, 'Ecumenism', in W.M. Abbott (ed.), *The Documents of Vatican II* (trans. ed. J. Gallagher; London: Geoffrey Chapman, 1966), p. 338. The text of the 'Decree on Ecumenism' (*Unitatis Redintegratio*) is on pp. 341-66.

12 See 'Decree on Ecumenism', in Abbott (ed.), *Documents of Vatican II*, p. 355 n. 45, italics added.

13 One example of this in the British context has been noted in the Baptist Union's (BU) Doctrine and Worship Committee document, *Believing and Being Baptized: Baptism, so-called re-baptism, and children in the church* (Didcot: Baptist Union, 1996), p. 22: 'the direction in much ecumenical debate is *from* the act of baptism *to* the nature of the Church and its ministry. The hope is often expressed that once the baptism of *individuals* has been mutually recognized, it might be possible to proceed to what are felt to be the "more difficult" matters of recognition of *ecclesial* realities, such as ministry and sacrament [presumably meaning the eucharist]. Bafflement is often expressed as to why Baptists will not apparently take what is widely seen to be the "easiest" step of recognising common baptism as the basis for unity', italics original. According to Paul Fiddes (details in A.R. Cross, *Baptism and the Baptists: Theology and Practice in Twentieth-Century Britain* [Studies in Baptist History and Thought; Carlisle: Paternoster, 2000], p. 361), the Baptists' ecumenical partners who have been steadily moving towards the position of a common baptism (see below) received *Believing and Being Baptized* with consternation when they realized that the majority of Baptists were still unwilling and unable to accept infant baptism and confirmation as equivalent to believer's baptism.

be worked out, the significance of this change is hard to underestimate,[14] though it appears less clear in the light of *Dominus Iesus*.

In many ways, *Dominus Iesus* can be seen as a step back to a pre-Vatican II position. In section 16 Ratzinger states that 'The Lord Jesus, the only Saviour, did not establish a simple community of disciples, but constituted the Church as a salvific mystery... [T]he fullness of Christ's salvific mystery belongs to the Church... And...just as the head and members of a living body, though not identical, are inseparable, so too Christ and the Church can neither be confused nor separated, and constitute a single "whole Christ".' He concludes from this that, 'Therefore, in connection with the unicity and universality of the salvific mediation of Jesus Christ, the unicity of the Church founded by him must be firmly believed as a truth of Catholic faith. Just as there is one Christ, so there exists a single body of Christ.' By 'Church' and 'one body of Christ' he means the Roman Catholic Church: 'The Catholic faithful are requested to profess that there is an historical continuity—rooted in the apostolic succession—between the Church founded by Christ and the Catholic Church.' Then quoting from the 'Dogmatic Constitution of the Church',[15] he elaborates: '"This Church, constituted and organized as a society in the present world, subsists in [subsistit in] the Catholic Church, governed by the successor of Peter and by the Bishops in communion with him".'

This is the basis of the following clause, 17, which has caused considerable concern among non-Catholics. He reiterates the dogma that 'there exists a single Church of Christ, which subsists in the Catholic Church, governed by the Successor of Peter and by the Bishops in communion with him.' As a result other 'Churches which, while not existing in perfect communion with the Catholic Church, remain united to her by means of the closest bonds, that is, by apostolic succession and a valid Eucharist, are true particular Churches.' He concedes that 'the Church of Christ is present and operative' in such Churches 'even though they lack full communion with the Catholic Church' due to their non-acceptance of the primacy of the Pope. But 'the ecclesial communities which have not preserved the valid Episcopate and the genuine and integral substance of the Eucharistic mystery, *are not*

---

14   A. Hastings, *A History of English Christianity 1920–1990* (London, SCM Press, 3rd edn, 1991), p. 525: 'There can be no question but that the Vatican Council was the most important ecclesiastical event of this century, not just for Roman Catholics but for all Christians.' See the whole of his discussion of the council, pp. 519-31 and *passim*. See also L. Vischer, 'The Ecumenical Movement and the Roman Catholic Church', in Fey (ed.), *Ecumenical Advance*, especially pp. 322-43; and A. Hastings (ed.), *The Second Vatican Council across 25 Years* (London: SPCK, 1990).

15   'Dogmatic Constitution of the Church' (*Lumen Gentium*) 8, in Abbott (ed.), *Documents of Vatican II*, p. 23.

Churches in the proper sense; however, those who are baptized in these communities are, by Baptism, incorporated in Christ and thus are in a certain communion, *albeit imperfect*, with the Church', that is, the Roman Catholic Church.[16] His conclusion from this is also unacceptable to Baptists and other such ecclesial communities:

'The Christian faithful are therefore not permitted to imagine that the Church of Christ is nothing more than a collection—divided, yet in some way one—of Churches and ecclesial communities; nor are they free to hold that today the Church of Christ nowhere really exists, and must be considered only as a goal which all Churches and ecclesial communities must strive to reach.'[17]

'[T]hese separated Churches and communities as such, though we believe they suffer from defects, have by no means been deprived of significance and importance in the mystery of salvation. For the spirit of Christ has not refrained from using them as means of salvation which derive their efficacy from the very fullness of grace and truth entrusted to the Catholic Church.'[18]

While some Baptists have on the whole emphasized the positive aspects of the document and largely welcomed it,[19] many have expressed disappointment at its language and tone,[20] and seeming reversion to pre-Vatican II views on the ecclesial nature of non-Catholic traditions. Still others have outright rejected it.[21] The considered position of British

---

16   The italicized section is that which Baptists have taken particular exception to.
17   Ratzinger is here quoting *Mysterium Ecclesiae* (1973), 1, see *Dominus Iesus*, n. 64.
18   This is a quote from the 'Decree on Ecumenism', 3, in Abbott (ed.), *Documents of Vatican II*, p. 346.
19   E.g. I. Murdoch-Smith, Moderator of the BU's Church Relations Group and member of the WCC Advisory Group on Church and Ecumenical Relationships, 'Why Baptists Should Welcome *Dominus Iesus*', *Baptist Times*, 21 September 2000, pp. 5 and 11, who welcomed the many positive aspects of the report though lamented the contentious Clause 17, regarding as unfortunate the tieing of 'the uniqueness of God's revelation in Christ to the unique role of the Catholic Church as custodian of that revelation'. He later questioned why Baptists should be bothered by the implications of this: 'Do we aspire to "ecclesiastical precedence"? I seem to remember Jesus saying something about not seeking to rule but to serve; about the first being last; about deliberately sitting in the place of honour at the banquet. After all we wouldn't want the Catholic Church to look upon the Baptist Union as a "sister church" would we—we are not a 'Church', but a Union of independent, local, "ecclesial communities" of faith!'
20   Such as Myra Blyth, Deputy General Secretary of the BU and former Executive Director of the WCC, as reported in M. Finnis, 'Vatican Statement a Major Blow', *Baptist Times*, 7 September 2000, pp. 1-2; and the European Baptist Federation, '"Disappointment" at Vatican document', *Baptist Times*, 5 October 2000, p. 4.
21   E.g. Mr N. Moore-Smith, '*Dominus Iesus* not welcome', *Baptist Times*, 12 October 2000, p. 6.

Baptists is perhaps best summed up by David Coffey: '[*Dominus Iesus*] saddens us, for whatever its intentions the Declaration appears to draw on the language and tone of a past era, and fails to show the kind of mutual respect for each others' traditions that has been the mark of our closer journeying together.' He continues by taking issue with Ratzinger's concessions:

> What does it mean to affirm one Church as 'proper'? Is the true Church really to be measured by having 'preserved the valid Epsicopate and the genuine and integral substance of the Eucharistic mystery'? As Baptists, we cannot recognise any 'proper' churches—only failed, flawed communities of sinners who stand in need of grace and redemption. In as much as these communities seek to follow in the footsteps of Jesus and to be faithful to his way of love, they dare to describe themselves as part of one Church of Jesus Christ throughout the world.[22]

Baptism in Contemporary Ecumenical Thought

The preceeding discussion is intended to show some of the theological and practical complexities with which ecumenical discussions must engage. But the focus of this paper is narrower, concentrating primarily on baptism, and it does so from a British Baptist perspective, though it recognizes the broader debates that are going on. In so doing it continues work begun under Professor's Briggs' supervision at Keele University into developments in twentieth-century British Baptist baptismal theology and practice, a study which identified the ecumenical movement as the most important context and influence on the development of Baptists' theologies and practices of baptism.[23]

One of the most important twentieth-century documents on baptism is Faith and Order's *BEM*. Its section on baptism falls into two parts: discussion of the theology of baptism, followed by issues of baptismal practice.[24] While a great deal of agreement has been registered from the various denominations on the theoretical first part, there has not been a corresponding level of agreement from Baptists on *BEM*'s call for

---

22 D. Coffey, General Secretary of the BU, reported in 'Ratzinger rattles the Protestant cage', *Free Church Chronicle* 53.2 (November, 2000), p. 9. Cf. Brian Haymes, 'Baptist and Pentecostal Churches', in P. Avis (ed.), *The Christian Church* (London: SPCK, forthcoming 2002), whose final paragraph begins, 'In the last anlysis, all our ecclesiologies are provisional.'

23 See Cross, *Baptism*, and 'Baptists and Baptism—A British Perspective', *Baptist History and Heritage* 35.1 (Winter, 2000), pp. 104-21. It is important to note the plural here: there is no single theology or practice of baptism among Baptists, British or otherwise, see Cross, *Baptism*, e.g. p. 463.

24 *BEM* sections I–III, pp. 2-4, and IV–V, pp. 4-7, respectively.

'common baptism',[25] also known as 'mutually recognized baptism'.[26] In Britain this move has been strongly advocated in the Churches Together in England (CTE) report, *Called to be One*,[27] but while there are a number of British Baptists who advocate common baptism,[28] the consequences of such a practice, for Baptists, would be that they refrain from so-called 'rebaptism'.[29] Though several Baptists have called for Baptists to refrain from 'rebaptism' for the sake of Christian unity,[30] the

---

25   *BEM*, Commentary (13), p. 5: 'In some churches which unite both infant-baptist and believer-baptist traditions, it has been possible to regard as equivalent alternatives for entry into the Church both a pattern whereby baptism in infancy is followed by later profession of faith and a pattern whereby believers' baptism follows upon a presentation and blessing in infancy. This example invites other churches to decide whether they, too, could not recognize equivalent alternatives in their reciprocal relationships and in church union negotiations.'

26   For a detailed discussion of the process leading up to and immediately following *BEM* from the Baptist point of view, see Cross, *Baptism*, pp. 266-78, especially the official reponse of the BU, pp. 275-78.

27   *Called to be One* (London: Churches Together in England, 1996), p. 70.

28   For discussion of common baptism, see Cross, *Baptism*, pp. 358-64. See also the recent discussion of C.J. Ellis, 'A View from the Pool: Baptists, Sacraments and the Basis of Unity', *Baptist Quarterly* 39.3 (July, 2001), pp. 117-18.

29   *BEM*, IV. A. 13, p. 4, and Commentary (13), p. 5; *Called to be One*, p. 70. On both documents, see Cross, *Baptism*, pp. 315-18, and the wider discussion of baptism in recent ecumenical developments, pp. 244-318. The practical implications of rebaptism have been further explored in the work of another CTE working party, *Baptism and Church Membership with particular reference to Local Ecumenical Partnerships* (London: Churches Together in England, 1997), e.g., pp. 26-30. To date there are two agreements on baptismal policy within LEPs: *Baptist/Methodist Agreement on Baptismal Policy within Local Ecumenical Projects* (n.d. [1991]) and *The Baptist Union of Great Britain/United Reformed Church Agreed Guidelines for Baptismal Policy in Local Ecumenical Partnerships* (1996). In both the person who is 'rebaptized' has to transfer to the Baptist membership roll. Discussions between the BU and Church of England are in progress.

30   Most notably G.R. Beasley-Murray, 'The Problem of Infant Baptism: An Exercise in Possibilities', in Faculty of the Baptist Theological Seminary, Rüschlikon (eds.), *Festschrift Günter Wagner* (Berne: Peter Lang, 1994), pp. 13-14: 'I make the plea that churches which practise believer's baptism should consider acknowledging the legitimacy of infant baptism, and allow members in Paedobaptist churches the right to interpret it according to their consciences. This would carry with it the practical consequence of believer-baptist churches refraining from baptizing on confession of faith those who have been baptized in infancy.' (Beasley-Murray's views have been welcomed by the Church of Scotland theologian, D.F. Wright, 'Scripture and Evangelical Diversity with Special Reference to the Baptismal Divide', in P.E. Satterthwaite and D.F. Wright [eds.], *A Pathway into the Holy Scripture* [Grand Rapids: Eerdmans, 1994], pp. 265, 267-68.) It should be acknowledged that in practice this is what many British Baptists do. Those churches which practise open membership, or have supplementary membership open to those from paedobaptist traditions, effectively recognize a person's

overwhelming number of Baptists continue to reject this.[31] Dr David Russell, for example, himself deeply involved in and committed to the ecumenical movement, notes that though *BEM* has indeed achieved 'a goodly measure of "convergence"', it nevertheless 'falls short of "consensus", not least in the report's interpretation of baptism and the nature of the Church to which baptism testifies'. *BEM* makes claims for the 'rite' of baptism 'which, in the Baptist mind, belong to the total process of Christian initiation which includes a responsible faith-commitment on the part of the one baptised'.[32] In response to claims made by the Eighth Assembly of the WCC in Harare which located Christian unity in baptism, Ruth Bottoms pointed out that member churches of the WCC were as divided over baptism as they were over the eucharist. Rather, she stated 'We Baptists would want to speak of our common faith in Jesus Christ as our basis for unity.'[33]

This is not intransigence on the part of Baptists, but reflects a commitment to one of their basic theological principles. Further, while Ratzinger seems to have left open recognition of communion 'with the

---

infant baptism if that person is convinced that their baptism as an infant is valid. Such a person is welcomed into membership 'on profession of faith'. However, the majority of Baptists would 'rebaptize', as far as paedobaptists are concerned, those who wish to be baptized as believers and who do not view their baptism in infancy as valid. Baptists, and their Anabaptist precursors and cousins, almost unanimously reject the charge of rebaptism on the grounds that the only valid faith in baptism is the faith of the baptized themself: the faith of parents or the church is, in Baptist theology, inadequate.

31 *Believing and Being Baptized*, p. 15: 'The majority of the committee...refused to regard the rite called "infant baptism" as baptism.' See the fuller discussion, pp. 13-16.

32 D.S. Russell, 'The Ecumenical Role of Baptists', in F.H. Littell (ed.), *The Growth of Interreligious Dialogue 1939–1989* (Toronto Studies in Theology, 46; Lewiston, NY: Edwin Mellen Press, 1989), p. 130. For the most recent Baptist studies into baptism as a process, Christian initiation, see *Believing and Being Baptized*, e.g. pp. 9-12; C.J. Ellis, 'Baptism and the Sacramental Freedom of God', and P.S. Fiddes, 'Baptism and Creation', both in P.S. Fiddes (ed.), *Reflections on the Water: Understanding God and the World through the Baptism of Believers* (Regent's Study Guides, 4; Oxford: Regent's Park College/Macon, GA: Smyth & Helwys, 1996), e.g., p. 31 and pp. 55-56 respectively; A.R. Cross, '"One Baptism" (Ephesians 4.5): A Challenge to the Church', in S.E. Porter and A.R. Cross (eds.), *Baptism, the New Testament and the Church: Historical and Contemporary Studies in Honour of R.E.O. White* (Journal for the Study of the New Testament Supplement Series, 171; Sheffield: Sheffield Academic Press, 1999), pp. 173-209; and A.R. Cross, 'Spirit- and Water-Baptism in 1 Corinthians 12.13', and P.S. Fiddes, 'Baptism and the Process of Christian Initiation', both forthcoming in S.E. Porter and A.R. Cross (eds.), *Dimensions of Baptism: Biblical and Theological Studies* (Journal for the Study of the New Testament Supplement Series; Sheffield: Sheffield Academic Press, 2002).

33 'Baptist concerns over baptism', *Baptist Times*, 17-24 December 1998, p. 1. Ruth Bottoms was the Moderator of the BU's Faith and Unity Executive.

Church' of 'those...baptized in these communities', albeit imperfectly, there is little doubt that he would reject believer's baptism as practised by Baptists and other credobaptists.[34] Similarly, Baptists and other believer-baptists would reject his view that their understanding and practice of baptism is imperfect in the sense he means of a deviation from Roman Catholic theology and practice. There is little likelihood that credobaptists in general will be predisposed to this concession which almost effectively unchurches them.

There seems, then, to be little prospect of a rapprochement in the foreseeable future—if ever. The questions that are seldom asked are whether such a rapprochment is possible, or desirable. Is this, then, the end of the road together, an impasse, or is there a way that could lead towards greater recognition and mutual respect of one anothers' theological and practical principles? A parallel project to *BEM*[35] has explored the possibilty of the common expression of the faith through the Niceno–Constantinopolitan Creed.[36]

An Old Path Revisited

For Baptists the problem with turning to the ecumenical creeds as the basis of Christian unity is their derivative nature to scripture. Some Baptists have been more appreciative of the usefulness of the creeds than others. For example, the General Baptist 'Orthodox Creed' of 1678 declares that 'The three creeds, viz. Nicene creed, Athanasius's creed, and

---

34 'Credobaptists' is the more embracing term than 'Baptists' as it includes those other traditions which practise believer's baptism, see K. Roy, *Baptism, Reconciliation and Unity* (Carlisle: Paternoster, 1997), e.g., pp. 11-12, though J.W. McClendon, *Ethics: Systematic Theology. Volume I* (Nashville, TN: Abingdon, 1988), pp. 19 and 27-35, uses the term 'baptist' in reference to the heirs of the Radical Reformation. Both terms can be used to include the Mennonites, Churches/Disciples of Christ, the Brethren, many Pentecostals and restorationist churches. What Ratzinger and the 'official' Catholic position, as expressed in *Dominus Iesus*, make of the Society of Friends and Salvation Army is not made explicit to my knowledge.

35 K.W. Clements, 'Towards the Common Expression of the Apostolic Faith Today: Baptist Reflections on this Faith and Order Project', *Baptist Quarterly* 33.2 (April, 1989), pp. 63-64, traces the origins of this project to 1920, antedating the first Faith and Order conference by seven years. See the whole of this article, pp. 63-71.

36 See *Confessing One Faith: Towards an Ecumenical Explication of the Apostolic Faith as Expressed in the Nicene–Constantinopolitan Creed (381)* (Faith and Order Paper, 140; Geneva: World Council of Churches, 1987); and also the preliminary studies, e.g., H.G. Link (ed.), *The Roots of Our Common Faith: Faith in the Scriptures and in the Early Church* (Faith and Order Paper, 119; Geneva: World Council of Churches, 1984); H.G. Link (ed.), *A Handbook for Study* (Faith and Order Paper, 124; Geneva: World Council of Churches, 1985).

the Apostles creed...ought throughly to be received and believed',[37] and there was the famous presidential address at the inauguration of the Baptist World Congress in 1905, when Alexander Maclaren said:

> I should like that there should be no misunderstanding...as to where we stand in the continuity of the historic Church. And I should like the first act of this Congress to be the audible and unanimous acknowledgment of our Faith. So I have suggested that, given your consent, it would be an impressive and a right thing, and would clear away a good many misunderstandings and stop the mouth of a good deal of slander—if we here and now, in the face of the world, not as a piece of coercion or discipline, but as a simple acknowledgment of where we stand and what we believe, would rise to out feet and...repeat the Apostles' Creed.

The report of the proceedings adds: 'The whole gathering then instantly rose and repeated, slowly and deliberately, after Dr. Maclaren the whole of the Apostles' Creed.'[38] Morris West is right, then, when he observes that 'A growing number of Baptists are content to use the classic creeds of the church in worship as community confessions of faith. This is particularly true of the Apostles' Creed and rather less true of the Nicene Creed.'[39]

In response to the hesitation of many Baptists to the direction taken by *BEM*, Keith Clements suggested that 'If in response to BEM many Baptists have evinced a degree of unease over what they see as an undue emphasis upon "sacramental" unity—or upon agreement on sacraments and orders as an essential prerequisite of unity—by the same token they might well look more eagerly at this new project which underlines that Faith is no less important than Order and in fact comes first in the search for unity.'[40] But he also identifies the major problem as far as Baptists are concerned: 'Theologically, Baptists have wished to assert unequivocally the authority of *Scripture*, and there is an instinctive fear that to elevate any later statement, of however venerable tradition, to high status would inevitably derogate from the attachment to Scripture.'[41] Baptist hesitation, he notes, is 'over the status of the creeds': when they

---

37 Article 38, 'Orthodox Creed', in W.L. Lumpkin (ed.), *Baptist Confessions of Faith* (Valley Forge, PA: Judson Press, rev. edn, 1969), p. 326.
38 *The Baptist World Congress. London, July 11–19, 1905. Authorised Record of Proceedings* (London: Baptist Union Publication Department, 1905), p. 20. The Apostles' and Nicene Creeds were later included in the most influential of the British Baptist service manuals, E.A. Payne and S.F. Winward, *Orders and Prayers for Church Worship: A Manual for Ministers* (London: Carey Kingsgate Press, 1960), pp. 28-29.
39 W.M.S. West, 'Foundation Documents of the Faith. VIII. Baptists and Statements of Faith', *Expository Times* 91 (May, 1980), p. 233.
40 Clements, 'Towards the Common Expression', p. 63.
41 Clements, 'Towards the Common Expression', p. 68, italics original.

explicate the biblical faith Baptists can welcome their use,[42] but when they are used, as historically they have been, 'in the formalization of faith' and 'by political power to compel uniformity of belief without regard to conscience',[43] then, in West's words, 'all (or almost all!) Baptists would resist the notion that the classic creeds should be enforced as doctrinal standards upon Christians'.[44]

It is not the form of words of the statement of faith in the Niceno-Constantinopolitan creed that is important for Baptists, but the voluntary nature of faith.[45] What is important to Baptists is not the acceptance of the creed as the baptismal creed, nor the rite of baptism per se, but 'that which it indicates, namely the union with Christ by faith'.[46]

> Baptists stress that faith, being our obedient response to God's grace, is an essentially free and personal relationship to God. While faith cannot be without its intellectual element of understanding, an emphasis on a credal formulary can lead to the intellectualization and formalization of belief to the loss of the personal, relational element which is the living heart of faith. Equally, while faith is never simply faith of the isolated individual, but a faith by which the believer is united with the community of the church, such faith cannot be coerced and compelled by external authority.[47]

---

42   K.W. Clements, 'A Response to the Faith and Order Commission Document No. 140', in W.H. Brackney and R.J. Burke (eds.), *Faith, Life and Witness: The Papers of the Study and Research Division of the Baptist World Alliance 1986–1990* (Birmingham, AL: Samford University Press, 1990), pp. 50-51: '[the Niceno–Constantinopolitan creed] will be significant for us in so far as it refers beyond itself to the Scriptures, within which is found the Word of God'.

43   Clements, 'A Response', pp. 49-50. The last point is forcefully made by another Baptist participant in the project, the American E.G. Hinson, 'The Nicene Creed Viewed from the Standpoint of the Evangelization of the Roman Empire', in S.M. Heim (ed.), *Faith to Creed: Ecumenical Perspectives on the Affirmation of the Apostolic Faith in the Fourth Century* (Grand Rapids: Eerdmans, 1991), p. 117.

44   West, 'Baptists and Statements of Faith', p. 233. This statement immediately follows on from the passage quoted above.

45   The importance of the voluntary principle for Baptists, and other Free Churches, has been discussed in detail by W.H. Brackney in a number of works: *Voluntarism: The Dynamic Principle of the Free Church* (Wolfville, NS: Acadia University, 1992), *Christian Voluntarism in Britain and North America: A Bibliography and Critical Assessment* (New York: Greenwood Publishing, 1995), and *Christian Voluntarism: Theology and Praxis* (Grand Rapids: Eerdmans, 1997).

46   Clements, 'A Response', p. 52.

47   Clements, 'A Response', pp. 49-50. Hinson, 'Nicene Creed', p. 117, concurs: 'From their predominantly Calvinist theology [Baptists] drew a theological principle that they made the axle around which their well-known concern for religious liberty turned. "God alone is Lord of the conscience," they insisted. "Therefore, to be authentic and responsible, faith must be free. If it is imposed, it is not faith." This voluntary

Clements raises further objections to the claim that 'the Nicene Creed served as an expression of the unity of the Early Church and is, therefore, also of great importance for our contemporary quest for the unity of Christ's Church'.[48] First is the historical justification for such a claim,[49] for how much 'unity' was there and of what kind was it in the fourth and fifth centuries; how much of this unity was due to the creed or to what extent was the creed part of this unifying process? Secondly, why should a fourth-century statement be understood to be crucial for our contemporary quest for unity? The subsequent history of the church shows that despite the existence of the Nicene Creed unity was neither achieved nor maintained. Further, the creed is not a full account of essential Christianity, as its neglect of such vital doctrines as the atonement make plain. 'What is more, does not the extent to which the creed now requires explanation indicate its inadequacy as a statement of unifying faith for today?'[50] This applies equally to those Baptists who hold a symbolic understanding of baptism and a sacramental one, for both 'regard the prevenience of God's grace in Christ as absolutely foundational to the meaning of baptism'.[51]

Both Glenn Hinson and Keith Clements have suggested that a positive contribution which Baptists can make to this ongoing project comes from their missionary emphasis. Hinson believes that 'Southern Baptists, and possibly others as well, will be more likely to undertake a sympathetic and objective reappraisal [of the Nicene Creed] if they can look at the fourth century in light of an understanding of the church as mission... When they hear the Johannine version [of the Great Commission, Mt. 18.19] in Jesus' "high priestly" prayer (John 17:21), their thoughts glide right past the petition "that all may be one" in order to get to the purpose clause "that the world may believe."'[52] Elsewhere Hinson describes this in terms of ecumenical pragmatism:

> The Baptist record in ecumenism, visible in a multiplicity of groups, clearly leans toward cooperation and away from union or merger, even with other Baptists. Baptists participate in ecumenical organizations which aid them in achieving their

---

principle stands behind Baptist rejection of infant baptism, for, in their view, infants could not voluntarily yield their wills to God.'

48 Cited by Clements, 'A Response', p. 50.

49 Made, for example, by J. Meyendorff, 'The Nicene Creed: Uniting or Dividing Confession?', in Heim (ed.), *Faith to Creed*, p. 8: 'what we now generally call the "Nicene Creed" emerged as a truly uniting text—accepted by the entire Christian world for centuries and (in principle) until our own time as the legitimate expression of the Christian faith.'

50 Clements, 'A Response', p. 50.

51 Clements, 'A Response', p. 53.

52 Hinson, 'Nicene Creed', p. 119. This is the whole thrust of Hinson's paper, pp. 117-28.

goals, without requiring too much commitment or threatening their autonomy or independence.[53]

Similarly, Clements remarks that 'to be "apostolic" has commonly been assumed to mean "faithful to what the apostles taught" and so it is—and more. It is to be faithful to what they did, and were sent to do, namely to be the witnesses of Jesus to all people and all creation... [E]ach generation is to be apostolic in this journeying, witnessing sense. Being apostolic means not remaining still but being sent "to the end of the earth" and "to the end of time". It means continuity with what the first apostles proclaimed—pursuing the direction they set, pointing towards what they first saw and heard...'[54]

But the study of the early creeds also suggests an alternative path to Christian unity.

Baptism, the Creeds and the Unity of All Christians in Christ

It is generally recognized that the great ecumenical creeds developed from the earliest credal material which is to be found in the New Testament and literature of the earliest church. The presence of such material has long been recognized[55] and its development has been traced to several life settings: the church's mission preaching, worship (including baptism and the Lord's Supper), catechetical instruction and the church's response to opposition.[56] In each setting the core of these credal statements was theological in that they are primarily

---

53   E.G. Hinson, 'William Carey and Ecumenical Pragmatism', *Journal of Ecumenical Studies* 17.2 (Spring, 1980), p. 73. He illustrates this mainly through the life and mission work of Carey, but also, p. 73, with reference to Southern Baptist, American Baptist and English Baptist examples. Cf. Haymes, 'Baptist and Pentecostal Churches', in his concluding section on 'Visions of the Ecumenical Future': 'Some Baptists will remain committed to the ecumenical movement. Those who do so will have the mission of the Church primarily in mind. The merger plans of the last century had little appeal since the deeper question remains that of the renewal of the Church in the mission of God.'

54   Clements, 'Towards the Common Expression', pp. 70-71.

55   Useful summaries of the New Testament material are to be found in J.N.D. Kelly, *Early Christian Creeds* (London: Longman, 3rd edn, 1972), pp. 6-29; R.P. Martin, 'Creed', in G.F. Hawthorne and R.P. Martin (eds.), *Dictionary of Paul and His Letters* (Downers Grove, Ill/Leicester: IVP, 1993), pp. 190-92; D.F. Wright, 'Creeds, Confessional Forms', in R.P. Martin and P.H. Davids (eds.), *Dictionary of the Later New Testament and Its Developments* (Downers Grove, Ill/Leicester: IVP, 1997), pp. 255-60; and W.J. Porter, 'Creeds and Hymns', in C.A. Evans and S.E. Porter (eds.), *Dictionary of New Testament Background* (Downers Grove, Ill/Leicester: IVP, 2000), pp. 231-38.

56   See Kelly, *Creeds*, pp. 13-23.

christological.[57] Further, it was the baptismal context which was central for the development of the creeds,[58] for from it the second and third century rules of faith developed and from them the creeds proper from the fourth century and onwards.

The earliest and most basic credal statement is 'Jesus is Lord' (Rom. 10.9), which is widely accepted as originating in a baptismal context,[59] though it was also used in other contexts.[60] A number of other credal statements are clearly baptismal (e.g. Eph. 5.14; Tit. 3.4-7; 1 Pet. 3.18-22). What is important for our purposes here is to notice that New Testament baptism is fundamentally defined in terms of christology and, in the case of Matthew 28.19, the Trinity. While, according to the book of Acts, the earliest baptisms were 'in the name of Jesus Christ' (Acts 2.38; 10.48; cf. Rom. 6.3; Gal. 3.27) or simply 'the name of the Lord Jesus' (Acts 8.16; 19.5), there is no need to see a conflict with this and Matthew 28.19's baptism in the threefold name, which is best understood as a semitism indicating that disciples are those baptized 'with reference to, for the sake of, or simply with the Father, the Son, and the Holy Spirit in mind'.[61] Further, much of the early credal material is binitarian in form

---

57 Martin, 'Creed', pp. 191-92, notes that the centre of the church's mission proclamation was 'the claim that God has exalted Jesus as sovereign Lord (Rom 10:9-10)'; that the baptismal confession was 'Jesus is Lord' (1 Cor. 12.3; Rom. 10.9-10, cf. Eph. 5.26); and that in response to resistance and challenge, 'the primary creed confessing the messiahship of Jesus gave way to longer expositions hailing his cosmic authority over demonic powers (Phil 2:6-11; Col 1:15-20; 1 Tim 3:16...)', and that part of Paul's response 'was to build on the Jewish monotheistic credo (Deut 6:4-5; Is 45:22) with its belief in one God (1 Cor 8:6) and to christianize it with a confession of the lordship of Christ, both pre-existent (Phil 2:6; 1 Cor 10:4; 2 Cor 8:9) and exalted (Phil 2:9-11; Rom 1:3-4).'

58 Kelly, *Creeds*, p. 31: 'It was precisely the need for a formal affirmation of belief to be rehearsed by the catechumen at baptism which instigated the Church to invent creeds in the first place. Whatever uses they may have been put to in the course of history, the true and original use of creeds, their primary *raison d'être*, was to serve as solemn affirmations of faith in the context of baptismal initiation.' So too F.M. Young, *The Making of the Creeds* (London: SCM Press/Philadelphia, PA: Trinity Press International, 1991), p. 6: 'The creeds took the form they did in response to the situation in which they arose, namely the context of catechesis and baptism.'

59 G.R. Beasley-Murray, *Baptism in the New Testament* (Exeter: Paternoster, 1972 [1962]), pp. 66, 87 and 100-102. W.A. Meeks, *The First Urban Christians: The Social World of the Apostle Paul* (New Haven, CN: Yale University Press, 1983), p. 152, sees baptism as the most likely setting.

60 J.D.G. Dunn, *Romans 9–16* (Word Biblical Commentary, 38B; Dallas, TX: Word, 1988), p. 607, widens this confession's use to include not just baptism but also worship (1 Cor. 12.3), evangelism (2 Cor. 4.5) and parenesis (Col. 2.6).

61 N.A. Dahl, 'Trinitarian Baptismal Creeds and New Testament Christology', in N.A. Dahl, *Jesus the Christ: The Historical Origins of Christological Doctrine* (ed. D.H.

(Father and Son; e.g., 1 Cor. 8.6; 1 Tim. 6.13-14; 2 Tim. 4.1),[62] but there are also 'trinitarian' statements (1 Cor. 12.4-6; 2 Cor. 13.14; Eph. 4.4-6; Pet. 1.2), the clearest of which is Matthew 28.19.[63] The whole issue of the authenticity of this 'formula' is not of concern here: what is, is the fact that Matthew 28.19 went on to have a determinative influence on the development of the creeds.[64] The later baptismal interrogations clearly developed from it,[65] as did the practise of threefold immersion.[66] The various rules of faith (summaries of the faith that were often given to baptismal candidates, cf. Tertullian, *On the Spectacles* 4), developed in second- and third-century writers such as Irenaeus, Tertullian, Hippolytus and Origen, and were increasingly given a trinitarian form, most likely on the basis of Matthew 28.19. Like the credal material before them and the creeds after them, these rules varied in wording and even in the order of their main points, but the 'essential message was fixed by the facts of the gospel and the structure of Christian belief in one God, reception of salvation in Christ, and experience of the Holy Spirit'.[67]

The study of the early credal material clearly shows that there was no uniformity in either the baptismal rite or the wording of the baptismal confession. But what is remarkable is how similar the baptismal liturgy, including the credal formulae, was throughout the entire Christian world. John Meyendorff notes that practically all the credal formulae from this period 'include elements that distinguish catholic Christianity from

---

Juel; Minneapolis, MN: Fortress Press, 1991), p. 177. Also Beasley-Murray, *Baptism*, pp. 89-91.

62   See Kelly, *Creeds*, pp. 19-22.

63   Commenting on these twofold and threefold patterns W.G. Rusch, *The Trinitarian Controversy* (Sources of Early Christian Thought; Philadelphia, PA: Fortress Press, 1983), p. 2, observes that in the New Testament there is no fixity of wording and no doctrine of the Trinity in the Nicene sense: 'However, the threefold pattern is evident throughout, in spite of the fact that there is usually nothing in the context to demand it. The conclusion seems obvious: the idea of the triadic manifestation of the Godhead was present from the earliest period as part of Christian piety and thinking.'

64   Cf. J.N.D. Kelly, *Early Christian Doctrines* (London: A & C Black, 5th edn, 1977), p. 89.

65   See Kelly, *Creeds*, pp. 40-49.

66   Dahl, 'Trinitarian Baptismal Creeds', pp. 176-77, notes that the threefold immersion accompanied by a threefold interrogatory creed is to be found in Hippolytus, Cyprian and Tertullian, and was likely presupposed by Irenaeus and Justin Martyr earlier in the second century, while *Didache* 7.1-3 shows that a threefold baptismal immersion was practised at the end of the first and beginning of the second century, though it is not possible to tell whether it was accompanied by a threefold interrogation.

67   E.F. Ferguson, 'Rule of Faith', in E.F. Ferguson (ed.), *Encyclopedia of Early Christianity* (New York: Garland, 2nd edn, 1999), pp. 1003-1004. On the rules of faith, see also Kelly, *Creeds, passim*, and R.P.C. Hanson, *Tradition in the Early Church* (Library of History and Doctrine; London: SCM Press, 1962), pp. 75-129.

Gnosticism', and that these are the unity of God the creator, the life, death and resurrection of Christ and the sending of the Spirit. 'There is little formalism about the wording, but there is a clear and universal concern for a doctrinally united, universal commitment to the one faith, accepted consciously and personally, as one entered the church.'[68] There was no attempt to standardize them and the three constant elements were trinitarian. According to Origen, these were 'The particular points clearly delivered in the teaching of the apostles'.[69] Jaroslav Pelikan adds, 'apostolic continuity...did not preclude discussion of other issues, but this central content was not negotiable'.[70]

The creeds as we now know them began to emerge in the fourth century, though they did not originally serve as tests of orthodoxy, but as 'summaries of faith taught to new Christians by their local bishop, summaries that were traditional to each local church and which in detail varied from place to place'.[71] Comparison of two of the most important creeds, the Niceno–Constantinopolitan Creed (which was a development of a local eastern creed adopted by the Council of Constantinople in 381) and the Apostles' Creed (which is descended from the Old Roman Creed) is their three-part structure—clauses on God the Father, God the Son and God the Holy Spirit.[72]

Clearly, then, it is not the creeds themselves which are the basis of the church's unity, rather it is that to which the creeds bear witness, a relationship with the triune God. As John Meyendorff puts it, the Niceno–Constantinopolitan creed 'was never an end in itself; it was a symbol of unity'.[73] To seek to locate Christian unity in any creed or confession of faith, is to make primary that which is only secondary. The rightful place of the creeds was eloquently identified by Philip Schaff: 'The Church is, indeed, not founded on symbols, but on Christ; not on any words of man, but on the word of God; yet it is founded on Christ as

---

68 Meyendorff, 'The Nicene Creed', pp. 5-6. Meyendorff, pp. 12-13, notes the Niceno-Constantinopolitan Creed only came to have a fixed form in the East following the Council of Chalcedon in 415 and that the West followed later. A.M. Ritter, 'Creeds', in I. Hazlett (ed.), *Early Christianity: Origins and Evolution to AD 600. In Honour of W.H.C. Frend* (London: SPCK, 1991), pp. 97-98, comments, 'this was very much only the outcome of a long process'. It was not until the sixth century that churches recited the creeds in worship, see E.G. Hinson, 'Creeds and Christian Unity: A Southern Baptist Perspective', *Journal of Ecumenical Studies* 23.1 (Winter, 1986), p. 35.

69 Origen, *On First Principles* Preface 4.

70 J. Pelikan, *The Christian Tradition: A History of the Development of Doctrine. 1. The Emergence of the Catholic Tradition (100–600)* (Chicago: University of Chicago Press, 1971), p. 117, conflates these three elements into two.

71 Young, *Making*, p. 3.

72 Young, *Making*, pp. 3-5. On the Niceno-Constantinopolitan Creed, see Kelly, *Creeds*, pp.205-262 and 296-367, and on the Old Roman Creed, pp. 100-166.

73 Meyendorff, 'The Nicene Creed', p. 15.

confessed by men, and a creed is man's answer to Christ's question, man's acceptance and interpretation of God's word.'[74] This is not to diminish either theology or the creeds, but rather to emphasize that the heart of Christianity is christological, a point also highlighted by Adolf Ritter:

> According to the New Testament, to 'confess' is equivalent to *homologein*. The noun derived from it, *homologia* (confession), does not mean an enumeration of diverse *credenda* (things to be believed), rather the acknowledgement of the divine One, the person of Jesus Christ; acceptance of him suffices to distinguish a Christian from a non-Christian.[75]

James Dunn similarly concludes his investigation into the unity and diversity of first-century Christianity, when he identifies

> *a fairly clear and consistent unifying strand* which from the first both marked out Christianity as something *distinctive* and different and provided the *integrating centre* for the diverse expressions of Christianity. That unifying element was the unity between the historical Jesus and the exalted Christ...the conviction that the wandering charismatic preacher from Nazareth had died and been raised from the dead to bring God and man finally together, the recognition that the divine power through which they now worshipped and were encountered and accepted by God was one and the same person, Jesus, the man, the Christ, the Son of God, the Lord, the life-giving Spirit.[76]

But we must ensure that this christological core is not separated from its own trinitarian nature: that christology is related to theology in the fullest sense of the doctrine of the person of the triune God. Nils Dahl cautions that

> New Testament Christology can be treated properly only if it is related to faith in God... [W]hat is said about Christ cannot be isolated from early Christian experience of the Holy Spirit, the Spirit of God and of Christ. Jesus is represented as the Christ of God, the Son and agent of God, the righteous sufferer who was vindicated by God; language used to speak about God is transferred to Jesus as well.[77]

The opening of the creeds is indicative of what the early church believed to be truly both crucial and distinctive. In J.N.D. Kelly's words:

---

74   P. Schaff (ed.), *The Creeds of Christendom: With a History and Critical Notes* (ed. D.S. Schaff; 3 vols; Grand Rapids, MI: Baker Books, 1983 [rev. edn, 1931]), I, p. 5, italics original.
75   Ritter, 'Creeds', pp. 92-93.
76   J.D.G. Dunn, *Unity and Diversity in the New Testament: An Inquiry into the Character of Earliest Christianity* (London: SCM Press, 1977), p. 369, italics original.
77   Dahl, 'Trinitarian Baptismal Creeds', pp. 179-80.

'The classical creeds of Christendom opened with a declaration of belief in one God, maker of heaven and earth', and 'The doctrine of one God, the Father and creator, formed the background and indisputable premiss of the Church's faith.'[78] This theological point cannot be overemphasized for it reveals the primary concern of the creeds: they are above all else theological in the fullest sense that they are about God— Father, Son and Holy Spirit. In a similar way, Glenn Hinson notes that 'the Niceno–Constantinopolitan Creed of 381, is *primarily personal and relational, not propositional*, although it contains propositions. *The central thrust of it is toward faith in God—Father, Son, and Holy Spirit...*'[79] He continues, noting how the Protestant creeds and confessions of the sixteenth century deviated from this when they came to focus more on the scriptures in their attempt to establish their basis of authority in debates with Roman Catholics.[80] Philip Thompson, however, has made the important observation that the earliest Baptists did not follow this general Protestant trend, and he shows that the major seventeenth-century Baptist confessions began by focusing on God: 'Significantly, in both the catechetical and confessional pieces produced by the early Baptists, treatment was almost always given first not to humanity or the Scriptures, as in similar documents of other Reformed bodies, but to God and the utter distinction between God and creation.'[81] This observation shows that by beginning with God early Baptist thought had more in common with the theological intention of the early Christian

---

78   Kelly, *Doctrines*, pp. 83 and 87.
79   Cf. D.A. Hagner, *Matthew 14–28* (Word Biblical Commentary, 33B; Dallas, TX: Word, 1995), p. 888, who also emphasizes the relational dimension when he comments that 'this baptism brings a person into an existence that is fundamentally determined by, i.e., ruled by, Father, Son, and Holy Spirit'. Beasley-Murray, *Baptism*, p. 91: 'Baptism...sets a man in that relationship which one has in view in the performance of it. On this analogy baptism, in the name of the Father, etc., sets the baptized in a definite relation to God; the Father, Son and Holy Spirit become to the baptized what their name signifies.'
80   Hinson, 'Creeds and Christian Unity', p. 33, italics added. He then warns that 'Protestants today need constantly to be reminded that they did not intend thereby to substitute faith in the Scriptures for faith in God'.
81   P.E. Thompson, 'Toward Baptist Ecclesiology in Pneumatological Perspective' (PhD thesis, Emory University, 1995), pp. 42-43 (forthcoming as *The Freedom of God: Toward Baptist Ecclesiology in Pneumatological Perspective* [Studies in Baptist History and Thought; Carlisle: Paternoster]). Such include, pp. 43-44, the Particular Baptists' 1644 'London Confession' and 1655 'Midland Confession', and the General Baptists' 1651 'The Faith and Practice of Thirty Congregations' and 1678 'Orthodox Creed', the one exception was the 1677 Particular Baptist 'London Confession' which was a slightly modified version of the 'Westminster Confession', and thus began with the scriptures. For the confessions themselves, see Lumpkin, *Baptist Confessions*, pp. 156-57, 198, 176-77, 298-301 and 248-49.

creeds than is usually recognized, and it is something which some modern Baptist writers are seeking to recover.[82]

This path through the creeds towards recognizing one another in Christ is supported by four other biblical and theological observations. We have already noted Hinson's point that the creeds are relational. He maintains that it is both important and helpful to think of the reciprocal interaction between the scriptures and the creeds 'in relation to the covenant concept which is so central both in the Hebrew Bible and the New Testament and in the history of the church. Both individually and corporately the central Christian concern is faithfulness to God according to the covenant into which believers have entered. The Scriptures, not by accident called the Old and New Covenants, relate the story of God's dealings with the covenant people and their responses.'[83] Covenant, biblically and theologically understood, is a two-way relationship of love and commitment between the triune God and his people. The former is reflected in the Hebrew covenant term *chesed*, 'steadfast love', the later in the summary declaration of covenant, 'I will be your God and you will be my people'. But covenant also relates to the relationships among his people who are one precisely because of their relationship to him. This dimension, too, is to be marked by love and commitment.

Secondly, the images employed by the New Testament writers for the people of God also support the position we are seeking to establish. The defining and distinctive feature of the church is the fact that it is God's: 'you are a chosen race, a holy nation, *God's own people*' (1 Pet.2.9); '[you]...are called *to belong to Jesus Christ*' (Rom. 1.6). The church owes its very existence to the triune God—Father, Son and Holy Spirit—and many of the images of the church found in the New Testament[84] make this relationship explicit. It is the church of God (1 Cor. 1.2; Acts 20.28 [a verse which brings together all three persons of the Trinity]; 1 Thess. 1.1 describes the church of Thessalonica as 'in God the Father

---

82   E.g. B. Haymes, A.R. Cross and R. Gouldbourne, *On Being the Church: Revisioning Baptist Identity* (Studies in Baptist History and Thought; Carlisle: Paternoster, forthcoming 2003), in which the authors ground their study of Baptist identity in the doctrine of God. Another example of this starting point for doing theology is P.S. Fiddes, *Participating in God: A Pastoral Doctrine of the Trinity* (London: Darton, Longman and Todd, 2000). I also believe that C.H. Pinnock's *Flame of Love: A Theology of the Holy Spirit* (Downers Grove, Ill: InterVarsity Press, 1996) could also be categorized as another example of this approach though it is primarily a study of the Holy Spirit. See, e.g., the first chapter 'Spirit & Trinity', pp. 21-48, the first section of which is entitled 'Why Begin Here?'

83   Hinson, 'Creeds and Christian Unity', p. 34.

84   P.S. Minear, *Images of the Church in the New Testament* (Philadelphia: Westminster, 1960), identifies ninety-six images, which are supplemented by J.D.G. Dunn, *The Theology of Paul the Apostle* (Edinburgh: T. & T. Clark, 1998), pp. 536-37.

and the Lord Jesus Christ'), while Galatians 1.22 speaks of the 'churches of Judea that are in Christ' (cf. Rom. 16.16 'the churches of Christ'); the people of God (Rom. 9.25-26); children of God (Rom. 8.14-17); the household of God (Eph. 2.19); 'we are the temple of the living God; as God said, "I will live in them and walk among them, and I will be their God, and they shall be my people"' (2 Cor. 6.16, cf. 1 Cor. 3.16-17); while in 1 Corinthians 6.19 the person of the Holy Spirit is mentioned: 'your [plural] body is a temple of the Holy Spirit'; God's servants, his field and his building (1 Cor. 3.9); and the bride of Christ (Rev. 19.7, cf. 2 Cor. 11.2). Acts 11.26 records that it was in Antioch that 'the disciples were first called "Christians"', a name which means 'Christ-people'.[85] The dominant theological image for the church in Paul's thought is 'the body of Christ' (e.g. Rom. 12.4-5; 1 Cor. 10.16-17; 11.24, 27, 29; 12.12-13, 14-27; Eph. 4.4; and Col. 1.24). Of this body, Paul tells us in Ephesians 5.23 and Colossians 1.18, Christ is the 'head', a metaphor which speaks of Christ's authority over the church (used in Eph. 1.22 in reference to Christ's supremacy and authority over the cosmos), but also the fact that he is its source or origin.[86] Not only is the church identified as belonging to God, but it gains its life, its very existence from him. This is reflected in Jesus' prayer: 'As you, Father, are in me and I am in you, may they also be in us' (Jn 17.21). This is underlined by Colossians 2.19 which shows us that the 'head' is the source of the body's ongoing life, 'growth'. Ephesians 4.4-6 explicitly brings together the church in its relationship with the three persons of the Trinity. The importance of all this must not be overlooked, for all discussions of the nature of the church must be based on this foundation.[87]

Thirdly, in an important study of 'Baptism and the Unity of the Church in the New Testament', James Dunn has further developed his wealth of work on the understanding of baptism as a part of the the total event of becoming a Christian: conversion–initiation. While scholars might well disagree on the exact relationships of the various elements of this process,[88] Dunn is unquestionably right when he states 'that the

---

85   Cf. F.F. Bruce, *The Book of Acts* (New International Commentary on the New Testament; Grand Rapids: Eerdmans, rev. edn, 1988), p. 228.
86   See A.T. Lincoln, *Ephesians* (Word Biblical Commentary, 42; Dallas, TX: Word, 1990), pp. 368-70.
87   So, e.g., the Baptist Union's report on episcopacy, *Transforming Superintendency* (Didcot: Baptist Union, 1996), pp. 3 and 9, opens with a discussion of the triune nature of God and it is from this that all else follows.
88   See, e.g., my forthcoming study 'Spirit- and Water-Baptism' in which I take issue with Dunn and others who separate Spirit- and water-baptism.

decisive factor in conversion–initiation was the gift of the Spirit'.[89] He draws out a number of important conclusions from his study which indicate 'some dangers of stressing the ritual moment'. Several of them are of particular note to the present discussion. He questions whether 'a theology of baptism which functions as a unifying factor among churches which honor the biblical canon as the norm also needs to observe the relative weight and emphasis which the NT writers placed on the different elements in conversion–initiation. *The centrality and sovereignty of the Spirit is particularly prominent, as also its correlative faith.* Whatever weight we judge ought to be placed on baptism should not be allowed to obscure or diminish *these centralities.*'[90] This leads him to an 'embarrassing question':

> Is our discussion of baptism and unity unhelpfully, or even misleadingly, focused? We say baptism is an act of God. But our disputes are all about the *humanly devised* rubrics which control the administration of the sacrament. Should our discussion not take our *theology* more seriously and orient itself in relation to *God's* action? What matters is whether God has acted in a human life. And where God has so acted, baptism is (properly speaking) a secondary consideration—still of major importance, but secondary.[91]

Dunn asks us to consider the acceptance of the Gentiles into the church as recorded in Acts 10–11: 'What settled all the questions was the manifest action of God in the life of Cornelius. Peter argued not *from* baptism, but from the evident work of the Spirit *to* baptism' (Acts 10.47). 'The basis of Christian *fellowship* is the *shared experience of* the Holy Spirit.' He therefore concludes:

> Ought we not to orient our conclusions to this most fundamental datum? Ought we not to be discussing such questions as: How may we better recognize the grace of God in a human life, and give that greater prominence as a criterion of unity than we have given it hitherto? And how may we better correlate the importance of 'the shared experience of the Spirit' for unity, with the issue of baptism and unity?[92]

This is in accord with the common Baptist practice of working with other Christians who share the same faith in God and concern for doing the work of God in the world, what is often termed 'grass-roots' ecumenism.

Finally, the import of what Paul says in 1 Corinthians 12.18 must not be overlooked: 'But *as it is*, God arranged the members in the body, each

---

89   J.D.G. Dunn, 'Baptism and the Unity of the Church in the New Testament', in M. Root and R. Saarinen (eds.), *Baptism and the Unity of the Church* (Grand Rapids: Eerdmans/Geneva: WCC Publications, 1998), p. 82.
90   Dunn, 'Baptism and the Unity of the Church', pp. 101-102, italics added.
91   Dunn, 'Baptism and the Unity of the Church', p. 102, italics original.
92   Dunn, 'Baptism and the Unity of the Church', pp. 102-103.

one of them, *as he chose*' (NRSV). The two italicized phrases are significant. The unity of the body is 'as it is'; it already exists and, according to Paul in Ephesians 4.3, is something which Christians must make every effort to maintain. And it is not the decision of any part of the church to decide who is in and who is outside *God's* church. This is God's prerogative alone. Through the ages Christians have found it difficult to acknowledge the Lord's teaching in, for example, Matthew 13.24-30 of the mixed kingdom, of wheat and weeds existing side by side. Various theologians down the ages have wisely developed the teaching of the visible and the invisible church. Contemporary ecumenical discussions would do well to try and avoid using such theologies to the purpose of excluding and instead seek to discern fellow members of God's people, in all their rich variety and diversity of theology and practice. The basis for this as a genuine 'ecumenical path' is to be found in those biblical passages which talk of the body of Christ (Rom. 12, 1 Cor. 12 and Eph. 4), for these very same passages are also those which recognize the body's legitimate diversity.

Christian unity, then, is not based on agreement on ecclesiology, baptism, eucharist or ministry (though this is not to imply that these are unimportant), but in our common life in God—Father, Son and Holy Spirit.

Conclusion

Recently, Christopher Ellis has explored the activity of the Holy Spirit as the basis for unity, though he admits that 'Incorporation into the life of the triune God could be argued as a fuller basis.'[93] Ellis, though, limits his discussion to the Spirit and offers three suggestions on how the Spirit creates unity and enables Christians to recognize other Christians. First, the Spirit is the Spirit of unity and draws people into Christ and towards one another. Secondly, becoming a Christian is the work of the Spirit, and when Christians recognize faith in others they are not validating their status as Christians but celebrating the work of the Spirit in them. Thirdly, Christians experientially recognize the work of the Spirit in others

---

93 Ellis, 'A View from the Pool', pp. 107-120, quote from p. 118. This was earlier argued for by Neville Clark, The Fulness of the Church of God', in A. Gilmore (ed.), *The Pattern of the Church: A Baptist View* (London: Lutterworth Press, 1963), pp. 95-96: '"Our fellowship is with the Father and with his Son Jesus Christ" [1 Jn 1.3] because there has been granted to us "participation (*koinonia*) in the Spirit." [Phil. 2.1; 2 Cor. 13.14] As at Pentecost, it is the corporate sharing in the Holy Spirit that makes the people of God... The Church for God is the fellowship of the Spirit... She exists...to actualize in her own life and being the kingly rule of Christ..., to mirror through communion the love that binds together the blessed Trinity.'

through the exercise of faith and other gifts, and through Christ-like fruit in their lives. To those who would object that these criteria are subjective or individualistic Ellis agrees, and points out that the focus of attention on external criteria in the search for unity on the basis of a common baptism—or, we may add, eucharist, ministry or ecclesiology—excludes some within the community and encourages nominalism. To this end, he practically argues for 'a vision of unity which can be described as "reconciled diversity" and a plurality of baptismal practices'.[94] This mutual recognition of the different theologies and practices of the various Christian traditions, I believe, is the inevitable outcome of recognition that Christian unity is based, not on uniformity in theology or practice which in any case, I believe, is never likely to be attained this side of the parousia, but on our common life with God in Christ in the power of the Spirit. This was expressed over forty years ago by George Beasley-Murray when he objected to the impression given by the Faith and Order report *One Lord, One Baptism* that there exists agreement on the subject of baptism. In response he identified Christian unity in trinitarian terms: 'If it be asked wherein the unity of the Church does lie, if not in one baptism, the answer, surely, must be: *in the common confession of that to which Biblical baptism points*, namely the redemption of God in Christ and participation in it through the Holy Spirit by faith.'[95]

This is wholly in accord with the evidence of the New Testament and patristic thought. According to J.N.D. Kelly the fathers of every school shared the conviction, which they derived from Paul's teaching, 'that Christians form a mystical unity with one another through their fellowship with, and incorporation into, Christ'.[96] Christian unity is a mystical unity. Ultimately only God knows who are truly his and the ecumenical preoccupation with unity based on matters of church order and conformity to a set formula are alien to the theology of the New Testament and the nature and intention of the early creeds. Further, I believe, that the ecumenical concentration on unity on the basis of

---

94 Ellis, 'A View from the Pool', pp. 118-19.

95 G.R. Beasley-Murray, *Baptism Today and Tomorrow* (London: Macmillan, 1966), pp. 159-60, italics original. It should be noted that Beasley-Murray was involved in the commission which produced this report, *One Lord, One Baptism: The Meaning of Baptism* (London: SCM Press, 1960). Also Haymes, 'Baptist and Pentecostal Churches', who, in his section on 'Unity, Catholicity and Apostolicity', notes that in their response to *BEM* 'Baptists raised the question of who is a Christian?' and, as I have also argued here, he rejects the widely held view in ecumenical discussions that the performance of any rite, baptism or any other, should be made the basis of Christian fellowship, asking, 'Can that really be the case in the light of Paul's letter to the Galatians?'

96 Kelly, *Doctrines*, p. 403.

ecclesiology, baptism, eucharist or ministry is predicated on a false assumption: namely, that these are in fact the bases of Christian unity. They are not and never were intended to be. Our unity is in God: Father, Son and Holy Spirit.

The understanding of Christian unity which is being proposed here is consistent with Hinson's 'ecumenical pragmatism', or what British Baptists often refer to as 'grass-roots ecumenism'. This is an ecumenism widely practised by Baptists even if not always articulated, though it has received eloquent expression from time to time. Morris West, another prominent Baptist within the ecumenical movement, wrote:

> The approach to visible unity is now not through union schemes but through the making visible of the unity *which all believers have by being in Christ together*. The motivating purpose is not to create one united structure but to see how the needs of the local church may best be met in the developing relationships and in their mission to the world: not structural union but realise [sic] and manifest unity in Christ in the congregations in their worship and on the frontiers of their mission is their aim.
>
> The way ahead envisaged in making visible the unity is through mutual recognition of members and ministries, a sharing of table fellowship and by a declaration of intent by all those Churches willing to build on such a foundation towards closer relationships and more effective mission.[97]

This is not just a Baptist way of understanding unity, but a viable theological and intensely realistic and practical paradigm for Christian unity. It is a position which is also consistent with the WCC's own basis of membership which is Trinitarian, and which incorporates the central components of the Nicene faith, namely, the triune God.[98] It is not one which seeks uniformity in matters of church order or necesarily in the

---

97 W.M.S. West, 'The New Approach', *Baptist Times*, 18 March 1976, p. 7, italics added. Cf. Myra Blyth's comment that in Britain Protestants and Catholics 'work, witness and worship together in a way which clearly acknowledges our common identity in Christ and our common vocation to be the Church on earth', in M. Finnis, 'Vatican Statement a Major Blow', p. 1.

98 WCC Constitution, I. Basis: 'The World Council of Churches is a fellowship which confess the Lord Jesus Christ as God and Saviour according to the scriptures and therefore seek to fulfil together their common calling to the glory of the one God, Father, Son and Holy Spirit.' Similarly, 'The Baptist Doctrine of the Church' (1948), in R. Hayden (ed.), *Baptist Union Documents 1948–1977* (London: Baptist Historical Society, 1980), p. 6, states that 'It is in membership of a local church that the fellowship of the one holy catholic Church becomes significant. Indeed, such gathered companies of believers are the local manifestation of the one Church of God on earth and in heaven... *The vital relationship to Christ* which is implied in full communicant membership in a local church *carries with it membership in the Church* which is both in time and in eternity, both militant and triumphant', italics added.

mode of expression of the Christian faith, but it is based on the recognition of brothers and sisters who are 'in Christ'. In 1926, the Baptist Union replied to the Lambeth Appeal, issued six years earlier, stating:

> We believe in the Catholic Church as *the holy Society of believers in our Lord Jesus Christ, which He founded, of which He is the only Head, and in which He dwells by His Spirit*, so that though made up of many communions, organised in various modes, and scattered throughout the world, *it is yet one in Him*.[99]

What is more, we need to take to heart the declaration of the Apostle Paul that we are already one in Christ and that what we are called to do is to maintain that unity. During a controversy in 1967 over whether evangelicals should share in ecumenical meetings with Roman Catholics, George Beasley-Murray justified such meetings when he declared

> Here is the ground of the unity of the people of God: We are sinners for whom Christ died. We have confessed our sins and have been brought out of our disunity with God in a unity of guilt *into unity with Christ our Saviour, who makes us one in Him and with each other by his Holy Spirit*.
>
> The Ecumenical Movement is a call to the people of God, not to become one, but to recognise that they are *one in Christ*, and to endeavour to give this unity a better expression than they have done in history. That's what this meeting is for.[100]

As one recent Baptist Union report succinctly expresses it:

> There is only one Church of Jesus Christ. The Church is one because it participates in the life of the one triune God. Its unity is grounded in the unity of God.[101]

The history of the development of baptism and the creeds lead us away from issues of church order to a christological and theological centre and provide a viable paradigm for constructive future ecumenical discussions, as we seek the unity of the church which, according to Paul, we already

---

99 'Reply of the Churches in Membership with the Baptist Union to the "Appeal to all Christian People" issued by the Lambeth Conference of 1920', in J.H. Rushbrooke *et al*, *The Faith of the Baptists* (London: Kingsgate Press, n.d. [1926]), pp. 86-87, italics added.

100 Cited by P. Beasley-Murray, *Fearless for Truth: A Personal Portrait of the Life of George Raymond Beasley-Murray, 10 October 1916–23 February 2000* (Carlisle: Paternoster, forthcoming 2002), in ch. 6, italics added.

101 *Transforming Superintendency*, p. 11. It continues: 'since the being of God is one then the Church that participates in the life of God is one regardless of the many congregations in which it finds expressions.' I believe that 'congregations' can be understood to incorporate all Christian denominations, and that the writers of the report would too.

have 'in Christ' and which we are to make every effort to maintain (Eph. 4.1-16).

CHAPTER 2

John Wesley—
Exemplar of the Catholic Spirit

Herbert B. McGonigle

When John Wesley published his sermon, 'Catholic Spirit', in 1755, it was much more than merely an addition to his sermon corpus. In content and intention, it expressed Wesley's understanding of what the essentials of Christian experience are, and his resolve to work with all those who honoured Christ and promoted his kingdom, even if he differed from them in some doctrinal matters. Earlier he had published another sermon along similar lines, 'A Caution Against Bigotry'. In both sermons Wesley spelt out his warning against the sectarian spirit that divides the people of God and prevents Christians from understanding that God is present and working in fellowships and parties and denominations other than their own. In this volume of essays that proclaims a true ecumenity of spirit and acceptance without sacrificing orthodox and evangelical truths, John Wesley has something to say to all of us in the twenty-first century. This contribution will look at what Wesley meant by the catholic spirit and how he practised that spirit in half a century of preaching, writing and setting up the Methodist Societies.[1]

The sermon on bigotry is based on Mark 9.38-39, where Jesus cautioned his disciples not to exclude the man casting our demons just because he did not belong to the circle of Jesus' disciples. Wesley defined bigotry as 'too strong an attachment to, or fondness for, our own party, opinion, Church, and religion'.[2] The reference to casting out demons is taken to mean the proclamation of the gospel in the widest

---

[1] In so doing, I am delighted to contribute a chapter in this presentation to John Briggs. He is a living example of the catholic spirit and I take this opportunity to thank him both for his freindship and his excellent academic supervision of my research.

[2] *The Bicentennial Edition of the Works of John Wesley* (ed. Frank Baker; 15 vols; Oxford: Clarendon Press/Nashville, TN: Abingdon Press, 1975–95), II, p. 76. Hereafter cited as Wesley,*Works [BE]*.

sense. The devil has set up his throne in every human heart and it is only the power of Christ, mediated in the gospel, which can evict him. Wesley here assumes a very orthodox understanding of original sin and the deep conviction that the gospel is God's power for our salvation. So the man casting out demons represents all those who truly and faithfully proclaim Christ's gospel. But how, Wesley asks, will we recognise such a man? The test is really quite simple. Have we sufficient proof of a particular man or woman, now unquestionably a Christian, and who was previously a 'gross, open sinner'? If there is also plain proof that this transformation of life came about by hearing a particular preacher, then that preacher unquestionably casts out demons. The point that Wesley wants to make is clear enough—such a preacher is exercising a gospel ministry and we should not hinder him. Having detailed the various ways in which Christians hinder one another because of bigotry, Wesley goes much further. It is not enough merely to tolerate the other preacher and refrain from attacking his methods and party and his particular theological stance; we must positively pray for him and speak well of his ministry. The sermon concludes with a very moving appeal:

> If you will avoid all bigotry, acknowledge the finger of God. And not only acknowledge but rejoice in his work, and praise his name with thanksgiving... Speak well of him wheresoever you are; defend his character and his mission. Enlarge as far as you can his sphere of action. Show him all kindness in word and deed. And cease not to cry to God in his behalf, that he may save both himself and them that hear him.[3]

Most of us will probably have to conclude, to our shame, that there have been too many occasions in the work of God when we have not treated colleagues and our brethren in the Lord in the way Wesley recommends.

A few years later John Wesley published his sermon, 'Catholic Spirit'. He based it on Jehu's question to Jehonadab: 'Is thine heart right, as my heart is with thy heart?' And Jehonadab answered: 'It is. If it be, give me thine hand.'[4] While acknowledging that Jehu was not exactly a model saint, yet Wesley urges that his example here is one that every Christian should imitate. Jehu's question is not about Jehonadab's opinions but about his spirit, his attitude and his affections. How does he regard his neighbour? In a word, is there love in his heart? And then Wesley writes a glorious sentence, pleading that even allowing our differences of opinions, we must not let this stand in the way of brotherly affection: 'Though we can't think alike, may we not love alike?'[5] John Wesley wrote much in defence of that understanding of Christian sanctification

---

3   Wesley, *Works [BE]*, II, p. 77.
4   2 Kings 10.15.
5   Wesley, *Works[BE]*, II, p. 82.

that he understood as love perfected, and this sentence is as good a practical summary of it as anything he argued elsewhere.

Wesley's sermon goes on to explain that while Christians have differing modes of public worship, differing ideas about church government and differing practices about the subjects and manner of baptism, yet far more important than any of these is the question: do you love God and all mankind? If you do, then, says Wesley, give me your hand, and I will seek, by God's grace, to love you in His name. This 'catholic spirit' is more important than denominational zeal, or distinctives or any of the outward characteristics of the various 'parties' that make up Christ's church. Where it is found, Christians go forward in God's work hand in hand, and the One great Head of the church is glorified in his people.

Like the sermon against bigotry, this sermon is a call to Christians to put away the party spirit, the unkind criticism, the harsh judgements and the censorious back-biting that Wesley knew only too well to be so prevalent in his own day. The first decade of the eighteenth-century revival had witnessed not only strong opposition from many of the clergy of the established church, but bitter controversy inside 'Methodism' itself. Hardly had Wesley's 'field preaching' begun in Bristol in 1739 when the 'Societies' of the converts were sharply divided over the doctrines of election and predestination. The long-standing friendship begun at Oxford between John and Charles Wesley and George Whitefield was strained to breaking point. There were rival claims about who really 'owned' the revival work in Bristol and allegations that John Wesley had usurped Whitefield's rightful leadership. Back in London the Moravians and the 'Methodists' were going separate ways, and the split among the members of the Fetter Lane Society epitomised the growing divide among these former good friends.[6] All these sad divisions, with the accompanying rancour and mutual suspicion, must have been in Wesley's mind when he published this sermon. If only Christians would love one another as their Lord had directed them! There was a great need to call fellow-believers back to the catholic spirit and that was the sermon's intention.

John Wesley knew that however well-intentioned this sermon was, its plea to 'think and let think'[7] could easily be misunderstood for theological and doctrinal indifference. The sermon concluded with a rejection of what Wesley called 'speculative latitudinarianism'. This

---

6 The origins and characteristics of the Fetter Lane Society are very fully discussed in C. Podmore, *The Moravian Church in England, 1728–1760* (Oxford: Clarendon Press, 1998), pp. 29-71.

7 In his 1742 apologetic, *The Character of a Methodist*, Wesley wrote: 'As to all opinions which do not strike at the root of Christianity, we "think and let think"', Wesley, *Works [BE]*, IX, p. 34.

meant uncertainty and indifference about the doctrines of the historic Christian faith. Wesley protested that the man of true catholic spirit is as 'fixed as the sun in his judgement concerning the main branches of Christian doctrine'. Among those who subscribed to the creeds of the church there had always been differences of opinion about ecclesiastical practices and those doctrines that did not directly affect our salvation. With many of high-Calvinist persuasion, Wesley did not share their opinions about absolute predestination, limited atonement and irresistible grace. Against Roman Catholic theologians John Wesley had no place for their teachings on papal infallibility, a propitiatory mass, the adoration of Mary, purgatory and other Roman doctrines. But with protagonists of both Calvinistic and Catholic Christianity, Wesley, while rejecting what he saw as their peripheral teachings, was at one in confessing with them such foundation doctrines as the holy Trinity, the deity of Christ, original sin, justification by faith, holy living and final destiny. But this catholic spirit, which strongly identified with all who asserted the historic doctrines of the faith, was not at all complacent about dangerous diversions.

This was well illustrated in Wesley's response to what he saw as the reductionist christology of John Taylor of Norwich. A popular Socinian preacher and writer, Taylor published his book *The Scripture Doctrine of Original Sin, Proposed to Free and Candid Examination*. Written in a lively and very readable style and showing a mastery of the biblical languages, it was the eighteenth century's most trenchant attack on the orthodox doctrine of original sin. As a corollary, it undermined the evangelical teaching on justification by faith and, as a pronounced Socinian, Taylor saw Christ as the world's greatest teacher and exemplar of God's grace but not as God incarnate.

As John Wesley itinerated across the four kingdoms of Great Britain, he lamented that Taylor's teaching was producing disciples who ridiculed evangelical Christianity.[8] He waited for some orthodox theologian to reply to Taylor, and when none appeared, Wesley took up the cudgels. Retiring for some ten weeks to a friend's house in London late in 1756, he wrote *The Scripture Doctrine of Original Sin according to Scripture, Reason and Experience* (1757). Running to some 522 pages, it was the single longest treatise that Wesley published. It was followed two years later by a summary in his sermon 'Original Sin' and there were letters to friends about this controversy, including a letter to Taylor himself. In all these publications Wesley did not attack Taylor in person; indeed he acknowledged that he esteemed his opponent a man of 'uncommon sense and knowledge'. But Wesley had no time for Taylor's

---

8 In his *Journal* for Sunday 28 August 1748, Wesley records his visit to Shackerley in Lancashire: 'Abundance of people were gathered before six, many of whom were disciples of Dr. Taylor, laughing at Original Sin, and, consequently, at the whole frame of scriptural Christianity', Wesley, *Works [BE]*, XX, pp. 245-246.

Enlightenment optimism about fallen mankind. No writer since Mahomet had given such a wound to Christianity.[9] Wesley unsheathed his controversial sword and threw away the scabbard. What was at stake was nothing less than our 'eternal peace'. The issue between himself and Taylor was, quite simply, 'Christianity or heathenism'. Either he had mistaken the whole of Christianity from beginning to end—or Taylor had. Wesley's scheme—or Taylor's—was as 'contrary to the scriptural as the Koran is'. If the scriptural doctrines of redemption, justification and the new birth are removed, or, alternatively, explained as Taylor explains them, then Christianity is no better than heathenism. If the doctrine of original sin means no more than John Taylor asserts, then Christianity is merely a system of good advice and the religion of St Paul has no pre-eminence over the teaching of Socrates or Epictetus.[10]

Having looked at John Wesley's plea for the catholic spirit to prevail among Christians, and noting that it did not mean indifference to plausible heresies, it is time to turn and see how far Wesley exemplified this spirit in his own life and work and ministry. An appropriate starting point is the year 1739 when Wesley first organised his followers into 'Societies'. Most of these men and women had been awakened by the Methodist preachers and they requested Wesley to help them in discipleship. In this way the Societies were begun and the conditions of membership were simple: 'a desire to flee from the wrath to come, to be saved from their sins'.[11] The rules of these Societies forbade, among other things, swearing, Sabbath-breaking, drunkenness and quarrelling. There were also positive injunctions about doing good, attending the means of grace, studying scripture and family and private prayer. But John Wesley imposed no doctrinal or theological test on those joining the Societies. They might be Calvinists or Catholics, Presbyterians or Moravians, Quakers or Dissenters of any colour—all this made no difference.[12] If their intention was to seek the salvation of their souls, then they were welcome in Wesley's Societies. Whatever opinions they held about other doctrines, provided these were not the occasion of conflict and controversy, Wesley made then welcome. With the help of his preachers and assistants and class-leaders, he watched over their souls, preached, taught and explained repentance and faith and then instructed the regenerate to grow in the love of God and man. In a famous passage he said of himself that in life he wanted to know one thing—'the way to heaven'.[13] Having found it, he spent the rest of his life helping others to

---

9   *The Letters of the Rev. John Wesley* (ed. J. Telford; 8 vols; London, 1931), IV, p. 48. Hereafter cited as Wesley, *Letters*.
10   Wesley, *Letters*, IV, p. 67.
11   Wesley, *Works[BE]*, IX, p. 70.
12   Wesley, *Letters*, IV, p. 297.
13   Wesley, *Works[BE]*, I, p. 105.

find it. Salvation was not in creeds, or dogmas, or styles of worship, or denominational labels but through faith in the Son of God. Taking the world as his parish,[14] he laboured to help men and women on the way to heaven, for the catholic spirit permitted no barriers among those who practised the love of God and man.

John Wesley's 'United Societies', as they were first called, had been preceded by the Religious Societies. These had come into existence in the late seventeenth century, mostly as the work of Dr Antony Horneck.[15] They, too, catered for those who wanted gatherings where prayer, fellowship and devotional reading were encouraged. But they catered mostly for a religious elite and offered little attraction to those who were not regular worshippers or acquainted with religious matters. In contrast, Wesley's Societies were open and democratic, and their pattern ensured that they were geared to help those who were mostly strangers to religious practices, forms and terminology. Indeed many of these early 'Methodists' were illiterate and the societies introduced them not only to the essentials of Christian doctrine but also spurred them on to learn to read and write.

In the late 1730s and early 1740s, the Methodists were divided by wrangles over election and predestination. An anonymous letter circulated among the converts in Bristol warning them not to listen to John Wesley because he preached against predestination. Although the accusation was false, the rumours spread and finally Wesley preached and then published his sermon, 'Free Grace'. It was a strong attack on absolute predestination but no names were mentioned. George Whitefield replied with his 'A Letter to the Rev. Mr John Wesley'(1740), censuring him for publishing a provocative sermon, and then attacked Wesley's theology. The outcome of this doctrinal quarrel among former friends was that the revival split into two groups; those who followed the Wesley brothers were designated Wesleyan Methodists and those who sided with Whitefield and his supporters became known as Calvinistic Methodists. This 'parting of the ways' among old friends hurt both parties and it bred mistrust and suspicion of fellow believers on both sides.

The record of this early, and lasting, breach in the work of the eighteenth-century revival constitutes a sad and depressing chapter. While this historic divide, usually but inaccurately, labelled the Calvinistic/Arminian dispute, had been part of Evangelicalism since the seventeenth century, its resurrection among the eighteenth-century

---

14   Wesley, *Works[BE]*, XXV, p. 616.

15   Anthony Horneck (1641–97) came to England from Bacharach in Germany in 1661. In about 1678 he began to organise meetings for young men in and around London in order that they 'might apply themselves to good discourse and to things wherein they might edify one another'. See J.S. Simon, *John Wesley and the Religious Societies* (London: Epworth Press, 1921), p. 10.

Methodists can never be an occasion of rejoicing for the evangelical historian or theologian. Former friends went their separate ways, fellowships were broken off, misunderstandings and half-truths proliferated and the work of God and evangelism suffered. If only John Wesley and George Whitefield had come together and, even if complete doctrinal agreement was not possible, surely there could have been a brotherly rapport that eclipsed discord and allowed the glorious work of soul-saving to prosper. Looking at both camps, with Whitefield, John Cennick and their supporters on one side, and the Wesley brothers and their preachers on the other, what potential there was to advance the work of God. What might have been achieved if these good and godly people had been catholic enough in spirit to agree to disagree on some theological interpretations in order to support each other in evangelising the land.

Writing to Whitefield in the midst of the warfare, John Wesley acknowledged that it was bigotry that divided the evangelicals.

> The case is quite plain. There are bigots both for Predestination and against it. God is sending a message to those on either side. But neither will receive it, unless from one of his own opinion. Therefore for a time you are suffered to be of one opinion and I of another. But when His time is come God will do what man cannot—namely, make us both of one mind.[16]

Over the next few years this dispute rumbled on and there was also a gap opening up between John Wesley and the Moravians. Ever since he had first met the Moravians on a voyage to America in 1735, John Wesley had been profoundly influenced by their teaching and example of holy living. His ties with them in Georgia were very strong, and when he returned to England early in 1738, he and Charles formed a close friendship with the Moravian Peter Böhler. The progress of the Wesleys' spiritual pilgrimages between February and May 1738 was directed by the counsel and teaching of Böhler and it climaxed at Pentecost that year. Charles Wesley found the assurance of sins forgiven on Pentecost Sunday while staying in a Moravian home in London. Three days later a similar experience of 'heart-warming' came to John while attending a Moravian gathering. His record of what happened that Wednesday evening in Aldersgate Street was couched in Moravian language: 'I felt my heart strangely warmed. I felt I did trust in Christ, Christ alone for salvation, and an assurance was given me...'[17]

The Wesley brothers and the Moravians worked together very closely in London and later in 1738 John Wesley visited the Moravian headquarters in Herrnhut in Germany and met the founder, Count

---

16   Wesley, *Letters*, I, p. 351.
17   Wesley, *Works[BE]*, XVIII, p. 250.

Zinzendorf and other leaders. When his itinerant preaching ministry began in Bristol in April 1739, he had the full support of the Moravian brethren and his many letters to James Hutton, a leading English Moravian, shows how close this friendship was. Differences began to emerge when a German Moravian, Philip Molther, introduced 'Stillness' practices into the Fetter Lane Society. This teaching advocated that seekers after God should refrain from all the means of grace, including scripture reading, prayer and hearing sermons, and wait for the Spirit to bring to them the gift of faith. The Wesleys opposed this emphasis, convinced that through these means of grace God mediated his Spirit to bring people to repentance and faith. There was a split in the Fetter Lane Society and a large number followed the Wesleys out of that Society and joined with them in a new fellowship, the first of the many Wesleyan Societies that would be organised in the years ahead.[18]

Although the Wesleys and the Moravians still shared some love-feasts together, there was disagreement among them on the question of the believer's sanctification. With their strong Lutheran background, the Moravians emphasised the imputation of Christ's righteousness to the Christian. Increasingly the Wesleys, while advocating imputation, were also stressing the transforming work of the Spirit in the Christian's life and spoke of imparted or inherent righteousness as well. The Christian is not only accounted righteous but he is being made righteous. This emphasis convinced John Wesley that the Moravian teaching, unless it was expressed very carefully, opened the door to antinomianism. This dispute with old friends who esteemed each other highly might well have been amicably resolved but for the intervention of Count Zinzendorf. On a visit to London in 1741 he met with John Wesley and was totally unsympathetic to any notion of imparted holiness. James Hutton's biographer later recorded that Zinzendorf openly disparaged what he called the Wesleys' 'self-made holiness'. In his capacity as 'bishop and guardian of the Church of the Brethren', he publicly branded John and Charles Wesley as 'false teachers and deceivers of souls' and declared that fellowship between the Moravians and Methodists could only be restored if the Wesleys dropped their delusions about 'Christian perfection'.[19]

It was John Wesley's growing unhappiness about these divisions between the three groupings of the revival movement that led him to propose a conference of all the parties in an attempt to heal the breaches.

---

18 The Wesleys brothers and their followers began to meet at the Foundery, a building which they purchased in the Moorfields district of London. The Foundery became the headquarters for the Wesleys' work for almost forty years. See *The Journal of the Rev. John Wesley* (ed. N. Curnock; 8 vols; London: Epworth Press, 1938), II, pp. 316-319. Hereafter cited as Wesley, *Journal*.

19 D. Benham, *Memoirs of James Hutton* (London, 1856), p. 112.

He took the initiative to call the leaders together in London in August 1743. George Whitefield responded positively and Howell Harris likewise. Harris, a recognised leader of the revival work in Wales, was a close friend of both Whitefield and the Wesleys and a man of a truly catholic spirit. Although his theological persuasions put him closer to Whitefield than to the Wesleys, both parties regarded him with warm affection.[20] Charles Wesley recorded that he was itinerating in Cornwall when John wrote and asked him to attend the conference. Whitefield, Harris and the Wesley brothers convened but the Moravians were not represented. John Wesley invited one of their leading preachers, August Spangenberg, an old friend of his from their days together in Georgia, but just before the conference was due to start, Spangenberg left England for America. This was a blow to John Wesley's high hopes that the gathering would resolve differences among brethren and bring about a closer co-operation in the work of evangelism and building up the work of God. The reason for the Moravians' refusal to take part was their condition that the Archbishop of Canterbury should be informed of the proposed meeting and that an Anglican bishop should be invited. Charles Wesley wrote of his disappointment when he arrived in London and heard that the meeting had been cancelled.

There is clear evidence that John Wesley was deeply disappointed that the divisions among the Methodists and between the Moravians and Methodists had not been resolved. Out of a 'strong desire to unite with Mr Whitefield as far as possible' and to 'cut off needless dispute',[21] he had proposed some modifications in his own doctrinal emphases. He reasoned that the two sides were divided over three main points; unconditional election, irresistible grace and final perseverance. He would accept a doctrine of unconditional election for some, provided it did not entail the necessary damnation of all the rest. Nor would he object to an interpretation of irresistible grace, unless it implied that those on whom it worked without apparently producing any response were therefore irrevocably damned. As to final perseverance, Wesley went even further in trying to effect a harmonious unity among the leaders of the revival. He confessed that he believed there was a state of grace from which the Christian could not fall away.

On any scale of measurement Wesley's olive branch was a remarkable gesture. In the history of theological disputes among Christian theologians, there are few examples of those who were willing to moderate previously-held views for the sake of co-operation and brotherly affection. Far more often these disputes have led to

---

20   Arnold Dallimore suggests that a very friendly letter from Harris to John Wesley in May 1743 may well have prompted Wesley's decision to call a conference. A. Dallimore, *George Whitefield* (2 vols; Edinburgh: Banner of Truth, 1979–80), II, p. 145.
21   Wesley, *Works[BE]*, XIX, p. 332.

protagonists hardening their attitudes, and, it is to be feared, also their hearts. John Wesley knew that many would interpret his proposals as a 'climb down' on his part, but there is no doubt that he genuinely wanted to be reconciled with Whitefield. He published this remarkable theological *eirenicon* in his *Journal* for all to see. Given the time of its composition, it looks as if John Wesley had prepared these propositions for the hoped-for conference in London. Sadly, nothing came from these proposals. John Wesley had taken considerable steps to bring old friends together and even though they failed, they were welcome examples of the catholic spirit.

Five years later there were still some lingering hopes that even now Whitefield and Wesley might yet establish some kind of union in the work of the revival. Whitefield had been in America for four years and on his return he wrote to both the Wesleys, expressing the hope that they would meet him in London. John Wesley was preaching in the north of England and Charles was in Ireland. Whitefield wrote another letter to John Wesley, expressing disappointment that they had not been able to meet in London and then asked Wesley if he had any further thoughts about union. Whitefield confessed that he felt he and Wesley were on 'two different plans'.[22] His own 'attachment' to America did not allow him to stay long in England and he expressed fears that even if he formed societies here he had no 'proper assistants' to take care of them. He hoped that he and John would meet soon and in the meantime he asked for his prayers, assuring John that he esteemed him 'most affectionately'.

While Whitefield's letter seemed to discourage any move towards a union of his people and Wesley's, yet the tone was warm and friendly and it breathed good will. In the hope of yet establishing a closer relationship with Whitefield, John Wesley proposed a meeting in Bristol. It was another olive branch in another attempt to settle differences and bring the leaders of the revival closer together. On Wednesday 2 August 1749, John and Charles Wesley met with George Whitefield and Howell Harris in the Wesleyan 'New Room' in Bristol. The first day was spent in discussing how they might establish 'a closer union in affection'. They agreed not to believe rumours about each other, to defend the other's reputation and not to speak about difference of opinion in a way that caused friction. Agreement was reached after 'some mild and friendly debate' on an understanding of justification. The next day predestination and perfection were on the agenda. Again there was a general spirit of agreement, particularly mentioning that both sides agreed, on the predestination question, not to use 'such terms as naturally tend to revive the controversy'. There was further harmony in agreeing that terms like

---

22   Wesley, *Works[BE]*, XXVI, p. 327.

'sinless' and the 'inbeing of sin' should be dropped and all Christians should be exhorted to 'press on to perfection in the holy law of love'.[23]

While this meeting of the four Methodist leaders seemed very promising in the agreements reached, it is difficult to gauge what good came from it. John Wesley made no record of it in his *Journal* and this might be the best indicator that the outcome was disappointing. Charles Wesley made a brief mention of the gathering in his *Journal*, saying that it 'came to nought, I think through their flying off'.[24] If this is an accurate observation on the conference, then certainly Charles Wesley felt that if Whitefield and Harris had been willing to stay longer in discussion, much more might have been achieved. Having convened the 1743 gathering in London and this meeting in Bristol six years later, John Wesley might well have felt he had done his utmost to bring about reconciliation. While the Bristol gathering seems to have concluded in good will and with mutual affection, it did not really bring the parties together in doctrinal harmony over the disputed matters of predestination and Christian perfection.

The history of Methodism shows only too clearly that the theological divisions continued to be subjects of polemic for the decades to come. John Wesley had certainly displayed a truly catholic spirit and both Whitefield and Harris seem to have responded in kind. But it must be said that so much more could (and should) have come from these gatherings of the evangelical leaders. Perhaps what was needed was an acknowledgement by Wesley and Whitefield that their publicised wrangling ten years earlier had had melancholy consequences. If both men had acted with less haste in vindicating their own positions, later hostilities might have been avoided. If only John Wesley had not gone to the printers with his trenchant sermon, 'Free Grace'! And if only George Whitefield had directed his 'Letter' to Wesley in private, rather than publishing it! All of us who truly long for open, honest, heart-felt and Spirit-inspired fellowship and co-operation among evangelicals in the twenty-first century, must learn from what happened in the eighteenth century. The catholic spirit certainly means that we will not attack and criticise one another openly, nor will we have any part in allowing unfounded rumours and innuendo to make us suspicious of one another. But the catholic spirit also means that, whatever convictions we hold personally on the questions of predestination, perfection theories, gifts of the Spirit, women in ministry, and such like, we will pray for, support and work with all those who believe and proclaim the great doctrines of historic orthodox Christianity.

---

23 'An Early Methodist Eirenicon', *Proceedings of the Wesley Historical Society* 5 (1905), pp. 108-10.

24 *The Journal of the Rev Charles Wesley* (2 vols; London, 1849), II, p. 63.

By the late 1740s, John Wesley found himself taking care of a rapidly-growing number of people who had joined his Societies in their search for salvation. To help them in that quest and confirm those already in the way of salvation, Wesley instituted class meetings, band meetings, love-feasts, quarterly meetings and other such means of grace. Full-time travelling preachers were recruited, assistants and local leaders were appointed and a circuit system was set up. John Wesley also began to compose, extract from other works, edit and publish many writings for the instruction of his preachers and the edification of his people. These publications ranged from popular evangelistic tracts like, *A Word to a Swearer*, *A Word to a Drunkard*, to reasoned apologetics like, *An Appeal to Men of Reason and Religion*. In 1749 he began a very ambitious publishing project. This was his *Christian Library*, fifty dudecimo volumes, subtitled *Extracts from and Abridgements of the Choicest Pieces of Practical Divinity which have been Published in the English Tongue*. Believing that 'reading Christians will be knowing Christians',[25] he edited extracts that began in the first century with Clement of Rome and extended to works written in the eighteenth century.

Wesley concentrated on what he called 'practical divinity'; those writings that were meant to confirm the Christian faith and build up believers in holy living. In his own words, this *Christian Library* would constitute 'Christianity reduced to practice':[26]

> I have endeavoured to extract such a collection of English Divinity, as (I believe), is all true, all agreeable to the oracles of God: as is all practical, unmixed with controversy of any kind; and all intelligible to plain men: such as is not superficial, but going down to the depth, and describing the height of Christianity. And yet not mystical, not obscure to any of those who are experienced in the ways of God... I take no author for better, for worse; (as indeed I dare not call any man Rabbi) but endeavour to follow each so far as he follows Christ.[27]

This *Christian Library*, a huge literary undertaking for a busy, travelling preacher, is a very good guide to John Wesley's understanding of both Christian truth and Christian practice. The *Christian Library* demonstrates how Wesley's hermeneutic, in a typical Anglican way, was constituted by scripture, tradition and reason. But there was a fourth dimension to this approach to Christian theology and practice—and that was experience. Wesley was sure that the 'experience' of sins forgiven and the indwelling Christ were privileges granted to Christians in every age. The *Christian Library* was intended not only as an instructor in Christian truth but also a means of confirming Christian practice and

---

25   Wesley, *Letters*, VI, p. 201.
26   J. Wesley, *Christian Library* (50 vols; 1749–55), II, p. 3.
27   Wesley, *Christian Library*, I, p. ix.

encouraging what Wesley often summarised as true Christian experience—the 'faith that works by love' (Gal. 5.6).

John Wesley's *Christian Library* was yet another illustration of his deep commitment to the catholic spirit. When the contents of the *Christian Library* are examined carefully, it gives a remarkable insight into the scope and depth of Wesley's Christian sympathies. The extracts represent the Apostolic Fathers, continental authors, Anglican and Puritan writers and some anonymous devotional writings. The Fathers are represented by Clement of Rome, Polycarp, Ignatius and Macarius. Wesley's appreciation of the fourth-century Macarius is typical of his penchant for practical Christian instruction:

> Whatever he insists upon is essential, is durable, is necessary. What he continually labours to cultivate in himself and others is, the real life of God in the heart and soul, that kingdom of God, which consists in righteousness, and peace, and joy in the Holy Ghost. He is ever quickening and stirring up in his audience, endeavouring to kindle in them a steady zeal, an earnest desire, an inflamed ambition, to recover that Divine image we were made in; to be made conformable to Christ our Head; to be daily sensible more and more...[of] such a victorious faith as overcomes the world, and working by love, is ever fulfilling the whole law of God.[28]

If Wesley's inclusion of the writings of Macarius in his *Christian Library* does not provoke much surprise, it is different with the writings of two medieval Roman Catholic writers. They were Antoinette Bourignon (1616–80), a Spanish Quietist, and Miguel de Molinos (1640–97), also a Spanish Quietist. While John Wesley took a vigorous stand against Roman Catholic doctrines such as transubstantiation, purgatory, indulgences, papal infallibility and all forms of maryolatry, yet he was willing to recognise that some Catholic writers were helpful in promoting practical Christianity. Although he was later castigated by Richard Hill and Augustus Toplady for promoting popery, Wesley defended his use of these writers. Whatever the deficiencies in their understanding of some Christian doctrines, they had deep, personal acquaintance with Christ through his Spirit. Both were exponents of a kind of meditative spirituality that placed great emphasis on waiting on God, and little of what could be described as distinctive Roman dogma was found in their pages. Wesley also made it plain that when he selected an extract from any particular book, it did not mean that he agreed with everything else in that volume, much less what that author might have written elsewhere. In compiling the *Christian Library*, Wesley made it plain that he was an editor, not an author. Wesley's attitude to these

---

28 Wesley, *Christian Library*, I, p. 71. Patristic scholarship is now fairly unanimous that these *Homilies*, traditionally attributed to the fourth-century Egyptian monk, Macarius, were almost certainly written by a disciple of Gregory of Nyssa.

Catholic mystics is well summarised in the preface he wrote in his extensively-edited *Life* of Madam Guyon. She was a French Catholic mystic and a self-confessed disciple of the writings of Molinos.

> The following contains all that is scriptural and rational; all that tends to the genuine love of God and our neighbour. In the mean time, most of what I judge to be contrary to Scripture and reason is omitted... The grand source of all her mistakes was this; the not being guided by the written word. She did not take the Scripture for the rule of her actions; at most it was but the secondary rule. Inward impressions, which she called inspirations, were her primary rule. The written word was not a lantern to her feet, a light in all her paths... Yet with all this dross, how much pure gold is mixed! So God did wink at involuntary ignorance...[29]

> There are excellent things in most of the Mystic writers. As almost all of them lived in the Romish Church, they were lights whom the gracious providence of God raised up to shine in a dark place.[30]

Given John Wesley's well-known predilection for Anglican authors, especially those of the Restoration period, 1660–1700, the inclusion of extracts from their writings would be expected in his *Christian Library*.[31] And they are there, including Thomas Ken, Jeremy Taylor, Simon Patrick, William Cave, John Tillotson, William Beveridge and many more. But there are just as many Puritan authors represented in his *Christian Library* and the list of names is impressive, including Richard Sibbes, Thomas Goodwin, Richard Alleine, Richard Baxter, Edmund Calamy, John Flavel, John Howe and others. Indications of the high esteem in which John Wesley held these and other Puritan writers can be found scattered throughout all his publications, and in the *Christian Library* he gave specific reasons for including them. He was not blind to what he believed to be both their literary and theological imperfections, but their practical value more than compensated for these weaknesses.

> They are exceeding verbose, and full of circumlocutions and repetitions. But I persuade myself, most of these defects are removed in the following sheets... But it should not be concealed, there are other blemishes in the greater part of the Puritan writers. They drag in controversy on every occasion, nay, without any occasion or pretence at all. Another is, that they generally give a low and imperfect view of sanctification or holiness... But abundant recompence is made for all their

---

29   Wesley, *Works*, XIV, pp. 276-77.
30   Wesley, *Works*, XIII, p. 25.
31   In 1789 Wesley wrote of the strong Anglican influences under which he grew up in Epworth, and indeed remained with him throughout his life. 'From a child, I was taught to love and reverence the Scriptures, the oracles of God; and, next to these, to esteem the primitive Fathers, the writers of the first three centuries. Next after the primitive church, I esteemed our own, the Church of England, as the most scriptural national Church in the world', *Works*, XIII, p. 272.

blemishes, by the excellencies which may be observed in them... Their judgement is generally deep and strong, their sentiments just and clear, and their tracts on every head full and comprehensive... More particularly they do indeed exalt Christ. They set him forth in all his offices... And next to God himself, they honour his Word. They are men mighty in the Scriptures, equal to any of those who went before them, and far superior to most that have followed them... They are continually tearing up the very roots of Antinomianism... But the peculiar excellency of these writers seems to be, the building us up in our most holy faith.[32]

Among the Puritan writers from whom Wesley extracted material for his *Christian Library* were some whose high Calvinism he had little sympathy with. But here he followed the same principle as when he made extracts from medieval Catholic writers; an extract did not necessarily mean Wesley's agreement with other parts of the writing. In both these examples, Wesley was putting the catholic spirit into practice. If the writer exalted Christ and, in particular, promoted practical holiness, then his or her attachment to doctrines not acceptable to Wesley was no bar to his using the 'good grain'. With reference to the English Puritans, Wesley's use of the writings of John Owen clearly demonstrates that for him the catholic spirit took precedence over personal opinions. Owen was unquestionably the most dogmatic Calvinist of the English Puritans and his book *The Death of Death* was the most extensively-argued presentation of the doctrine of limited atonement that could be found. He was, not unnaturally, a vigorous exponent of the doctrine of absolute predestination and did not shy away from the doctrine that consequently flows from it—reprobation. To John Wesley, any concept of the doctrine of reprobation was utterly irreconcilable with his understanding of the love of God. He vehemently rejected the doctrine of unconditional election because 'it necessarily implies unconditional reprobation. Find out any election which does not imply reprobation, and I will gladly agree to it.'[33]

Although Owen was the acknowledged defender of high Calvinist doctrines, yet Wesley included extracts from Owen's writings in his *Christian Library*. When he used the Catholic mystics, he carefully avoided any extracts that promoted Catholic doctrine or mysticism. Likewise with his use of Owen. From the many volumes of the Puritan's works, Wesley avoided all controversial matter, and selected what was calculated to glorify Christ and incite the Christian to holy living. He made use of four of Owen's publications. They were his *Mortification of Sin in Believers*, *Of Temptation, the Nature and Power of it*, *A Declaration of the Glorious Mystery of the Person of Christ, God and Man*, and *Of Communion with God the Father, Son and Holy Ghost*. In

---

32   Wesley, *Christian Library*, IV, pp, 106-107.
33   Wesley, *Works*, X, p. 211.

these writings the Christian met with 'practical divinity'. Wesley could recommend these works of Owen to every Christian seeking instruction in scriptural truth and guidance on the holy life. Wesley's catholic spirit prompted him to include extracts from the writings of this magisterial Calvinist theologian, but extracts that carefully avoided what Wesley considered to be unhelpful, and often confusing, theological speculation.

Two more examples of John Wesley's catholic spirit are worth noting briefly. In 1749 he published 'A Letter to a Roman Catholic'. It acknowledged that Protestants and Roman Catholics held many prejudices about each other but it was not opinions on either side, or a particular mode of worship, that made a man a true Christian. All those who call themselves Protestants but in practice are 'common swearers, drunkards, whoremongers, liars... in a word, all who live in open sin', are really heathens. The true Protestant worships God in spirit and truth, loves God and his neighbour and walks in holiness. Wesley then challenges his Roman Catholic reader. Can he find fault with this description of a Christian? Is he following Christ in like manner? Is his whole life a sacrifice to God and is he delivered from both outward and inner sin? This alone is 'the old religion, true, primitive Christianity'.[34]

Wesley then proceeded to offer a remarkable *eirenicon* of Christian good will to Roman Catholics:

> Are we not thus far agreed... If God still loveth us, we ought also to love one another... Let the points wherein we differ stand aside; here are enough wherein we agree, enough to be the ground of every Christian temper, and of every Christian action. O brethren, let us not fall out by the way! I hope to see you in heaven. And if I practise the religion above described, you dare not say I shall go to hell. Then if we cannot as yet think alike in all things, at least we may love alike. Herein we cannot possibly do amiss. For of one point none can doubt a moment. 'God is love, and he that dwelleth in love, dwelleth in God, and God in him.'[35]

John Wesley was seeking what common ground he could find between Roman Catholics and himself. He was making a very important distinction between Roman Catholic dogma, which he repudiated, and Roman Catholic people whom he loved for Christ's sake. Their dogmas were 'a heap of erroneous opinions delivered by tradition from their fathers'.[36] The true gospel of salvation by faith had effectively driven popery out of England and that gospel alone could keep it out.[37] Wesley openly declared that he 'detested and abhorred the fundamental

---

34 Wesley, *Works*, X, p. 85.
35 Wesley, *Works*, X, p. 85.
36 Wesley, *Works*, VI, p. 199.
37 Wesley, *Works[BE]*, I, p. 129.

doctrines of the Church of Rome',[38] but his attitude to Roman Catholic people was one of good will, concern for their bodies and souls, and a ready acknowledgement that in character and conduct many of them gave indisputable evidence of being true Christians.[39] Here again there is testimony of how John Wesley endeavoured to distinguish between opinions and true faith. He was as forthright as any eighteenth-century English Protestant in exposing what he believed to be the numerous and dangerous errors of Roman Catholicism, but his love for his neighbour warmly and genuinely embraced Roman Catholics. Throughout his ministry he strongly maintained that there is a very important distinction between essential Christian doctrine and personal opinions. There can be no compromise on vital doctrines but opinions are another matter. He spelt it out in a letter to John Newton in 1765. 'You have admirably well expressed what I mean by an opinion contradistinguished from an essential doctrine. Whatever is "compatible with a love to Christ and a work of grace" I term an opinion.'[40]

Our final look at how John Wesley demonstrated the true catholic spirit is concerned with his hopes for a practical working unity among England's evangelical clergy. Following a friendly meeting in March 1761 with Henry Venn, Vicar of Huddersfield, Wesley took positive steps towards bringing about a fraternal union among evangelical ministers. Writing to George Downing, an Essex rector, he spoke about how he had laboured for many years 'to unite, not scatter, the messengers of God'. Now he voiced the hope that all those who embraced essential Christian doctrines might come together in the kind of harmonious unity that would greatly enhance the work of God.

> I think it great pity that the few clergymen in England who preach the three grand scriptural doctrines—Original Sin, Justification by Faith, and Holiness consequent thereon—should have any jealousies or misunderstandings between them. What advantage must this give to the common enemy! What an hindrance is it to the great work wherein they are all engaged! How desirable is it that there should be the most open, avowed intercourse between them![41]

Three years later John Wesley took this plan for unity among the evangelical clergy a step further. He wrote a letter to almost fifty of the leading evangelical clergy in the Church of England, including George Whitefield, William Romaine, John Newton, Walter Shirley, Henry Venn and John Berridge. The plea was for a coming together of all those who were 'fellow labourers in His gospel'. Wesley reasoned: 'Ought not those

---

38   Wesley, *Works*, I, p. 456.
39   Wesley, *Works*, III, p. 312.
40   Wesley, *Letters*, IV, p. 297.
41   Wesley, *Letters*, IV, p. 146.

who are united to one common Head, and employed by Him in one common work, be united to each other?' After naming those he wished to unite, Wesley added that this proposal included any other clergy who agreed on the doctrines of original sin, justification by faith and holiness of heart and life.[42]

Wesley then set out the kind of union he had in mind. It was not a unity of opinions, or expressions or outward order; rather a unity of good will and mutual support. Hindrances would be removed when ministers did not judge or envy each other, were not displeased with others who had greater success than they had, and did not gossip about the faults, mistakes and infirmities of their brethren. But Wesley was concerned that this evangelical fraternity would be marked, not only by its avoidance of critical and judgmental attitudes, but positively by the way it manifested the fruits of the Spirit. These brethren would love, think well of and honour each other. They would speak respectfully of one another, defend each other's characters and help one another in every possible way. It would require an earnest effort on the part of all concerned to desire this unity, and it would require the grace and power of God working through them to accomplish it.

> All nature is against it, every infirmity, every wrong temper and fashion; love of honour and praise, of power, of pre-eminence; anger, resentment, pride, long-contracted habit, and prejudice lurking in ten thousand forms. The devil and all his angels are against it... All the world, all that know not God, are against it... But surely 'with God all things are possible.'[43]

John Wesley was deeply disappointed that most of the clergy to whom he wrote did not even bother to reply to him. Just as he done in earlier years in trying to bring the Methodist and Moravian preachers together, now he was attempting to unite the evangelical clergy in the Church of England. He longed for a unity of purpose and vision among his brethren that would strengthen their united efforts in evangelism and in building up the work of God. His vision and hope and prayer was that the catholic spirit might characterise all those who truly loved God and their neighbours. As he repeatedly said: 'If we cannot think alike, then at least let us love alike.' If that catholic spirit was needed among the people of God in Britain in the eighteenth century, it is needed no less in this twenty-first century. And it is fitting that this attempt to demonstrate what John Wesley meant by the catholic spirit should conclude with words by his brother Charles, words expressing that what unites us in Christ is far more important than our denominational labels or our theological slogans.

---

42 Wesley, *Works[BE]*, XXI, p. 456.
43 Wesley, *Works[BE]*, XXI, pp. 457, 458.

Sweetly now we all agree
Touched with softest sympathy
Kindly for each other care
Every member feel its share.

Love, like death, hath all destroyed
Rendered all distinctions void
Names, and sects, and parties fall
Thou, O Christ, art all in all.[44]

---

44   G. Osborn (ed.), *The Poetical Works of John and Charles Wesley* (13 vols; London, 1868–72), I, p. 362.

CHAPTER 3

Worlds of Ambiguity: the YMCA, the YWCA, the WSCF and Mission, Nationalism, Ecumenism and the Explosion of Empire

J.C.G. Binfield

An organization is a collective memory, it has a history, it is a repository. A movement is an organization inspired by a theme, it is memory impelled to vision. The movements examined in this paper are the Young Men's Christian Association (YMCA), the Young Women's Christian Association (YWCA) and the Student Christian Movement (SCM). Their international organizational expressions are alliances, or federations, and their themes are appropriate variants on what, when first translated from the original French into English in 1855 for the new World's Alliance of YMCA's, became known as the Paris Basis. That basis provides my text:

> The Young Men's Christian Associations seek to unite those [young men] who, regarding Jesus Christ as their God and Saviour, according to the Holy Scriptures, desire to be His disciples in their faith and in their life, and to associate their efforts for the extension of his Kingdom [amongst young men].[1]

In 1955 the World's Alliance, in an apparently pedantic change, turned itself into the World Alliance. The World's YWCA and the World's Student Christian Federation (WSCF) had done likewise. Those changes suggest a confident world view. The old world's alliances had been Protestant Euro–American constructs, admittedly reflecting increasingly far-flung fellowships but of as yet like-minded Christians, who from time to time came conveniently together. A world alliance, however, suggested

---

1 This remains one of two key texts which form the basis on which national movements affiliate to the World Alliance of YMCAs; the bracketed words were deleted in 1969. See, e.g., 'Statements of YMCA Aims and Purposes', *Life Right Now: The Reports of the National Council Review Group* (London: YMCA England, 2001), Appendix B, pp. 25-26.

a discovery of what it meant to be international. These three alliances may have been forged in the West but they were now global in their outworking, fired in the crucible of war, some of their elements destroyed but others created in the process, their balance profoundly, perhaps permanently, affected. All this was reflected in their common setting: Geneva.

Geneva is a challenge, a world of ambiguity in itself. It is a topographical deception. It is in Switzerland but the mountains which define its views are in France. It is small, delighting in its claims to be the smallest of the great capitals, its land mass the size of Manhattan, its population that of Belfast or Tel Aviv. For over 450 years it has attracted religious, political and economic refugees, but its own record has been variable. Stamped by the systematic genius of John Calvin, this nerve centre of the Reformation has long had more Catholics living in it than Protestants. An old republic, home to one of the Enlightenment's two most representative figures (Voltaire) and birthplace of the other (Rousseau), it developed as conservative an oligarchy as could be found. The first convention of the Red Cross met there in 1864 and the 'Alabama' dispute was settled there in the wake of the American Civil War by pioneering international arbitration, yet its communication network remained meagre and its international status was assured only after the Great War when it accommodated the League of Nations. Even that pride of place was ceded to New York when the United Nations replaced the League after 1945. This city of refuge and inexpensive repository for innumerable international agencies now became the ultimate expression of secularized western values, elegant, well-groomed and cosmopolitan. Finance was its motor. No sensible organization with a shoestring budget would choose to settle there. It was the perfect testing ground for Christian citizenship.

The YMCA's international citizenship had been tested there since January 1879 in a succession of rented quarters culminating in the Palais Wilson which the State of Geneva took over from the League of Nations in 1937 for the use of international bodies. The Second World War brought a neighbouring hotel into the picture. The Swiss Confederation needed the Palais for some of its Federal Administration. The Bellevue, an elegant building of the Belle Epoque, balconied and bourgeois, was to hand for the displaced tenants, and the octogenarian John R. Mott, whom contemporaries viewed as the Wesley and St Paul of roving ecumenists, turned necessity into vision. He visited the Bellevue and the view entranced him. Here was the ideal headquarters for ecumenical youth organizations: the World's Alliance of YMCAs, of which Mott had been President since 1926, the World's Student Christian Federation, of which he had been a founder in 1898, General Secretary to 1920, and Chairman to 1928, and the World's Alliance of YWCAs, which had been in Geneva since 1930. In the event, the YMCA first used the Bellevue in 1942–43, the YWCA joined them in October 1945 and the WSCF came only in 1970–71. Thus the Bellevue became John R. Mott House, though the mutual cooperation—and economies of scale—which, like the views, had fired Mott's imperial vision, proved fitful. Nonetheless the purchase demonstrated the flair with which Mott pushed practicality to its limits, the grandeur which left lesser men gasping and the enlightened capitalism on which such enterprises relied. The principal donors included the charitable distillation of English Methodist flour-milling, the Joseph Rank Benevolent Trusts, and the James Stokes Society, which administered the estate of an American whose imagination had been seized by Russia and the Latin races and whose property was to be used for the YMCA.[2]

The house's furnishings were representative. 'I am not certain whether you are the Pedro Celestino whom I met at the International Older Boys' Camp in Tsingtao in 1935, or not', one of the staff members wrote in acknowledgement of bamboo curtains from the Philippines. 'If you are then I have never forgotten you and I must say that the thing that has kept your memory ever fresh was the way in which you signed your name with little pictures in the midst of the signature. Some place I still have a copy of that signature which has now gone through a Japanese war, a communist revolution and several inflations in China.'[3] Japan also sent bamboo curtains. There were gifts, or promises, from South Africa, Australia, Canada, New Zealand and Scotland (a tartan carpet), with an Egyptian tour-de-force: furniture and prints which would have done justice to Aida and perhaps were contemporary with it. There was also a chapel, a cream-painted, barrel-vaulted combination of symbol and simplicity. Its table was from Greece. Here, for it represented Christ's table tomb (and his monogram and those of the four evangelists were incised on its white marble top), was the beginning and end of Christian life. From this gospel base the eye rose to three windows from the Swedish YMCA, each illuminating the Holy Catholic Church. In the centre was the crucifixion, the darkened sun veiled at Christ's side while, from his flesh, blood trickled over Adam's skull as fallen creation was redeemed. That was the Protestant window. To one side Mary, the human mother who wears the crown of heaven, holds Jesus, the boy who is the world's hope; so Mother Church, earthly yet divine in word and

---

2   For John R. Mott see C.H. Hopkins, *John R. Mott 1865–1955: A Biography* (Grand Rapids, MI: Eerdmans, 1979). James Stokes was a philanthropic New York executive with what John R. Mott described to his parents as 'objectionable peculiarities', Hopkins, *John R. Mott* , p. 245. See also *Association Men* 45 (February, 1920), p. 334.

3   Robbins Strong to Pedro C. Celestino, 11 February 1959, Geneva, World Alliance Archives.

sacrament, holds Christ, our life and our salvation, in her arms a cloth shaped like a boat, for Christ sits in its stern, steering his church between rocks and breakers. At the window's base kneel men singing and pointing in world's alliance to the world's church, Catholic in glory and praise. This was the Catholic window. The Orthodox window mingled the twin motifs of Orthodox art, Christos Pantokrator and the Risen Christ. The latter held the cross in his hand, symbol of death yet sign of victory, while under his feet was the cave of hell, where those imprisoned by death—a king, a soldier, a woman, a youth, an older man, people of the old covenant, the first man—escaped towards life at the call of life's firstborn. Christos Pantokrator had the book in one hand, while the other was raised in blessing, for from God comes the word of salvation and in Christ is man blessed.

How much of that was grasped by those who gazed? All passed the chapel because the lavatories were beyond it, but the staff worshipped there. Its designer and its donors bore some responsibility for what shaped the World Alliance while their chapel was in use.

Forty years on the YMCA, YWCA and WSCF had dispersed, much reduced, to separate premises. The YMCA's new home was a villa in the English style, almost as much Bournemouth as Geneva, which, as the Pension Melrose, had been the occasional home at the end of his life of the Olympic pioneer, Coubertin. It was thus still archetypally Geneva, a place of refuge and discreet retirement to be teased out by determined visitors. It contained no designated chapel. Cost and convenience precluded its removal into the house.[4]

When John R. Mott House was in formation the World's Alliance comprised thirty-two members, mostly national movements although the South American Federation was itself a transcontinental alliance of national movements. It was growing. Four members (Burma, now Myanmar, Egypt, Liberia, Malaya) were received in July 1953. That was the formal picture. The informal picture was much larger: YMCAs could be found in seventy-seven countries. The growth was insistent. Eight members were received in 1961, most of them witnessing to a post-imperial world struggling to be free: Hong Kong, Lebanon, the British Caribbean, with five in Africa, Dahomey, Ethiopia, Ghana, Kenya, the Rhodesias (as they were still known). By 1977 there were eighty-six national movements and related associations: 'It would be safe to project a number of over 23 million members and registered participants.'[5]

That figure was projected from a survey to which sixty-five movements had responded with details of 18,443 men and women in full-time

---

    4   The windows have been incorporated into a basement common room in 12 Clos Belmont, and the marble table is (2002) in the front garden.
    5   *YMCA Year Book* (New York: YMCA of USA, 1954), p. 132; *YMCA Year Book* (1962), p. 109; *YMCA Year Book* (1967), p. 98; *YMCA Year Book* (1977), pp. 73-74.

service; 663,055 voluntary leaders and committee members; 9,414 local associations with 690 hostels, 71,615 beds, 1,000 'food service operators', 1,364 swimming pools, 1,621 gymnasiums and 715 camps; of the 65% male members and users and 35% females, just over half were under eighteen years old and 29% were over thirty.[6] No big battalion could be formed from what were at best suggestive estimates, but they pointed to a movement with its finger on the pulse of change, and movement presupposes change and encourages a distinctive mentality. 'In human relationships the whole is greater than the sum of all its parts', wrote Paul Limbert, the Alliance's American Secretary-General to a largely sceptical American audience in 1960: 'The World Alliance is a living demonstration of christian unity and diversity. It provides opportunities for coordinated planning and concerted action on a world scale.'[7] It was a body with authority. In 1973 Limbert's Swedish successor, Fredrik Franklin, adopted a contemporary UNESCO aphorism ('technology is universal, culture is local') to identify its path-breaking possibility:

> The exportation of a technology—so often fails unless it is acceptable to the culture of the other society. The medical profession grapples in the transplanting of organs, with the problem of rejection. Yet the YMCA might claim that it is part of a super culture, the Christian faith, and certainly this is the one factor that binds all Movements together and gives our world brotherhood its strength.[8]

That sort of certainty was at its peak in 1980: 'If...the YMCA succeeds in raising the consciousness of its more than 24 million members...in 90 countries, then... We would be creating a force of world-minded people who know that local actions need global perspectives...and that problems at the local level are often symptoms of global problems...'[9] To buttress this an army of reports, surveys, study-guides and handy compilations flowed from Geneva on structural, religious, social and regional issues. In the quarter century after 1965 these focused on Christian unity, Christian witness in a multi-religious context, or in an Islamic context, or in a secular context. They also focused on social justice and human rights, apartheid, South Africa, Palestine, Central America, as well as the North–South divide and resource sharing. They were impressive evidence of responsibility, whatever their success as communication.

For Geneva was a culture shock, especially for North Americans. Paul Limbert was grateful that his theological training as a minister of the Reformed Church in the United States enabled him to work with Germans

---

6 *YMCA Year Book* (1977), pp. 73-74.
7 *YMCA Year Book* (1960), p. 138.
8 *YMCA Year Book* (1973), pp. 134-35.
9 *YMCA Year Book* (1980), p. 71.

and Scandinavians. He could cope with the significantly different mentality, and spirituality, of the European movements.[10] A Canadian's first impression of discourse at John R. Mott House was its 'churchiness'. He found the experience salutary but narrow. The Canadian movement had put that sort of thing behind it. Another Canadian, struck by the Eurocentric mind-set, reflected on how much more democratic things would be if everybody had to speak through an interpreter. That would make people reflect more on the cultural dimension to their conflicts.[11]

These impressions reflect what in retrospect appears as a distinctive stage of ecumenical endeavour, when informal fellowship still played a larger part in the structure of World Alliance life, invaluably so where true development can only be achieved at the speed of the most diffident. But the pace of Genevan life was stepping up. The Alliance's Secretary for Refugees had a post which regularly took him into areas of personal and political danger, requiring instant decision. Paul Limbert estimated that he spent up to half of his time out of Geneva, but he also recognised that he had been called to a post which offered space for statesmanship. He had come prepared by all the frustrating opportunities which the presidency of a smallish American Liberal Arts College could afford, to find himself 'in touch with currents of thought and life that affect the whole world', and with time to write about them.[12] Such horizons were constantly enlarging. So were the built-in frustrations.

Thus the setting and the constituency for worlds of Christian ambiguity in the latter half of the twentieth century. What lay behind them?

The YMCA has been summarized as 'the oldest ecumenical organization, next to the Evangelical Alliance...and without exception, the oldest international Christian body with a federative type of organization'.[13] Two dates stand out. The first is 6 June 1844, when a group of young men from London business houses formed a Christian association. The second is August 1855, when a larger group, among them the moving spirit of the London group, met in Paris under the wing of the Evangelical Alliance to formulate a basis for a world's alliance of young men's Christian Associations, a confessionally united cooperation of separate entities. However unwittingly they drew on nearly four hundred years of Protestant young men's activity across Europe and latterly in North America in such a way that their interdenominational but confessionally united alliance quite quickly and naturally became

---

10   P. Limbert, *Reliving a Century* (Asheville, NC: Biltmore Press, 1997), p. 14.
11   Personal conversation and correspondence, 11-12 May 1993.
12   P. Limbert to F. Franklin, 5 April 1961. Limbert MSS (I am indebted to the late Dr Paul Limbert for transcripts and copies).
13   P. Limbert 'Preface', in C.P. Shedd *et al*, *History of the World's Alliance of Young Men's Christian Associations* (London: SPCK, 1955), p. xvii. But how ecumenical was the Evangelical Alliance?

interconfessional, a pacesetter in the earlier stages of the ecumenical movement. They were a hinge in Christian development. They interwove strands in Protestantism which encouraged localised Christian associations outside the councils of the church. There were common threads. Their guiding spirits knew, or knew of, each other. They shared knowledge. There were overlapping concepts. Prayer, Bible study, moral and social reclamation, concern for mission and evangelical unity, and a relative unconcern for ecclesiology, marked them out.

The London Association was the catalyst in this. Its active protagonists were young laymen, discreetly supported by influential clergymen and usefully placed grandees. They combined firm evangelicalism with determined self-improvement. Signally helped by the Great Exhibition of 1851 and energised by the implications of working in the imperial capital of the world's prime urban and industrial nation, the London Association seemed to encircle the globe. It was swiftly replicated in Britain, North America and Australia. Its eighth report listed eight London branches, twenty-two provincial branches, and branches in Boston, Geneva, New Orleans, New York and Paris. Its ninth report could barely contain itself: 'The resting beams of the morning sun first fall on the Calcutta branch and linger latest on that of California.'[14] Here was a gold rush indeed.

Yet there were other cities and factors in the frame. On the continent work for young artisans, businessmen and intellectuals, all of it Protestant, most of it pietist, some of it cushioned by benevolent patrons but much of it self-supporting, reflected contemporary distinctions of class and culture, unified by an increasingly recognised similarity of aims and cemented by the useful networks of family, business and religious confession. Work in Francophone Europe was hampered by its focus on a beleaguered, self-conscious Protestant minority, part indigenous, part immigrant evangelical islands in a Roman Catholic sea shot through with ever stronger secularist currents; but that work was also helped by the solidarity common to minorities—a largely Francophone web of educated, multi-lingual, often surprisingly cosmopolitan pastors backed by strategically networked laymen. In northern Europe there were the easier benefits of belonging to an establishment culture. There was thus throughout Protestant Europe a suggestive counterpart to the influential backing from which the British movement benefitted. As in Britain it was spiced by the expectations of youth, with its generational nonconformity, and by the nonconformity inherent in minority status. This balance of established and dissenting values, prudently tipped in favour of the former, but never to the point of imbalance, marked and on the whole helped the YMCA in its European crucible and later served it similarly in

---

14   Shedd et al, *History*, pp. 34-36. The ninth report listed the Associations in Australia and the United States as 'Provincial Branches'.

Asia, the Middle East, Latin America and Africa. In North America the balance differed. Evangelical Protestantism and interdenominationalism were foundational but there were not the fault lines which penetrated British church life, neither was there the business-house focus which characterised the early English associations, nor the artisan emphasis of some of the continental European work. It was more community-centred.

The prime agents were charismatic individuals, their enthusiasm best caught in two letters written while dreaming of a conference which was shaping in Paris for 1855 by William Chauncy Langdon, a twenty-one-year-old Washington patent office clerk and Episcopalian. He wrote first to the twenty-one-year-old Genevan banker, Henry Dunant, with a young American's breathlessly accurate hyperbole: 'Now we find ourselves bonded as one vast institution reaching over Protestant Christendom. I am awestruck with the magnitude of the movement which God has raised up for his own work.' And then in his infectious over-the-top way he wrote to the Anglo–French Methodist, Jean-Paul Cook, who was also in his twenties: 'the occasion is too good to miss...for an assembly of Christian young men which will take its place in the history of the world and the results of which will never be forgotten... Several of our young men would go as far as Siberia for a conference of this sort.'[15]

Langdon got neither to Paris nor Siberia in 1855, but that international, evangelical, Christian, young men's meeting remains a remarkable feat, even if in reality it was pretty small beer, tapped in the wash of the meetings of the Evangelical Alliance. The Alliance expected 1,200; the Young Men expected ninety-nine, eight of them from North America. Those ninety-nine, however, were seasoned correspondents from nine countries now meeting, most of them for the first time. Their average age was twenty-three.[16] The way was open for a mentality to be shared and shaped. A structure was outlined. A basis was agreed. That basis was simple, comprehensive and marvellously, if unintentionally, elastic. It expressed where the participants were in their own lives: personal faith, Christian brotherhood, and the missionary work to which faith and brotherhood beckoned. It was undogmatic, but hardly untheological, Protestant in commitment, catholic in grasp, celebrating a vital, trinitarian Christianity.

The context should also be noted. The accents of class and politics could not be banished from the discourse of bright young men at the

---

15 Shedd *et al, History*, pp. 75, 79, 80. For an exploration of the familial, spiritual and Genevan context of Henry Dunant (1828–1910), see Gabriel Mützenberg, *Henry Dunant le prédestiné* (Geneva: Editions Robert-Estienne, 1984).

16 The emerging conference is explored in Shedd *et al, History, passim*, esp. pp. 102-37. The stress on youth needs one qualification, prompted by the surviving photograph's middle-aged look: many of these young men had been working for their living since their teens. They were not, in worldly terms at least, inexperienced.

cutting edge of newly politicising societies. The continent of Europe was in a state of constant redefinition. The United Kingdom was snagged by Ireland. The United States might become the Untied States should slavery become inextricably entangled with States' rights. In Paris the recent reality had been war in the Crimea with France and Great Britain ranged uncomfortably with Turkey against Russia. Such issues forced a practical ecumenism on seriously confederating Christians and they flicker across the rhetoric of one of the younger participants, the nineteen-year-old Edouard Barde: 'while outside two great peoples were celebrating a military alliance, we were within ratifying ours for a conquest also, that of our younger generation, and we are certain that one day we will conquer with the Church. We have projected the basis of a vast missionary association in the midst of Protestant Christianity.'[17]

The new Alliance's stage moved to London, its structures subsumed into those of the London Association. In these years new movements evolved and were recognised. The Euro–American construct began to bulge in unlikely places. International conferences became a regular feature. Issues were faced, more often circumvented. Broad-based programmes began to feature. Associations were reported from the 1850s in Calcutta and Colombo, from the 1860s in Beirut and Kandy, from the 1870s in Trivandrum, Lahore, Bombay and Jerusalem. Initiatives were reported in Russia, Italy, Spain, Syria, Persia, China and Japan. These were largely expatriate groups, the work of serious-minded businessmen or officials, sometimes the offshoot of overseas mission, but they gave substance to the claims of an international movement, even if the international conferences remained firmly European.

As for difficult issues, the American Civil War (1861–65) brought race and military conflict into sharp focus, and the American YMCA into high profile, for its mobile units for the service of soldiers were the first placed in the field by any organization in wartime;[18] and the Franco–Prussian War (1870) saw two national movements on opposing sides. The long standing personal wounds were arrested but not healed.

By 1878 the World's Alliance needed more than a clearing house for correspondence and conference preparation. The French proposed an 'International Committee'. Some deft palace-revolutionary footwork at the Geneva World's Conference brought that into being, backed by 350 delegates from seventeen nations (forty-two of them Americans over on a Cook's tour), and serviced by having a young, if heavily bearded,

---

17   Shedd et al, History, p. 117.
18   Shedd et al, History, p. 164. For America see C.H. Hopkins, History of the YMCA in North America (New York: Association Press, 1951).

salaried secretary, who also happened to be a multi-lingual Swiss banker.[19]

Between the Russo–Turkish War and the Great War there were nine World's Conferences, all of them in Europe. If the executive ceased to be a coterie of *bien pensant Genevois* (the Dutchman who insisted in 1881 that it was 'an impossible illusion that a centre in Geneva will be able to influence the work from Spain to Russia' spoke for many),[20] it remained overwhelmingly European.

For the movement as a whole, however, this period was one of almost unbounded growth. One measure is attendance at World's Conferences: Geneva 1878 included an African American and a Chinese. London 1894, believed to be 'the largest delegated evangelical convention of all lands ever held', included twenty-one from India, and one each from Sierra Leone, China and Japan.[21]

Money, politics and convenience dictate conference attendance. There are other ways of tracing growth. For a start it was transcontinental. By 1913 there had been hopeful inroads into southern and eastern Europe, Latin America and Africa. Those in Europe and Latin America would eventually have interconfessional implications. It was Asia, however, which saw startling advance.

In large part this reflected the extraordinary and interlinked missionary and student impulse which characterised the North American and British Movements from the late 1880s and from which Geneva seemed curiously remote, however much the World's Conferences throbbed with it. In significant part it also liberated indigenous energies, allowing for some apparently mealy-mouthed but in fact creative constitutionalism.

The first of these elements can be identified in India, which by 1899 had twenty-four YMCA secretaries, eight of them American, six British, one Danish, but nine Indian.[22] In the Indian V.S. Azariah, the American G. Sherwood Eddy, and the British J.H. Oldham, the Indian movement in 1899 had pioneers of international status. Azariah was a founding father of the modern world's proto-ecumenical church. Eddy exemplified the

---

19   The story is told in *World Communiqué* (April, 1953), pp. 4-5. Cook's Tours, like the World's Alliance, took off in the 1850s. Thomas Cook (1808–92; no relation of J.P. Cook) was an English General Baptist; a granddaughter of his married a son of George Williams, the London YMCA's founder. Williams played a significant mediating role at Geneva in 1878 and his choice as the Alliance's new Secretary was the usefully connected Charles Fermaud (1855–1937).
20   Shedd *et al*, *History*, p. 240.
21   Shedd *et al*, *History*, pp. 214, 337. For an account of the 1894 conference see also C. Binfield, *George Williams and the YMCA: A Study in Victorian Social Attitudes* (London: Heinemann, 1973), pp. 5-8.
22   Shedd *et al*, *History*, p. 363.

mutuality of true Christian missionary work. Oldham is the representative pioneer of the ecumenical movement.[23]

Nonetheless the transformation into a truly international movement was far more measured than this geographical expansion might suggest. It inched forward. Although the Alliance's central committee had had an Asian member in Tokyo's Taizo Miyoshi since 1891, and the indigenous potential of the Chinese, Indian and Japanese movements was widely recognised, only one of the twenty-three Asian representatives at London 1894 was in fact Asian. It was S.K. Datta's presence at Christiania (Oslo) 1902 which might be seen as a watershed. Datta was not just the first Indian to represent India at a World's Conference, he became the first Indian (and Asian) to become a World's Alliance Secretary in Geneva.[24]

Growth brought constitutional problems, puny in the sight of eternity but awkward at the time and suggestive of leaps forward. Was Scotland a nation, or was it a nationality? That question remained unanswered, but in 1894 some determined ingenuity allowed for a Scottish presence on the Alliance's central committee *de facto* but not quite *de jure*.[25] It could be seen as analogous to Finland, which was part of Russia, or to Burma and Ceylon (now Myanmar and Sri Lanka), which were parts of India. The way was opened for it, and Wales and Ireland too, to achieve independent membership. This was not quite a storm in a teacup. A movement whose *raison d'être* was union could be at a disadvantage when confronted by politically-edged cultural claims, but with the whole world in constant redefinition precedents like the Scottish 'solution' had their uses. They were politically neutral amidst competing imperialisms.

Growth in a youth movement is bound to have a generational dimension. These years saw phenomenal growth in student work. It was this which precipitated the movement into a new age. The continental movement had attracted students from the first. Their presence helps to explain the intellectual vigour of the debate at Paris in 1855. The four framers of the Paris Basis were students. It was the American movement which fostered the greatest student growth.

The American Inter-Collegiate YMCA had been formed at Princeton in 1877, but it tapped into a much older missionary student concern. By 1888 it had nearly 15,000 members and was arguably 'the largest

---

23 For India, see M.D. David, *The YMCA and the Making of Modern India (A Centenary History)* (New Delhi: National Council of YMCAs of India, 1992). See also K.W. Clements, *Faith on The Frontier: A Life of J.H. Oldham* (Edinburgh: T. & T. Clark, 1999).

24 In 1928, followed by S.N. Ghose in 1929. Cost and distance contributed to this as well as race and colonialism. Thus the delegates at Barmen—Elberfeld (1909) included an Indian (from Rangoon), a Japanese, and two Chinese, but the Chinese were at the Universities of Yale and Michigan: Shedd *et al, History*, p. 450.

25 Shedd *et al, History*, pp. 237, 335-36.

fraternity of students in the world'. Its associations were 'the spiritual nerve centres of the whole American Movement...evangelistic, Bible-centred, missionary minded and socially concerned...unique at this moment among the YMCAs of the world'.[26]

Their leadership had already produced its apostolic succession. Their founder, Luther D. Wishard (1854–1923), embarked from 1888 on a missionary world tour. In his place Richard C. Morse (1841–1926), already instrumental in securing the appointment of the World's Alliance's twenty-three year old General Secretary, now appointed the twenty-two year old President of Cornell University YMCA, John R. Mott, as American National College Secretary. A global strategy was in train.[27]

From the first Wishard had a missionary role for his student movement. In 1879 he wrote, with Japan in mind, 'convert the colleges of foreign mission lands into strongholds and distributing centres of Christianity; make them academies of the Church Militant to train leaders for the present crusade of evangelism'.[28]

His travels, followed by Mott's, precipitated a new breed of secretary, young, educated and ablaze for mission. They harnessed the enthusiasms of innumerable volunteers, all of them self-consciously the future of North America, to whom the world was now open. At the same time students world-wide, so obviously also the nations' future leaders, were targeted. Here lay the future of each national movement and each church as well as each nation. This was a strategy which presupposed training alongside vocation. Thanks to its students the movement was becoming a forum for experts.

This was a largely American odyssey. Geneva, strapped for cash, its leadership stretched, its mindset centred on Europe, was effectively bypassed. Yet the platform of World's Conferences and the criss-crossing webs of movement connexion were invaluable in opening its world to this student enthusiasm and in making the 1890s as crucible a decade as the 1840s and 1850s. Amsterdam 1891 saw Mott at his first World's Conference, together with Wishard, hot from world travel, and two resonating Swedes, Nathan Söderblom (1866–1931), future archbishop and architect of the Life and Work Movement that would feed into the World Council of Churches, and Karl Fries (1861–1943), who thirty years later became the Alliance's General Secretary. With their names we turn to 'the first international student and ecumenical organization', the World Student Christian Federation.[29]

---

26   Shedd *et al*, *History*, p. 278.
27   Shedd *et al*, *History*, p. 280.
28   P. Potter and T. Weiser, *Seeking and Serving the Truth: the First Hundred Years of the World Student Federation* (Geneva: WCC Publications, 1997), pp. 4-5.
29   Potter and Weiser, *Seeking and Serving*, p. xi.

Although its largest component was North American, with Mott shaping the Student Volunteer Movement for Foreign Mission (1888) and its electric slogan, 'The evangelization of the world in this generation', there were also significant British and continental components. Mott's leadership, however, demonstrated Geneva's isolation from too much energising activity and Mott, once convicted, was unstoppable. He convinced key leaders from Britain, Sweden and Germany of a Federation's potential, and one was duly formed at Vadstena in August 1895.

Thanks to Fries, Mott, and Wishard relations with the Alliance were close. Each gained from the other. From the YMCA's point of view the Federation allowed for a more conscious missionary and ecumenical strategy than had previously been possible. Unlike the Alliance, the Federation had an avowed duty to unite 'in common purpose and work the coming leaders of church and state in all lands' and Mott's tour of Europe, the Middle East and Asia made 'possible for the first time a thorough and comprehensive study of the religious state of the students of the whole world'.[30] China hit him as 'the greatest mission field in the world'; Japan was 'the most difficult field we have ever visited'; in India 'he made the discovery that there might be those in the East who could themselves make a contribution to the cause of Christ'.[31] And Mott's definition of evangelization, so grandly and Americanly Protestant, at least liberated it from clerical or organizational control:

> By evangelization we...mean... [t]he presenting of the gospel in such a manner to every soul in this world that the responsibility for what is done with it shall no longer rest upon the Christian church, or any individual Christian, but shall rest on each man's head for himself.[32]

The Federation was pacesetting. Its Williamstown (USA) Conference, 1899, was chaired by a Japanese—'probably the first world Christian gathering at which an Oriental had presided'.[33] At Versailles, 1900, the social issue was to the fore: 'It is not merely for ourselves that we are saved, not only to preach a set of doctrines—but that the very life of Christ may through us permeate the whole fabric of our social and civic life'.[34] Oxford, 1909, understood evangelization 'as the redeeming of persons and of the societies in which they live towards justice and human

---

30 Potter and Weiser, *Seeking and Serving*, p. 14.
31 Potter and Weiser, *Seeking and Serving*, pp. 16-17.
32 Potter and Weiser, *Seeking and Serving*, p. 15.
33 Thus Mott, Potter and Weiser, *Seeking and Serving*, p. 20.
34 Potter and Weiser, *Seeking and Serving*, p. 23.

dignity, in love'.[35] None of this was absent from Alliance rhetoric, but it was more sharply focused in the Federation.

Tokyo, 1907, was claimed to be the first international conference of any kind to have been held in the Far East. One note struck by a conference garden-party's speech deserves to be left ringing: 'If you wish Christianity to dominate the thought and life of the whole Orient, it is indispensable that it should be done by the might of the Japanese people.'[36] Other notes were struck at Constantinople in 1911 and Lake Mohonk in 1913. The former was remarkable for the prominent and reasoned participation of Orthodox Christians and the latter included four native and thirteen African–Americans.[37] The Federation could begin to claim that it was international, inter-racial and ecumenical. These were not stray threads, left hanging. They were picked up and woven by young men who became leaders in church and nation.

And not only young men. Women had been related to the Federation from the first but at Zeist in 1905, attended by 145 students from thirty countries, there were thirty-two women from fifteen countries. They met separately at first, but then shared in four plenaries; and Ruth Rouse, the future historian of ecumenism, was appointed secretary for women students, with a women's committee to advise her.[38]

That degree of integration was neither achieved nor sought by the Alliance and yet the emergence in the 1890s of the World's YWCA was as suggestive for YMCA work as for the WSCF. The three movements should not be seen as isolated or self-regarding elements in their world of Christian endeavour.

The YWCA was both parallel and counterpoint to the YMCA. It too was 'Protestant in origin, in temper, and in method'.[39] It too was a Euro–American construct in which a foundational European Christian culture was braced and balanced by a large New World element and the imperatives 'of a new country cut off from close connections with its origin',[40] and vast in resources. It too developed a determinative rhythm of conferences. It too had a missionary thrust promoted by epic journeys, and a marked practical and social thrust. And its pioneers were literally the wives, sisters and daughters of YMCA pioneers. Crucially, however, it

---

35 Potter and Weiser, *Seeking and Serving*, p. 31.
36 Thus Count Okuma, in Potter and Weiser, *Seeking and Serving*, p. 28. En route to Tokyo Mott visited Korea which, he decided, 'will be the first nation in the non-Christian world to become a Christian nation', see Potter and Weiser, *Seeking and Serving*, p. 27.
37 Potter and Weiser, *Seeking and Serving*, pp. 33-5, 43.
38 Potter and Weiser, *Seeking and Serving*, p. 26.
39 Anna V. Rice, *A History of the World's Young Women's Christian Association* (New York: The Woman's Press, 1947), p. 4.
40 Rice, *History*, p. 5.

reflected the differing but rapidly changing perceptions of women's role in society at large and Christian society in particular. If the YMCA began in London business houses in the 1840s, the YWCA had two British beginnings in the 1850s. One was as a prayer union, the other as a provider of accommodation for the young, single, respectable, self-supporting woman. Like the YMCA it spread rapidly from London to North America. Helped by that now vanished army of governesses, it spread through Europe. In Asia it found more to do than occupy the time of expatriate wives. In India it developed a work with Eurasian women.[41]

As with the YMCA many distinctive trends were tested, intensified and radicalised by the YWCA's American experience. That too had a significant student emphasis, and recognised the value of purpose-built premises and a professionally trained and salaried leadership.[42] Such emphases explain the social awareness.[43]

The emergence of an international structure took longer for the YWCA but it was achieved in London in November 1894. For the next thirty-six years the new body's headquarters were in London; its Presidents were British, its General Secretaries were American, all were formidably well-connected.

Three points might be noted. First, whatever the official ambivalence, indeed disapproval, of the World's Alliance and World's YWCA, five national movements in the Alliance included 588 mixed associations in their membership in 1908.[44] These could not now be wished away. Secondly, the wide span of YMCA work made it harder to reach the sort of accommodation with the YWCA which both reached with the WSCF. Thirdly there was the unalterable conviction that the YWCA's call was to 'a work for and with young women by women' in the contemporary context of changes in women's lives which were far more revolutionary than the changes in men's lives.[45] The YWCA was a women's movement as well as a young Christian's movement. Its leadership needed to gain and transmit organizational skills. This would not realistically be achieved in a mixed movement with subordinate provision for women's activities.

---

41   The Bombay (Mumbai) Association of c. 1875 had four founders: English, Eurasian, Indian, and Scottish. Rice, *History*, p. 15.

42   Thus, in 1893 its American Convention was addressed by Mrs William Boyd (Corabel Tarr) on 'A New Profession for Women and How to Enter It'. See Rice, *History*, p. 43.

43   Memorably voiced by Florence Simms with her conviction 'that the Y.W.C.A. should openly declare itself for social righteousness and constitute itself one of the organs of social reclamation'. See Rice, *History*, pp. 106-109, 126-29.

44   They were Austria (46 associations), Finland (42), Norway (450), Scotland (20), Sweden (30). Shedd op. cit., p. 447.

45   Rice, *History*, pp. 142-43.

These factors, together perhaps with the recognition that since ecclesiastical leadership remained a male preserve, what women might do together was less threatening to ecclesiological order, conditioned the YWCA's increasingly ecumenical stance. Like the WSCF, the new World's YWCA accepted the Paris Basis almost verbatim. Yet the issue of relations with both Orthodox and Roman Catholics predated its formation and a doggedly careful pragmatism had led by 1914 to the adoption of three constitutional articles which opened the way for ecumenism rather than an eirenic but Protestant inter-denominationalism.[46] The World's YWCA had reached a similar position to the WSCF.

And the World's Alliance? One of its most impressive expressions of ecumenism, a masterwork of Protestant catholicity, rooted in the Réveil, had been voiced at Paris in 1855 by Emile Laget of Nîmes.[47] It affirmed tradition yet potentially transformed it. From the 1880s the increasing engagement with radically different cultures from the Evangelical Protestantism which had hitherto formed the movement's leadership led to a real grappling with such union. There were tensions in Sweden. There were concerns, which peaked in 1904–05, that the German movement was too church based. The Alliance resolved them by declarations which made explicit the interconfessional, ecumenical meanings that were arguably implicit in the Paris Basis and which reaffirmed the movement's mission as a lay movement, an arm of the church but not the church. Theirs was 'the spirit of evangelical alliance according to John XVII. 21'. The use of that phrase was masterly. It picked up Laget's theme of 1855. It affirmed tradition and transformed it.[48]

At Paris 1905 the Alliance stepped into deeper waters than those of northern Europe's state churches. Constantinople's Professor Eliou made the startling proposal that 'evangelical' might be defined to include Roman Catholic and Orthodox Christians.[49] At Barmen-Elberfeld 1909 the call was to cultivate 'the fields of the Roman and Greek Catholic countries in Europe, aiming to develop in them as soon as possible efficient, self-supporting national organizations'.[50] At Edinburgh in 1913 the emphasis changed: 'the attitude of the Association towards the ancient Christian Churches in these lands will require careful and prayerful study'.[51] By now the Alliance's leadership in such matters had fallen to Mott who was convinced that there must be links with Orthodoxy and that the Paris Basis allowed for this. The WSCF and

---

46 Rice, *History*, p. 132.
47 A full version is given in Shedd *et al*, *History*, pp. 121-22.
48 Shedd *et al*, *History*, pp. 405-16, esp. p. 415.
49 Shedd *et al*, *History*, p. 423.
50 Shedd *et al*, *History*, p. 438.
51 Shedd *et al*, *History*, p. 438.

World's Alliance were thus in step. Mott's role in the famous Edinburgh Missionary Conference of 1910 and its aftermath belongs to the wider history of ecumenism but its participants showed the part played by YMCA and WSCF leaders in creating the right climate.

In a lay movement practice shapes ecumenism. The Alliance's practice of emergent programme and mission, refracted through its uneasy yet unavoidable response to contemporary social and political pressures and exercised, aired, and hot-aired at world's conferences, was bound to affect the movement's spirit of evangelical alliance. How this might appear in the movement's rhetoric is suggested by the title of Mott's early WSCF text, *Strategic Points in the World's Conquest: The Universities and Colleges as Related to the Progress of Christianity* (1897). Intellectual conquest was alluring to students out to conquer life, but the language of conquest, however up-ended into paradox by the Christian faith, sat uneasily with emerging nations and transforming societies in the age of empire.

The missionary explosion, ecumenical transformation, and social engagement of the YMCA, YWCA and WSCF were set in a doubly imperial expansion. The evangelization of the world in this generation was a war cry of Christian imperialism, the world's rhetoric appropriated and neither entirely purged nor transformed in the process. It was also helped along its way by secular imperialism. That was inevitable when the world was coloured by empires, British, Dutch, French, German, Russian, with Japan and the United States joining them and YMCAs in all of them. Thus the Alliance's 1907 London Plenary was informed and literally enlarged by the parallel meetings of the British YMCA's Intercolonial Council, with representatives from Australia, Burma, Ceylon, India, Malaysia and New Zealand. But explosions cannot be contained, even by strategists, although their results can sometimes be transmuted by statesmen; and explosion is the word. It was not just that students were to be evangelized for church; they might become professional secretaries in the process, a consciously formed, educated young professional élite. Wishard's missionary tours; Mott's appointment; the arrival in Japan in 1888 of Swift, the first foreign secretary sent by any national movement and thus the pioneer of that honoured yet misunderstood tradition, the long succession of fraternal secretaries; the arrival in India in 1890 of David McConaughy Jr; the setting up of the American Movement's Foreign Department in 1889 (perhaps the single most significant step for the world movement taken by any national movement), followed in 1891 by the English National Council's Foreign Committee and in 1892 by the sending out of the first two English fraternal secretaries, to Bombay and Egypt and Palestine; all these developments opened dimensions of work undreamed by the expatriates who had founded the first Asian associations.

Such Christian imperialism, coloured by natural patriotism and fired by unthinking adventure, can be as easily dismissed as once it enthralled. It was a complex phenomenon. The personnel of imperial expansion, the settlers, adventurers, administrators, soldiers, businessmen, tourists, scholars, missionaries, teachers, had too many conflicting aims to be the shock troops of any master plan. They exploited and were exploited. The true communicators among them received as well as gave, therefore they learned. Like those with whom they communicated, they emerged as quite different men and women. As Emile Laget of Nîmes would have recognised, this implicit transformation was the heart of the matter. It gave the YMCA, YWCA and WSCF an independence of which they did not always take advantage. England's W.H. Mills recognised this in 1892:

> In their character as missionary societies, they have the precious privilege of being able to work without being preoccupied with inherited ecclesiastical or religious traditions; they are not bound to any particular type of organization... It is this simplicity of organization which permits them to adapt themselves to the economic, social, or political situation of the different countries and that will make them increasingly the means for the evangelization of young men of the entire world...[52]

Two years later the Swedish Karl Fries and the American David McConaughy conveyed the essence of mission whatever the empire. For Fries, himself a thwarted missionary, trained in the Swedish navy, 'It should be the aim of YMCAs to turn out young men who, in the political and commercial relations in which they may come to people outside the boundary line of Christendom, will do honour to the name of Christ and form, as it were, an object lesson to the words of divine truth proclaimed by the missionaries. By upholding Christian principles, by showing honesty and esteeming the human rights of the natives in every dealing with them, such men will form a check upon those scoundrels who, without conscience, use their superiority as representatives of European civilisations for the satisfying of their own lusts and greediness to degrade, morally and socially, those who stand before them nearly defenceless.' And McConaughy cut to the heart of the matter:

> There is no such thing as the foreign field... Come with me to Calvary, and stand under the Cross of Christ...and, if you will, take your stand there with me upon that only point on all the earth high enough to see that there is no such thing as a foreign field and a home field.[53]

These two speeches mark the point at which the Christian imperative confronts politics. To give one further brief example: the nineteenth

---

52 Quoted in Shedd *et al*, *History*, p. 328.
53 Shedd *et al*, *History*, p. 342.

century saw an increasingly migrant world. It was not just Christians students who were on the march. The turn of the new century saw the Alliance's assumption of work with migrants. Twisted by war into work with refugees, this grew into its most far-reaching twentieth-century commitment, uncontroversially humanitarian, yet inseparable from further social exploration.

All the main issues of the Alliance's second half century were thus forming or in place in its first half-century and to the forefront of the World's YWCA's and WSCF's first two decades. Indeed the issues of its third half-century (and of their second half centuries) were already there in embryo. So were their responses. I have ended on the eve of the Great War when it would have been better to have ended, as I began, with the aftermath of the Second World War. But my ending at least allows for a degree of perspectival swivel. By 1914 the YMCA's figures of 1855 had become elder statesmen and had died. Through them there were links with almost unimaginable pasts and futures. Lord Shaftesbury, the English movement's most famous supporter from the 1840s, celebrated in his surprising combination of conservative politics, conservative evangelicalism and social radicalism an aristocratic world which remembered the French Revolution; he lived to address London 1881. J.H. Gladstone, the London Scot who had been at Paris 1855, was the scientist father-in-law of Britain's first socialist Prime Minister, in a world reeling from Bolshevik revolution.[54] Fries, Söderblom and Mott, striding into their first prime in the 1890s, were men who coloured the high twentieth-century's ecumenical movement. Azariah, Datta and Oldham, young in India in 1899, were not far behind. They bridged the movement's tensions as well as its years. They defined its life, its mission and its relationships with the church for which it witnessed and the world in which it witnessed. They explain why in 1955 the Alliance had a President who was a West African and why its Secretary General would have been an African–American had the man who had been approached as first choice accepted.[55] With them we return to that microcosmic world

---

54   For John Hall Gladstone FRS (1827–1902), father-in-law of James Ramsay MacDonald FRS (1866–1937), Prime Minister 1924, 1929–35, see *The Compact Edition of the Dictionary of National Biography* (London: Oxford University Press, 1975), II, p. 2656.

55   The President was Charles Dunbar Sherman of Liberia (1918–1986, President 1955–64). The preferred choice for Secretary General was Benjamin Elijah Mays (b. 1895), President of Morehouse College, Atlanta, from 1940, author of *The Negro's Church* (1933) and *The Negro's God as reflected in his Literature* (1938). His pupils included Martin Luther King. Mays declined and Paul Limbert (b. 1897), President of Springfield College, MA, was appointed, and served 1953–62. Limbert, *Reliving a Century*, p. 169.

of ambiguity, Geneva and its John R. Mott House: where Secretary General and World President operated.

CHAPTER 4

Edinburgh 1910 and the *Oikoumene*

Brian Stanley

Student essays and examination answers on the history of the modern ecumenical movement almost invariably begin with the World Missionary Conference, held in Edinburgh from 14 to 23 June 1910. Their assumption that the ecumenical movement originated in 1910 is an understandable one. Much of the literature designed for students and general readers reinforces the assumption. The chapter on the ecumenical movement in Alec Vidler's volume in the Pelican History of the Church notes at the outset that 'it is generally agreed that the movement, as it is now known, dates from the International Missionary Conference [*sic*] that was held at Edinburgh in 1910'.[1] B.G. Worrall's *The Making of the Modern Church* similarly begins its chapter on the ecumenical movement with an account of Edinburgh 1910, though properly situating that account in the context of the developing history of co-operation in mission and evangelism by evangelical Protestants over the preceding century.[2] Most accounts give at least some such recognition to the fact that the 1910 conference was the culmination of a long tradition of evangelical ecumenism, and many do so by making the fortuitous connection with William Carey's chimerical proposal of 1806 that 'a general association of all denominations of Christians' should meet every ten years or so at the Cape of Good Hope, commencing in 1810, a notion famously dismissed by Andrew Fuller as 'one of bro^r Carey's pleasing dreams'.[3]

---

1   A.R. Vidler, *The Church in an Age of Revolution: 1789 to the Present Day* (Harmondsworth: Penguin, 1961), p. 257.
2   B.G. Worrall, *The Making of the Modern Church: Christianity in England since 1800* (London: SPCK, 1998), pp. 203-207.
3   See R. Rouse, 'William Carey's "pleasing dream"', *International Review of Missions* 38 (1949), pp. 181-92.

By making such a connection, these accounts encourage the false supposition that the Edinburgh conference was indeed 'a general association of all denominations of Christians'. To a possibly greater extent than any other event in modern Christian history, the conference suffers from the distortions of hindsight. Because the institutions of modern Protestant ecumenism can trace their descent so clearly from 1910, the temptation is irresistible to interpret the conference in the light of what followed, while paying inadequate attention to its origins in the Protestant missionary movement. The purpose of this essay is to suggest that the World Missionary Conference was more seriously limited in its scope than either its formal title or the ascription 'ecumenical' would imply, and to reflect briefly on the lasting consequences of those limitations.

It hardly needs to be said that the World Missionary Conference was representative of only one segment of the world Christian community. There were, of course, no delegates from the Roman Catholic, Orthodox, or ancient eastern churches. The only contribution from a Roman Catholic source was a remarkable message of greeting from Bishop Geremia Bonomelli of Cremona, sent at the invitation of Silas McBee, a lay American Episcopalian with a vision for ecumenism, and a member of the American executive committee, who had been introduced to the bishop in April 1910. Significantly, the elderly Bonomelli was a friend of a young priest, Angelo Roncalli, later to become Pope John XXIII.[4] The conference was, of course, a decidedly Protestant gathering, the sole exceptions being those amongst the thirty-five members of the Society for the Propagation of the Gospel (SPG) who would have regarded themselves as Anglo–Catholic rather than Protestant,[5] and their supporters on the episcopal bench—principally Charles Gore of Birmingham and E.S. Talbot of Southwark—who attended as special guests of the British executive committee.

Neither was the conference geographically representative of the composition of the world church in 1910, for the simple reason that delegates represented not churches but Protestant and Anglican missionary societies, and societies were allocated places on the basis of their annual income. Hence the big battalions of the Anglo–American missionary movement dominated the field. Thus, of the 1,216 official delegates, 510 were British, 490 were North American, 171 originated from continental Europe, 28 came from the white colonies of South

---

4   J.M. Delaney, M.M., 'From Cremona to Edinburgh: Bishop Bonomelli and the World Missionary Conference of 1910', *Ecumenical Review* 52 (2000), pp. 418-31.

5   The SPG, under pressure from many supporters opposed to the conference, declined to send any official delegates, but permitted individual members of its committee and staff to attend if they chose.

Africa and Australasia, and only 17 were from the non-western world. 1,009 of the delegates were men, and 207 were women.[6] Of the seventeen non-western delegates, ten attended as representatives of American mission boards, only three as representatives of British missionary societies, three were invited specially by the American executive committee, and one (V.S. Azariah) by the British executive committee. All seventeen were Asians—of whom eight were Indians, four were Japanese, three were Chinese, one was Korean, and one Burmese.[7] As will be discussed below, South America and the Caribbean were not represented at all. Although many contemporary accounts of the conference implied that Africans were present, nobody appeared to notice that Africa was in fact represented only by expatriate missionaries, though two of these were non-white: Alexander Camphor, a black Methodist Episcopal missionary to Liberia, observed by Temple Gairdner as being of 'immense size and glorying in his African race', and John Rangiah, a Telegu Baptist missionary to Natal.[8]

The international committee responsible for preparations for the conference had suggested as early as July 1908 that missionary societies should be asked to include in their delegations 'if practicable, one or two natives from mission lands'.[9] Most missions, however, failed to fulfil even this modest injunction. The case of one society, the London Missionary Society (LMS), is instructive in illuminating the decision-making processes that lay behind this failure. In January 1910 one of its leading China missionaries, W. Nelson Bitton, wrote to J.H. Oldham from Shanghai, alerting him to the concern felt by some of his missionary colleagues in China, in view of the rising tide of anti-foreign sentiment in the Orient, about the inadequate provision made to include indigenous

---

6 These figures are compiled from the list of delegates in World Missionary Conference, 1910, *Volume IX: The History and Records of the Conference* (Edinburgh and London: Oliphant, Anderson, & Ferrer, n.d. [1910]), pp. 39-71. Figures will vary slightly depending on how one counts a few missionaries from one region or continent who served under a mission whose home base was in another region or continent.

7 See W.R. Hogg, *Ecumenical Foundations: A History of the International Missionary Council and its Nineteenth-Century Background* (New York: Harper & Bros, 1952), p. 396. An eighteenth Asian, C.C. Wang, then a student in Edinburgh, was present at the conference, but not an official delegate.

8 W.H.T. Gairdner, *'Edinburgh 1910': An Account and Interpretation of the World Missionary Conference* (Edinburgh and London: Oliphant & Ferrer, 1910), p. 58. On Rangiah, see below pp. 93-94. For examples of statements that Africans were present, see Gairdner, *'Edinburgh 1910'*, p. 56; *The Missionary Review of the World* 33 (1910), p. 649; and *Missionary Herald* (Boston) 106 (1910), p. 351.

9 Third Ecumenical Missionary Conference (June 1910), Minutes of International Committee, 14-20 July 1908, p. 9, Ecumenical Centre, Geneva.

Christians in the conference delegations.[10] Oldham acted promptly, forwarding Bitton's letter to John Mott, together with a letter from Dr Arthur Brown, of the Presbyterian Board of Foreign Missions in New York, which appears to have made a similar criticism.[11] Oldham also sent a copy of Bitton's letter to Ralph Wardlaw Thompson, the venerable Foreign Secretary of the LMS. The LMS, however, was in dire financial straits in 1910, needing to reduce its expenditure by about £10,000 a year. Thompson's reply to Oldham pointed out that every Asian delegate would cost the society an additional £100, and informed him merely that he had written to China inviting the society's churches to send one or two representatives at their own expense.[12] The LMS Board agreed in February 1910 that four of its thirty-eight allocated places should be reserved for native delegates, two from China and two from India, but that their expenses should be met entirely from local funds.[13]

Two Chinese delegates were subsequently put forward: Ch'eng Ching-yi (Cheng Jingyi), a twenty-nine year-old pastor from Beijing who had studied at the Bible Training Institute in Glasgow, and had unusually fluent English for a Chinese at that time; and Moses Chiu, who was currently studying for a Doctor of Philosophy degree in the University of Berlin. In the event, Chiu was unable to attend the conference owing to a clash of dates with his doctoral examination.[14] Ch'eng Ching-yi did attend, financed by the LMS churches in China, and, as is well known, made a great impact at Edinburgh with a speech calling for the imminent formation of a united Christian church in China. Seventeen years later, his vision was realized through the formation of the Church of Christ in China, with Ch'eng as its first moderator (and later general secretary).[15]

---

10 Copy of Bitton to Oldham, 12 January 1910, Mott Papers, Yale Divinity School, Special Collections 45 [hereafter Mott Papers], Box 63, Folder 1169; also in Henry Martyn Centre, Westminster College, Cambridge [ECM 3/15].

11 Copies of Oldham to Mott, 2 February 1910, and Oldham to Brown, 2 February 1910; Mott Papers, Box 63, Folder 1169; copies also in Henry Martyn Centre [ECM 3/16 and ECM 3/17]. Brown's letter appears not to have been preserved.

12 Thompson to J.H. Oldham, 7 February 1910, LMS Home Office Outward Letters, Box 2, Council for World Mission archives [hereafter CWMA], School of Oriental and African Studies, University of London. I am grateful to the Council for World Mission for permission to cite these archives.

13 LMS Board Minutes, 15 February 1910, Box 53, CWMA. Only ten places were allocated to serving missionaries.

14 Thompson to K. Maclennan, 12 May 1910; Thompson to E. Curwen, 17 May 1910; and Thompson to M. Chiu, 18 May 1910; LMS Home Office Outward Letters, Box 2, CWMA.

15 The speech is recorded in World Missionary Conference, 1910, *Report of Commission VIII: Co-operation and the Promotion of Unity* (Edinburgh and London: Oliphant, Anderson, & Ferrer, n.d. [1910]), pp. 195-97. Ch'eng became secretary of the China Continuation Committee (1913–22) and general secretary of the National

The LMS Indian churches, being substantially poorer even than their Chinese counterparts, had no realistic prospect of raising the funds to send any representatives to Edinburgh. Hence Ch'eng Ching-yi was the sole LMS delegate from the non-western world. The financial crisis facing the LMS in 1910 was real enough, but the society never considered reducing its conference expenditure by foregoing some of its thirty-eight places. What proved decisive was Thompson's conviction that the 'younger' churches were not yet ready to take their place in such exalted company: 'I do not think the time is ripe for the inclusion of delegates appointed by the Churches in non-Christian lands in any great Conference such as ours. Ten years hence I hope there may be such a development of independent Church life as will make it necessary to have representation from various parts of the world.'[16]

The LMS case is illustrative of an assumption shared by most, though not all, of those involved in Edinburgh 1910: the conference was a gathering of mission executives and missionaries; indigenous Christians were a dubious luxury whose presence was not integral to the character of the event. The other major British societies did no better than the LMS: the Church Missionary Society included in its vast delegation of eighty-nine persons just one Asian, R.K. Sorabji,[17] a prominent lawyer from Allahabad; the SPG similarly had one Asian representative, the Rev. S. Ghose of the Cambridge Mission to Delhi. The Wesleyan Methodist Missionary Society, the Baptist Missionary Society, and the Foreign Mission Committees of the Church of Scotland and United Free Church of Scotland were unable to muster a single non-Westerner between them.

Happily, there were those in 1910 with a larger vision. The American mission boards, as Oldham noted in February 1910, did rather better than their British counterparts;[18] the American Baptists spectacularly so. It may give the recipient of this Festschrift some pleasure to note that five of the seventeen Asian delegates (more than from any other denomination) were Baptists, all of them delegates of the American Baptist Foreign Mission Society. The Rev. John Rangiah was not simply the first missionary sent (in 1903) by the Telegu Baptist Home Missionary Society to the Telegu-speaking workers of the sugar

---

Christian Council (1924–33). See H.L. Boorman and R.C. Howard (eds.), *Biographical Dictionary of Republican China* (5 vols; New York & London: Columbia UP, 1967–79), I, pp. 284-86; C. Boynton, 'Dr Cheng Ching-Yi', *Chinese Recorder* 70 (1939), pp. 689-98; N. Bitton, 'Cheng Ching-yi: a Christian statesman', *International Review of Missions* 30 (1941), pp. 513-20.

16   Thompson to Oldham, 7 February 1910, LMS Home Office Outward Letters, Box 2, CWMA.

17   On the Sorabji family see E. Stock, *The History of the Church Missionary Society* (4 vols; London: Church Missionary Society, 1899–1916), IV, p. 217.

18   Oldham to Brown, 2 February 1910, Mott Papers, Box 63, Folder 1169.

plantations in Natal, but also the first overseas missionary sent out by any of the mission churches of the American Baptists. The Rev. Yugoru Chiba, a graduate of Colby College and Rochester Theological Seminary, was President of the Southern Baptist Theological Seminary at Fukuoka, Japan, and Dean-elect of the new Japan Baptist Seminary in Tokyo. He later became chairman of the National Christian Council of Japan, and the most prominent leader in twentieth-century Japanese Baptist life. Thangkhan was an evangelist from the Garo Hills of Assam who had formerly served on the staff of the teacher training institution at Tura; he had studied at the Newton Theological Institution (now Andover Newton Seminary) in Massachusetts. Professor L.T. Ah Sou from Rangoon Baptist College in Burma had been a student for two terms at the Moody Bible Institute. Professor Tong Tsing-en (Tong Ching-an) from the recently founded Baptist Theological Seminary in Shanghai, is described by Temple Gairdner as a 'sturdy nationalist' resplendent in skull-cap, pigtail and peacock-blue silk jacket.[19]

In the LMS, Nelson Bitton felt keenly the virtual exclusion of Asian voices. The September 1910 issue of the LMS *Chronicle* contained an article by Bitton which regretted the lack of opportunity given at Edinburgh for the expression of indigenous Christian viewpoints; one suspects that the criticism was aimed in part at Bitton's own society.[20] One of Bitton's travelling companions from Mukden in Manchuria all the way across Siberia and Europe to Edinburgh had been Che'ng Ching-yi, an experience which left an enduring imprint on Bitton.[21] Bitton's commitment to non-western representation was shared by both Mott and Oldham. Oldham later testified that 'it was Mott above all others who insisted in the face of a good deal of conservative opposition that the younger Churches should be represented at the Edinburgh Conference in 1910'.[22]

---

19 On the five Baptists as a group see *Missions* 1 (1910), pp. 189-90; World Missionary Conference, *Monthly News Sheet* 7 (April 1910), p. 142. On Rangiah see A.W. Wardin (ed.), *Baptists around the World: A Comprehensive Handbook* (Nashville, TN: Broadman & Holman, 1995), p. 57; S. Hudson-Reed (ed). *Together for a Century: The History of the Baptist Union of South Africa 1877–1977* (Pietermaritzburg: South African Baptist Historical Society, n.d. [1977]), p. 86. On Chiba see F.C. Parker, *The Southern Baptist Mission in Japan, 1889–1989* (Lanham, MD: University Press of America, 1991), pp. 19, 64, 72, 78-80, 155-56, 169; K. Lodwick (comp.), *The Chinese Recorder Index: A Guide to Christian Missions in Asia, 1867–1941* (2 vols; Wilmington, DE: Scholarly Resources Inc., 1986), I, p. 85. On Tong Tsing-en see Gairdner, *'Edinburgh 1910'*, p. 57; Lodwick, *Chinese Recorder Index*, I, p. 479.

20 *The Chronicle of the London Missionary Society* 75 (1910), pp. 165-66.

21 Bitton, 'Cheng Ching-Yi', pp. 515-16.

22 J.H. Oldham, 'John R. Mott', *Ecumenical Review* 7 (1955), p. 258; cited in C.H. Hopkins, *John R. Mott 1865–1955: A Biography* (Grand Rapids: Eerdmans, 1979), p. 348.

As for Oldham himself, another of his responses to Bitton's letter in January 1910 appears to have been to issue, on behalf of the British executive committee, a special invitation to his former colleague in the Indian YMCA, V.S. Azariah, founder of the Indian Missionary Society and National Missionary Society, and the future Bishop of Dornakal.[23] Azariah was even better known to Mott, who had tried without success to secure Azariah's presence in Britain in July 1909, at the Oxford conference of the World's Student Christian Federation, and it is probable that Mott had a hand in the Edinburgh invitation also.[24] It is worthy of remark that when, on the eve of the conference, Oldham and his wife, Mary, went on retreat to the Yorkshire village of Goathland in the company of John Mott and some of the key figures involved in the organization of the conference, Azariah (but not, apparently, his minder, the formidable Mrs Isabel Whitehead, wife of the Bishop of Madras) was invited to join the party. This young, newly ordained and still largely unknown Indian priest thus formed one of the select few who were invited to set the spiritual tone of the conference by prayer and silent reflection amidst the beauty of the Yorkshire Moors.[25]

Although as late as April 1910 the conference organizers were expressing the hope that 'the number of delegates from non-Christian countries' would be 'considerably larger' than the twelve names recruited at that stage, it needs to be emphasized that Edinburgh 1910 was at no stage conceived as a comprehensive gathering of spokespersons for the world church.[26] It was rather a conference in which self-appointed representatives of western Protestant missions, particularly from Britain and North America, consulted together, with only minimal interaction with a handful of selected Asian Christians, about the prospects for the evangelization of the world in their generation. Nevertheless, it may still be asked, was not the conference noteworthy for the seriousness with which it devoted attention to the challenge presented to Christian mission by the current state of the world? Was not the conference, even if not ecumenical in its representation, truly 'ecumenical' in the alternative

---

23 K.W. Clements, *Faith on the Frontier: A Life of J.H. Oldham* (Edinburgh: T. &. T. Clark, 1999), p. 89.
24 Azariah to Mott, 25 May 1909, Mott Papers, Box 4, Folder 61.
25 Postcard from John R. Mott to Leila Mott, 7 May 1910, Mott Papers, Box 107, Folder 1835. The others present at Goathland included Kenneth Maclennan (assistant conference secretary), George Robson (chairman of the business committee), the Methodist, W.H. Findlay (a member of the international committee), and Mrs Alexander Whyte of Edinburgh. Azariah had been ordained to the Anglican priesthood on 5 December 1909. On Azariah and Mrs Whitehead see S.B. Harper, *In the Shadow of the Mahatma: Bishop V.S. Azariah and the Travails of Christianity in British India* (Grand Rapids: Eerdmans/Richmond: Curzon Press, 2000), pp. 121-22, 139-47.
26 World Missionary Conference, *Monthly News Sheet* 7 (April 1910), p. 142.

sense that it sought to promote a co-ordinated and reflective Christian response to the needs of the entire inhabited globe? Does it not deserve to be remembered, therefore, as the first gathering of the modern era in which Christians endeavoured in a scientific fashion to apply the gospel to what would now be termed the *oikumene*?

What we remember as the World Missionary Conference of 1910 was originally planned as, and entitled 'The Third Ecumenical Missionary Conference'. It followed two even larger but now virtually forgotten conferences in London in 1888 and New York in 1900.[27] The Edinburgh conference, like its predecessors in London and New York, was to be designated as 'Ecumenical' in the original sense of the word that it would include the whole human race in its scope. It was to be concerned, according to the first major planning paper drafted in December 1907, with 'the missionary future of the world'.[28] Unlike its two predecessors, however, the 1910 conference was to be, not an inspirational jamboree for mission enthusiasts, but a serious consultative gathering of experts. It was modelled, not on the large public events of 1888 and 1900, but on the Indian Decennial Missionary Conference held in Madras in 1902 and the Shanghai Missionary Conference of 1907. The Edinburgh conference was to proceed on the basis of detailed reports prepared in advance by eight appointed study commissions. The first of those commissions was originally given the title 'Carrying the Gospel to all the World'.[29] In September 1908 it was decided that the title of the conference be changed to 'The World Missionary Conference' in order to avoid any misunderstanding arising from the fact that 'the word "Ecumenical" has acquired a technical meaning'—in other words, its modern meaning, associated, ironically, with the very movement for church unity to which Edinburgh gave birth.[30]

Formally, therefore, Edinburgh 1910 might appear to have been originally concerned to discuss how the good news of Jesus Christ could be more effectively proclaimed to the whole world, to humanity in its entirety. If such had been substantially the case, it could hardly be faulted on theological grounds. In reality, however, the scope of the conference was implicitly limited from the outset by a decision taken in March 1908 that representation at the conference was not simply to be on a financial

---

27   The London conference in 1888 had 1517 delegates; the New York conference in 1900 had over 2,500.

28   Third Ecumenical Missionary Conference (June 1910), Memorandum Suggesting Constitution and Procedure of Conference, 12 December 1907, p. 6, Ecumenical Centre, Geneva.

29   Third Ecumenical Missionary Conference (June 1910), Minutes of International Committee, 14-20 July 1908, p. 3, Ecumenical Centre, Geneva.

30   World Missionary Conference (1910), Minutes of General Committee, 23 September 1908, p. 21, Ecumenical Centre, Geneva.

basis but also confined to 'Societies and Boards administering funds and sending out missionaries for the propagation of the Gospel among non-Christian peoples'. In the case of societies which worked in part in 'professedly Christian countries', only that portion of their income 'expended on work among non-Christians' could be counted.[31] In September 1908 the first (American) meeting of Commission I, supposedly entrusted with the topic 'Carrying the Gospel to all the World', accordingly took a decision that its sub-committee on statistics should exclude 'missionary work carried on on the Continent of Europe, with the exception of the Turkish Empire and southeastern Europe'. The meeting considered the possibility of excluding *all* missions in Catholic and Orthodox countries, but rejected the idea, ostensibly on the grounds of 'practical difficulty', though one suspects more substantial reasons for the American decision.[32] It is important to note that even before the question of the geographical scope of the conference became a bone of contention between Anglo–Catholics and evangelical Protestants, the principle had been conceded by all, including the Americans, that most of Europe (and also, implicitly, North America itself) should be excluded from its purview as being 'Christian' lands. In practice, therefore, it had been decided that the conference was not in fact about *world* mission but rather about mission from 'Christendom' to 'heathendom'. There was no dispute that the two could be differentiated on a territorial basis: the only issue was where to draw the boundaries.

In February 1909 J.H. Oldham as secretary of the conference found himself on the receiving end of an episcopal onslaught from Charles Gore of Birmingham, Edward Talbot of Southwark, and H.H. Montgomery of the SPG in protest against the intention to include in the conference statistics (for whose compilation the Americans were wholly responsible) of Protestant missions working in Catholic or Orthodox territory. Unless such an intention were revoked, it was clear that all Anglo–Catholic participation in the conference would be forfeited, and the hopes of Oldham and Tissington Tatlow, secretary of the Student Christian Movement, that this conference, unlike its forbears in 1888 and 1900, could claim the full endorsement of the Church of England, would be dashed.[33] The nub of the issue was whether the (mainly North American) Protestant missions in Latin America were to be included or

---

31 Third Ecumenical Missionary Conference (June 1910), Minutes of Executive Committee, 12 March 1908, pp. 14-15, Ecumenical Centre, Geneva.

32 World Missionary Conference Papers, Box VII, Folder IV, Minutes of Commission I, 9-10 September 1908, Union Theological Seminary, New York.

33 See Clements, *Faith on the Frontier*, pp. 81-85; T. Tatlow, *The Story of the Student Christian Movement of Great Britain and Ireland* (London: SCM Press, 1933), pp. 404-10. The correspondence between Talbot, Gore and Oldham is in the Oldham Papers (Box 1, Folder 2), New College, Edinburgh.

not. Oldham warned Mott that, 'if the leading men in the Church of England were to withdraw, the whole attitude of the Press and of the general public in this country toward the Conference would be altered. The blow would be a very serious one indeed'.[34] Ultimately, however, there was little doubt that the Anglo–Catholic case would triumph, because, if Europe and North America were deemed to be within Christendom and hence beyond the scope of mission, how could the same status logically be denied to Latin America? As Oldham commented to Mott, 'If you admit work among the Roman Catholics in South America why should we exclude such work in papal Europe?'[35]

Under pressure from Oldham, who made a special journey to New York for the purpose, the Americans caved in and the crucial support of the leaders of the Anglo–Catholic party was retained. On the suggestion of the Americans, the title of Commission I was changed to 'Carrying the Gospel to all the Non-Christian World'. A subtitle was added to the conference as a whole: 'to consider Missionary Problems in relation to the Non-Christian World'.[36] Latin America was excluded from the scope of the conference, with the exception of missions among the aboriginal tribes and 'non-Christian immigrants'. On similar grounds all missions among African American people in the West Indies were excluded, though work among Asian immigrants to the Caribbean was included.[37] In the cases of the Turkish empire, Persia, and Egypt, the British section of Commission I reached a compromise of strange logic. All statistics of Protestant church membership were omitted, on the grounds that these Christians were primarily proselytes from the ancient Oriental or Orthodox churches. However, 'in view of the direct bearing of the work in these countries upon the Mohammedan population', statistics of the missionaries who were working towards making such converts from the ancient churches *were* included, 'as indicating the agencies and forces which are influencing, and in a measure are directed to effect the ultimate conversion of the non-Christian populations'.[38] One wonders whether such illogic was not a sop to the Americans, who, having had one of their areas of missionary predominance swept from the agenda by the British,

---

34   Oldham to Mott, 2 March 1909, Box 1, Folder 2, Oldham Papers.

35   Oldham to Mott, 10 March 1909, Box 1, Folder 2, Oldham Papers.

36   World Missionary Conference (1910), Minutes of Executive Committee, 30 June 1909, p. 44, Ecumenical Centre, Geneva.

37   World Missionary Conference papers, Box VII, Folder 11, Minutes of the British Section of Commission I, 4 May 1909, Union Theological Seminary, New York.

38   *Statistical Atlas of Christian Missions* (Edinburgh: World Missionary Conference, 1910), p. 61; World Missionary Conference papers, Box VII, Folder 11, Minutes of the British section of Commission I, 4 May 1909, Union Theological Seminary, New York. On 20 May the American section of Commission I agreed to apply the same principle to the Philippines.

might well have jibbed at seeing another such region—the Near East—disappear altogether as well.

From the standpoint of present-day ecumenical orthodoxy, the overall outcome seems highly desirable. Protestant proselytism of Roman Catholics, and, rather less clearly of Orthodox, had been implicitly declared to be no valid part of Christian mission. In point of fact, however, all had accepted from the beginning the principle that only mission funds expended on work among non-Christians should be counted in the determination of representation. The real division was between those who defined Christian identity primarily in terms of an act of personal commitment to Christ and those who thought in terms of belonging by territorial and baptismal affiliation to the church catholic. The decision to restrict the territorial scope of the conference drew strong criticism in Britain from the leaders of the Baptist and Wesleyan Methodist Missionary Societies, and the China Inland Mission.[39] In the United States, one of the mission leaders who found the decision most difficult to swallow was the Rev. Dr Thomas Barbour, Foreign Secretary of the American Baptist Foreign Mission Society, the mission board which had done more than any other to ensure inclusion of indigenous representation in its delegation.[40] Barbour's case raises the question of who in 1910 in fact stood more clearly for the unity of the world church—those who were jealous for catholic principle or those who were in practice prepared to allow unity in Christ to transcend divisions between church and mission, and East and West.

Yet the majority of leaders of denominational Protestant missions appear to have regarded the limitations imposed by Anglican scruples as a price worth paying, perhaps because they were themselves more or less ambivalent about the acceptability of the notion of Christendom. R. Wardlaw Thompson, for instance, in defending to Lord Kinnaird the concession made to the Anglo–Catholics, referred to his regret at the necessity for restricting the sphere of the conference to missions 'working among non-Christian peoples'.[41] We have seen that a few weeks earlier, Thompson had used a similar phrase—'non-Christian lands'—to resist the arguments of Oldham and Bitton in favour of increasing indigenous representation.[42] The idea that the world could be divided into Christian and non-Christian nations had become widely accepted even amongst those whose theology of church and state logically ruled out such concepts. Many outside the Anglican tradition in 1910 willingly accepted the notion of Christendom in relation to the supposedly godly

---

39   Oldham to Mott, 21 May 1909, Oldham Papers, Box 1, Folder 3.
40   Oldham to Mott, 13 April 1909, Oldham Papers, Box 1, Folder 3.
41   Thompson to Lord Kinnaird, 24 May 1910, LMS Home Office Outward Letters, Box 2, CWMA.
42   On which see above p. 93.

commonwealths of Protestant Europe or North America; tacitly accepted it even in relation to Catholic Europe; and then found as a result that they had no option but to accept the extension of the boundaries of Christendom to Latin America. Areas such as the Balkans and the Near East were left uncomfortably poised, half in Christendom and half outside it, depending on which set of statistics one looked at.

Edinburgh 1910, therefore, was concerned, not with the mission of the church to the entire inhabited globe, but rather with mission to those portions of the globe which everybody could agree were beyond the frontiers of Christendom. Indeed, the conference was to a large extent preoccupied with one continent only: Asia. The introduction to the section on Africa in the Report of Commission I on 'Carrying the Gospel to all the Non-Christian World' referred to India and China as 'the two great mission fields of the world'. In comparison, the population of Africa was deemed to be sparse (only two-thirds that of India and less than half of the Chinese population) and its social conditions were dismissed as 'primitive'.[43] The conference assumed that African paganism was 'doomed' to succumb to the 'higher' and more dogmatic monotheistic religions.[44] The only real issue for discussion was whether Islam or Christianity was going to win the race for the soul of the animist. In comparison to Asia, whose ancient faiths were held to pose much more serious questions for the mission of the church, Africa received slight and superficial attention, both in the commission reports and in the conference itself.

In substantial measure, therefore, the conference was a gathering in which western Protestants talked to each other about the evangelization of the Orient. It is no wonder, therefore, that at least one of the seventeen Asian delegates found it a not entirely happy experience. At the evening session on Monday 20 June a now celebrated address was given by V.S. Azariah on 'The Problem of Co-operation between Foreign and Native Workers'. Azariah complained of 'a certain aloofness, a lack of mutual understanding and openness, a great lack of frank intercourse and friendliness' between European missionaries and national Christians, citing examples of experienced Indian missionaries who had never once been invited to share a meal with any of their European brethren. He insisted that 'friendship is more than condescending love' and argued that no substantial change would be possible unless the dependent financial relationship which bound Indian workers to missionaries as servants to their masters were severed. He concluded with a searching application of the apostle Paul's words in 1 Corinthians 13: 'Through all

---

43 World Missionary Conference, 1910, *Report of Commission I: Carrying the Gospel to all the Non-Christian World* (Edinburgh and London: Oliphant, Anderson, & Ferrer, n.d. [1910]), pp. 204-205.
44 *Report of Commission I*, pp. 20-21.

the ages to come the Indian Church will rise up in gratitude to attest the heroism and self-denying labours of the missionary body. You have given your goods to feed the poor. You have given your bodies to be burned. We also ask for *love*. Give us FRIENDS!'[45]

This prophetic word was received in what Temple Gairdner called 'an electric silence, broken now by a sort of subterraneous rumbling of dissent'. Applause broke out only when Azariah conceded that the failing he was alluding to was not typical. But he immediately qualified the concession by an impromptu: 'At the same time it would be a mistake to think that it was exceptional!', and there was some nervous laughter and further applause.[46] At the conclusion of the address, the chairman of the meeting, Lord Reay, a former Governor of Bombay, Under-Secretary of State for India in the Liberal government of 1894–95, and a prime mover in the steps then being taken to found a School of Oriental Studies in the University of London, rose to say that some of *his* best friends were Indians. Perhaps they were, but the scholars and princes whom Donald Mackay had welcomed to the Governor's residence in Bombay were not the same sort of Indians of whose treatment by missionaries Azariah was complaining.[47] Reay asked Azariah to take back to his church the assurance that this conference of Christians was prepared 'at all times to shake the hand of fellowship with them' (Hear, hear).'[48]

Whether anyone present actually shook Azariah's hand at the end of the meeting we do not know. What we do know is that Isabel Whitehead later wrote to Azariah's wife, Anbu, reporting that the speech had struck the company 'like a bomb', with half of the audience being delighted 'and the other half very angry'. Mrs Whitehead counted herself in the former camp, 'little realizing that she was part of the problem'.[49] Azariah's indictment of missionaries as being deficient in the essential Christian motivation of fraternal love had caused such a sensation that an informal meeting was called to discuss what should be done. Some pressed for 'something in the nature of a public protest' or, at least an explanation that would reassure the faithful that reality on the mission field was not as this unknown Indian had suggested. In the end, it was agreed simply that Sherwood Eddy, the American Congregationalist and YMCA evangelist who was Azariah's closest confidant, would administer

---

45   World Missionary Conference 1910, vol. IX, *The History and Records of the Conference*, pp. 306-15.
46   Gairdner, *'Edinburgh 1910'*, p. 110.
47   On Mackay, 11th Baron Reay, see *Proceedings of the British Academy* 10 (1921–23), pp. 533-39; *Journal of the Royal Asiatic Society* (1921), pp. 665-73; and *Dictionary of National Biography*.
48   *The Scotsman*, 21 June 1910, p. 10.
49   Harper, *In the Shadow of the Mahatma*, p. 148.

a 'fatherly admonition'.[50] In fact it is possible that Eddy had helped him write the speech in the first place.[51] Whether Eddy himself really believed that an admonition was necessary is not known. There is evidence, almost certainly autobiographical in nature, that Azariah had been diffident about speaking so frankly, but had been urged by John Mott to 'tell out freely what lay on his heart'. One may speculate that he felt that his initial doubts had been amply vindicated. In later years he told J.Z. Hodge, his biographer and the secretary (under Azariah's chairmanship) of the National Christian Council of India, Burma, and Ceylon, that he had spoken 'under a severe nervous strain, and, while he did not regret having entered his remonstrance, he mentioned that were he called to take similar action again he would do it more circumspectly'.[52]

Azariah had long since learned, like many others, that Christian professions of the unity of redeemed humanity were too often belied by the realities of missionary behaviour. In 1910 he further discovered to his cost that the truly ecumenical fellowship he had experienced on retreat at Goathland was not mirrored in the spirit of the conference which followed. Himself a missionary in India of uncommon gifts and effectiveness, he was denied that status at Edinburgh because he stood on the wrong side of a division between the Christian and the non-Christian world that had come to be defined in territorial and hence racial terms. If the acid test of Christian fellowship is the capacity to receive in humility an uncomfortable truth spoken in love by a fellow Christian, then Edinburgh 1910 must be judged to have failed that test of ecumenicity.

There is plentiful evidence to suggest that much popular understanding of mission in the western churches even now remains imprisoned within a mental framework constructed around the opposition between a white Christian West and the 'heathen' mission fields overseas. Nearly a century after the Edinburgh conference, such attitudes are even less appropriate now than they were then. Missions conducted by Christians from the non-western world, already in 1910 far more substantial than the organisers of the conference realised, now dwarf the missionary endeavours of the western churches in both scale and significance. Christian profession in Europe and much of North America has receded, at the same time as it has exploded in Africa, Oceania and parts of Asia. Over 60 per cent of all the world's Christians now live in the so-called Third World. The old territorial division between the Christian and non-Christian worlds no longer corresponds with statistical reality, nor, in the aftermath of the end of the western colonial empires, does it possess

---

50 J.Z. Hodge, *Bishop Azariah of Dornakal* (Madras: Christian Literature Society for India, 1946), pp. 4-5.
51 R.L. Nutt, *The Whole Gospel for the Whole World: Sherwood Eddy and the American Protestant Mission* (Macon, GA: Mercer University Press, 1997), p. 72.
52 Hodge, *Bishop Azariah*, pp. 3, 6.

moral acceptability. The polarities between (white) Christian and (non-white) non-Christian populations so engrained in western Christian discourse in 1910 have been consigned to the dustbin of history. No Christian theology of mission deserves a hearing today unless it is explicitly committed to the unity of humanity and to the multi-directionality of mission.

In response to the distortion of the Christian understanding of humanity represented by what might be termed the 'racialization' of redemption, mainstream theological thinking in both Protestant and Catholic traditions has in the last forty years come to place more and more emphasis on the unity of humanity as the central theological principle that should animate Christian mission. The radical shift that took place during the 1960s from a church-centred to a world-centred approach to mission, which drew particularly on J.C. Hoekendijk's missiology of the kingdom in confrontation with the world, can be understood as a reaction against the racial and colonial implications of the fatal merger between church and Christendom exemplified at Edinburgh. Hoekendijk's *The Church Inside Out* (1964) was in part a protest, grounded firmly in biblical theology, against the current tendency to divide the one apostolic task of mission to the world into two spheres—that of 'evangelism', conducted within the political–linguistic frontiers of Christendom, and 'missions', conducted beyond those frontiers.[53] After a century in which the increasingly sophisticated human structures of western missionary agencies had dominated the scene, the *Missio Dei* now resumed centre stage. This was long overdue, but in the markedly secular climate of the 1960s and 1970s, humanization became the central objective and motif of mission, and the sending of missionaries across the territorial boundary separating the old Christendom from the old heathendom now appeared at best a marginal activity and at worst a perpetuation of colonialism.

In order to repudiate the ideology of western Christendom it now seemed to many theologians necessary to go one step further and question the legitimacy of the call to conversion to Christianity itself. Thus the Indian Protestant theologian Stanley Samartha affirmed in 1981: 'If it is recognized that real conversion is not from one religion to another but from unbelief to God, and that "mission" is not the church's work but God's, then the implications of this in the context of religious pluralism must be more openly acknowledged.'[54] More recently, Samartha has made the point still more explicitly: 'In a

---

53 J.C. Hoekendijk, *The Church Inside Out* (ET, London: SCM, 1967), pp. 13-17, 39. See T. Yates, *Christian Mission in the Twentieth Century* (Cambridge: Cambridge University, 1994), pp. 163-64, 196-97.

54 S.J. Samartha, *Courage for Dialogue: Ecumenical Issues in Inter-Religious Relationships* (Geneva: World Council of Churches, 1981), p. 32.

religiously plural world the mission of the church is not to make other people Christian but to invite people to enter the Kingdom of God.' In fairness to Samartha, it should be noted that he goes on to explain that the kingdom is present wherever people are being transformed by Jesus Christ, showing 'the marks of love and self-sacrifice in their commitment of human liberation', even if, for many in countries such as India, such transformation does not lead to baptised membership of the institutional church.[55] Samartha would say that the call to conversion to *Christ* stands, even if the call to conversion to Christianity does not.

The ultimate implication of the Christian pluralist position is, however, to suggest that distinctively Christian faith and worship are of value for those who, through accident of birth or other people's evangelistic witness, belong to the Christian tradition, but are not of such pre-eminent value that they deserve to be commended to all human beings. In other words, Christianity is the tribal religion of those who are fortunate enough to have it already—Christendom still rules OK. For all the radicality of its reaction to the racial divisions of the colonial era, the pluralist theology of humanity has concealed within it a chasm between what is appropriate for Christendom and what is appropriate for what used to be called the heathen world. This chasm is disintegrative of the very heart of Christianity. As Jürgen Moltmann has said recently, 'If Christianity loses its missionary character anywhere in a given civilization, or at any time in a given era, or in any society, it is forgetting its origin and surrendering its identity.'[56] Or, to cite another author of an earlier generation and a very different theological tradition, Frank Lenwood, the Congregationalist and former Foreign Secretary of the LMS, and by the time he wrote this an avowed Unitarian in belief: 'Better a propagandist Christianity that is exclusive than a Christianity that is merely tribal.'[57]

If we repudiate the call to bring the good news of Christ to those beyond the frontiers of the church, we shall end by destroying the Christian basis for the unity of humanity. The World Missionary Conference of 1910 was conceived out of a laudable concern to accelerate the church's fulfilment of its commission to bring the gospel to the world, but in several key respects failed to give adequate expression

---

55   S.J. Samartha, *One Christ—Many Religions: Toward a Revised Christology* (Maryknoll, NY: Orbis Books, 1991), p. 153.

56   J. Moltmann, 'The mission of the Spirit—the gospel of life', in T. Yates (ed.), *Mission: An Invitation to God's Future* (Calver: Cliff College Publishing, 2000), p. 19. See also J. Moltmann, *God for a Secular Society: the Public Relevance of Theology* (London: SCM Press, 1999), pp. 226-44.

57   F. Lenwood, *Jesus—Lord or Leader?* (London: Constable, 1930), p. 331, cited in B. Stanley, 'Manliness and mission: Frank Lenwood and the London Missionary Society', *Journal of the United Reformed Church History Society* 5 (1996), pp. 458-77, quotation from p. 474.

either to the unity of the body of Christ or to the unity of humankind. In today's contrasting ecumenical climate, the threat to the unity of the *oikumene* is concealed under different guise: for the church to abandon the imperative to bring the gospel of Christ to *all* the world may conceivably leave intact the central Christian claim that only in Christ and his kingdom can the eschatological vision of a restored humanity and a renewed creation be realized; but what it undeniably does is to sever the ties that bind the kingdom of Christ to the body of Christ and to reinforce the dangerous notion that religion is inextricably linked to ethnicity and territoriality.

CHAPTER 5

The Christian World Communions: Denominational Ecumenism on a Global Scale

Richard V. Pierard

An important alternative to conciliar ecumenism was the international links that had developed among the denominational or 'confessional' families. Ans J. van der Bent, the director of the World Council of Churches library in Geneva and respected scholar in his own right, correctly declared that in their early days these organizations were in fact the principal forms of the ecumenical movement, and they gave the members of their churches a new consciousness of universality through an understanding of the worldwide dimensions of their own fellowships.[1] Some of the associations dated back to the later nineteenth century, the earliest being the General Conference of Seventh-day Adventists, formed in 1863. The World Presbyterian Alliance (formally known as the Alliance of Reformed Churches Throughout the World Holding the Presbyterian System) was founded in 1875, and in 1970 it merged with the International Congregational Council, organized in 1891, to constitute the World Alliance of Reformed Churches (Presbyterian and Congregational).[2] In 1867 Anglicans inaugurated the practice of a decennial Lambeth Conference of bishops from their worldwide community, which its convenor, the Archbishop of Canterbury, made clear was to be a consultative body, not a synod or deliberative body that legislated for the whole church. However, over the years the need to maintain the international bonds became more keenly felt and eventually (1963) a central office in London was established called the Advisory

---

1 A.J. van der Bent, 'Christian World Communions', in A.J. van der Bent (ed.), *Historical Dictionary of Ecumenical Christianity* (Metuchen: Scarecrow Press, 1994), pp. 79-80.
2 See A.P.F. Sell, *A Reformed Evangelical Catholic Theology: The Contribution of the World Alliance of Reformed Churches, 1875–1982* (Grand Rapids: Eerdmans, 1991), and M. Pradervand, *A Century of Service: A History of the World Alliance of Reformed Churches* (Edinburgh: St Andrews Press, 1975).

Council on Missionary Strategy. The 1968 conference approved converting it into a formal agency, the Anglican Consultative Council.[3] British and North American Methodists began holding decennial Ecumenical Methodist Conferences in 1881 and in 1951 the delegates decided it would be advisable to establish a permanent structure known as the World Methodist Council.[4]

In the twentieth century other international denominational associations formed, the largest being the Baptist World Alliance in 1905 and Lutheran World Federation (LWF) in 1947.[5] International agencies created by smaller denominations included the Disciples Ecumenical Consultative Council of the Christian Church–Disciples of Christ, World Convention of the Churches of Christ, Friends World Committee for Consultation, Reformed Ecumenical Council, Mennonite World Conference, Pentecostal World Conference, and Salvation Army.[6]

The Confessional Families and Founding of the World Council

The early ecumenists struggled to find a suitable label for the 'structured visible expressions', to use Harold Fey's term, of the denominational groupings. A widely used one was that of 'confessional' organizations or families.[7] However, the word meant various things to different groups, and the Anglicans in particular denied that they were a confessional church at all. Nevertheless, regardless of what one called them, the

---

3   The developments are sketched out in O. Chadwick, 'The Lambeth Conference: An Historical Perspective', *Anglican and Episcopal History* 58 (September, 1989), pp. 259-77.

4   *Encyclopedia of World Methodism* (Nashville, TN: United Methodist Church, 1974), pp. 2600-2602.

5   J.H. Schørring, P. Kumari, and N.A. Hjelm (eds.), *From Federation to Communion: The History of the Lutheran World Federation* (Minneapolis: Augsburg Fortress, 1997). A multi-author centennial history of the Baptist World Alliance is scheduled for publication in 2005, to which John Briggs will be a contributor.

6   Descriptive articles on many of these groups may be found in the N. Lossky *et al* (eds.), *Dictionary of the Ecumenical Movement* (Grand Rapids: Eerdmans, 1991), and van der Bent, *Historical Dictionary of Ecumenical Christianity*. A comprehensive history of the global denominational families in Protestantism remains to be written.

7   H.E. Fey, 'Confessional Families and the Ecumenical Movement', in H.E. Fey, (ed.), *The Ecumenical Advance: A History of the Ecumenical Movement. Volume 2, 1948–1968* (Philadelphia: Westminster Press, 1968), p. 117. Fey's discussion of the role of the confessional families in the founding of the World Council (pp. 118-21) is quite helpful. Another useful account of the early history of their development and relationship to the WCC are the three essays by Y. Ishida, H. Meyer, and E. Perret, that comprise the symposium, 'The History and Theological Concerns of World Confessional Families', *LWF Report* 5 (August, 1979).

confessional world organizations, which varied widely in their distinctive character and organizational structures, had a strong sense of obligation to foster their own respective traditions and church consciousness. Their existence constituted a major problem for the World Council of Churches (WCC) from its very beginning. At the planning meeting in Utrecht, The Netherlands, in 1938 that laid out a structure for the future WCC, Lutherans argued that membership should consist of churches and seats in its Assembly and Central Committee should be allotted on a denominational basis. Their contention was that the World Council's united testimony before the world would be more forthright and effective if the churches associated in confessional groups were permitted to speak freely with one another in friendly comparison of views—certainly more quickly and firmly that if Christians spoke with one another as national or geographical groups. They felt that the way to a united Christian testimony would be rendered more difficult by sectionalism or regionalism than by sectarianism as such.

After the war the Lutherans reiterated their position that membership should be by confessional blocs. However, W.A. Visser't Hooft, the General Secretary of the provisional committee for the WCC, appeared before the founding assembly of the Lutheran World Federation in 1947 to defend the idea of representation by churches as such. He said:

> The World Council is deeply aware of the fact that the ecumenical task can only be performed if the main confessional federations and alliances perform their task of bringing the churches of their confessional family together in close fellowship and so prepare the way for the even greater and more difficult task of establishing the wider ecumenical Christian brotherhood.[8]

He had essentially called for a 'both–and' instead of an 'either–or' approach to the question of representation. The Amsterdam Assembly ratified this by adopting the provisional committee's recommendation: 'Seats in the Assembly shall be allocated to the member churches by the Central Committee, due regard being given to such factors as numerical size, adequate confessional representation and adequate geographical distribution.'[9] This was a compromise formula that recognized the existence of confessional groups but made the basis of membership that of formally organized 'Churches'.

The founding assembly offered an olive branch to the confessional bodies by authorizing the new WCC 'to establish consultative

---

8   *Proceedings of the Lutheran World Assembly, Lund, Sweden, June 30–July 6, 1947* (Philadelphia: United Lutheran Publishing House, 1948), p. 186.

9   W.A. Visser't Hooft (ed.), *The First Assembly of the World Council of Churches: The Official Report* (London: SCM Press, 1949), p. 113. This was incorporated into Article V, Section 1, of the WCC constitution.

relationships with denominational federations (world confessional associations'. They would be invited 'to send representatives to the Assembly and the Central Committee in a consultative capacity', and they 'should especially be consulted with regard to membership of churches of their confession'. Further, because 'in their manifold approaches to the churches the activities of the Council and of the confessional federation overlap to some extent', it would be 'most desirable' to maintain regular contacts with the executive officers. The federations were encouraged to set up offices in Geneva or at least send special representatives there.[10]

A resurgence of confessional groups occurred parallel to the new World Council of Churches and its task in the next years was to harness their energies to the ecumenical movement. At the Evanston Assembly in 1954 the Central Committee 'noted with satisfaction' in its report 'that almost all world confessional associations have gone on record as wishing to support the ecumenical movement', and suggested that the general secretary should 'arrange for informal consultations from time to time, with three or four representatives from each association, to discuss the implementation of that desire and other common problems'.[11] Within three years this would result in the calling of the first meeting of representatives of the 'world confessional organizations'.

Beginnings of the Conferences of World Confessional Families

The post-war relief efforts of the various international church bodies, especially the Baptist World Alliance and the Lutheran World Federation, distracted attention from the matter of ecumenical/confessional relationships, but after Evanston it became increasingly obvious that it needed attention. Dr John A. Mackay, President of Princeton Theological Seminary and the World Presbyterian Alliance during the mid-1950s, took the lead in attempting to direct the competitive possibilities of the denominational groups into an ecumenical channel. Both he and Visser't Hooft recognized the need for consultations among the leaders of the confessional fellowships and the WCC, but agreed that it would be too risky for the WCC to call such a meeting. Mackay commented at the 1956 executive committee meeting of the Presbyterian Alliance about confessionalism and insisted that this was a positive factor since there was no disposition to 'absolutize their several confessional structures or loyalties. No single confession believes that it represents the one and only

---

10   Visser't Hooft (ed.), *First Assembly of the World Council of Churches*, p. 131.
11   *The Evanston Report: The Second Assembly of the World Council of Churches, 1954* (New York: Harper & Brothers, 1954), pp. 184-85.

Church of Christ, the Una Sancta.' But each seeks to make its specific contribution to the 'ecumenical treasure house of Christian faith and life'. He proposed a motion, unanimously accepted by the body, which expressed the hope 'that in the near future an informal gathering can be arranged between representatives of the several world confessional bodies in the Protestant family of churches. The object of this meeting would be to provide an opportunity for the representatives of each confession to interpret to their brethren of the other confessions the nature, objective, and development of the group to which they belong.'[12]

In his paper at the meeting entitled 'The Confessional Resurgence and the Ecumenical Movement', Mackay pointed out that the two were growing side by side and asked what was to be the future relationship of the two endeavours. 'The Confessional Movement could develop in such a way as to wreck the Ecumenical Movement or at least reduce the World Council of Churches to a venerated façade.' On the other hand, the Confessional Movement, 'if wisely directed', could enrich the Ecumenical Movement. 'The several confessions must at the same time define their nature in relation to the other Confessions and begin to think through their role in the world of our time.' Their leaders must 'come together for the exchange of information and the discussion of policies in an atmosphere of Christian confidence.'[13]

The result was that a two to three hour informal gathering of the secretaries of seven denominational groups took place during the meeting of the WCC Central Committee at Yale Divinity School in New Haven, Connecticut, on 1 August 1957. (They were there in their capacity as observers.) Although no official minutes were kept, a discussion of it at the Presbyterian Alliance's executive committee meeting a few days later revealed that Mackay had actually convened it. The motion adopted authorized him to seek a further conference at which both the chair or president and the executive secretary of each confessional group should be present. Such a conference

> would engage in frank and friendly discussion of the place of confessionalism in the ecumenical movement; the contributions which resurgent confessionalism can make to the enrichment of that movement; the points at which, if any, confessionalism becomes a threat to that growing oneness in Christ which the ecumenical movement seeks; and the ways in which the commitment of the churches to the ecumenical movement presupposes some restraint on the

---

12 Excerpts from the minutes of the World Presbyterian Alliance Executive Committee, Prague, 7-11 August 1956, quoted in Fey (ed.), *Ecumenical Advance*, p. 121, and E. Parret, 'The Conference of Secretaries of World Confessional Families: 1957-1977,' *LWF Report* 5 (August, 1979), pp. 45-46.

13 *The Reformed and Presbyterian World* 24 (September, 1956), pp. 107-108, 110-11

consciousness and practice of mission on the part of the confessional groups with reference to each other.

The consideration of these issues 'might well eventuate in the drawing up of an agenda to be undertaken by further conferences'.[14] The idea here was such a meeting, involving additional officials of the bodies, would take place during the WCC Central Committee sessions, not only to avoid unnecessary travel expenses but also to emphasize the link between the confessional groups and the larger ecumenical movement.

However, a second meeting followed on 14-15 November 1957 which was proposed by WCC General Secretary Visser't Hooft and called by the LWF General Secretary Carl E. Lund-Quist. Attending were the secretaries of the seven confessional alliances with which the WCC had relations—the Baptist World Alliance, Friends World Committee for Consultation, International Congregational Council, Lutheran World Federation, World Methodist Council, Disciples of Christ Ecumenical Consultative Council, and World Presbyterian Alliance. Some WCC staff members were present and it focused on matters of cooperation and the contribution of the world confessional groups to ecumenical life and church union movements.[15] The WCC seemed to be taking a larger role in the confessional groups and how they might be utilized to advance the ecumenical cause.

Next year, the general secretaries gathered at the annual WCC Central Committee session, this time in Nyborg, Denmark, on 22 August 1958, and held a luncheon meeting where they exchanged information about their upcoming denominational conventions and discussed a request for preparing books containing their main confessional documents. It is noteworthy that an Anglican and a representative of the Orthodox Church joined their conversations.[16] Feeling that not enough could be accomplished in such a short time, the 1959 meeting was scheduled at a different time and at the Ecumenical Centre in Geneva. Then no conferences were held in 1960 and 1961 as the New Delhi assembly was being planned, and the 1975 meeting was cancelled because the date originally chosen coincided with the Nairobi assembly. Over the next years the numbers of participants increased as additional confessional groups became involved, and the two or three day long sessions now highlighted sharing of each body's work and consideration of matters of ecumenical concern. WCC staff officials were present and contributed to the dialogue. Meetings in 1965, 1973 and 1974 involved issues of relations with the Roman Catholic Church, foreign missions, and bilateral

---

14 Quoted in Fey (ed.), *Ecumenical Advance*, p. 122, and Parret, *LWF Report* 5, p. 47.
15 Parret, *LWF Report* 5, pp. 48-49.
16 Parret, *LWF Report* 5, p. 49

dialogues, and 'experts' came to assist in the discussions. The 1963 and 1978 gatherings were essentially enlarged consultations on world confessionalism.[17]

As the number of participants multiplied (by 1978 sixteen bodies were represented, including the Orthodox and Roman Catholic Churches), the problem of definition became more complex. First, the informal association was designated as World Confessional Church Groups. In 1962 it became World Confessional Groups, and in 1965 World Confessional Bodies. From 1967 it was World Confessional Families. The problem of defining 'world confessional body', a concept recognized in Article XIII of the WCC constitution, was an enormous problem, and it was accentuated by the challenge from Asia, to be mentioned below. Having not met for over two years, twenty-five representatives of the world confessional organizations assembled in Geneva on 3-4 April 1962 to respond to their critics. It was pointed out that two circumstances made a definition necessary. First, each world denominational grouping had a different understanding of what united it and used a variety of terms, including communion and fellowship, and they adopted such diverse names for their international organizations as council, alliance, conference, federation, convention, and so forth. Second, most of them would not ordinarily apply to themselves the title of 'confessional body', even though the WCC used the term.

The 'working definition' that they accepted was drafted with the help of the WCC General Secretary, Dr Visser't Hooft, and was widely disseminated in the ecumenical and denominational press:

We understand the term 'confessional bodies' as used in the Constitution of the World Council to mean the organizations which represent families of churches. While each of these bodies has its own specific conception of the nature of the link that binds its members together and of its role in the total ecumenical life of the churches, these bodies have this in common:

a) that their member churches share together not only the general tradition which is common to all Christian churches, but also specific traditions which have grown out of spiritual crises in the history of the Church; and

b) that they desire to render witness to those specific convictions of doctrinal or ecclesiological character which they consider to be essential for the life of the whole Church of Christ.[18]

---

17 Parret, *LWF Report* 5, pp. 50-51. Parret, pp. 73-77, provides an appendix listing the dates and locations of all meetings between 1957 and 1978, the number of participants, presentations made, and topics dealt with.

18 Text in Parret, *LWF Report* 5, p. 56, and *Lutheran World* 10 (January, 1963), p. 35

In the long run, however, this effort at formal definition failed to resolve the matter. The increasing diversity of this international association of denominational representatives was such that none of these labels were adequate, and in 1979 it formally adopted as its name the Conference of Secretaries of Christian World Communions. This was the recommendation that Prof. Harding Meyer of the Lutheran Ecumenical Institute, Strasbourg, made in a paper he gave at the meeting on the group's self-understanding. The WCC constitution was changed to recognize this nomenclature.[19]

The Asian Challenge to Global Confessionalism

The idea of confessional world organizations linked with the ecumenical aspirations of the WCC suffered a severe blow when the East Asian Christian Conference ([EACC], since 1973 the Christian Conference of Asia) issued a strong statement at its assembly in Bangalore, India, in November 1961 that declared 'the very vitality of these confessional loyalties often creates serious obstacles to the younger churches'. It went on to say: 'The strength of the younger churches lies in increasing their missionary consciousness. A sense of this missionary responsibility goes hand in hand with an urgent sense of church unity. In the confessional perspective this remains out of focus.'[20] The declaration called attention to the simultaneous rise of the ecumenical movement and growth in the strength of the confessional bodies, and the EACC's apprehension that denominationalism exported from the West placed a roadblock in the path of uniting churches locally in Asia. In another portion of the statement the EACC advanced the criticism: 'However good the intention, it seems that the expression of world confessionalism, in increasingly complex institutional structures, results in the perpetuation and

---

19 Article XIII. Christian World Communions, in *World Council of Churches Yearbook 2000* (Geneva: WCC, 2000), p. 87:
    1. The World Council of Churches recognizes the role of Christian World Communions or world confessional bodies in the ecumenical movement.
    2. Such Christian World Communions as may be designated by the Central Committee and which express their desire to this effect:
    a) shall be invited to send a delegated representative to the Assembly; and
    b) shall be invited to send an adviser to meetings of the Central Committee; and
    c) shall be provided with copies of all general communications sent to all World Council member churches.
    3. The Central Committee shall establish and review as appropriate guidelines for relationships and cooperation with Christian World Communions.
20 Quoted in Fey (ed.), *Ecumenical Advance*, p. 124.

reinforcement of patterns of paternalism and continued exercise of control.'[21]

The EACC threw down the gauntlet at its Bangkok meeting in February 1964 where it recommended that representatives of the confessional fellowships and the younger churches should come together in a consultation and help the Asian churches in their own families to move toward unity. The council stated that three hard questions needed to be addressed:

> 1. Do the world confessional organizations rest on a theological principle or do they simply gather together Churches because of a common history and tradition?

> 2. Even where world confessional organizations are seeking to preserve for the universal Church some fundamental insight into an aspect of Christian truth, is this best done by an organization built around that truth?

> 3. Are the confessions and doctrines which are the historical basis of these world confessional organizations living realities among the people in the confessional families?[22]

The criticisms were particularly directed at the World Methodist Council, the Anglican communion, and the Lutheran World Federation, and the EACC called on them to give whole-hearted support to their member churches in Asia that were moving toward unification.

In October 1963 the annual meeting was replaced with a WCC Consultation on 'Confession and Confessionalism' which wrestled with the charges. The participants included forty-nine representatives from world confessional bodies, regional councils of churches and the WCC staff. The basic questions discussed were: how may a young indigenous church make its true confession of Christ to a surrounding non-Christian society, and how can the present world denominational families, all of them centred in the West, help the young churches undertake joint action for mission?[23] The general argument was that this confessionalism was a

---

21 Quoted in Perret, *LWF Report* 5, p. 66. He notes, p. 66, that the WCC Youth Department made a similar criticism in 1963: 'The tendency of the confessional institutions is to encourage self-sufficiency among denominational groups and to reinforce exclusiveness.'

22 Fey (ed.), *Ecumenical Advance*, p. 125. See also the symposium 'World Confessionalism and the Ecumenical Movement,' in *Lutheran World* 10 (January, 1963), pp. 35-67; and Paul C. Empie, 'Dilemmas of World Confessional Groups with Respect to Engagement in Mission and Unity', *International Review of Missions* 25 (April, 1966), pp. 157-70, which affirmed the commitment of the Western denominational leaders to ecumenism and rebutted the charges of the Asians.

23 A. J. van der Bent, *Six Hundred Ecumenical Consultations 1948–1982* (Geneva: WCC, 1983), p. 5.

'movement within the ecumenical movement'[24] and the organizations regarded themselves as being in agreement with the WCC in its articulation of the meaning of ecumenism. A further response was made in a conference of the denominational bodies and the WCC in October 1965 on the relation of the confessional movements to the conciliar ecumenical movement and the future of the total mission of the church. The report affirmed 'that the present situation offers unprecedented challenges to the churches which call for a new and urgent response, both in the confessing of the faith and in the structures of church life'.[25]

However, the tensions between the programmes of the individual denominational groupings and the WCC could not be easily resolved and the debates over confessionalism continued for the next fifteen years. A report received at the Nairobi assembly in 1975 stated that the relation between the WCC and the World Confessional Families required 'new attention', but recognized their many contributions to the ecumenical movement. It called for fuller cooperation between them and the WCC in such matters as inter-church aid programmes, international affairs, human rights, and religious freedom, and commended them for their support of church unity endeavours and involvement in bilateral dialogues. It 'welcomes' the proposal that the World Confessional Families, in close collaboration with the WCC's Faith and Order Commission, should establish a forum for the regular evaluation of bilateral conversations. Also, there needs to be further discussion 'on the unity we seek and the witness we present in the world'.[26]

In response to this call for re-examination of the WCC-WCF, a joint consultation took place at the annual meeting on 23-25 October 1978. It expressed the conviction 'that the WCC and the WCFs are called to play together constructive and complementary roles in the search for the visible unity of the Church, in one faith and in one eucharistic fellowship'. It also affirmed 'that the WCC is...the most nearly comprehensive instrument of the ecumenical movement in the world today...[and] is the only forum where all aspects of the ecumenical movement have the opportunity to encounter one another'.[27] The WCC's General Secretariat greeted the report with enthusiasm at its January 1979 meeting and detailed a wide range of ways in which the WCFs could work with the Faith and Order Commission to find a common expression of the one faith we share, procure and evaluate responses to the study on 'Baptism, Eucharist, and Ministry', engage in a fresh reflection on the

---

24   The phrase of Norman Goodall in the *Lutheran World* symposium, p. 57.

25   See the report 'Statement of a Joint Consultation Concerning Confessional Movements and Mission and Unity', *Ecumenical Review* 18 (January, 1966), pp. 91-93.

26   David W. Paton, *Breaking Barriers: Nairobi 1975* (London: SPCK, 1976), pp. 195-98.

27   The text of the report is in *LWF Report* 3 (December, 1978), pp. 73-87.

question of authority, tradition, creeds, and koinonia, and participate in programmatic studies. They could also assist in projects of the Commission on World Mission and Evangelism and the Commission for Inter-Church Aid, Refugees, and World Service, collaborate with the Commission of the Churches on International Affairs' study on human rights and consider establishing a joint monitoring committee on religious liberty, and take part in a variety of other common ventures.[28] However, what the authors of this ambitious set of recommendations failed to take into account was that the confessional bodies currently were in the process of a sweeping change in their relationship with the World Council.

From World Confessional Families to Christian World Communions

The confessional bodies are a loosely organized group. As indicated above, the general secretaries meet once a year for two or three days, and the only real structure is a chair who serves a two-year term, rotated among the constituent groups, and a secretary, also elected for two years. This person is eligible for re-election, and the current secretary, Dr Bert Beach of the General Conference of Seventh-day Adventists, has served for over a quarter century. WCC General Secretary Visser 't Hooft and Dr Lukas Vischer, who headed the Faith and Order Commission from 1965 to 1979, endeavoured to tie the body more closely to the WCC, but by the late 1970s this was becoming less and less possible.

One factor was the changing character of the membership. Not only was the Greek Orthodox Ecumenical Patriarch of Constantinople represented, but also, from 1967, the Moscow Patriarchate as well, and from time to time someone from the Oriental Orthodox Churches taking part in the meeting. Moreover, in 1968 a representative of the Pontifical Secretariat (now Council) for Promoting Christian Unity of the Roman Catholic Church began attending the meetings, and in 1977 the conference even took place in Rome and attendees had an audience with the Pope. The International Old Catholic Bishops' Conference brought another group to the table that was outside the traditional ecumenical Protestant orbit. The often more conservative free churches rapidly were drawn into the network: the Salvation Army, Seventh-day Adventists, Reformed Ecumenical Council, Mennonite World Conference, Church of the Brethren, World Convention of the Churches of Christ, and the World

---

28 Report included as an Appendix in Perret, *LWF Report* 5, pp. 78-79.

Evangelical Alliance (formerly Fellowship).[29] Occasionally a Pentecostal figure attends as an observer, and a representative of the United Bible Societies also comes with observer status. Because both the Anglicans and the Orthodox, as well as some other liturgical as well as free church people were uncomfortable with the term World Confessional Families, the secretaries decided, as mentioned above, to adopt the name Christian World Communions.

Already by the 1970s the WCC leadership was becoming aware of the heterogeneity of the group. There was a shift away from speaking of the 'WCFs and the ecumenical movement' to the formulation 'the WCFs in the ecumenical movement'. It is one movement and the WCFs are simply part of it. However, some regarded themselves as the true ecumenical movement, while others saw them as 'unecumenical'. Anti-doctrinal and anti-institutional ecumenists regarded the claims of confessional families as reactionary and arrogant. More 'secular' ecumenists, who were engaged in the struggle against world hunger and for peace and justice for all people, looked upon the task of unifying divided churches as essentially irrelevant. Many non-Western Christian leaders saw the missionary and financial policies of the denominations as perpetuating Western divisions and hindering the united witness of a united church.

Because of the vast differences among these churches, would it ever be feasible to make any material or substantive statement that would be representative of all or that all could accept? The apparent impossibility of this led to greater emphasis on bilateral dialogues. The Conference of Secretaries of World Confessional Families sponsored a world-wide survey of bilateral conversations during the period 1959–1974 and identified literally hundreds of them. Sometimes theological and pastoral agreements were achieved and sometimes not. Often they were a sharing of views and getting to know one another better. The WCF itself did not sponsor them—it lacked any structure or mandate to do so—but rather individual world denominational bodies or churches in individual countries. It was found that these proved to be more effective in resolving specific problems separating two traditions than were the usual multilateral approaches. They offered greater possibilities for personal acquaintance and for focused exploration of controversial issues. Because they have had an official and representative character, they could not so easily be dismissed as the fantasies of theologians out of touch with churchly realities. It also implied a public commitment on the part of the sponsoring bodies to achieve specific results or at least some sort of a

---

29   The *World Council of Churches Yearbook 2000*, pp. 56-57, lists the addresses of nineteen 'international organizations of churches of the same tradition or confession' that participate in the 'annual informal gatherings of the secretaries' of such bodies. Missing from the list are the Oriental Orthodox Churches, although individuals from these churches do come to the meetings occasionally.

rapprochement. The bilaterals usually involved an exercise in mutual presentation and interpretation and then went on to focus on specific issues—doctrinal, liturgical, structural, or ethical—which separate the traditions concerned, probe the intentions behind divisive formulations and attitudes, and push forward to some sort of affirmation of shared faith. Whether these will lead to any really meaningful sort of church unity is an open question, but such dialogues are a continuing process.[30]

The aims of the annual meetings of secretaries are quite modest.[31] A secretary may come alone or bring one or two 'consultants' from his or her communion, but the sessions are not open to the public or the press. The meeting lasts for three days, and each person talks about his or her church group's polity, history, and beliefs, and may also give an oral or written report about what the body has done in the past year and expects to be doing in the future. Thus it is primarily a time of openness, sharing and networking. Each individual speaks for him or herself—and they can take suggestions from the others back to their home bodies for consideration. They also invite their colleagues to attend their own church conventions as observers.

The group has no dues, no constitution, no delegated or decision-making power as such. The members only meet in a consultative capacity, but they have on some occasions drafted a letter of concern about an issue like human rights and how that might affect churches. The reports themselves cover a variety of topics, depending on the occasion and amount of time available. Topics dealt with in recent years include religious liberty and persecution, bilateral dialogues that have occurred, problems of proselytism, the declining position of Christianity in the Middle East, African Instituted (or Independent) Churches, and the situation of local churches in the country where they are assembled. A few years ago the Conference of Secretaries adopted the policy of meeting every other year in a venue beside Geneva, such as South Africa, London, Jerusalem, and in 2002 Hendersonville, North Carolina, USA.

The WCC provides staff assistance when needed, allows the conferences to meet in its facilities, and disseminates information about its activities. However, the body has no formal connection with the World Council or the Faith and Order Commission. One of my informants emphasized strongly that several of the more conservative or evangelical

---

30 Nils Ehrenström, 'The World Confessional Families in the Service of Unity', *Ecumenical Review* 26 (April, 1974), pp. 264-77; Nils Ehrenström and Günther Gassmann, *A Survey of Bilateral Conversations among World Confessional Families 1959-1974* (Geneva: WCC, 1975).

31 The information on the inner workings of the Conference of Secretaries of the Christian World Communions was provided in interviews with Dr Denton Lotz, General Secretary of the Baptist World Alliance, on 12 January 2002, and Dr Bert Beach, the Secretary and Seventh-day Adventist representative, on 20 January 2002.

representatives would not attend the meetings if that were the case. Some other participants would drop out if the body did become a policy or decision-making agency.

Conclusion

The Christian World Communions are a unique type of ecumenical venture. In the early years they were linked to conciliar ecumenism and were seen as a means of harnessing the confessional or denominational aspect of Christianity to the broader movement for achieving church unity. As the meetings of secretaries came to encompass increasingly diverse churches, it took on a new character. The Christian World Communions functioned as a means of communication and interaction among churchly bodies, and the annual sessions helped to foster understanding and sympathy for each other's traditions and values. The association itself did not contribute materially to the cause of organic unity, but it did bring Christians closer together.

The Conference of Secretaries of the Christian World Communions evolved into an institution which recognized and honoured the richness and diversity that really is the kingdom of God. It enabled us to learn that organic and theological differences do not keep us from acknowledging the one Lord and Saviour who has created and redeemed us, regardless of who we are or where we live. Even though we cherish our distinctives and unique qualities, we still can affirm our oneness in Christ. May it ever be so.

CHAPTER 6

The Church and Salvation: A Comparison of Orthodox and Baptist Thinking

Paul S. Fiddes

'There is no salvation outside the church' (*extra ecclesiam nulla salus*). This aphorism of the early church fathers is immediately identifiable as part of the teaching of the Orthodox Church in all ages, and indeed Georges Florovsky in modern times regarded it as a simple tautology, since 'salvation *is* the Church'.[1] For the Orthodox, to be in God, in salvation and in the church are theologically inseparable concepts. Many modern Baptists, however, are likely to greet the phrase, not so much with outright disagreement, as with a sense of bewilderment. The intimate linking together of the concepts of church and salvation is likely to be unfamiliar to them, and they may think more naturally in terms of a kind of sequence: that those who experience God's salvation have a duty to become members of the church, though some will regrettably choose to 'go it alone'.

This lack of resonance between Orthodox and much modern Baptist thinking may make the title of this paper seem rather odd. What meaningful 'comparison', as distinct from stark contrast, can there be? Yet earlier Baptists would have generally approved the view of the Reformer John Calvin that membership in a true visible church was 'ordinarily necessary to our salvation',[2] and it can be argued that it was this very conviction which motivated the emergence of Baptists as a separate group in the first place. They were concerned, not with personal preferences or mere tastes in worship and church organization, but with the life-and-death issue of salvation as they saw it. The way that the church was ordered was a matter of obedience to God, and leading an

---

1   Georges Florovsky, 'The Catholicity of the Church', in *Bible, Church, Tradition: an Eastern Orthodox Tradition*, in *The Collected Works* (12 vols; Belmont, MA: Nordland, 1972–89), I, pp. 37-8.
2   J. Calvin, *Institutes of the Christian Religion*, Bk. IV, ch. 1, s.8; cf. also s.4.

obedient life was a mark of assurance of salvation.[3] The nature of the church has been at the heart of Baptist convictions, and is logically prior to insistence on believers' baptism, which follows as a mark of a community of believers. There is, then, much potential gain in comparing Orthodox and Baptist beliefs about the relation between ecclesiology and soteriology, not least because the Orthodox and the Baptist views of the nature of the local church have a striking affinity, as I hope will become evident. Baptists should here take up the challenge of the Romanian Orthodox theologian Dumitru Staniloae, that both Roman Catholic and Protestant traditions might well be guided by the 'essential characteristics of Orthodox ecclesiology' if they want to 'penetrate more deeply into the very roots of their own form of Christianity'.[4]

Staniloae makes this challenge because his own observation has been that 'as often as some one or other group of these Christians sketches the image of the Church that it is seeking, the result, in principle, usually resembles Orthodox ecclesiology'. How far this claim can be established should become clear as we proceed, but I aim to write in the spirit of a mutual exploration of traditions that Staniloae commends. And there seems nowhere better to attempt this than in a paper written in honour of my friend and colleague, John Briggs, who has combined skilful studies of Baptist history with appreciative journeys into the heritage of others in the milieu of the World Council of Churches.

However, to continue at all with this comparison between Orthodox and Baptist beliefs, we will need to clarify the sources of what I am identifying as 'Orthodox' and 'Baptist'. I am exploring Orthodox thought largely, though not entirely, through the eyes of three modern interpreters of their own tradition: Vladimir Lossky (Russian), John Zizioulas (Greek) and Dumitru Staniloae (Romanian). As dialogue partner with Orthodoxy, I myself am taking the part of an interpreter of Baptist thought, though I am drawing material from those Baptist confessions of faith and other Baptist writings which deliberately place themselves within the story of the Radical Reformation in sixteenth-century Europe from which the early Baptists sprang. I suggest that one of the reasons why the link between church and salvation seems alien to many Christians who call themselves Baptists today is that they find their understanding of salvation and spiritual authority adequately covered by one of the several 'statements of belief' produced by modern international evangelical movements. In making this point, I am not intending to be critical of

---

3   See Stephen Brachlow, *The Communion of Saints: Radical Puritan and Separatist Ecclesiology 1570–1625* (Oxford: Oxford University Press, 1988), pp. 54-55.
4   Dumitri Staniloae, 'Trinitarian Relations and the Life of the Church', in *Theology and the Church* (trans. R. Barringer; Crestwood, NY: St Vladimir's Seminary Press, 1980), pp. 11-12.

these 'strategic alliances' in themselves,[5] or to suggest that Baptists should not be involved with them. I am simply making the observation that as 'non-denominational' movements, without interest in ecumenical convergence, they attempt to state the meaning of salvation, develop a christology and declare the nature of 'final authority in faith and practice' without any reference to the community of the church or the means of grace in the sacraments. Early Baptists, whether Particular (Calvinist) or General (mildly Arminian) could not have taken this theological approach, as their confessions of faith demonstrate.

There are, admittedly, some problems with the phrase *extra ecclesiam nulla salus* with which we began. Any who are engaged in ecumenical relations, who live in multi-cultural societies, and who are concerned for respectful inter-faith dialogue, are bound to feel some discomfort with it. I am going to suggest that it may still be a useful form of expression, *if* we understand it in a modified way, and indeed Orthodox thinkers have moved in the same direction.[6] In its terseness it has at least the advantage of putting forcefully the point that 'no one is saved alone. He [or she] is saved in the Church, as a member of it and in union with all its other members' (Alexis Khomiakov, a Russian Orthodox).[7] That is, salvation is about being part of a renewed human community, sharing in the continuing body of Christ on earth and participating in the communion of the triune God.

Salvation and the Church as the Body of Christ

The image of the church as the body of Christ has been central to the ecclesiology of all churches since it was formulated (it seems) by the Apostle Paul.[8] The notion of 'one body, many members' has been constantly drawn upon to explore the relation between unity and diversity in the community, and to affirm the value of every kind of gifting within it. But it has been the Orthodox tradition that has, perhaps most clearly, developed the implications of the image for salvation, weaving together union with Christ, participation in the life of God, membership of the

---

5   But for an analysis of the difference between alliance and covenant, see Richard Kidd (ed.), Paul Fiddes, Brian Haymes and Michael Quicke, *On the Way of Trust* (Oxford: Whitley Publications, 1997).

6   See section 2 below; also, Timothy Ware, *The Orthodox Church* (Harmondsworth: Penguin, new edn, 1997), pp. 307-11.

7   Alexis Khomiakov, 'The Church is One', in William J. Birkbeck (ed.), *Russia and the English Church during the Last Fifty Years* (London: Eastern Churches Association, 1895), section 9.

8   See, e.g., 1 Cor. 12 and Rom. 12; John A.T. Robinson, *The Body: A Study in Pauline Theology* (London: SCM Press, 1952).

church and sharing in the eucharist. To be on the way of salvation and to be part of the church as the body of Christ is identical, because salvation is understood as *theosis* ('deification') and because the deifying of human nature in the person of Christ is extended into the life of human persons in the church.

In this theological account, the relation between 'nature' and 'person' is a key concept, though it has been handled a little differently by Orthodox theologians in recent years. In Orthodox thought, human nature before salvation is bound to decay and death through fallenness from the divine glory. In Christ, divine nature transfuses human nature and so gives it eternal life, raising it to share in the very life of God. As clarified by Gregory Palamas,[9] this is not a 'becoming God' in the sense of complete identity with the divine *substance*, but rather a participation in the divine *energies* that shine out from the ineffable being of God. Orthodox theology lays stress on the formulary of Chalcedon that the human and divine natures in Christ unite 'without separation and without confusion' in one hypostasis or person.[10] Orthodox thought also makes a fundamental point of what Chalcedon implies (though does not explicitly state)—that this one hypostasis *is* the Logos, the Son of God who is a person in the divine Trinity.[11] Human nature has been deified through being assumed into the person of the divine Son; thus a created nature, but not a created 'person', has entered into the union. So the way for all human natures to be transformed is to be 'in' the hypostasis of the Son, or to share the personal existence of Christ. Our death-laden and corrupt natures are to be 'hypostasized' by Christ.

But how is that to be communicated to all human persons? How is all human nature to be deified? Early theologians like Athanasius and Gregory of Nyssa tended to lean here on a philosophical notion of universals: if a particular human nature had been glorified in the person of Jesus Christ, this must involve all human nature as a universal reality.[12] The Orthodox tradition, however, while not neglecting this insight, has laid stress on the church as being the link. The church as the body of Christ, especially through its sacraments of baptism and eucharist, brings human nature into the personal life of the Son of God, and so into the communion of the triune God. Vladimir Lossky thus speaks of human

---

9   Gregory Palamas, *Theophanes*, in J.-P. Migne (ed.), *Patrologia Graeca* (166 vols; Paris: Petit-Montrouge, 1857–83) (hereafter *PG*) CL, 932D, 937D. For an earlier version of the idea, see Maximus the Confessor, *De Ambiguis*, *PG* XCI, 1076C.

10   Text in J. Stevenson (ed.), *Creeds, Councils, and Controversies: Documents Illustrative of the History of the Church A.D. 337–461* (London: SPCK, 1973), p. 337.

11   Prior to Chalcedon this had been the clear view of Cyril of Alexandria: see e.g. *Contra Didorum et Theodorum* (*PG* LXXVI, 401).

12   E.g. Athanasius, *Contra Arianos* 3.33 cf. 2.61; Gregory of Nyssa, *Oratio Catechetica* 16.

persons having an 'ecclesial being',[13] and John Zizioulas envisages an 'ecclesial hypostasis' that stands in contrast to the merely 'biological hypostasis' with which we are born as human beings.[14] Interestingly, however, these twentieth-century Orthodox theologians place the emphasis differently in the relation between nature and person, and we shall see later that this has some relevance to our own enquiry in this paper.

Lossky begins rather traditionally with the concept of nature. Just as God is three persons in one nature, so there are many human persons in one nature—that is, rooted through the church into the one deified human nature of Christ. The church as the body of Christ is a reality with two natures, its created nature suffused with the fulness of uncreated grace.[15] Two natures always work together in the church, in its sacraments, ceremonies and ministries. This is most evidently the case in the eucharist, but even the human act of the ascent of the presiding bishop to the altar is an image of a divine event—the ascension of Christ to heaven.[16] Lossky affirms that, united to the body of Christ through baptism, and nourished by the body of Christ in the eucharist, we too can become *two-natured persons*.[17] As Maximus the Confessor urged, our human natures, while not suppressed or confused with the divine nature, are reunited to the uncreated nature through love.[18] Lossky finds, of course, the divine hypostasis in Christ to be the key to this union of natures. It is because the church has a 'created nature inseparably united to God in the hypostasis of the Son' that its nature is transformed. We share in a deified human nature by being 'received into the person of Christ'.[19] But the centre of Lossky's vision of salvation lies in the union of two *natures*.

By contrast, John Zizioulas conceives the process of salvation as a matter of having our human nature directly transformed by the *hypostasis* of Christ. In a subtle shift of focus, he stresses that 'person constitutes nature' (rather than one nature transforming another through

---

13   Vladimir Lossky, *The Mystical Theology of the Eastern Church* (London: James Clarke, 1957), p. 175.
14   John Zizioulas (Metropolitan John of Pergamon), *Being as Communion: Studies in Personhood and the Church* (London: Darton, Longman and Todd, 1985), pp. 51-54.
15   Lossky, *Mystical Theology*, pp. 175-77, 184-85.
16   Lossky, *Mystical Theology*, p. 189.
17   Lossky, *Mystical Theology*, p. 185.
18   Maximus, *De Ambiguis, PG* XCI, 1308B; cf. *The Church's Mystagogy*, in *Maximus Confessor. Selected Writings* (trans. G. Berthold; New York: Paulist Press, 1985), pp. 193-95.
19   Lossky, *Mystical Theology*, p. 183.

being in one person).[20] Zizioulas always begins with the priority of person over nature, since in the triune life of God the divine nature—which is communion—is formed by the activity of one person, the Father. The tragedy of the human person, in its natural state, is to be bound by the cruel necessity of a nature which is orientated towards death. So even the ecstatic love of the human person is corrupted into egocentricity, and the self becomes a fortress of individualism.[21] When we are identified with the hypostasis of Christ, we are delivered from the ontological necessity of nature. His person determines our nature, and we are enabled to overcome all separation from each other to live truly in communion, in the image of the Trinity. Our new hypostasis may be called an 'ecclesial hypostasis', because the church embodies this trinitarian community in history. Moreover, the church is the 'womb' of the new person, since the identification of our hypostasis with that of Christ, and so our adoption into God, happens in baptism.[22] As our birth by nature gave us a biological hypostasis, so our new birth from the church as our mother gives us a new hypostasis, an authentic personhood, by which we can relate to others in love in a way that is freed from the restraints of the laws of nature. These relations are focused and re-made in the event of the eucharist:

> The eucharist is first of all an assembly (*synaxis*), a community, a network of relations, in which man [sic] 'subsists' in a manner different from the biological as a member of a body which transcends every exclusiveness of a biological and social kind.[23]

In their own way, both Lossky and Zizioulas are urging a kind of catholicity that includes genuine acceptance of differences and distinctions within the community of the church. This is what Orthodox call 'sobornicity', a unity which exists in the freedom of diversity. Lossky tends to locate the aspect of unity in the union of human persons with the deified human nature of Christ. *Diversity* is the work of the Holy Spirit, 'filling' the many persons who belong to the one body, bestowing a variety of spiritual gifts freely upon all (Eph. 1.23).[24] Staniloae, however, criticizes Lossky strongly for what he believes to be a division of the work of the Son and the Spirit.[25] For Staniloae, the key image is that of the Spirit proceeding from the Father to 'rest' on the Son. As we share in the relation between the Father and the Son in the triune life, the

---

20 Zizioulas, *Being as Communion*, pp. 40-44, 46-47.
21 Zizioulas, *Being as Communion*, pp. 51-52.
22 Zizioulas, *Being as Communion*, pp. 56-8.
23 Zizioulas, *Being as Communion*, p. 60.
24 Lossky, *Mystical Theology*, pp. 184-85, 191-92.
25 Staniloae, 'Trinitarian Relations and the Life of the Church', p. 39.

Spirit rests on us, accentuating in his hypostatic fulness what is particular to us as persons. Thus the Spirit certainly stimulates diversity, as Lossky states: but as the one whom the Father sends to rest upon, and shine out from, the Son, the Spirit is the 'flowing current of love of the Son and Father'.[26] This means that the Spirit is equally a source of unity. We see that like Zizioulas, Staniloae is more interested in the church as mutuality of personal relations than as the means of communication of a nature, but all three theologians are concerned with the salvific effect on human life of the divine hypostasis, received in the church.

Now, is there any parallel in Baptist thought to the Orthodox concept that human persons are connected with the saving work of Christ through being in his 'body', the church? Is there any deep ontological connection between church and salvation? There seems, to be sure, no development in Baptist tradition of the relation between person and nature in the church, as in Orthodox thought. But we need to look in another direction from this. There is another way of affirming that the church is a sphere of salvation *prior* to the salvation of particular persons. If the church is the body of Christ, then Christ is its head, and Baptist thought here follows the Reformation concept that Christ exercises this 'headship' through his threefold office of prophet, priest and king.[27] Rather than conceiving the salvific relation of Christ to the church through a divine hypostasizing of human nature, Baptist thought conceives of this relation as the *presence and activity of Christ in his household*.

We need to take a step back from modern, individualized concepts of salvation here, and to enter into the perspective of early Baptist confessions of faith. If we turn first to those which come from the Calvinist tradition, they begin their explanation of salvation with a triune God who is already in relationship with a human community, the 'people of God'. Old Israel is mainly in view here, united to God by a covenant which has been constantly and tragically broken from the side of faithless human beings. God thus determines to make a new covenant with human hearts, and its mediator is Jesus Christ. Salvation is achieved through the establishing of a new agreement by Christ, whose mediatorial activity is defined as being 'the Prophet, Priest and King of the Church of God'.[28]

---

26 Staniloae, 'Trinitarian Relations and the Life of the Church', p. 25.

27 See S.F. Winward, 'The Church in the New Testament', and N. Clark, 'The Fulness of the Church of God', in A. Gilmore, *The Pattern of the Church: A Baptist View* (London: Lutterworth Press, 1963), pp. 55-63 and pp. 97-100 respectively.

28 See, e.g., 'The London Confession' (1644), chs x, xiii, in W.L. Lumpkin (ed.), *Baptist Confessions of Faith* (Philadelphia, PA: Judson Press, 1959), pp. 159-60.

It is characteristic, here and in many other places, that the phrase 'of the church' is connected to the threefold office.[29]

According to 'The London Confession' (1644), salvation has a threefold form: as prophet, Christ reveals the whole will of the Father 'that is needful for his servants to know'; as priest he makes a once-for-all sacrifice for sin, making 'his people a spirituall house, an holy priesthood'; as king he governs the church, 'exercising his power over all Angels and Men'. This, we notice, is an office to which Christ is appointed *in the church*, whose boundaries have been widened beyond natural Israel to include all who have saving faith. But there is no question of salvation happening somewhere outside from, or apart from the 'church', that is the assembly of God's people in the present, in continuity with the covenant community of the past. All those who 'acknowledge him to be their Prophet, Priest and King' are 'inrolled amongst his household servants...to have communion here with the saints'.[30]

The 'Second London Confession' (1677), influenced strongly by the wording of the Westminster Confession, echoes the earlier language of the threefold office as an exposition of the meaning of salvation:

> It pleased God in his eternal purpose, to chuse and ordain the Lord Jesus Christ his only begotten Son, according to the Covenant made between them both, to be the Mediator between God and Man; the Prophet, Priest and King; Head and Saviour of his Church...unto whom he did from all Eternity give a people to be his seed, and to be by him in time redeemed, called, justified, sanctified and glorified.[31]

This passage, from the beginning of the chapter on 'Christ the Mediator', also gives the context, in Calvinistic terms, for the salvific relation of Christ to the church. The church is the company of the elect, whom God has in mind from before the foundation of the world. But the more Arminian confessions that come from the General Baptists, in Amsterdam and England, also describe the mediatorial work of Christ in terms of his being 'the only King, Priest and Prophet of his church'.[32] According to the 'Short Confession' probably written by John Smyth in 1610, this 'holy office...is to help, govern, and preserve, by His Holy Spirit, his holy

---

29 In addition to the examples cited below, see, e.g., 'Propositions and Conclusions concerning True Christian Religion' (1612–1614), art. 30, in Lumpkin (ed.), *Baptist Confessions*, p. 128; 'The Orthodox Creed' (1678), art. xvii, in Lumpkin (ed.), *Baptist Confessions*, p. 310.
30 'The London Confession', ch. xxxiv, p. 166.
31 'The Second London Confession' (1677), ch. viii.1, in Lumpkin (ed.), *Baptist Confessions*, p. 260.
32 'A Declaration of Faith of English People Remaining at Amsterdam' (1611), art. 9, in Lumpkin (ed.), *Baptist Confessions*, p. 119

church and people in the world'.[33] According to a declaration written in the following year, the various particular congregations of the one church 'have Christ given them, with all the meanes off their salvacion...[and] Are the Bodie off Christ.'[34] The point is that the concept of Christ as 'mediator' is not essentially that of being a bridge between a wrathful God and individual sinners, as the image has been used in evangelical preaching. Christ is 'mediator' in the sense of being the establisher of a covenant between God and the church. Of course, persons must repent and exercise their own faith in Christ, but this is faith in one who is creating a community, one who is head of a household. This is a common concept, whether or not the exact list of members of the community are thought to be chosen, or even known, by God from all eternity.

The salvation of the individual person within community is thus expressed in 'hypostatic' language within Orthodoxy and by covenant language within the Baptist tradition. It is evident, however, that there are at least hints of convergence. This is not just because Orthodox theologians can themselves use the language of the threefold office of Christ, such as the Greek theologian Christos Androutsos, who writes that the church is 'the centre and organ of Christ's redeeming work...nothing else than the continuation and extension of his prophetic, priestly and kingly power'.[35] Ideas of salvation through the divine hypostasis and the divine covenant come together when the assuming of human nature into the life of God is understood to be the continuous activity of the Christ who is actually *present* here and now in his church.

For Baptists, a key text here for the nature of the church has been Matthew 18.20: 'where two or three are gathered together in my name, there am I in the midst of them.' This has seemed to define the character of the gathered congregation, the believers' church.[36] It is the risen Christ, standing in the midst of the congregation in the authority of his threefold office, who gives his people the seals of the covenant, and so the right to celebrate the sacraments (as priests), to call some to the ministry of the word (as prophets), and to exercise a mutual discipline among each other (sharing the kingly role of Christ). Orthodox theologians too write

---

33 'A Short Confession of Faith' (1610), art. 17, in Lumpkin (ed.), *Baptist Confessions*, pp. 106-107.

34 'A Declaration of Faith', art. 11, p. 120.

35 Christos Androutsos, *Dogmatic Theology* (Athens, 1907), pp. 262-65, cited by Ware, *Orthodox Church*, p. 241.

36 E.g. 'A Declaration of Faith' (1611), art. 11; 'The London Confession', ch. xxxiii; see Ernest A. Payne, *The Fellowship of Believers: Baptist Thought and Practice Yesterday and Today* (London: Carey Kingsgate Press, enlarged edn, 1952), p. 23.

that 'the church is Christ with us'.[37] Staniloae quotes this same Gospel text and comments that through the Spirit, who *is* the 'midst' between the Father and the Son, 'we are related among ourselves as brothers, and Jesus Christ is brother to us all in our midst'.[38] In accord with this reflection on the meaning of Christ 'in the midst', Staniloae affirms the 'continuous saving presence of Christ in the midst', and finds that the church 'experiences the pressure of revelation as a continuous act through which the same Christ is ceaselessly present in her midst with all his treasures of grace and truth'. The Holy Spirit, he adds, maintains the church in being by 'keeping this same active presence of Christ continuously visible to the eyes of faith'.[39]

As concepts of hypostatic union and covenantal union converge in the idea of saving presence, so there is a similar coming together in the concept of the eucharist. As Zizioulas puts it, the eucharist is an 'assembly' in which the participants are liberated from self-centred existence and become 'a true expression of community—the body of Christ, the body of the church, the body of the eucharist'.[40] Salvation is experienced through new relations of love with each other, cutting across all differences of race, class and gender. In Baptist tradition, those who assemble at the Lord's Table and share in the bread are themselves the body of Christ, and so may seek for his mind among them in mutual decision-making about their life and mission. This is why in many early Baptist meeting houses the church book, recording the discussions of the church meeting, was kept in a drawer in the 'table pew', the seat nearest the communion table. In both bread and fellowship the body of the crucified and risen Christ can be discerned. As Zwingli concluded in commenting on 1 Corinthians 10.17, 'We eat bread so that we are made into one bread... What we become by this eating...is the body of Christ.'[41] In this sense, Baptists as well as Orthodox may consider themselves to be a 'eucharistic community'.

There are, of course, large divergences as well as some signs of convergence here. For instance, Orthodox ecclesiology regards the

---

37   E.g. Christos Androutsos, *Dogmatic Theology*, cited by Ware, *Orthodox Church*, p. 241.
38   Dumitru Staniloae, 'The Holy Spirit and the Sobornicity of the Church', in *Theology and the Church*, p. 63.
39   Dumitru Staniloae, *The Experience of God: Volume 1. Revelation and Knowledge of the Triune God* (trans. I. Ionita and R. Barringer; Brookline, MA: Holy Cross Orthodox Press, 1998), p. 64.
40   Zizioulas, *Being as Communion*, p. 64.
41   Zwingli, 'Letter to Matthew Alber', 16 November 1524, in E.J. Furcha and H.W. Pipkin (eds. and trans.), *Selected Writings of Huldrych Zwingli, II. In Search of True Religion: Reformation, Pastoral and Eucharistic Writings* (2 vols; Allison Park, PA: Pickwick, 1985), p. 141.

presence of the bishop standing 'in the midst' of the congregation in apostolic succession, presiding over the eucharist, as essential for Christ to be experienced in the midst. But as these models of the church are brought into interaction with each other, each tradition may gain from the other. Baptists need to take seriously their own tradition of Christ's saving activity as prophet, priest and king. All too often this is reduced to the priestly function alone, and this itself is confined to a narrowly forensic understanding of a satisfaction of the demands of divine sovereignty, owing more to the image of the Roman law court than to the Hebrew temple. Bringing this covenant mediation into relation with the Orthodox concept of *theosis* will open up the saving significance of the presence of Christ within his household. Orthodox, for their part, perhaps need to be sensitive to the way that this presence can be reduced to an idea of the communication of 'nature' through the structure and sacraments of the church; when this happens, the more dynamic concept of encounter with the divine person (hypostasis) of Christ can be attenuated into the transmission of some kind of divine–human substance. Emphasis, that is, may be laid unhelpfully on the sacrament as 'food of immortality' rather than 'encounter with the eternal Lord'.

Salvation in the Invisible and Visible Church

Earlier I indicated some unease with the phrase *extra ecclesiam nulla salus*. Positively, it places salvation firmly in the context of a redeemed community, but it has the negative implication of apparently excluding some from even the possibility of salvation. While broadly affirming the phrase, both Orthodox and Baptist tradition has given it a theological spin by appealing to a contrast between the church 'invisible' and the church 'visible.' This in turn has interacted, sometimes in a confused way, with the contrast between the church 'local' and the church 'universal' (or catholic).

According to Orthodox thought, the 'visible church' is the church here on earth, composed of many specific congregations. The title 'invisible church' essentially refers to the church in heaven, the glorified saints and the angels. Orthodoxy strongly insists that there are not two churches but only one. In its theology and in its liturgy, it affirms one communion, one continuous reality. Entering the inner sanctuary, beyond the icon-screen, to consecrate the elements for the eucharist, the bishops, priests and deacons are sharing in the heavenly worship. The deacon appears through the 'royal doors' of the icon-screen like an angelic messenger, coming from the heavenly sanctuary to bring the word of God to the waiting congregation on earth, who form one assembly with those who have finished their earthly course. It is thus only in human terms that one speaks of 'the church visible and invisible'. In Orthodox thinking, the phrase 'invisible church' does not indicate some ideal, indivisible church which at present exists only in heaven in contrast to a divided church on earth. The true church exists here and now on earth, visible and undivided; it must be one because God is one.[42] Its unity is not maintained, however, by some superior bishop endowed with a universal jurisdiction; it is united through communion. The local church is unified by its gathering to celebrate the eucharist, gathered round its bishop. The church universal is unified by the communion of the bishops with each other, as the heads of the local churches. While the communion of churches is the Catholic Church, *each* local church is also the Catholic church, the church in wholeness, showing the marks of the overcoming of all human barriers between people of different backgrounds.[43]

Orthodoxy thus claims to be the one visible church on earth, and since God's saving power is mediated through Christ's body, it appears that outside this church there can be no salvation. Few Orthodox, however, have wanted to deny the working of God's grace and mercy freely in the world, and so there have been two ways of understanding this wider saving activity; they are both implied in a statement of Alexis Khomiakov, written well before the beginning of the twentieth-century ecumenical movement:

> Inasmuch as the earthly and visible Church is not the fullness and completeness of the whole Church which the Lord appointed to appear at the final judgement of all creation, she acts and knows only within her own limits... The rest of humankind, whether alien from the Church, or united to her by ties which God has not willed to reveal to her, she leaves to the judgement of the great day.[44]

The first approach here is to appeal to the eschatological reality of the church, the church as it will be in its 'fulness and completeness'. One can then envisage the gracious activity of God among those who are being *led towards* participation in the church in its glorious destiny. There is 'no salvation outside the church' because finally those who are saved *will be included* in the community of the body of Christ. The church 'invisible' thus includes the church in its future reality, and in the eucharist the church already enjoys a foretaste of its eternal state of being. This kind of view has been most clearly developed in the thought of Staniloae in recent years, who affirms that it is difficult to distinguish between a divine providence that 'acts to preserve and protect' the world,

---

42 Ware, *Orthodox Church*, p. 245.
43 Zizioulas, *Being as Communion*, pp. 147-53, 235-36.
44 Khomiakov, 'The Church is One', section 2.

and a providence that 'leads the world to deification'.[45] Creation and salvation cannot be driven apart. Staniloae goes beyond other Orthodox writers in offering more than a concession to the idea that God's grace and mercy might be at work outside the church. Basing his thought on the primary Orthodox notion of salvation as the deifying of human nature as a universal reality, he finds the providential activity of God in leading all human beings to deeper relations of love and justice among themselves.[46]

This can be understood as the work and presence of the 'cosmic Christ', who has entered into history and has 'placed himself in a personal relation with all of humanity', leading human life to a recapitulation in himself.[47] In line with this Staniloae can say that 'the Christian must see Christ in every man [sic] and hear Christ's cry for help in every human cry'.[48] The whole of humanity and all material creation is 'destined for transfiguration through the power of the risen body of Christ'; the universe belongs both to Christ and to human beings, 'to Christians and non-Christians alike, who suffer and advance towards salvation'.[49] Here he quotes from the Orthodox medieval mystic, Nicholas Cabasilas, who says that 'the blood flowing from [Christ's] wounds...has cleansed the whole cosmos from the taint of sin'.[50]

In itself, this vision of a universe on the path towards final salvation does not affirm anything about membership of the church here and now. A more conservative, more concessionary, version of this approach therefore concludes that those who are not baptized members of the one Orthodox Church are not presently members of the church of Christ at all, whatever divine grace is at work within them. Staniloae takes a more ambiguous stance, urging only that 'the spirituality of the Christian East represents the method by which advancement in the direction willed by God's providence is *best assured*...'[51] Orthodox who want to say something explicit about the connection of other Christians to the Catholic Church, especially those involved in the contemporary ecumenical movement, tend to take the second approach sketched out by Khomiakov, that those outside the visible church may be 'united to her

---

45 Dumitru Staniloae, *The Experience of God: Volume 2. The World: Creation and Deification* (trans. I. Ionita and R. Barringer; Brookline, MA: Holy Cross Orthodox Press, 2000), p. 192.
46 Staniloae, *Experience of God*, II, p. 196.
47 Dumitru Staniloae, 'The Problems and Perspectives of Orthodox Theology', in *Theology and the Church*, p. 223.
48 Dumitru Staniloae, 'The Orthodox Doctrine of Salvation', in *Theology and the Church*, p. 209.
49 Staniloae, 'Orthodox Doctrine of Salvation', p. 211.
50 Staniloae, 'Orthodox Doctrine of Salvation', p. 212.
51 Staniloae, *The Experience of God*, II, p. 200.

by ties that God has not chosen to reveal to her'. In the words of Kallistos Ware, who takes this view, 'Many people may be members of the church who are not visibly so; invisible bonds may exist despite an outward separation'.[52] Ware is careful not to say that such make up an 'invisible church' on earth—it is the *bonds* to the one visible church that are invisible.

Perhaps Staniloae also intends to include this view when he says that 'the universe belongs to Christ; it is mysteriously attached to his crucified and risen body'.[53] But there seems something inconsistent in speaking of an invisible membership of the church but no invisible church. Generally Staniloae seems to stand closer here to the way that Apostle Paul uses the phrase 'body of Christ', in a threefold sense: for Paul there is the glorious risen body of Christ, who is the person in continuity with Jesus of Nazareth; the company of his disciples which is the church; and the eucharistic bread. These three bodily realities interweave and overlap inseparably, but they are not simply identical. Taking this perspective, people outside the Christian church may still be connected to the body of Christ in the first sense, in relation with the cosmic Christ who 'draws the world towards himself in a state of continuous change...[who] reveals himself to the world at every step of the way in some new perspective even though for the world he may remain someone *incognito*'.[54]

Baptists, in thinking about the saving work of God, also reflected from their earliest days on the relation between the 'invisible church' and 'visible saints'. Unlike the Orthodox, they *did* think that there was an invisible church here and now on earth as well as in heaven, but they did not use this concept as a justification for rejecting wider visible structures of the church beyond the local congregation. This is, to be sure, the way that the contrast between the 'visible' and 'invisible' church has been drawn upon by many Baptist groups in modern times: only the single local unit is claimed to be visible, and the search of the ecumenical movement for 'visible unity' is dismissed in the name of an 'invisible' church universal. Even claims that associations or unions of churches in fellowship together have an ecclesial character are likely to be suspected of having fallen into the error of attempting to make the 'invisible' church visible in some other place than the local congregation. The church universal is said to be invisible in the sense of being a 'purely spiritual' union of all regenerate people, not to be confused with any outward forms beyond the local level.[55]

---

52   Ware, *Orthodox Church*, p. 308.
53   Staniloae, 'Orthodox Doctrine of Salvation', p. 211.
54   Staniloae, 'Orthodox Doctrine of Salvation', p. 205.
55   An influential voice here was Augustus Hopkins Strong, *Systematic Theology* (Philadelphia: Griffith & Rowland, 1909), pp. 887-91.

Early Baptists certainly understood the 'invisible church' to be the total company of all the redeemed, whether they were inside or outside the visible church, and whether they lived in the past, present or future. Those in the Calvinistic tradition understood the 'invisible church' or the 'spiritual kingdom'[56] simply to be God's elect, those named for salvation from before the beginning of the world and for whom Christ had died. It was the church in the mind of God, and was the universal church in its fulness. Saints became 'visible' when they gathered in 'particular congregations' to live under the covenant rule of Christ, and when their profession of faith and their ethical behaviour gave visible evidence that they were indeed chosen to be sons and daughters of God.[57] They became visible in 'right gathering' and in obedience to Christ, and so showed themselves to have an 'effectual calling' and to be on the way of salvation. While the 'Second London Confession' treats the contrast between the invisible church and visible saints in its article on the church (ch. XXVI), it clarifies the scope of membership of the invisible body of Christ in its earlier article on 'Effectual Calling' (ch. X), including among the regenerate 'elect infants dying in infancy...[and] all other elect persons who are uncapable of being outwardly called by the Ministry of the Word'.[58]

Baptists in the Arminian tradition also understood the 'invisible church' to be the whole number of the regenerate, and were usually content to regard this also as the company of the 'elect', as long as it was understood that the effectiveness of the atonement made in Christ was not restricted to a fixed and predetermined number of elect persons. They thus took a more relaxed view of the mysterious interaction between the electing grace of God and human freedom and duty to respond in faith.[59] John Smyth in 1612 affirmed that the 'outward church visible consists of penitent persons only', and is a 'mystical figure outwardly, of the true, spiritual, invisible church; which consisteth of the spirits of...the regenerate'.[60] The later 'Orthodox Creed' of some General Baptists contains an article headed 'Of the invisible catholick Church of Christ' (XXIX) which affirms that 'There is one holy catholick church, consisting of, or made up of the whole number of the elect, that have been, are, or shall be gathered by special grace.'[61] The accompanying article on 'Of the catholick Church as visible' states that 'we believe the visible church of Christ on earth, is made up of several distinct

---

56   'The London Confession', ch. xxxiii, p. 165.
57   'The London Confession', ch. xxxiii. See also 'The Second London Confession', ch. xxvi.2, p. 285.
58   'The Second London Confession', x.3, p. 265.
59   See, e.g., 'The Orthodox Creed', art. ix, p. 303: 'a great mystery indeed'.
60   'Propositions and Conclusions', art. 64, p. 136.
61   'The Orthodox Creed', art. xxix, p. 318.

congregations, which make up that one catholick church, or mystical body of Christ'.[62]

The advantages of a contrast between an 'invisible' and 'visible' church were at least three. First, it stressed the mixed nature of the church as it appeared to human eyes; any congregation was bound to be made up of the regenerate and the unregenerate, and this was explained by the fact that the visible church was not exactly identical with the invisible church. Second, it recognized the freedom of a sovereign God to be in a saving relationship with whomever God wished, regardless of their membership in earthly organizations. These first two points introduced a necessary dose of humility into the hearts of those who regarded themselves as 'visible saints'. Third, it laid stress on the importance of the local church as a place where the universal church became visible. As with the Orthodox ecclesiology, the local assembly was not a deficient fragment of a larger structure, but the 'whole church'.

However, the positive affirmation of the local congregation as making the invisible catholic church visible did not imply the negative—that there was no visibility anywhere else. The catholic church was visible nowhere in its *completeness*, and one could be sure of finding it visible in particular congregations, but this did not mean that the body of Christ could not *also* be made manifest in wider groupings of churches. 'The London Confession' of 1644, a Particular Baptist statement, envisages a communion of local churches that certainly seems to make the body of Christ manifest together:

> ...though we be distinct in respect of our particular bodies, for conveniency sake, being as many as can well meet together in one place, yet are all one in communion, holding Jesus Christ to be our head and Lord...and although the particular congregations be distinct and several bodies, every one a compact and knit city in itself; yet are they all to walk by the same rule, and by all means convenient to have the counsel and help one of another in all needful affairs of the church, as members of one body in the common faith under Christ their only head.[63]

The theological point here about authority is that the local church has liberty to order its life, not because of any human-centred freedom, but because it stands under the direct 'rule' of Christ. But likewise, other congregations also exist under the same rule of the one Christ, and so they are all 'one body...under Christ their only head'. The General Baptist confession quoted above ('The Orthodox Creed'), which speaks of the church universal as being made visible in 'several distinct

---

62   'The Orthodox Creed', art. xxx, p. 319.
63   'The London Confession', extracts from the introduction and ch. xlvii, pp. 155, 168-69.

congregations', is careful to keep the word 'congregations' in the plural, reading: 'such a visible church, *or congregations...*'.[64] In line with this it refers to the representatives to general councils or assemblies of churches as making 'but one church'.[65] A modern statement of the Baptist Union of Great Britain on 'The Baptist Doctrine of the Church' (issued in reply to the famous 'Cambridge Sermon' on unity by the Archbishop of Canterbury in 1946), keeps the same openness about the nature of the visibility of the church universal. Gathered companies of believers are said to be 'the local manifestation of the one Church of God on earth and in heaven', but this clearly does not exclude translocal manifestations, as the document goes on to say that a local church which fails to seek communion with other churches 'lacks one of the marks of a truly Christian community'.[66]

What emerges, then, if we place Baptist and Orthodox ecclesiologies alongside each other, on this issue of salvation and the visibility of the church? Both traditions are clear that God's saving relationship to humankind is wider than the boundaries of the visible church as it is at present. God is engaged in a work of transforming human lives and relationships, and leading them towards a climax of God's creative project. Both Orthodox and Baptist thinkers of the present day build on earlier theological ideas in their tradition here, expanding them beyond the intentions of earlier thinkers. Baptists will find a point of departure in the affirming of God's freedom to make covenant relations with whom God wills; Orthodox find seminal the ideas of the deification of human nature and the recapitulation of all things in Christ. Both traditions may affirm *extra ecclesiam nulla salus* in the sense of a denial of individualistic salvation, and in an eschatological perspective.

If each tradition is allowed to influence the other, then Baptists ought to take seriously the Orthodox urging that the church here and now on earth is always visible. Despite elements of their traditional thinking, Baptists might think more in terms of a constant *becoming* visible of the whole catholic church. While we never have the universal church in its fulness here on earth and in our time, there is a momentum *towards* visibility, towards making the face of Christ known in the world through the many features of his members, first at the local level but also in intercommunion.[67] The many gifts are distributed among the many churches, and for the body to work as one we must work for structures, assemblies, where this unity becomes manifest.

---

64 'The Orthodox Creed', art. xxx, p. 319.
65 'The Orthodox Creed', art. xxix, p. 327.
66 'The Baptist Doctrine of the Church' (1948), in Roger Hayden (ed.), *Baptist Union Documents 1948–1977* (London: The Baptist Historical Society, 1980), p. 8.
67 The image of the features of a face is used by John Chrysostom in *Epist.1 ad Corinthios Homilia*, 30.3 (*PG* LXI, 253-54).

Where Baptists will take issue with Orthodoxy is in its equating of visibility with *indivisibility*. It is the tragedy of the church to have been broken through the contingencies and conflicts of history. It is visible indeed, but in pieces whose fragmentation is a scandal to the world and which enters the heart of God as a cause of grief and pain. It is an aspect of the divine humility, we may say, to allow the church to be divided, and a dimension of God's experience of the cross. The Orthodox claim to be the one and only indivisible Catholic Church will seem to Baptists to be a too swift moving on from the Good Friday of history, which must always be held in tension with the brightness of Easter morning. The church is indeed an icon of the Trinity, as the Orthodox perceive, mirroring the unity and diversity within God's own communion of life. The mutual indwelling of the divine persons in one God has a parallel in the mutual indwelling of many members in the one local eucharistic assembly, and the coinherence of many local churches in the one catholic communion. We cannot appeal to trinitarian diversity to justify the *divisions* of Christian churches among themselves. The ecumenical hope for reconciled diversity reaches beyond the present situation of diversity-in-separation. The present division of the church cannot reflect the multiplicity within the triune life; but it does reveal the brokenness of fellowship within God's life, which is there because God willingly takes into God's own self the destructiveness of human sin. As Hans Urs von Balthasar peceives, the 'gulf' of divine love in God which is the 'otherness' in the relations of Father, Son and Spirit, makes room for the painful gap of alienation.[68] As part of that situation of alienation, the church must be the object of God's salvation as well as its medium, for it is an all-too human as well as a divine reality.

Something of the scandal as well as the realism of the division of the church is expressed in one of the 'propositions' of John Smyth, written in 1612. This is an interesting piece for Baptists, as it clearly assumes that the 'outward', that is *visible*, church is far wider than the local church. There is no sense here that the body of Christ is only visible in a particular congregation; indeed, since all those who profess true repentance and faith are 'visible saints', this would make little sense. But what *is* visible is 'rent' asunder; the body is indeed broken.

> That all penitent and faithful Christians are brethren in the communion of the outward church, wheresoever they live, by what name soever they are known, which in truth and zeal, follow repentance and faith, though compassed with never so many ignorances and infirmities; and we salute them all with a holy kiss, being heartily grieved that we which follow after one faith, and one spirit, one Lord, and

---

68 Hans Urs von Balthasar, *Theodrama: Theological Dramatic Theory. Vol. IV. The Action* (trans. G. Harrison; San Francisco: Ignatius Press, 1994), pp. 323-24.

one God, one body, and one baptism, should be rent into so many sects and schisms: and that only for matters of less moment.[69]

Salvation: A Process in the Church

If salvation is essentially about the restoring of communion with the triune God and an enabling of deeper participation in the life of God, then the church as a network of relations between God and humanity must be deeply involved in salvation. As Zizioulas expresses it, 'the church's ministry realizes here and now the very saving work of Christ, which involves the very personal life and presence of the one who saves'.[70] But this ministry, as part of a human (and broken) community, will have a human as well as a divine character, and to understand this duality is to explore the meaning of salvation itself. It leads us, I suggest, to understand salvation as marked by process and by the co-working of divine grace with human response. Looking at these linked characteristics will also return us to the themes of the body of Christ and the visibility/invisibility of the church that we have already explored.

In the first place, the integration of church and salvation makes clear that salvation is not a single point but a process or—in more graphic terms—a journey. The Orthodox perspective is shaped by the concept of salvation as a deifying union with God, and this 'has to be fulfilled ever more and more in this life, through the transformation of our corruptible and depraved nature and by its adaptation to eternal life' (Lossky).[71] The life and power given through the human nature of Christ to our natures is 'a principle of growth, a gift and a promise implying eschatological development' (Staniloae).[72] Salvation is thus a continuing struggle, full of tensions, until the *theosis* of the created is realized completely in the age to come, and the church is the context for this process.

In the age-old language of Orthodoxy, nature is constantly being transformed by grace. As Lossky puts it, 'in Eastern spirituality "a state of grace" has no absolute or static sense. It is a dynamic and shifting reality' because the life in Christ is 'an unceasing struggle for the acquisition of that grace which must transfigure nature'.[73] This idea of process is thus linked with an understanding of the co-working of divine and human wills, to which I will come in a moment. The point here is that the setting of the church both discloses the phenomenon of the struggle

---

69 'Propositions and Conclusions', art. 69, p. 137.
70 Zizioulas, *Being as Communion*, pp. 211-12.
71 Lossky, *Mystical Theology*, p. 196.
72 Staniloae, 'Orthodox Doctrine of Salvation', p. 186.
73 Lossky, *Mystical Theology*, p. 180.

and provides a way to resolution. As a 'two-natured reality' (Lossky), the life of the church reveals the tension between human nature which is only partly transformed, only partly open to the power of grace, and the deified human nature of Christ which is all the time being communicated to human life. As Ephrem the Syrian commented, 'the whole Church is the Church of the penitent; the whole Church is the Church of those who are perishing.'[74] Lossky concludes that 'The church is both a stable and definite reality, but also a reality in becoming.'[75] On the one hand, as the body of Christ it has its hypostasis in him and is united as a creature with God; on the other hand, 'in the human persons who are the multiple hypostases of its nature' the church has only partially attained perfection. Yet in its sacraments there is a foretaste of full *theosis*, for here—according to Lossky—there is provided a perfect unity of natures, the created nature of bread and wine totally united with the deified human nature of Christ. Here, as we participate, our natures are united both with Christ and with all members of the church. Here, 'Christ has mingled his body with ours that we may be one, as a body joined to the head' (John Chrysostom).[76]

We may feel, however, that the traditional Orthodox focus on human and divine natures, summed up brilliantly in Lossky's synthesis, actually tends to undermine the dynamic process of transfiguration which is expressed in the event of the eucharist itself. Talk of 'nature' seems to place stress on static substance. John Zizioulas, as we have already seen, prefers to concentrate on the transformation of nature by *person*. For him, then, the process of salvation inheres in the tension between the 'biological hypostasis' of a human being, given in birth, and the 'ecclesial hypostasis' given in new birth.[77] Zizioulas recognizes, of course, that the biological hypostasis, with its tendency to exclusivism, does not cease to exist in the new relations of the church. Human beings do not cease to age and die. Zizioulas is thus concerned to express the paradoxical relationship of the one hypostasis to the other in authentic personhood, and he finds this to lie in an eschatological identity. In his or her ecclesial hypostasis, the person appears 'as that which he [sic] *will* be'. The situation created by this paradox can be described, Zizioulas suggests, as a 'sacramental or *eucharistic* hypostasis'.[78]

Zizioulas means that the eucharist is not only an *assembly* in one place, but a *movement* towards the goal of the ecclesial hypostasis in God's future. In the movement of the liturgy, 'The ecclesiastical hypostasis

---

74 Cited by Lossky, *Mystical Theology*, p. 185.
75 Lossky, *Mystical Theology*, p. 185.
76 John Chrysostom, *Hom. in Ioannem*, XLVI (*PG* LIX, 260).
77 Zizioulas, *Being as Communion*, pp. 50-54.
78 Zizioulas, *Being as Communion*, p. 57.

reveals man [sic] as a person which has its roots in the future.'[79] The dialectic of 'already and not yet' that pervades the eucharist, combining the presence of Christ with the appeal 'Come, Lord Jesus', also characterizes the human hypostasis in process of being saved. The element of struggle is there because the ecclesial hypostasis resists the biological hypostasis; yet it does not deny the biological *nature* of existence but re-hypostasizes it in the hypostasis of Christ. So the eros of the body, as an ecstatic movement of love towards others, is not suppressed but given its true place in the eucharist. In the eucharistic movement, biological life is no longer tragic but is rooted in the future where person has final priority over nature. This, we may add, is why the visible church is united in the eucharist with the invisible church; no persons who have lived in the non-exclusive relations of love can be lost through the natural necessity of death, and so they are remembered in the eucharistic assembly.[80]

The Orthodox appeal to deification as the central concept of salvation does not, of course, exclude the rich range of models of atonement that we find in scripture and tradition. It rather acts as a gathering point for them. For instance, we may say that Christ offers himself in pure *sacrifice* to the Father to create the conditions for our own total surrender to the Father; Christ draws us into his sacrificial nature so that we can sacrifice our own selfish existence, in order to receive communion in the triune life.[81] Thus he makes access for us to the Father, and this is expressed in the image of justification, or right relationship. To take a third image of atonement—victory over death and all hostile powers—Christ accepts death into his deified human nature in order to overcome it there for us in the power of the resurrection.[82] *Theosis* is thus a comprehensive idea, and in all its aspects it clearly involves the community of the church in the process of salvation. As Staniloae comments, 'Christ is the central hypostasis which connects all human hypostases with each other.'[83]

By contrast, the primary model of salvation in Baptist thought, stemming from the Reformation, has probably been that of reconciliation, closely connected to the image of justification. Staniloae points out (in commenting on Lutheran thought) that this term, which is not often used in Orthodoxy, has the special advantage of stressing the nature of human beings and God as persons in the economy of salvation. It makes clear that 'salvation is brought about by the re-establishment of a normal personal relationship between man [sic] and God'.[84] The image

---

79 Zizioulas, *Being as Communion*, p. 69.
80 Zizioulas, *Being as Communion*, pp. 64-65.
81 So Cyril of Alexandria, *de Adoratione in Spiritu et Veritate*, 9.
82 So Athanasius, *de Incarnatione*, 20.
83 Staniloae, 'Orthodox Doctrine of Salvation', p. 191.
84 Staniloae, 'Orthodox Doctrine of Salvation', p. 184.

can, unfortunately, be evacuated of its personal relational content when it is treated as a narrowly forensic concept, leaning too heavily on the language of the law-court. It becomes even more narrow when interpreted in terms of highly transactional theory, such as Calvin's doctrine of penal substitution, though it should be said that Baptist confessions of faith over the years have in fact shown a remarkable openness in seeking to understand how reconciliation is achieved through the death of Christ.[85]

Another problem with the language of reconciliation is that it can relapse into the loneliness of the soul before God. Absorbed with the right standing of the individual person before the divine tribunal, salvation can become a matter of 'inner peace with God' and lose contact with the power of salvation to transform relations in community. A sign of this isolation, Orthodox critics of Protestantism suggest, is the separation of 'justification' from 'sanctification'; at the same time this absolute distinction tends to regard salvation itself as a single act of imputation, or being *declared* in the right with God.[86] Kallistos Ware comments that 'Orthodox usually have little to say about justification as a distinct topic...salvation is not a single event in our past life but an ongoing process of growth in Christ.'[87] Staniloae suggests that Orthodoxy might well learn from the Reformation concern about being 'righteous' before God, but this is best seen as an increasing and ever-growing righteousness which is founded on a relationship of peace between human beings and God.[88] It is probably true to say that a good deal of Baptist thought has regarded justification by faith to be an individual and isolated event in which an individual stands alone before Christ, while sanctification or growth in grace is seen as a corporate experience in the fellowship of other believers.

However, there is also much in Baptist thought that *does* regard reconciliation with God as process, and this becomes clear in ways of thinking that relate salvation to the church. Notably, there is the experience of assurance and the place of baptism itself in the development of Christian discipleship, both of which involve the

---

85 For evidence of this statement, see Paul S. Fiddes, 'The Understanding of Salvation in the Baptist Tradition', in Rienk Lanooy (ed.), *For Us and For Our Salvation: Seven Perspectives on Christian Soteriology* (Utrecht/Leiden: Interuniversitair Instituut voor Missiologie en Oecumenica, 1994), pp. 33-34.

86 *Salvation and the Church: An Agreed Statement by the Second Anglican–Roman Catholic International Commission* (London: Church House Publishing/Catholic Truth Society, 1987), pp. 15-19, argues that 'justification and sanctification are two aspects of the same divine act', thus helping to resolve a historic split at the time of the Reformation.

87 Ware, *Orthodox Church*, p. 125.

88 Staniloae, 'Orthodox Doctrine of Salvation', pp. 185-86.

community. To take the issue of assurance first, early Baptist churches which stood in the Calvinist tradition discerned a kind of process between the act of turning in faith to Christ and the moment when believers receive the assurance of salvation (or 'make their calling and election sure'). These stages are graphically portrayed in John Bunyan's story of the *Pilgrim's Progress*, for when the Pilgrim enters the narrow 'wicket gate' of conversion he is still carrying his heavy burden of guilt. It is not until some while later that he arrives at a wayside cross, and

> his burden loosed from off his shoulders and fell from off his back; and began to tumble, and so continued to do till it came to the mouth of the sepulchre, where it fell in, and I saw it no more. Then was Christian glad and lightsome, and said with a merry heart, 'He hath given me rest, by his sorrow, and life, by his death'.[89]

This exact pattern of salvation experience was not universal among Baptists, even among Particular Baptists, and among Baptists of today a waiting for such a 'moment of inner assurance' is very rare. But similar patterns, in which assurance of dying and rising with Christ is found in sharing in the lifestyle of the community, in studying scripture together and in mutual care of fellow-disciples ('watching over each other'), point to a story of salvation which is more complicated and extensive than conversion alone. Perhaps this is why in our modern age the movement of charismatic renewal, with its emphasis upon further stages of filling with the Holy Spirit beyond the moment of conversion, usually received in worship in the community, has had such a powerful influence on Baptist life in many parts of the world.

Indeed, believers' baptism itself implies that salvation is a story or journey, since a candidate for baptism who is already a believer must already have experienced the transforming grace of God in his or her life, must be already regenerate, and be already therefore a member of the body of Christ. Yet in the act of baptism in the midst of the congregation, the disciple shares in the death of Christ in order to rise with him to new life (Rom. 6.1-3). The New Testament describes baptism as an act of salvation, of baptism in Spirit, of new birth and of adoption as a child of God;[90] baptized into the triune Name, the believer is being changed by encounter with a gracious God. The many Baptists who understand baptism to be an act of God, as well as a human confession of faith, will see it as a high point in the process of 'being saved' which does

---

89   John Bunyan, *The Pilgrim's Progress* (ed. Roger Sharrock; Harmondsworth: Penguin, 1965), p. 70.
90   See, e.g., 1 Pet. 3.21; 1 Cor. 12.13; Tit. 3.5; Jn. 3.5; Gal. 3.26-27.

not deny previous entrance into the saving grace of Christ.[91] Understanding salvation as a process like this must begin to break down any neat distinction between 'justification' and 'sanctification'. It will recognize that justification is not merely a legal declaration of being 'in the right' with God and a legal transfer to us of the righteousness of Christ, but also part of the ongoing story of being *made righteous* in the image of Christ, through the transforming power of the Spirit of God in the community of the church.

Salvation: As Cooperation with God in the Church

One significant reason why salvation is a *process* is because human nature may at various moments either yield to the pressure of the grace of God or resist it. It seems that the journey, whether of deification or reconciliation, involves both divine grace and human freewill working together and this is what Orthodoxy calls *synergy*. The Eastern tradition has never polarized grace and freewill in the way that has happened in the West under the influence of Augustine and Calvin. Rather it has always affirmed their 'cooperation' in salvation, recalling the words of Paul that 'we are fellow-workers (*synergoi*) with God' (1 Cor. 3.9). Gregory of Nazianzus, for instance, states that our incorporation into Christ depends both on God and on ourselves: 'There is need both of that which lies in our own power and of the salvation granted by God.'[92] The Orthodox view is not, of course, that our acts of freewill earn grace as a reward; as Lossky points out: 'it is not a question of merits but of a cooperation, of a synergy of the two wills, divine and human, a harmony in which grace bears ever more fruit and is appropriated...by the human person.'[93] While what God does is infinitely more important than the human response, yet 'our voluntary participation in God's saving action is altogether indispensable' (Kallistos Ware).[94]

The Orthodox doctrine of synergy has long fallen under suspicion in western theology, the most notable recent critic being Karl Barth, deeply concerned that the sovereignty of God be not impuned.[95] But the heart of

---

91 See *Believing and Being Baptized: Baptism, so-called re-baptism and children in the church. A Discussion Document by the Doctrine and Worship Committee of the Baptist Union of Great Britain* (London: Baptist Union, 1996), pp. 9-12.
92 Gregory of Nazianzus, *Orations*, 37:13.
93 Lossky, *Mystical Theology*, p. 198.
94 Kallistos Ware, 'The Understanding of Salvation in the Orthodox Tradition', in Lanooy (ed.), *For Us and For Our Salvation*, p. 117.
95 K. Barth, *Church Dogmatics* (13 part-vols; ed. and trans. G.W. Bromiley and T.F. Torrance; Edinburgh: T. & T. Clark, 1936-77), IV/1, p. 113; cf. II/2, pp. 193-94; III/3, pp. 139, 144, 147.

the Orthodox idea is not some kind of sequence between human and divine actions (as in semi-Pelagianism), but a mysterious *simultaneity*. Gregory of Nyssa speaks, for instance, of human effort and the grace of the Spirit 'running together to the same place'.[96] This concurrence is due to the fact that all human acts of will, while genuinely free, are already interwoven with the gift of divine grace. As Kallistos Ware expresses it strongly, 'in every good desire and action on our part, God's grace is present from the outset'.[97] One way of understanding this interaction is christologically, as the union of two natures which also (as Maximus the Confessor insisted)[98] include two wills. Staniloae, considering the idea of synergy, thus roots it in the central concept of *theosis*: the human will has been conformed to the divine will in the single hypostasis of Christ. In human nature, assumed into the divine hypostasis, 'human will has become the will of the Son of God who directs it towards the Father'.[99] Thus Staniloae is not content only to appeal to the Orthodox view that human freewill has not been completely destroyed by the fall. Also, in some way, a new human will has been communicated to all humanity, as a 'leaven working secretly within the whole body of mankind'.[100] Here he seems to echo the words of St Macarius of Egypt, that grace permeates the human personality like yeast in bread and 'becomes fixed in a man like a natural endowment, as though it were one substance with him'.[101] This is the subjective aspect of the Orthodox concept of union with God, what St Seraphim of Sarov calls 'acquisition of grace'.[102]

Now, in the Orthodox view it is in the church that the synergy of wills, human and divine, has the greatest scope to operate. If we ask how divine grace is to be appropriated through human acts of freewill, the immediate answer is, according to St Seraphim, through 'prayer, fasting, vigils, alms and other Christian practices'.[103] This is the ascetic or spiritual tradition of Orthodoxy, centred upon the divine liturgy. Orthodoxy does not neglect the service of the church in society (*diakonia*), but this is regarded as flowing from divine service, as 'the liturgy after the liturgy'. Thus, Lossky affirms that the whole church is a reality not only with two natures, but two wills. In this synergy, 'the sacramental unions which the church offers us...are gifts which must be realized, acquired, and become

---

96 Gregory of Nyssa, *De Instituto Christiano*, PG XLVI, 289.c.
97 Ware, 'The Understanding of Salvation in the Orthodox Tradition', p. 119.
98 See 'The Trial of Maximus', in Berthold (ed.), Maximus Confessor, *Selected Writings*, pp. 23-24.
99 Staniloae, 'Orthodox Doctrine of Salvation', p. 188.
100 Staniloae, 'Orthodox Doctrine of Salvation', p. 191.
101 Macarius, *Spiritual Homilies*, 37.10, cited by Lossky, *Mystical Theology*, p. 199.
102 Cited by Lossky, *Mystical Theology*, p. 199.
103 Lossky, *Mystical Theology*, p. 196.

fully ours, in the course of constant struggles wherein our wills are conformed to the will of God in the Holy Spirit present in us'.[104] Lossky also points out that perception of divine truth in councils of churches also involves a 'harmony of two wills', appealing to the formula of Acts 15.28, 'It seemed good to the Holy Spirit and to us.' While Lossky here has in mind the mysterious harmony of will between the *bishops* and the Spirit,[105] we may recall that there is a quite widespread Orthodox opinion (and notably in the school formed by Khomiakov) that the decisions of councils can only be regarded as dogma when there is evidence, over time, that they have been accepted by the whole people of God. This assent is not expressed formally, as in a Baptist church meeting, but is 'lived' in the will of the people.[106]

Within the Baptist story, it may seem at first sight that there was much more affinity to the Orthodox idea of synergy within the General (or mildly 'Arminian') Baptist approach to salvation than among Particular Baptists. In fact, however, there were signs of convergence between these two traditions over the matter of grace and freewill long before the emergence of 'evangelical Calvinism' with Andrew Fuller and his friends in the late eighteenth century. On the one hand, General Baptists agreed with Calvinists that divine initiative was needed to activate human freewill. So the General Baptist 'Orthodox Creed' of 1679 affirms that

> justifying faith is a grace, or habit, wrought in the soul by the holy ghost, through preaching the word of God, whereby we are enabled to believe...and wholly and only to rest upon Christ.[107]

On the other hand, Particular Baptists agreed that a willed response of faith was necessary to actualize a covenant relationship with God here and now. We find the Particular Baptist theologian Benjamin Keach arguing that while a covenant agreement exists between God and the elect by eternal decree, it is only when by the Spirit we 'choose Jesus Christ as the only Object of our Affection' that 'we enter into an *actual* Covenant with God', and 'the Reconciliation becomes mutual'.[108]

Indeed, it is in covenant theology that there is the most interesting possibility of dialogue with Orthodox thinking about synergy of wills, for here the human will to make covenant interacts in a mysterious way with the eternal covenant decree of God. Moreover, this cooperation only makes sense in the context of the church community. To see why this is,

---

104 Lossky, *Mystical Theology*, p. 183.
105 Lossky, *Mystical Theology*, p. 188.
106 See Ware, *The Orthodox Church*, pp. 252-53.
107 'Orthodox Creed', art. xxiii, p. 314.
108 Benjamin Keach, *The Display of Glorious Grace. Or, The Covenant of Peace Opened* (London: 1698), p. 282.

we must recall that for early Baptists (and for other dissenters of the period), the term 'covenant' had a threefold meaning. First, it referred to an eternal 'covenant of grace' which God had made with human beings for their salvation. Calvin was influential in developing this idea, although for him the covenant was restricted to those whom God had elected to be saved.[109] We have already explored this idea in considering Christ as mediator of the new covenant for the church. Second, it seemed to Christian thinkers that if God had made an eternal covenant with human beings and that this was based on a costly act of God's grace costing nothing less than the death of Christ, then there must have been agreement *within* God about this.

There is then a covenant *in God*, between the Father and the Son in the love of the Spirit. In theology following the Reformation, this covenant referred to a kind of transaction between the Persons of the triune God, in which the Son is envisaged as consenting to the will of the Father to undertake the work of the salvation of human beings.[110] I suggest that in our theological thinking today we need to get away from rather legal ideas of transaction and any ideas about the elect which restrict the free and extravagant grace of God; but we still need to keep the central idea of a covenantal relationship in God, a harmony of will and purpose within the communion of God's triune life. Covenant in its primary meaning is about fellowship in the being of God, about a God who is open in relations within God's self and towards creation. Covenant is about the purpose of the Father to send out the Son in mission into the world, about the glad and obedient response of the Son, saying 'yes' to the Father,[111] and about the surprising energy of the Spirit who is always opening up this covenant relationship into new depths and into a new future.

The third sense of 'covenant' in Baptist tradition is an act of *consent* between people gathered in a particular place to be a church there. In the words of many early Baptist covenant documents it is the pledge to 'give up themselves to the Lord in a church state'. This is the covenant made and signed when a local church is first formed and agreed subsequently

---

109 E.g. John Calvin, *Institutes of the Christian Religion* (2 vols; trans. H. Beveridge; London: James Clarke & Co, 1949), Vol. I, VI, 293-98; Vol. II, 3.XXI, pp. 208-11.

110 Thus, while the Particular Baptist 'London Confession' of 1644 refers only to 'the blood of the everlasting covenant', 'The Second London Confession' of 1677/89 specifies the eternal covenant as a being 'a transaction between the Father and the Son about the Redemption of the Elect'. In his treatise on the covenant, *The Display of Glorious Grace* (1698), pp. 285, 294, Benjamin Keach regards the 'federal' agreement between the Father and the Son as the primary meaning of the covenant of grace.

111 This has been a pervasive theme in Karl Barth: see, e.g., *Church Dogmatics*, II/2, pp. 161-74.

by new members who enter it through the years. The early Baptist John Smyth defined the church in this way, in 1607:

> A visible communion of Saincts is of two, three or more Saincts joyned together by covenant with God & themselves...[112]

It was no accident of words that the very same term 'covenant' was used for the mutual agreement of church members and the eternal decree of God, that is both for the eternal covenant and a local covenant. In some mysterious way, the assent of God to human creation and salvation was intersecting with a promise-making of a small human congregation.[113] God's decision in eternity, and the inner life of God, were bound up with the response of a few people in a little town or village. It was becoming actual in a time and place.

In this covenant theology, God's making of covenant *with* the church is simultaneous with the making of covenant *by* the church. This is a mystery of synergy that stretches the mind and the imagination. The way that these aspects of covenant are connected was not worked out systematically by early Baptists and it remains tantalizing not only in Smyth's thought, but in the later model covenant of Benjamin Keach at Horsley Down (1697). This begins with the pledge

> to give up ourselves to the Lord, in a Church state according to the Apostolical Constitution that he may be our God, and we may be his People, through the Everlasting Covenant of his Free grace, in which alone we hope to be accepted by him, through his blessed Son Jesus Christ, whom we take to be our High Priest, to justify and sanctify us...[114]

In this drama of the 'solemn covenant of the church', the members are not just recalling that they *have been* included in God's eternal covenant, but envisage themselves as somehow entering it at that very moment. Moreover, we catch a glimpse here of the second theme of covenant, the inner fellowship of God: this local fellowship of believers is somehow participating at this moment within the inner communion of the triune God.

---

112 John Smyth, *Principles and Inferences Concerning the Visible Church* (1607), in W.T. Whitley (ed.), *The Works of John Smyth* (2 vols; Cambridge: Cambridge University Press, 1915), I, p. 252.

113 See Paul S. Fiddes, 'Walking Together. The Place of Covenant Theology in Baptist Life, Yesterday and Today', in W.H. Brackney, Paul S. Fiddes and J.H.Y. Briggs (eds.), *Pilgrim Pathways: Essays in Baptist History in Honour of B.R. White* (Macon, GA: Mercer University Press, 199), pp. 58-63.

114 Benjamin Keach, *The Glory of a True Church, And its Discipline display'd* (London: 1697), p. 71.

But the practice of church covenant-making did not only preserve the mystery of divine grace and human freedom. I suggest that it imprinted on Baptist minds the sense that salvation was not merely a point but a process or a story. In the terms used by Benjamin Keach, the eternal covenant is 'actualized' when someone 'embraces' or 'lays hold' of Christ ('when God gives Christ to a Sinner, the whole Covenant is performed to that Person'),[115] and this actualizing of the covenant in conversion is then 'renewed' in the event of church covenant-making, as it is also in the church acts of baptism and the Lord's Supper. This story of eternal purpose, actualization in time and renewal along the way is the story of a 'pilgrim's progress'.

This account of Baptist ideas of covenant, with regard to the process and the synergy of salvation, reinforces a conclusion that I hope has emerged from every part of this paper. Covenant theology and a doctrine of *theosis* have a remarkable potential for interaction. Here both Baptists and Orthodox envisage salvation as a participation in the interweaving relationships of the triune God. Nor can either concept be understood without the corporate nature of salvation as a healing of relations, and so the intimate connection of salvation with the community of the church. This does not mean that Baptist and Orthodox ecclesiologies are simply the same, nor that a Baptist can hold the naïve expectation that Orthodox can without further ado accept Baptist churches as part of the One Church. But we may affirm Staniloae's belief that traditions other than Orthodox can deepen their own understanding of the church through exposure to Orthodox ecclesiology, with the hope that there may also be some gain in the other direction. And this dialogue may surely, in itself, be seen as part of the journey of salvation.

---

115 Keach, *Display of Glorious Grace*, p. 296.

CHAPTER 7

Disciples and Baptists: A Study in Comparative Polities

William H. Brackney

I am pleased to present this contribution to a Festschrift for my esteemed colleague, John H.Y. Briggs. In the two decades I have known Professor Briggs he has actively engaged an ecumenical vision of the church from a Baptist perspective. I have selected this topic because it provides an American context for a comparison of two Free Church groups in ecumenical relationships, and because both the Disciples and Baptists have origins in the religious cultures of Great Britain.

Introduction

The Disciples of Christ and the Christian Church began as reformation streams in American Protestantism in the early nineteenth century. By the twentieth century these two streams had converged into a single ecclesial tradition that understood and organized itself as a church. Having adopted, under the leadership of Alexander Campbell, an essentially congregational polity, Disciples did not have biblically-conceived or historic regional and national structures.[1] Hence, much time and energy has been devoted to developing and making sense, both administratively

---

This study was originally commissioned by a grant from the Lilly Foundation for a denominational study of the Christian Church (Disciples of Christ) held at Christian Theological Seminary in Indianapolis, Indiana, 1986. It has been substantially revised. I wish to espress appreciation to David McWhirter of the Disciples Historical Society, James Lynch of the American Baptist Historical Society, and Richard Gladden in the office of the General Secretary, American Baptist Churches in the USA, in the preparation of this study.
  1   D. Newell Williams, *Ministry Among Disciples: Past, Present, and Future* (St Louis, MO: Christian Board of Publication, 1985), pp. 7-10, argues that Barton Stone and the Christians adopted an essentially Presbyterian polity.

and theologically, of extra-congregational structures. A principal question has been how, without violating the essence and purpose of gathered local congregations and believers, do congregations with a common purpose and spiritual heritage achieve permanent cooperation and accountability?

This essay recovers and evaluates the stages in the structural evolution of Disciples from the late nineteenth century to the 1970s. In order to understand better the Disciples, the structural evolution of Northern/ American Baptists is also examined. While their paths began in somewhat different contexts, there was constant cross-fertilization of ideas and concerns and a remarkable similarity between these two groups.

It is evident from this comparative examination that structure for Disciples, prior to the 1960s, reflects a series of pragmatic responses to program and administrative difficulties. Only through restructure did a fully rationalized ecclesiality emerge.[2]

Common Development in an American Environment

The Disciples of Christ and American Baptists, with roots in transatlantic revivalism, both emerged from the early nineteenth century as religious movements rather than clearly structured and/or integrated polities inclusive of congregations and extra-parish ministries. Borne along by frontier informality, a heightened emphasis upon local and regional concerns and a predominantly self-educated leadership, resistance in both groups to either a connectional or cooperative denominational structure was great. Indeed, some historians among both groups have reduced the concept or theology of the church to 'nothing other than local congregations'.[3] Such local church protectionism blended well with the Spirit of Jacksonian America. Eventually the growth of missionary opportunities at home and abroad and the efforts of influential leaders would challenge this disposition.

---

2   By 'ecclesiality' I mean not only the doctrine or theological basis of the church, but also its form and expressed self-understanding. Both Baptists and Disciples have exhibited the desire to look like a 'church' while retaining the freedom of individual parts of their original movements.

3   On the Disciples, see W. Barnett Blakemore (ed.), *The Renewal of the Churches* (St Louis, MO: Bethany Press, 1963), pp. 63-64. It was actually the original notion of Thomas Campbell that 'The Church of Christ upon earth must necessarily exist in particular and distinct societies, locally separate from one another.' For the Baptists, a similar story is recounted in Winthrop S. Hudson, 'Stumbling into Disorder', *Foundations* 1.2 (April, 1958), pp. 45-72. A combination of the New Hampshire Confession of Faith, the work of Francis Wayland and 'landmarkism' ensured that no convention would compete favorably with a local Baptist church.

From roughly 1840 to 1880 both groups uncertainly experimented with specialized organizations, missionary societies and associations, which were in no sense considered 'church' but appendages of the outreach and authority of local churches. Among the American Baptists, these groups proliferated and became highly competitive with each other for the limited resources and loyalty of all the local churches. Moreover, effective leadership and the accumulation of financial resources within the major mission organizations began to provide an identity independent of local clergy. Similarly, within the Disciples there was an influential group of churches and editors who desired a more mature organizational life but who were staunchly opposed by local church protectionism and hindered by insufficient resources of their own.

There were two catalysts for change within the American Baptist family, beginning in the 1880s. The first was the farsighted leadership of Henry L. Morehouse and the second was the reality of insufficient funds for all of the mission societies to operate without some coordination of efforts. Morehouse was a long-term figure in the Home Mission Society who nursed a national vision for Baptists of the North.[4] Unlike earlier proponents of this viewpoint, he had an uncanny ability for organization, fundraising and interpretation. In a series of successive steps, Morehouse negotiated a comity plan with Southern Baptists about the territory of each other's missionary organization, he formed nationally cooperative bodies for education and planning and sought out wealthy individual Baptists like John D. Rockerfeller to provide seminal funding for his schemes. As Robert T. Handy has rightly observed, Henry L. Morehouse was the parent of the Northern Baptist Convention and he lived long enough to chart its original course and personify its objectives. It was his idea in 1907 to ensure that the autonomy and independence of every local congregation was completely protected in the Northern Baptist Convention preamble and by-laws, while also skillfully providing for new common planning processes, education and pension boards.[5]

Unlike the Baptists who had a seventeenth-century theology of the local church, the Disciples movement actually early on assumed a symbolic and yet invisible cohesion about itself that they called 'brotherhood'. The idea may have had its origin in Thomas Campbell's 'Second Proposition' that distinct societies (congregations) be 'perfectly joined together in the same mind, and in the same judgment'.[6] The

---

4 For a biography of Morehouse, consult Lathan A. Crandall, *Henry Lyman Morehouse: A Biography* (Boston, MA: American Baptist Publication Society, 1919).

5 Handy's comments are found in a headnote in William H. Brackney (ed.), *Baptist Life and Thought 1600-1980* (Valley Forge, PA: Judson Press, 1983), p. 290.

6 Thomas Campbell, *Declaration and Address of the Christian Association of Washington* (Washington, PA: Brown and Sample, 1829), p. 23. See also, Lester G.

earliest formal definition of the term 'brotherhood' among the Disciples is to be found in a James Mathes editorial, 'The Spirit of Brotherhood', in which he asserted, 'there is among real religious philanthropists a spirit of brotherhood, which makes labor easy, suffering agreeable and association delightful'.[7] Later, George W. Kerr, a pastor in Hoyleton, Illinois, took the relational principle a further step by modelling what he called a 'Christian Brotherhood' on the teachings of Christ. Brethren owed each other a kinship and mature faith, grounded in the word of truth and a maintenance of orderliness in the affairs of the church. For Kerr, 'as soon as we commence the work of coming together [Christ] is in our midst. If we have not the spirit of Christ, we are none of his. Let us, then, work by his direction, that the brotherhood may be in Christ.'[8] This sense of the 'brotherhood' was an informal, spiritual form of union that would lend itself to more formal cooperation for some after 1870, and to schism from ecclesiastical unity for others in the continuing Churches of Christ movement.

The first manifestation of structural unity among the Disciples may be seen in the controversial Louisville Plan of 1869. Twenty years before the Northern Baptists achieved their convention, the Disciples had to respond to declining funds and an unclear perception of their only benevolent organization, the American Christian Missionary Association. An innovative blue ribbon committee of twenty, under the direction of William T. Moore, recommended a loosely cooperative arrangement of the Brotherhood congregations to channel funds for both domestic and foreign missions from local sources to the fields of endeavor. Borrowing a vehicle originally from Baptist parlance, the committee recommended that a General Christian Missionary Convention be formed to meet annually and be administered by a General Board. Moreover, each state would have a board and be divided into districts for promotional purposes. Delegates would be chosen from the states for the General Convention, thus insuring both equality of representation and communication in both directions. The American Christian Missionary Society would be retained only as the legal corporation.[9] With this new, highly integrated structure and concomitant theology of the church,

---

McAllister, *Thomas Campbell: Man of the Book* (St Louis, MO: Bethany Press, 1954), p.117.

7   James Mathes, 'The Spirit of Brotherhood', *Christian Record* 2.5 (November, 1844), p. 120.

8   George W. Kerr, 'The Brotherhood, No. 1', *Christian Standard* 5.13 (March 26 1870), p. 97; 'The Brotherhood, No. II', *Christian Standard* 5.18 (April 20 1870), p.137.

9   The connection with Baptists came through Campbell's experience in the Redstone Association. For the origin of the term, see my paper, 'The General Missionary Convention of the Baptist Denomination, 1814-1845: An American Metaphor', presented to the Southern Baptist Historical Society, April, 1989, pp. 2-3.

proponents of the Louisville Plan hoped to 'pass an act of oblivion on all past indiscretions in missionary work'. Somehow the committee hoped that the more egalitarian thrusts of a 'convention' would unite the various forces of the Christian Churches and silence the 'anti-society' factions.[10]

Unfortunately, just the opposite occurred. Symbolically, ten days before the first meeting of the new General Convention, the Great Fire of Chicago (1871) left several prominent Disciples bankrupt and thus unable to lend their significant support to the new venture. Second, a debate arose over foreign versus domestic missionary endeavor and the proportional amounts which congregations contributed to each and to the General Convention. Finally, scarcely enough funds were received to support the administrative staff, and the whole scheme appeared doomed in its infancy.[11] While the Louisville Plan recognized the supremacy of the church and provided for cooperation, it was still criticized as a 'human' invention and opposed by the very people who opposed the old society model because it was not representative of the churches. J.H. Garrison, a turn of the century editor, actually saw the Louisville Plan as a negative force in Disciples' development because it did not placate the anti-society view and it crippled the work of the societies themselves by calling for their combination.[12]

Advance to Denominational Status

Both the Northern/American Baptists and the Disciples of Christ progressed in the early decades of the twentieth century to an unmistakable 'denominational' status in American Protestantism. For the Baptists, this was intentional; one of their prophets reflected in 1912, 'there is a divine timing of events in the development, step by step, stage by stage of denominational life and power'.[13] Conversely, among the Disciples there has often been a strong disinclination to the concept of 'denomination'. From Alexander Campbell's writing about a 'community of communities' to the more modern proponents of

---

10 'The Louisville Plan', in J.H. Garrison (ed.), *The Reformation of the Nineteenth Century: A Series of Historical Sketches* (St Louis, MO: Christian Publishing Company, 1901), p. 297.

11 Lester G. McAllister and William E. Tucker, *Journey in Faith: A History of the Christian Church (Disciples of Christ)* (St Louis, MO: Bethany Press, 1977), pp. 256-57.

12 'Louisville Plan', in Garrison (ed.), *Reformation of the Nineteenth Century*, p. 304.

13 *The Making and Mission of a Denomination* (Philadelphia, PA: American Baptist Publication Society, 1912), p. 8.

restorationism, the Christian Church (Disciples of Christ) was the fundamental antithesis of denominationalism.[14]

But, if one follows the sage advice of Sidney Mead or Richard Niebuhr for instance, the Disciples movement qualifies well as a 'denomination', especially after the successive changes in its polity from 1919 to 1956. Disciples are indeed historically 'a voluntary association of like-hearted and like-minded individuals united for the propagation of their point of view'. And, they are to be identified with specific segments of the social structure.[15]

Once the rather major step was taken toward the establishment of a general, comprehensive structure among both the Disciples and the Northern Baptists, other pieces of denominational life began to fall into place. Northern Baptists had originally provided in 1910 for an executive committee empowered to act on matters of general interest between annual sessions of the Convention, a nominating committee, a finance committee to coordinate budgetary proposals for all cooperating societies, and a corresponding secretary for the Convention. Between 1919 and 1930 four boards were also established or reconstituted from earlier organizations to administer special interests: the Board of Education, the Ministers and Missionaries Benefit Board, the Board of General Promotion, and the Board of Missionary Cooperation.[16] The Board of Education and the Benefit Board remained discrete entities while the other two evolved from necessary modifications.

Toward the end of the decade of the 1920s, two factors had an impact upon Northern Baptist polity. These were the organized fundamentalist efforts in 1921–32 and overall economic realities of the Depression. Anti-modernist forces sought to reorganize the Convention beginning in 1920 as a strict confessional body and to protect fully the rights of local churches against prerogatives of new national bodies. The churches which joined this movement were generally opposed to the merger of the Northern Baptist Convention and the Free [will] Baptists in 1911, the entry of the Convention into the Federal Council of Churches of Christ in 1913 and the establishment of the New World Movement, a missionary expansion program of the Convention following World War I. As receipts fell in the late 1920s and the Executive Committee of the Convention

---

14   Royal Humbert (ed.), *A Compend of Alexander Campbell's Theology* (St Louis, MO: Bethany Press, 1961), pp. 158-59; also see Ralph G. Wilburn (ed.), *The Reconstruction of Theology* (St Louis, MO: Bethany Press, 1963), pp. 25-26.

15   Sidney E. Mead, *The Lively Experiment: The Shaping of Christianity in America* (New York: Harper, 1963), p. 104; H. Richard Niebuhr, *The Social Sources of Denominationalism* (New York: H. Holt, 1928), pp. 26-27.

16   Robert G. Torbet, *A History of the Baptists* (Valley Forge, PA: Judson Press, 1963), pp. 439-42; W.C. Bitting (ed.), *A Manual of the Northern Baptist Convention* (Philadelphia, PA: American Baptist Publication Society, n.d.), pp. 97-110.

wrestled with a better plan for stewardship cooperation, the Board of General Promotion was created to unify the budgets of all approved agencies and to present a single financial campaign to the churches. Many saw in this move a not-so-subtle attempt to control the independence of the historic mission societies and/or a threatened budgetary imposition upon the local churches.

Northern Baptists took a bold step in 1933–34 to remedy their problems in light of Convention needs. A commission was charged with creating a plan to revise the Convention, favoring function over conservation. Further the commission was requested to work on a design for both democracy of representation *and* simplicity and economy. The result was a new structure which continued the Boards of Education and Ministers and Missionaries Benefits Board but abolished the Board of Missionary Cooperation in favor of a Council on Finance and Promotion; in this plan a General Council replaced the Executive Committee. The latter Council was given broad discretion in constitutional revision, appointment of sub-committees, property management for the Convention, control of the annual agenda and approval of all special financial campaigns. To offset the ongoing charge that Northern Baptists were adopting a presbyterial model of national church government, it was argued that lay and clergy, small and large churches and all regions of the Convention, plus all officiating organizations, were represented on the Council.[17]

The conclusion of the Northern Baptist advance to a full denominational status symbolically came in 1944 when the Convention authorized a national conference center at Green Lake, Wisconsin, and in 1947 when a Commission of Review was charged to 'canvass thoroughly the whole form of operation...looking toward a mighty future of our faith'.[18]

Historian Robert G. Torbet described this gradual evolution against local opposition as 'American Baptists Coming of Age' in his much-quoted *A History of the Baptists*.[19] For him, and many other pro-convention voices, American Baptists had achieved a functional polity and presence as a member of the American Protestant community.

From 1917 to the mid-1950s the Disciples of Christ ran a parallel course. Although the Louisville Plan was aborted, the General Christian Missionary Convention sessions it inaugurated did survive and these regular meetings became the focal point for general Disciples identity from 1871 to the formation of the International Convention of the

---

17 *Annual of the Northern Baptist Convention* (Philadelphia: American Baptist Publication Society, 1933), pp. 56-66.

18 *Yearbook of the American Baptist Convention* (Philadelphia: American Baptist Publication Society, 1950), pp. 153-72.

19 Torbet, *History*, p. 470.

Disciples of Christ in 1917. Although the substance of the General Conventions was fellowship and preaching, the Convention also provided a forum for championing the agencies that expanded the benevolent ministry of Disciples. These included the Foreign Christian Mission Society, Church Extension Fund, Board of Ministerial Relief, National Benevolent Association, Christian Women's Board of Missions and enthusiastic involvement in the interdenominational Young People's Society of Christian Endeavor.[20]

One of the major shifts in Disciples' polity occurred in the two year period 1917 to 1919 with the respective establishment of the International Convention of the Disciples of Christ and the United Christian Missionary Society. Inextricably linked, these twins met the concerns of egalitarian consent and review of denominational thrusts plus stable, consistent, integrated administration of Disciples' programs. As Garrison and DeGroot point out, 'the International Convention [represented] the will of the Disciples as an instrument for assessing their mind on brotherhood affairs and for directing the agencies that implement that mind in action'.[21] Its role was largely to review and provide a vehicle for popular ownership. On the other hand, the United Christian Missionary Society (UCMS) for a period between 1920 and 1940 enjoyed the status of an administrative umbrella for many of the tasks of the Disciples' Brotherhood. Not only was the structure concerned with missions *per se*, it also included in its four divisions church erection, the ministry, education, promotion, and finances and management.[22] Like the Baptists, Disciples placed a high regard in the 1920s on efficiency and good stewardship. To all intents and purposes this dual structure defined the Christian Church (Disciples of Christ) until the reorganization and renaming of the International Convention in 1956. Notable revisions were made as the Board of Higher Education and the Pension Fund withdrew from the UCMS to become separate entities, though each continued the reporting process to the International Convention.

General American religious trends also had an impact upon the Disciples. Most notable were the continual primitivist, local church protectionist, and later the quasi-fundamentalist movements which became loosely known as the Churches of Christ and the Independent Christian Churches respectively. As early as 1880 division among the Christian Churches was pronounced over organized societies and the use of instrumental music in worship services. By 1906 the degree of

---

20 McAllister and Tucker, *Journey*, pp. 268-271 and *passim*; in 1895 the General Convention became again the American Christian Missionary Society.

21 Winfred E. Garrison and Alfred T. Degroot, *The Disciples of Christ: A History* (St Louis, MO: Bethany Press, 1947), p. 527.

22 McAllister and Tucker, *Journey*, pp. 387-94.

disaffection was recognized in the religious census though each of the groups continued to claim a common heritage. Some leaders of the Christian Church (Disciples of Christ) persisted in believing that the 'non-cooperating brethren' were part of what was meant by the 'Brotherhood'. This retarded any full-scale move toward a unified ecclesial system until a later period.

Symbols of Denominational Identity

As the inevitable evolution of administrative structure and democratic representation moved forward through the first half of the twentieth century, two respective institutions within each group emerged to identify the maturation of both the Christian Churches and American Baptists. These were the establishment of the Disciples of Christ Historical Society and the National City Christian Church. For American Baptists, the American Baptist Historical Society and the National Headquarters Building served the same purpose. Each had a profound impact upon the image of its sponsoring group.

The Disciples of Christ Historical Society was established in 1941 by the International Convention following a report of its 1939 Historical Commission. At first the sole purpose of the organization was the collection and preservation of the historical materials of the Campbell–Stone movements and service as the official archives of the International Convention. Thus it identified with both the mainstream and dissenting traditions. By 1952 the Society was moved from Culver–Stockton College in Missouri to the Joint University Library community in Nashville, Tennessee, to facilitate greater use of its resources by graduate students. In 1957 the Thomas W. Phillips family (identified with the Independent Christian Church) provided a major gift to erect a handsome gothic building in Nashville to house not only the library and records, but also a museum and interpretive center for the Society.[23]

In the years since its founding the Disciples Historical Society has moved from a mere conservation function to a significant interpretive role primarily for the heritage and ministry of the Christian Church (Disciples of Christ). Without adequate recognition or support, it also provides significant historical resources for the other branches of the Campbell–Stone Movement, including the Churches of Christ and many of the Independent Christian churches which claim their origin in the restorationist tradition. Recognition of the value of the Historical Society's work primarily among Disciples, is perhaps most vividly seen in

---

23 *Directory of the Disciples of Christ* (St Louis, MO: Bethany Press, 1957), p. 51; Errett Gates, 'A Letter', *Discipliana* (January, 1973), p. 36.

its 'emerging fiscality': zero in 1941 to $1.3 million support by 1967, and in the circulation of its journal, *Discipliana*, now estimated at 6,000.[24]

For Disciples, the National City Christian Church in Washington, DC, is another tangible evidence of the faith and strength of the Brotherhood, and also, quietly, of the ecclesial maturity of the movement. Following the establishment of the mother congregation of the Christian Church in the nation's capital in 1844, congregational leaders in 1884 dedicated their edifice as a memorial to President James A. Garfield, a well-known Disciples minister. In 1930 an imposing new structure was erected just blocks from the White House 'to bear witness to the faith of Disciples where cross the crowded ways of both men and nations' in the 'nation's symbolic city'.[25]

While at first it appeared that this project was of interest primarily to the Washington congregation, in 1945, and again in the 1960s when the membership declined substantially, a national campaign was approved to raise funds to restore and maintain, through an endowment, the ministry of the church. A total of $150,000 was requested from ministers across the Brotherhood to sustain a witness in Washington which 'more than any other city in the land reflects the intelligence, the culture, the unity, and the hopes of America'.[26] In the 1960s, the potential membership of President Lyndon B. Johnson who visited the church from time to time, was an important incentive for the renewal of the congregation. As other groups like Baptists, Methodists, Episcopalians, Roman Catholics and Presbyterians created a symbolic national center for their identity and mission in the District of Columbia, so also Disciples joined the tradition of blending the ideals of civil religion with the 'hopes of prominent Disciples dating back to Alexander Campbell'.[27]

American Baptists have similarly looked for the appropriate symbols of a denominational culture. Their pilgrimage to found an historical society has been far less focused, but their long debate over a suitable denominational headquarters structure culminated in an attractive symbol of the polity of the denomination when the American Baptist Historical Society was founded in 1853 by missionary historians John Mason Peck and Howard Malcolm, with its charter to preserve and enjoy the historical memorabilia of the 'people called Baptists' and American Baptists in

---

24 David McWhirter, 'Historical Outline of the Disciples of Christ Historical Society', file paper, Disciples of Christ Historical Society [DCHS].

25 J. Edward Moseley, 'Attention, Ministers Only!', p. 2. Typescript circular dated August 1945, files, DCHS.

26 Moseley, 'Attention', p. 2; McAllister and Tucker, *Journey*, pp. 355-56.

27 Moseley, 'Attention', p. 1; Presbyterians built a national center in the 1950s; the Episcopal Church had nearly completed its 'National Cathedral', the Roman Catholic Church consecrated the National Shrine of the Immaculate Conception in 1959, for example.

particular. For about a century, the Society was limited to a small library on two seminary campuses serving mostly limited numbers of students. In 1961 the society became the Department of Archives and History of the American Baptist Convention, which placed it in the budget of the Convention, and in 1973 the board of the society became synonymous with the General Board of the denomination.[28]

While the historical community has generally accepted the value of the society's work and resources (it is now the official archives of the denomination with offices in Rochester, New York, and Valley Forge, Pennsylvania), the denominational leadership has not discovered its potential for heritage education and the creation of an adequate image. The society still suffers from being under funded, understaffed and unclear in its purposes and constituency. Moreover, it competes unfavorably both with enterprising program sections of the mission boards and with other more successful historical agencies in the wider Baptist community. This has greatly hindered its impact as an agency of Baptist heritage.

Much more successful than the American Baptist Historical Society in symbolizing American Baptist denominational and structural identity has been the Headquarters Building in Valley Forge, Pennsylvania. Following the renaming of the Convention in 1950, a prolonged debate arose in the next decade over what should be the program staff cooperation pattern of the various boards and agencies and where they should be located. At that time major offices were scattered in New York, Boston and Philadelphia and there was a desire to bring all of them together in a single location. In the annual convention meeting at Cincinnati in 1958, the delegates preferred Chicago with proximity to the historic Baptist university, combined with the facility of travel to both coasts. However, parliamentary maneuvering by members of the Board of Publication led to the unique design of a circular building with an historic address in Valley Forge, Pennsylvania.[29] Each of the separate major organizations would have all three stories to itself as interconnected arcs of a circle. Independent, yet interdependent (connected by corridors and glass partitions) the building took the name 'Statement in Stone' to symbolize the fundamental concerns of American Baptist polity. In the American Baptist popular mind, 'Valley Forge' connotes freedom (borrowed from the nearby Revolutionary War reservation), 'cooperation' (all the

---

28 'The American Baptist Historical Society—History and Purposes' (pamphlet, n.d.) in ABHS files; *Yearbook of the American Baptist Convention, 1961* (Philadelphia: American Baptist Publication Society, 1961), p. 70; *The Final Report of Study Commission on Denominational Structure of the American Baptist Convention* (Valley Forge, PA: American Baptist Convention, 1971), pp. 50-51.

29 'Cincinnati, 1958...Togetherness', *Crusader* 13 (Summer, 1958), p. 3; Brackney, *Baptist Life and Thought*, p. 387.

national agencies under a single roof) and 'centralization' of the ecclesiocracy (usually a negative factor of recognition).[30]

In different ways, then, both the Disciples and American Baptists have used heritage interpretation, architecture and geographic location to provide symbols for their denominational unities in diverse Free Church communities.

The Second Frontier: Regional Organization among American Baptists and Disciples

Another evidence of an emergent denominational identity among both American Baptists and Disciples is in the substructure of regional organizations. In both cases regional life developed as a response to particular needs, later adopting a new agenda that ultimately must be accounted for in the restructuring of both denominations in the 1960s and 70s.

Among American Baptists state organizations emerged from two circumstances. In the era of rapid denominational growth from 1815 to 1850 there was a two-pronged effort to organize Baptist congregations in each state east of the Mississippi. Some in the national society community wished to see such organizations as auxiliaries to their programs primarily for fund-raising purposes. The first state conventions were organized from 1821 to 1840 according to this design. Secondly, some of these groups were actually transformations of state-wide Baptist associations that originally had been confessional bodies but had a broad regional constituency. Among these were the Virginia and Philadelphia Associations. This early type of state convention raised funds, held annual fellowship and enrichment meetings, considered resolutions on social, political and sometimes ecclesiastical issues, and kept statistical records. Later, between 1850 and 1910, a third set of state conventions was intentionally organized by the American Baptist Home Mission Society (ABHMS) to coordinate new church development in the western territories. Initially, these organizations were the field offices of the ABHMS and the staff were paid missionaries. Eventually, those of all three types which survived would develop their own programs, budgets and staffing which would form ideally 'a bridge between local churches and the national organizational life'.[31]

The evolution of a regional leadership style symbolized a new era in American Baptist polity. A fundamental change occurred with the advent

---

30 'Statement in Stone' (printed commemorative booklet, American Baptist Convention, 1962).

31 Charles L. White, *A Century of Faith* (Philadelphia, PA: Judson Press, 1932), pp. 244-61.

of state convention secretaries. This role, previously an unpaid, part-time responsibility, usually designated 'corresponding secretary', became increasingly important in inter-society communications, fund-raising and new church development after 1880. Where a pastor or layman might have served in this capacity in the East or Ohio Valley regions, the norm for the western states was a full-fledged missionary appointee of the ABHMS. As a field staff employee of that organization, each made regular reports to the ABHMS regional secretaries and supervised missionary pastors and missionary collections in the churches. When the Northern Baptist Convention was organized in 1907, these staff persons from the states or territories became strategic members of the General Board of Promotion, the Council on Missionary Cooperation, and later, the General Council. Through representatives, they served on subsidiary Northern Baptist councils and administrative committees. Further, each of the state conventions and city societies elected not only lay and clergy delegates to the annual national meetings, but also to what had become their chief executive officers. This was the general pattern until denominational reorganization in 1972–76.

With the formation of the Northern Baptist Convention, national program organizations also made significant forays into regional life. The Home Mission Society and later the Council on Missionary Cooperation utilized field personnel to coordinate mission education programs and encourage denominational fundraising. Later in 1961 when the Division of World Mission Support of the American Baptist Convention was organized, these nationally-focused efforts were combined so that regional staff members had a dual role in the national Convention as well. With a continuing interest in self-identification, the regional ministers eventually organized themselves in 1974 as the Regional Executive Ministers Council and they were formally recognized as part of the national structure in 1976 with membership in the General (National) Staff Council.

Among the Disciples, a strong regional organizational life also emerged. The first regional organizations were conferences (usually annual) of Stonite ministers and Campbellite Baptist associations. Gradually, as the number of cooperating and sympathetic congregations increased, Alexander Campbell called for regular regional and state meetings. Local church delegates would meet to appoint and raise funds for traveling evangelists. A list of approved organizations for Bible distribution and other evangelical thrusts characterized Disciples' cooperation by 1850. On a state basis, Indiana was the first group of congregations to develop a statewide meeting in June 1839.[32]

---

32 Williams, *Ministry Among Disciples*, pp. 21-23.

Three states, Kentucky, Indiana and Arkansas, represent the diversity of regional polity evolution. In Kentucky the first general organization of the Disciples was the American Christian Bible Society, begun in 1845. Four years later, several Kentucky Disciples lent their enthusiastic support to the establishment of the national body, the American Christian Missionary Society. In 1850 a Kentucky auxiliary to the national group was launched to aid in promotion. This eventually became the Kentucky Christian Missionary Society or State Body of Disciples.[33]

Similar patterns may be seen in Indiana and Arkansas. In Indiana in the 1850s, Disciples added to their simple State Meeting, a home mission society and a special missionary board. The State Meeting provided fellowship, laid plans for the upcoming year and employed agents to raise funds and hold evangelistic rallies. Although attendance waned during the late 1850s and there was widespread apprehension over the authority of a State Meeting, the hiring of an effective full-time corresponding secretary in 1861 who traveled thousands of miles himself and organized seventy-three evangelists helped to ensure the future of state work.[34]

Arkansas represents the type of state development from the later nineteenth century. Although Disciples congregations had been started as early as 1832, there were no district 'cooperations' until 1880. At the impetus of the General Christian Missionary Convention, Arkansas Christian pastors began to collect statistical data and planned to hold a state missionary meeting in 1883. The Arkansas Christian Missionary Convention was thus formed to hold fellowship sessions, plan for new church development and promote the interests of the General Convention. Almost immediately, division arose over musical instruments, settled pastors and ecclesiastical organizations, and many of the Arkansas churches opted to follow the non-aligned 'Churches of Christ' pattern.[35] The continuing work of state bodies like Arkansas in the next decades would focus upon evangelism and missionary promotion.

The ill-fated Louisville Plan would have done much to have strengthened regional organizations at an early period. As indicated earlier, district representatives would have been accountable to the State Meeting that in turn would send representatives to the General Convention. When this plan failed, the state meetings or conventions did

---

33 Alonzo W. Fortune, *The Disciples in Kentucky* (Lexington, KY: Convention of Christian Churches in Kentucky, 1932), p. 346.

34 Henry K. Shaw, *Hoosier Disciples: A Comprehensive History of the Christian Church (Disciples of Christ) in Indiana* (St Louis, MO: Bethany Press, 1966), p. 173.

35 Lester G. McAllister, *Arkansas Disciples: A History of the Christian Church (Disciples of Christ) in Arkansas* (n.p., 1984), p. 195. This work is one of the few up to date original studies. Far too little is known, and almost no published works exist, for this significant part of church life.

meet regularly (usually annually) as gatherings of delegates and pastors from the local churches. Special agents or corresponding secretaries collected funds for both the larger mission of the Disciples and local and state needs. Thus a pattern was born where state organizations became the clearinghouses for evangelistic and other forms of benevolence by collecting monies directly from the churches. A portion of the income obviously went to cover small overhead and salary expenses. Often when opposition set in to this arrangement, the state meeting or convention leaders took the position that only contributing churches and individuals were entitled to membership in the organization, thus effectively disenfranchizing those dissident churches that criticized incorporation.[36]

An example of highly successful regional development among the Disciples occurred in Indiana between 1875 and 1920. Disciples were numerous in the state (third behind Illinois and Kentucky) and their benevolent programs were extensive, including a State Women's Board of Missions, a Ministerial Association, a Sunday School Association and Butler University. Moreover, in the US presidential campaign of 1880, James A. Garfield's election brought much publicity to the Disciples movement in Indiana. To manage all of its concerns, the Indiana Christian Missionary Convention meeting of 1871 divided the state into five missionary districts and large sums were raised for missions, evangelism and building construction. By 1878 the annual meeting of the State Convention became the combined meeting of the Women's, Sunday School and Ministerial Association, with nearly a thousand people in attendance for preaching, reports and a picnic.[37] Eventually this type of growth, and particularly the organizational generosity of the Christian Women's Board of Mission, would lead to Indiana's becoming the new national center for Brotherhood life, as Henry Shaw termed it.[38]

Against the fears of some that a strong regional organization would lead to self-sufficiency, gradual progress was made both internally and as part of the larger connection among the state bodies. In 1930 the National Association of State Secretaries was formed to coordinate the interests of regional staffs. As steps were taken to modify the national bodies in the 1940s and 1950s, so also unification of staffs, programs and state auxiliary organizations took place. Willard Wickizer eventually observed in the 1960s that the primary purpose of state bodies should be to provide practically all services to the local churches, which increased both their visibility and financial needs.[39] As the regional units were purposely drawn into Restructure in the 1970s, tension predictably

---

36   McAllister, *Arkansas Disciples*, p. 100.
37   Shaw, *Hoosier Disciples*, pp. 204-206.
38   Shaw, *Hoosier Disciples*, p. 468.
39   Willard Wickizer, 'Ideas for brotherhood Restructure', in W.B. Blakemore (ed.), *The Revival of the Churches* (St Louis, MO: Bethany Press, 1963), pp. 117-19.

occurred as regional needs competed with national/general priorities for limited financial resources. While regional executive ministers felt a partnership in decision-making with the General Church, regional (and by implication, local) priorities yet await a clear definition of their relevance to the overall structure and program.[40]

From Denomination to Ecclesiality

In the process of organizational self-assessment, something larger had transpired among Baptists and Disciples, namely the growing sense of ecclesiality or 'churchliness'. In part this has happened as people, churches and organizations have worked together; in part it is also a product of participation in ecumenical endeavor, especially as Disciples and Northern Baptists took a long hard look at each other in merger conversations in the 1950s. The process of review and evaluation is therefore of critical importance for understanding the evolution of structure among Baptists and Disciples.

Disciples and American Baptists have approached their respective needs to evaluate the success of their organizations and mission in different ways. The Baptists have relied regularly and heavily upon internal review committees and later consultants from various non-theological perspectives. Disciples, in contrast, have created program objectives on a multi-year basis which have produced definite structural modifications and new directions. In recent years, programs have regularly been evaluated not just by administrators, but by teams of theologians and educators as well.

As noted earlier, Northern/American Baptists revised their polity and structure in the 1930s and again in 1950, 1961 and 1972. The most recent review prior to 1970 was actually a twelve-year process 1950–61 which modified the senior administrative and committee levels in the national program community. Prior to World War II, the chief concern was for adequate promotion and the development of a general, national effort. The constant critique of conservative and fundamentalist factions from 1920 to 1945 hampered serious attempts to forge any sort of national ecclesial structure which might have diminished the autonomy of local congregations. In this twenty-five year period approximately 1,000 congregations disaffiliated with another 500–600 churches unresponsive to the convention's overtures and programs.[41]

---

40 Based upon an unnamed 'Regional Ministers' Report to Regional Board 6-12-88', pp. 3-5, in my possession.
41 Torbert, *History*, pp. 435-36; W.H. Brackney; *The Baptists* (Westport, CT: Greenwood Press, 1988), pp. 31-32.

Disciples and Baptists

With a new generation of leaders like Luther W. Smith, Edwin Dahlberg, Reuben Nelson and Roy Madsen, Northern Baptists significantly changed their course in the post-war years. Utilizing what would become a regular review commission process (prominent lay persons with external consultants, all appointed by the Convention presidents) successive structural changes were made in the interests of 'efficiency for mission', growth of a national identity and conciliar control of nominations and general denominational decisions. What emerged by the 1970s was about as highly an integrated decision-making process as independently incorporated societies could allow.

The work of the 1948–1950 Commission of Review produced recommendations which ranged from changing the name from the regional 'Northern' to the American Baptist Convention (an historical signal to other US Baptists), the elevation of the corresponding secretary to an executive general secretary with platform skills, to a thoroughgoing revision of collection policies among the state and city organizations which then retained too much of what each collected prior to payment of national commitments. Perhaps the most important of the changes in 1950 was the new procedure for amendment of the by-laws only after recommendation of the General Council and reference to a 'law committee'.[42] This doubtless came in response to the repeated attempts of theologically conservative elements to alter radically the Convention's directions.

The impetus for structural review begun in the post-war years continued in the 1950s. One of the long-term problems in American Baptist missionary organization was the separation of women's home and foreign societies from their historic counterparts, ABFMS and ABHMS. As early as 1910 discussions were held seeking cooperation, but not until 1954 did positive results ensue. On the sesquicentennial anniversary of the Baptist missions movement, the officers of the two women's societies and the original mission agencies voted to integrate their work, to become effective from 1955.[43] The spirit of this merger was in keeping with the general trend toward organizational streamlining.

At the same time as the planning for the mission society integrations, the General Council in 1953 commissioned the American Institute of Management to do a thorough inventory of all American Baptist Convention organizational life. Then General Secretary, Reuben E. Nelson, explained that this was necessary 'in order to get a just and

---

42 *Annual of the American Baptist Convention* (1950), pp. 153-72.
43 *Yearbook of the American Baptist Convention* (Philadelphia: American Baptist Publication Society, 1955), pp. 64-72; Robert G. Torbet, *Venture of Faith: The Story of the American Baptist Foreign Mission Society and the Woman's American Baptist Foreign Mission Society, 1814-1954* (Philadelphia, PA: Judson Press, 1955), tells the story in narrative form.

neutral picture of our operations'. Initially, the report found that the management practices of religious organizations were 'appallingly archaic' and several structural modifications were proposed to bring about 'greater managerial efficiency within democratic action'.[44] It actually took about six years to move some of the changes through the Convention. In 1955 initial steps were taken to broaden the supervisory role of the General Council, increase the number of staff to the General Secretary and to clarify the role of the General Council Executive Committee. By 1961 further changes were made in the composition of boards, agencies and the General Council to ensure that the Council became the integrating force in all Convention bodies; further the Council fostered a 'family relationship' where the still relatively independent parts of Convention life were brought into closer accountability like the American Baptist Historical Society, the divisions of men's and women's work and various educational agencies. For the most part these groups were either attached to the Office of the General Secretary, or the Board of Education and Publication, or dropped from Convention support.[45] By 1962 when all of the offices of the national programs were moved to the Headquarters Building in Valley Forge, Pennsylvania, American Baptists had created the maximum amount of organizational interlocking possible without vacating historic corporate charters. The changes in this era were influenced mainly by progressive business models with little formal theological reflection. That would wait yet another decade.

In contrast to the Baptists, the process of denominational review and restructure among Disciples may be seen best as a function of a series of (usually) decennial programs which the church leadership proposed from time to time, and the respective outcomes. In sequence, there were the Men and Millions Movement (1913–1919), the Crusade for a Christian World [Order] (1947–1950), the Decade of Decision (1960–1970), and the Committee for 1970 and Beyond (1970–75).[46] Each of these programs provided the Brotherhood with a common set of goals, measurable objectives and a review process that was far-reaching. Additionally, each produced a sense of ecclesial flexibility beyond the

---

44 Paul M. Harrison, *Authority and Power in the Free Church Tradition: A Social Case Study of the American Baptist Convention* (Princeton: Princeton University Press, 1959), pp. 5, 91.

45 *Yearbook of the American Baptist Convention* (Philadelphia: American Baptist Publication Society, 1961), pp. 70-74.

46 Spencer P. Austin, 'Digest of Long Range Programs Among Disciples of Christ' (Correspondence Papers, Disciples of Christ Files, Archives of the National Council of Churches of Christ, PHS). Austin combines the five biennial emphases between 1950 and 1960 into a category called 'Long Range Program'. At times the word 'order' is used, at other times it was omitted.

routine administrative channels and each gave impetus to the next logical stage of denominational development.

The Men and Millions Movement was basically an outgrowth of the Christian Church's missionary experience in China. In 1912, a group of Disciples missionaries and board personnel reported that the Chinese mission was desperate for equipment and additional personnel. This led to plans to raise $200,000 in five years for China, followed by a businessmen's compact to provide $1 million. Finally, in 1913 a Brotherhood-wide campaign sought $6.3 million for missions, benevolence, education and the campaign expenses.

The Men and Millions Movement, though interrupted by World War I, became the first national crusade for the Christian Church and a significant force in unifying the Brotherhood. An every member canvas was developed to reach the financial goal, with the futuristic idea in mind that general stewardship would be increased permanently after the campaign. Planners also promoted a 'Joint Budget' for every local church, which greatly facilitated the collection and projection of resources. Finally, the administration and disbursement of 'Men and Millions' called into being an organizationally-representative Executive Committee which fostered inter-agency cooperation and a Businessmen's Commission to allot the funds received for education.[47] This latter group comprised the significant lay leadership of the Brotherhood. State organizations insured the overall success of the Men and Millions drive. Teams of fifteen to twenty select persons per state coordinated the efforts with no public appeals or mass meetings to receive funds. During 1918, when institutional resources hit their lowest ebb, the Executive Committee called for a War Emergency Drive which successfully forestalled bankruptcy for several Disciples Colleges. In the end, 2,342 persons pledged a total of $5.5 million to Men and Millions, meeting the matching gift promised by R.A. Long at the Toronto Convention.[48] Perhaps the greatest achievement of the campaign was not financial, but structural. More Disciples than ever before had participated in an effort which had educated the constituency to its potential.

From an historical perspective, Men and Millions had a profound impact upon the Christian Church (Disciples of Christ). In a major way, the United Christian Missionary Society (1920) was born out of the cooperative effort in missions and need for coordinated administration. The International Convention was given greater impetus by the successful completion of the campaign. Five troubled Christian Church periodicals were combined in the new *World Call*, first published in 1919. The Men

---

47 *Report of the Men and Millions Movement 1913-1919* (Pamphlet, DCHS), p. 8.
48 *Report of the Men and Millions Movement 1913-1919*, p. 5.

and Millions crusade had produced in the Disciples a truly national and coordinated sense of identity.

The Crusade for a Christian World [Order] grew out of the international social and political agenda at the conclusion of World War II. Manifestly it reflected Christian cooperation at every level, even as the United Nations generated political cooperation among the Western powers. An early position paper for the crusade declared, 'We shall succeed or fail...in breathing the spirit of life into the letter of the Charter of the United Nations as we are able...to vitalize thought and action at the level of the local parish.'[49]

While the theologically progressive elements of the Christian Church (Disciples) found in the crusade an opportunity to promote ecumenism through the Federal and World Councils and issues of peace and social renewal, more traditional leaders saw yet another agenda. Programs were arranged to start two hundred churches, to hold effective Sunday Schools, recruit and train a new generation of ministers, create renewal strategies for rural churches and modernize facilities of church related institutions. When the crusade concluded in April 1951, over $8 million (the goal was $14 million) had been raised and genuine revitalization of local, regional and national Disciples' ministry could be demonstrated.[50] All of this lacked the contextual feature of the Chinese mission which had been at the heart of consciousness raising in the Men and Millions movement.

Once again, the post-crusade planning process had a bearing upon the Christian Churches in the next decade. The success of numerous agencies working together during the three year crusade urged the conviction that more integral cooperation of the national societies was needed. In 1949, delegates to the International Convention authorized a Council of Agencies, representing every group reporting to the Convention; the purpose of this council was 'to make more effective the corporate life of the Brotherhood'. This goal took definite shape as a series of biennial emphases for the next decade; each of the major denominational interests benefitted. In the end, the Council on Agencies succeeded in blending the long-range planning and stewardship processes of all Brotherhood organizations. In recognition of greater structural and spiritual unity, in 1956 the International Convention of Disciples of Christ changed its name to Christian Churches (Disciples of Christ), and greatly expanded the role of the Convention office to include all public relations, ecumenical activity and the annual assembly.[51]

By 1955, the Disciples leadership was already beginning to focus on the 1960s, and this eventually produced yet another decennial emphasis,

---

49   'The Crusade for a Christian World Order' (typescript paper, DCHS files), p. 18.
50   *Christian Evangelist*, April 25 1951, p. 399.
51   McAllister and Tucker, *Journey*, p. 414.

the Decade of Decision. This new effort utilized twenty-two 'listening conferences' across the country to determine the mindset of the Brotherhood and it was the first time that a major national program was presented for review to the state secretaries. With a comprehensive foundation laid by 1958, a distinguished committee of men like Dale Fiers, Willard Wickizer and Gaines Cook was assigned by the Council of Agencies the task of bringing the 'Advance of the Christian Church (Disciples of Christ) for the Decade of Decision 1960–1970' to full fruition.

The goal of the Decade of Decision included adoption of a ten year promotional strategy, a full statement of capital needs across the Brotherhood, a stepped up stewardship campaign, correlation of new church development, recruitment for Christian vocations and the Churches in Transition program. Significantly, every agency—state, regional and national—was to make a full commitment to the Decade of Decision. In order to reach the goals, the Coordinating Committee arranged scores of training conferences which involved ministers and lay persons at work in local churches across the United States.[52]

On a separate but related track to the Decade of Decision, the prominent national leaders of the Disciples were also working during the 1960s on a long-range restructuring plan which would unify the entire program community of the national level, integrate the regional bodies and create for the first time a true sense of 'church'. One of the results of the listening conferences preparatory to the Decade of Decision had been the widespread feeling that restructure was needed, so the Council on Agencies responded by naming a Study Commission on Brotherhood Structure, to be chaired by Willard Wickizer, also a prominent personality in the management of the Decade of Decision program. When the Wickizer Study Commission report was accepted by the International Convention in 1960 (it called for a formal restructure process), the churches knew that the Decade of Decision meant more than just a new decennial program emphasis. The parent of change had indeed become the child itself!

New Structures and New Churches

Through the decade of the 1960s American Baptists continued their search for a more unified polity, a style which would include others of like mind. One of the significant advances in polity during this era was the acceptance of dually-aligned congregations as members of the

---

52 'How Came the Decade of Decision?' (typescript historical paper, DCHS files), p. 4.

American Baptist Convention. This measure helped to diversify the predominantly white membership with black and ethnic churches, though their first loyalty has been to their original alliances.[53]

Within the Convention, however, there was still the concern over independence of the societies and the unclear relationships for the state and city organizations. Some also held that while the General Council was representative of all the organizations in the American Baptist Convention, local churches expressed a sense of disenfranchisement. Finally, many leaders pressed for a completion of the 1961 process that seemed to point to full integration of the societies.

In 1968 the Convention authorized the creation of a Study Commission on Denominational Structures (SCODS) that was charged to review all American Baptist Convention organizations, not being limited to existing patterns. Norman R. DePuy, *American Baptist* editor, described the end of the century task as 'an attempt to get the fat out of administration, inertia out of mission, muscle into our money and people into our polity'.[54] In actuality, in the final report in 1972 SCODS recommended the most radical structural changes in the history of American Baptist life. The foundation of the plan created a national election district process of laymen, laywomen and clergy gathered as a General Board with full legislative powers; this met the longstanding Baptist concern for 'democratic decision-making'. The General Board would have a dual role as the collectivization of the national program boards (the former societies) and would conduct specific program reviews as well as oversee general concerns. Election districts replaced the historic associational patterns from region to region. The national annual conventions were superseded by a Biennial Meeting whose purpose was fellowship, inspiration and final action on by-laws revisions. In response to the criticism that SCODS was creating a presbyterial, connectional executive system of governance, the General Secretary's office was relieved of all program responsibilities and the name of the denomination was changed from Convention to 'American Baptist Churches in the USA' (ABCUSA). The latter came only after a national survey whereby it was determined that SCODS must reverse recent trends and 'accept and build upon the local church as the constituency of the denomination'.[55] Having arrived at the point of a fully integrated ecclesiology, the

---

53 *Annual of the American Baptist Convention*, 1965, pp. 525-26. The dual alignment movement was a response to the formation of the black Progressive National Baptist Convention in 1961. This body was founded on the basis of cooperation with other Baptist bodies.

54 *Report of the Study Commission on Denominational Structures* (Valley Forge, PA: American Baptist Publication Society, 1972), p. 2 [hereafter cited as *SCODS Report*].

55 *SCODS Report*, pp. 9, 57-59.

ratifying convention opted for a symbolic affirmation of local congregations.

It took only two years for the regional leaders of the new American Baptist Churches, USA to determine that SCODS had pertained primarily to national polity. Still, their relationship to the new structure was unclear. Consequently, in 1974 the Biennial Meeting authorized a Study Commission on Relationships (SCOR) to create the appropriate plan of relationships for the region, state and city organizations to participate fully in the ABCUSA. By 1976 SCOR recommended that each regional organization establish a covenant with the national ABCUSA, that new regional names be adopted (e.g. 'American Baptist Churches in the Central Region') and that regional executive ministers become also Associate National Secretaries who meet regularly with National Secretaries in a General Staff Council. In return, the regions would be guaranteed up to 55% return on all funds collected for United Mission Budget purposes within a given region.[56]

Alongside SCODS and SCOR was a third review process, the Study of Administrative Areas and Relationships (SAAR) which from 1962 to 1968 worked on a modification of regional life. SAAR was laid aside until after SCODS completed its work on national revision; ultimately many of its proposals were informally folded into the SCOR. Essentially, SAAR's purpose was to reduce the number of regional organizations from fifty to fifteen, and eliminate promotional duplication between national and regional interests by creating one staff in each region to promote national, regional and local concerns.[57] The anxiety among regional executives over the radical implications of SAAR created a new influence bloc, the Regional Executive Ministers Council in 1976, which continues to preserve the integrity of regional interests. Ironically, as of 1988, 75% of SAAR's proposed regional combinations have been achieved through budgetary reductions and the continuing concern over stewardship of personnel resources. In essence, SAAR is a dormant reminder of what the future must hold for American Baptist regional life.

In the wake of SCODS, SCOR and SAAR, American Baptists still struggle with an overly national emphasis in their polity, a representative process which somewhat artificially reflects the constituency, and a widespread feeling among clergy that the denomination has disenfranchised them.

The Restructure Process for the Disciples of Christ was equally far-reaching and in many ways a more clearly-defined evolution. Guided by

---

56   *The Report and Recommendation of the Study Commission on Relationships of the American Baptist Churches in the U.S.A.* (Valley Forge, PA: n.p., 1976), pp. 150-51, 224.

57   'Study of Administrative Areas and Relationships' (Typescript, Office of the ABC General Secretary, August 1968), p. 6.

what Anthony Dunnavant has termed 'restoration, unity, liberty and mission',[58] the shapers of the new church adopted a new doctrine of the church which was to be manifest at congregational, regional and general levels. Built into the provisional design were lessons learned from previous eras: feedback from listening conferences among the regions, and in-depth theological reflection and study on the theology, polity and heritage of Disciples by a Panel of Scholars and later the Association of Disciples for Theological Discussion.

Foundational to the new design for the Christian Church was a bicameral decision-making process involving church delegates in a biennial General Assembly and a programmatically and regionally representative General Board, the core of which functions as an executive or administrative committee. Through a series of covenantal relationships, program agencies of the International Convention became administrative units of the new church, twenty in number.[59] Significantly, the black National Christian Missionary Convention voted to join with the Provisional Design for the Christian Church one year after its near unanimous adoption at Kansas City in 1968. To the credit of those who shepherded 'Restructure' into reality, leadership played a significant and symbolic role. The first moderator of the Provisional Assembly was Ronald Osborn, perhaps the most articulate theologian of the 1960s; A. Dale Fiers served as the first general minister and president, having been intimately involved in the entire 'Restructure' process; Kenneth L. Teegarden, an outstanding regional minister, was permanently installed in that office in 1973. Delegates to the early general assemblies made important racial/ethnic and gender statements by electing as moderators a well-known black pastor and a laywoman. As a result of 'Restructure', the Christian Church (Disciples of Christ) had advanced to both a theological and structural unity far beyond what its nineteenth-century leaders allowed, but one which reflected some of the lost vision of Alexander Campbell.

Restructure for the Christian Church (Disciples of Christ) and American Baptists has not been accomplished without major and continuing dissent. American Baptists have absorbed a steady loss of membership and churches, obfuscated only by claiming large numbers of dually-aligned African–American congregations. The establishment of a centralized personnel placement system, recognition of quasi-episcopacy functions for regional executive ministers, and overwhelming budgetary inflation have proved too much for several hundred churches. In a planned five year review of SCODS and SCOR in 1982, another

---

58   Anthony L. Dunnavant, 'The Restructure of the Christian Church (Disciples of Christ) in the Light of Historic disciples Emphases' (PhD dissertation, Vanderbilt University, 1982).
59   McAllister and Tucker, *Journey*, pp. 449-50.

Denominational Review Commission identified regional competition with national bodies, bureaucratization, clergy disenfranchisement, and the lack of democratic decision-making as the principal issues confronting the denomination in the wake of reorganization as the American Baptist Churches in the USA.[60]

Likewise, the Disciples have a continuing debate. Beginning with the 'Atlanta Declaration' of 1967, 'loyal' leaders have dissented on the issue of lost freedom, local church autonomy, latent ecclesiasticism and the replacement of 'brotherhood' with authoritarianism.[61] During the 1970s the overall membership statistics have declined and with them the financial means to operate at the level anticipated in programs like 'Committee for 1970 and Beyond'.[62] With 'Restructure' firmly in place, Disciples theologians are now making every effort to move the Christian Church away from its early motifs of 'restoration' and individualism to a theology of community and fellowship.[63] Seemingly, their hope is to diminish the relevance of numerical decline by strengthening the bonds of ecclesiality.

Conclusions

Several conclusions may be drawn directly or by implication from this study. They are relevant not only to the two groups which are the subject of this study, but also to other Free Church polities in the mosaic of American Protestantism.

1. Disciples, like American Baptists, recognize the local congregation as the 'fundamental unit' of their identity. All of the structural and ecclesiological modifications notwithstanding, this is still pragmatically

---

60   'Report of the ABC Commission on Denominational Review' (Typescript files, ABC General Secretary's office); Minutes of the Regional Executive Minister's Council, 1984–1986 (Archives, American Baptist Historical Society). Other than a Commission on Life and Theology (COLT), there is little theological reflection inherent in these changes.

61   *Atlanta Declaration of Convictions and Concerns, with Commentary Authorized by the Atlanta Progress Committee* (file copy, DCHS), pp. 1-3; 'Freedom or Restructure: An Open Letter to Christian Churches and Churches of Christ' (Indianapolis: Committee for the Preservation of the Brotherhood, n.d.), p. 9; 'The Truth about Restructure: A Second Open Letter' (Indianapolis: Committee for the Preservation of the Brotherhood, n.d.), pp. 20-23.

62   'Report No. 41—The Committees for 1970 and Beyond', in *Yearbook and Directory—Christian Church (Disciples of Christ)* (St Louis, MO: Bethany Press, 1968), pp. 46-50.

63   W. Clark Gilpin, 'The Integrity of the Church: The Communal Theology of Disciples of Christ', in Kenneth Lawrence (ed.), *Classic Themes of Disciples Theology* (Fort Worth, TX: Texas Christian University Press, 1986), pp. 29-32.

the case. Historically both groups have struggled with the independence of the congregations versus the theological and sociological meaning of extra-parish organizations. Neither figured out quickly what was the nature of authority beyond the churches. Power was exercised by the societies and later the conventions on the basis of an annual consensus of interested advocates.

2. Leadership with a progressive perspective has been a key element in modernization and structural evaluation. At the turn of the twentieth century, there was a coterie of gifted persons who developed strategies to build national and regional structures which resembled other mainstream Protestant bodies. There were always a few who knew where the future lay.

3. The development of a denominational self-understanding at different times for each group, was an initial important step in the evolution of a full ecclesiality. Baptists and Disciples were greatly hindered in their advance to this status by anti-modernization factions within each family. Symbolic gestures like the establishment of historical agencies or the shape of a headquarters building were important statements about the maturation of denominations.

4. Regional development in both cases has provided an important link between national, general evolution and the bedrock of local congregations. The regions themselves have evolved as a substructure and have demanded recognition in the ecclesial identity. Uncertain financial resources have placed boundaries on the development of regional identities.

5. The radical restructure process which both denominations experienced between 1958 and 1972 reflected a common desire to be a 'church'. But the fundamental question still exists as to whether congregations in a Free Church polity are energized by ecclesiality or the mission imperatives which initially brought into being the organizational structure. Disciples have been far more theologically reflective about this issue than have American Baptists, but both groups have yet to develop fully a sense of ecclesiality in their local churches.

6. Lacking a biblically or historically well-defined structure, Disciples have spent large amounts of their time, energy and financial resources debating and studying what the appropriate structure should be. American Baptists have run a similar course. At times it would appear that structure became an end in itself, with mission and local church renewal as lesser priorities. Ironically, just as ecclesiality has been achieved, vitality has declined in line with other mainstream American denominations; leaders speak of the need to experience a renewal movement, which is precisely the point at which both the Christian Church (Disciples of Christ) and American Baptists originated.

CHAPTER 8

Making Too Little and Too Much of Baptism?

Brian Haymes

Baptism remains one of those important issues over which Christians do not agree. Detailed learned studies and important ecumenical consensus statements still cannot bring the church to a shared mind and practice. There seems little likelihood of that situation changing, given the way the issues are usually addressed.

In 1996 a group of British Baptists published a collection of papers under the general title of *Reflections on the Water*.[1] The contributors were not of one mind on all the issues they tried to address but their hope was that by looking at baptism again Baptists, as well as others, might be able to go beyond some entrenched positions which frustrate further growth towards unity.

All six contributors are committed to the search for Christian unity and honour those British Baptists who have played a significant part in national, European and international councils of churches.[2] Baptists understand the grounding of this ecumenical commitment in the divine call to mission, the will of Christ and the fundamental doctrine of the one holy catholic and apostolic church. With Jürgen Moltmann the contributors do not think that unity brings salvation but that the church, living in the salvation of God, both receives and experiences unity.[3] Thus the quest for unity is no optional extra to the life of the church, as if it

---

1   P.S. Fiddes (ed.), *Reflections on the Water: Understanding God and the World through the Baptism of Believers* (Regent's Park College Study Guides, 4; Macon, GA: Smyth & Helwys/Oxford: Regent's Park College, Oxford, 1996). The contributors are Christopher Ellis, Paul Fiddes, Roger Hayden, Brian Haymes, Richard Kidd and Hazel Sherman, with a response by Christopher Rowland.
2   John Briggs is another outstanding example of this tradition.
3   J. Moltmann, *The Open Church: Invitation to a Messianic Lifestyle* (London: SCM Press, 1978), p. 116.

were a module on the margins of the real theology course. Rather, the ecumenical challenge is a call for the church to be the church of Jesus Christ in the power of the Spirit. To any who say that being part of the ecumenical movement is an inevitable compromise, the contributors argue, first, that participating in the journey towards unity is a matter of obedience to Christ and, second, the paradox is that by participating they have come to appreciate all the more the insights of their own tradition. They would claim that their sense of Baptist identity has grown because they have had to test it in the ecumenical context. Baptism, however, remains one of the crucial issues.

In any case, none of the six contributors believes that the Baptist tradition is so complete that we should simply wait for others to see the light and return to the true faith. There is properly a provisionality about all ecclesiologies, including the Baptist. Hence they had no desire wilfully to bring a conflictual attitude of mind to discussion on these matters. It is precisely because, with ecumenical discussion partners, Baptists cannot or will not move beyond historic positions that the arguments go on as they do, almost as if there were sides and one had to win all the prizes. The contributors therefore took the risk of putting their heads above the denominational parapet in the hope that there might be new things to see. They knew perfectly well that, as the debate about baptism had been presented, the solution to the problem was beyond them, assuming the issue to be the reconciling of two or more modes of baptism. But are there ways of keeping the debate going, even of creatively recasting the questions? And are the accepted questions the right ones anyway? The concern in *Reflections on the Water* was to pursue the theology of believers' baptism as the Baptists understand and practise it, in the knowledge of what others are saying and doing. Can Baptists, in fact, develop their own baptismal understanding beyond simply repeating the valued but ancient ways?

To summarise the volume's affirmations, it begins by looking at baptism as a sacrament. Generally Baptists have been cautious of this word.[4] By downplaying any suggestion of the work of God in baptism they have often offered a very human centred understanding of baptism, emphasising the new candidate bearing public witness to her or his faith. The contributors to *Reflections on the Water* argue that God is active in

---

4   For a full discussion of this matter see A.R. Cross, *Baptism and the Baptists: Theology and Practice in Twentieth-Century Britain* (Studies in Baptist History and Thought; Carlisle; Paternoster Press 2000), and Stanley K. Fowler, *More Than a Symbol: The British Baptist Recovery of Baptismal Sacramentalism* (Studies in Baptist History and Thought; Carlisle; Paternoster Press 2002). Also see the forthcoming collection of essays from the Baptist perspective on the various dimensions and understanding of sacrament, A.R. Cross and P.E. Thompson (eds.), *Baptist Sacramentalism* (Studies in Baptist History and Thought; Carlisle: Paternoster, 2002).

baptism and that in this sense it is sacramental. This does not mean that the church controls the grace of God and determines the channels of the divine operation for what happens in baptism is an expression of the freedom of God.[5]

Baptism, it is argued, is a lens through which we might see and share the life and mission of God. Baptism in water relates to five important motifs: birth, cleansing, conflict, refreshment and journey. These find focus in baptism but expand the meaning of God's salvation by evoking experiences connected with these motifs in everyday life.[6] Far from baptism being a closed ecclesiastical event, it is about living in the creative redemptive work of God in the world of nature and human community. This seriously qualifies the individualism which has often been a dominant way of viewing believers' baptism.[7] So it is argued that baptism is a political event, in the sense that an owner is named and a new community shared.[8] By confessing that Jesus Christ is Lord and becoming part of a community whose life is shaped by the constant retelling of his story in the fellowship of the Holy Spirit, the church becomes an alternative society, with different values befitting the resident aliens who are exiles seeking the good of the city in which they presently live. The incarnational, sacramental, communitarian nature of baptism makes it a political event.

The contributors tried to reflect on baptism and the boundaries of the church. Frankly, here they had the greatest difficulty and internal disagreements. We shall take up this issue later, but they did agree together that, theologically, the affirmation of the centre of the church's life in the triune God is more important than the boundaries the church might find it appropriate to impose. That led to a chapter that asked why it is important that we are baptised into the name of the triune God. The answer given stresses that, again far from baptism being an individual or

---

5   A crucial theme in early Baptist thought but not so commonly expressed today. See Philip Thompson, *The Freedom of God: Towards Baptist Theology in Pneumatological Perspective* (Studies in Baptist History and Thought; Carlisle: Paternoster, forthcoming). This is a revised version of his doctoral thesis, 'Toward Baptist Ecclesiology in Pneumatological Perspective' (PhD thesis, Emory University, 1995).

6   P.S. Fiddes, 'Introduction: Reflections on the Water', in Fiddes (ed.), *Reflections*, p. 3. See Fiddes' essay, 'Baptism and Creation', pp. 47-67.

7   While appreciating W.B. Shurden's study, *The Baptist Identity; Four Fragile Freedoms* (Macon, GA: Smyth & Helwys, 1993), it seems to me to overstress the issue of individual freedom and does not say enough about the corporate accountablitiy within the church as members one of another. Perhaps he is writing in a context where such freedom is being questioned.

8   B. Haymes, 'Baptism as a Political Event', in Fiddes (ed.), *Reflections*, pp. 69-83.

even limited ecclesial event baptism is into the life and mission of God. 'The language of Trinity is not a remote speculation, but the way we talk about our experience of a God of super abundance, a God who is always breaking boundaries.'[9]

It may well be that to those outside the Baptist circles all this might amount to a very small offering. At last, some British Baptists have discovered the meaning and gift of sacrament! Eventually they have begun to recognise the social implications of Christian existence and the critical importance of the Trinity! Maybe so.[10] However, the contributors were not looking for a theological fight so much as to walk a different way in hope of seeing new possibilities. They know the old conflictual models, with their temptations to feelings of superiority, and that they do not work because they have been tried and found ecumenically wanting. What really is at stake in these baptismal controversies?

In this connection another document from British Baptists, this time published by the Doctrine and Worship Committee of the Baptist Union of Great Britain, merits attention. It is entitled *Believing and Being Baptized: Baptism, so-called re-baptism and children in the church*.[11] As partners in the World Council of Churches (WCC), Baptists are aware of the call for all churches to consider 'a way for the mutual recognition of each other's baptism'. Could we recognise a 'common baptism' that then might be understood to be the 'focus of unity' for the church and the world? In British local ecumenical partnerships the issue of baptism and rebaptism remains painful. Moreover, all this discussion sharpens the question of boundaries and, in particular for Baptists, the place of the child in the church.[12] The ecumenical hope in the World Council of Churches' call was that if we can be clear about the mutual recognition of one another's forms of baptism then we might move to the other issues of ecclesiology and ministry. Hence the understandable emphasis on mutual recognition of baptism and the desire for baptism to be viewed as the foundational basis for unity.

It might be thought, at this point, following the WCC train of thought, that the problem for Baptists is simply whether or not they could

---

9 Fiddes, 'Introduction', p. 5. See H. Sherman, 'Baptized—"in the Name of the Father and of the Son and of the Holy Spirit"', pp. 101-16.

10 The contributors would argue that they are only bringing to light some themes that have been part of the Baptist understanding of baptism but may have been down played in more recent years. See Cross, *Baptism, passim*, and Folwer, *More Than a Symbol, passim*.

11 *Believing and Being Baptized: Baptism, so-called re-baptism and children in the church* (Didcot: Baptist Union Doctrine and Worship Committee, 1996).

12 An Anglican response to *Reflections on the Water* by Christopher Rowland raised the question of children in the church, 'A Response: Anglican Reflections', pp. 117-34.

in *Jesus and the Spirit*.[19] His case is that Christian initiation, in the New Testament, involved conversion, baptism and receiving the Holy Spirit. These three 'events' do not have to happen in any particular chronological order but together they constitute initiation into the church, the body of Christ. In this article he argues that, for all of Paul's emphasis on baptism, the reception of the Spirit is the more fundamental.

> Paul, like Luke, repeatedly emphasised these two features of Christian beginnings—faith and the Spirit. Quite how he correlated baptism within the process is less clear. That he saw baptism as the expression of faith is quite probable... The baptizand handed himself over (in and by baptism) to belong to the one named over him. Otherwise Paul says nothing explicit about the correlation of faith and baptism—itself an interesting feature in one who saw the response of faith as such a crucial and sole defining element in the acceptance by God and the reception of the Spirit.[20]

Dunn argues against over stressing 'the ritual moment' of baptism. He warns against imposing a rich sacramental theology upon texts which speak only of the water rite for this in itself can lead to that old temptation of supposed ecclesial control over the means of grace. For Dunn, the New Testament writers placed their emphasis on the centrality and sovereignty of the Spirit and its correlative of faith. 'Whatever weight we judge ought to be placed on baptism should not be allowed to obscure or diminish these centralities.'[21]

For all that we may argue that baptism is a work of God, our baptismal disputes focus on devised forms by which we apparently claim to determine the boundaries of God's grace. But supposing that what really matters is the free sovereign work of God, then the act of baptism becomes a derivative matter, important, but secondary. For example, on the crucial question of whether or not Gentiles might become part of the church the argument moved not *from* baptism but *to* baptism: 'can anyone withhold the water for baptising these people who have received the Holy Spirit just as we have?' (Acts 10.47). The gracious work of God is primary. In Galatians 2.7-9 baptism is not even mentioned. Indeed, acts of baptism may even reflect those personal loyalties which can divide the church (1 Cor. 1.14-17). The basis of Christian fellowship in the New Testament is not baptism but the work of God, the shared experience of the Holy Spirit, and not the actions of the church.

---

19   J.D.G. Dunn, *Jesus and the Spirit: A Study of the Religious and Charismatic Experience of Jesus and the First Christians as Reflected in the New Testament* (London: SCM Press, 1975).
20   Dunn, 'Baptism and the Unity of the Church', pp. 100-101.
21   Dunn, 'Baptism and the Unity of the Church', p. 102.

Have we then given too great a place to baptism and been unwise in arguing that acceptance of common baptism is the starting point for the ecumenical journey? Should we not give greater emphasis to the recognition of the grace of God, focused in Jesus Christ, active in human life by the Spirit? Along with the human rites of our institutional initiations should we not also give more attention to matters of discerning the authentic signs of God at work in human lives? How might the varied experience of the fellowship of the Holy Spirit be correlated with baptism and the question of the unity of the church? This question is all the more urgent in the light of the growing Pentecostal churches, largely still outside the ecumenical movement, which simply do not accept the usual ecumenical agenda and questions. Who says that baptism, eucharist and ministry are the crucial questions concerning the unity of the church? Might not mission, evangelism and works of the Spirit be as important?

In drawing attention to Dunn's argument I am not proposing the sidelining of baptism, or suggesting that it is not important. I am suggesting that it is not first in matters of being the church of Christ. Negatively I am arguing that our focus on baptism and unity, baptism and membership, as the prior question, may be misleading.[22] Because the church in its various forms decides who can be baptised, then we have a high measure of control, but the bird of heaven cannot so easily be caged. And because the wind blows where it wills we will always have these 'difficult' cases of people in whom God is at work by the Spirit without the benefit of baptism.

I said earlier that there were two contributions which argued for caution when it comes to attempting to ground unity in the act of baptism. The second takes us back to the British Baptist document, *Believing and Being Baptized*. Often, to the surprise and dismay of other Christians, it has been Baptists who have refused to agree to the recognition of common baptism as the focus for unity. We have responded in this way, however, for what seem to us good theological reasons. Much discussion of baptism and unity in ecumenical debates moves from baptism to the church. Baptists are uneasy about this approach for two reasons.

First, we do not see that baptism is the foundation that others take it to be. If it is so to be understood, then it will exclude those whom we would not wish to forget or forsake. There are Christians who have not been baptised but who know and share the fellowship of the Holy Spirit, amongst whom are members of the Salvation Army and the Society of Friends. In fact, in England we have a large number of Baptist congregations practising 'open membership' which means that they

---

22 See the discussion by Christopher J. Ellis, 'A View from the Pool: Baptists, Sacraments and the Basis of Unity', *Baptist Quarterly* 39.3 (July, 2001), pp. 107-20.

admit into membership those who confess repentance towards God and faith in Jesus Christ as Saviour and Lord, who are committed to walk the way of faithful discipleship within the fellowship of the church, but are not baptised believers. Open membership churches do not insist on baptism. In practice, the vast majority of their members are baptised but they resist saying that people have to be baptised to be a member of Christ's Church. From the days of John Bunyan onwards there have been those who have argued that *Differences in Judgement about Water Baptism [are] no Bar to Communion*.[23]

Returning to Dunn's reflections on Paul and baptism, others have claimed that the argument of the letter to the Galatians means that no religious rite in itself can ever be the basis of Christian fellowship. Should we insist on baptism, then the church and its membership is being defined in terms of something we do and have turned into a law. That is the danger inherent in all formal acts of religion, namely, that the sign substitutes for the reality it signals. Personally, I believe this argument can be overstated, falling into the common trap of not being wrong in what it affirms but in what it is taken to deny. I shall return to it.

However, the second reason why Baptists have been uneasy about the argument that moves from baptism to the church is that our route is the reverse. For Baptists, ecclesiology defines baptism. It is not the other way around. It is the doctrine of the church that leads to the doctrine of believers' baptism. Thus the first issue is not who are the fit subjects for baptism, but how does the church ever come into being. Here is part of the influential Second London Confession of Particular Baptist churches (1677).

> 1. The Catholic or Universal Church, which (with respect to the internal work of the Spirit, and truth of grace) may be called invisible, consists of the whole number of the Elect, that have been, are, or shall be gathered into one, under Christ the head thereof; and is the spouse, the body, the fullness of him that filleth all in all.
>
> 2. All persons throughout the world, professing the faith of the Gospel, and obedience into God by Christ, according unto it; not destroying their own profession by any Errors everting the foundation, or unholyness of conversation, are and may be called visible Saints; and of such ought all particular congregations to be constituted.[24]

The confession goes on to make some references to impurity in the church and uses language only extremists would use today of other

---

23 The title of a famous tract written by John Bunyan in 1673.
24 'Second London Confession' (1677), in W.L. Lumpkin (ed.), *Baptist Confessions of Faith* (Philadelphia, PA: Judson Press, rev. edn, 1969), p. 285.

Christian denominations. But then it continues on the theme of the significance of the Lord Jesus Christ, the head of the church.

> 5. In the execution of this power wherewith he is so instructed, the Lord Jesus calleth out of the World unto himself, through the Ministry of his word, by his Spirit, those that are given unto him by his Father; that they may walk before him in all the ways of obedience, which he prescribeth to them in his Word.[25]

This is the theological argument that it is God who calls and gathers the church. Being the church is not a matter of the like-minded getting together, or the rest following a particular leader, but 'the church (is) constituted by God's act in Christ and the free human response to that gracious, initiating act'.[26]

Baptists claim that these two aspects of the one ecclesial reality are important to hold together, for they are what God has joined. So the church is both divine and human, of grace and faith. A potential weakness in Baptist ecclesiology with its stress on the voluntarist principle is that we over burden the personal individual centre of decision. Baptists have argued that only freely given consent is necessary to true faith. Compelled religion, however pure and correct it may be in its doctrines and practices, is unreal without the response, freely given, of faith in the one to whom worship is offered. Faith to be faith must be free. And yet there is a sense in which those who come to faith receive the trusting relationship of obedience as a gift. It is almost as if we find ourselves to be believers. God too has his freedom, sovereign freedom, and theologically the initiative always lies with God. We would have no call to answer and no one to trust had not God made himself known in Jesus. Again, none of this would be real to us unless the Holy Spirit did not go on taking up the things of Christ and showing them to us. There is a way of speaking of being Baptist that so emphasises the personal decision, the 'democracy' of it all, that the centre of the church can appear to be our deciding and not the gracious invitation of God. For all that there would be no church if there were no response to the call to discipleship, even more would there be no church if there were no divine invitation, no searching or meeting or knowing of God in Christ. Early Baptists in England, ready to face persecution, imprisonment and even death, had about them the sense that they were called, chosen and graced undeservedly by God. They were saved by grace and they rejoiced in faith as a gift. The affirmation of both grace and faith together remains essential. God has the initiative. Grace is prevenient. Hence the church begins in the call of God who, in his freedom, elects to be for us in Christ.

---

25 'Second London Confession', in Lumpkin (ed.), *Baptist Confessions*, p. 286.
26 S.M. Heim, 'Baptismal Recognition and the Baptist Churches', in Root and Saarinen (eds.), *Baptism and the Unity of the Church*, p. 151.

The church exists among humankind in those who, hearing and believing the gospel, freely respond in faith. Such faith in the Christ-like God shows itself in trust and obedience, that is, in discipleship.

Let me now return to the issue of the boundaries of the church. There were those who contributed to *Believing and Being Baptized* who were not able 'to regard the rite called "infant baptism" as baptism'. Their reasons for this had to do not with baptism in the first place so much as with the doctrine of the church. The church is composed of those who have freely responded to God's gracious work in Jesus. They are believers. They are disciples. They share the fellowship of the Holy Spirit. They have repented towards God and confessed faith in Jesus Christ. Upon making such confession they are baptised.

So goes the believers' church tradition. It is recognised that there are no pure churches under heaven but all are a mixture in practice and doctrine.[27] Those who are members in the believers' church tradition do not always believe, neither is their active discipleship always marked by faithfulness. This is the humanity of the church from which Jesus Christ does not turn away. As, indeed, he does not turn away from children.

What is the place of the child in the believer's church tradition? This is an important test case for Baptists. Are not those who baptise infants expressing that prevenient grace of God, that love with which the Son of God regarded children and described them as first in the kingdom, which is all in keeping with the gospel story?[28] Children do have a place in the community of faith. In their own way they believe. They often speak of their church, their minister, because they have a sense of belonging. The church of Christ needs to welcome, teach and nurture them as they are and not for what potentially they might be.

Baptists would want to affirm the truth in the doctrine of prevenient grace for all children. They have no wish to put a boundary around the freedom of God's activity, least of all by the actions of the church. So pastorally and liturgically we look for services of celebration, welcome, affirmation for every child. For every child Christ Jesus has died and been raised, whether the child and parents believe it or not. Some Baptists wish we could recapture the concept of the catechumenate.[29] All recognize that there are things appropriate to ask of a child that honours them as children and things that are not. To ask them to take up the whole commitment of Christian discipleship which baptism expresses is not one of them. Baptism has to do with making radical life-commitments that are not appropriate to children. With others, I wish that

---

27 'Second London Confession', in Lumpkin (ed.), *Baptist Confessions*, p. 285.
28 Heim, 'Baptismal Recognition and the Baptist Churches', p. 162.
29 See W.M.S.West, 'The Child and the Church: A Baptist Perspective', in W.H. Brackney, P.S. Fiddes and J.H.Y. Briggs (eds.), *Pilgrim Pathways: Essays in Honour of B.R. White* (Macon, GA: Mercer University Press, 1999), pp. 75-110.

every person might have the opportunity to hear the great words spoken over them as they stand of their own free will in the baptismal pool: 'Upon your profession of repentance towards God and of faith in our Lord Jesus Christ, I baptise you in the name of the Father and the Son and The Holy Spirit.'[30] Infant baptism denies this to many. More positively, the church can care, teach, nurture and encourage all those, young and old, who seek to be part of the church as they honestly can.

The question of boundaries is difficult. Theologically and pastorally, children are part of the church. We can hope and pray that they will become those in whom the Spirit is increasingly at work, calling them to an obedient discipleship that is implied in baptism. None of this is tidy and it does not fit with those who control and count numbers, but it is part of the humanity of the church God is calling into being and sustaining by his gracious word.

What then of the open church position which does not require baptism? The majority of those who prepared *Believing and Being Baptized* urged 'that Churches reconsider the place of baptism within Christian discipleship, and that they no longer accept without baptism those who have not yet been initiated in any way into membership of the Church of Christ'.[31] I cannot myself think of any reason why we would not make baptism essential for church membership, except that of it being seen as a church rite we declare to be necessary for participation in the fellowship of the Spirit. I do not think baptism is necessary for salvation, as if the church in this practice must do something in addition to the work of Christ. But it is particularly at this point that I want to return to the themes of the freedom of God, the freedom God gives and baptism as a sacrament.

Although I am resisting making baptism legalistically necessary for church membership, I am sure Dunn is right when he argues that full Christian initiation involves baptism. Of course, if you take a non-sacramental view of baptism, allowing the action only symbolic content as an act of witness, then it certainly becomes merely legalistic to insist upon it. But is baptism only a rather elaborate way of witnessing to my faith? If we can countenance a sacramental approach to baptism then the call for baptism is related to the freedom and grace of God.

As a working definition the contributors to *Reflections on the Water* settled for the modest proposal that 'the term "sacrament" suggests the power of symbols to link us to the depths of reality, and points us to the use by God of material means to mediate his saving action'.[32] We would

---

30   See my argument in 'Baptism: A Question of Belief and Age?' *Perspectives in Religious Studies* 27.1 (Spring, 2000), pp. 121-26.
31   *Believing and Being Baptized*, p. 29.
32   C.J. Ellis, 'Baptism and the Sacramental Freedom of God', in Fiddes (ed.), *Reflections*, p. 36.

argue that early Baptist confessions and practice imply a more sacramental view, the anti-sacramental view coming more to the fore mainly in response to the Tractarians in the nineteenth century.

The contrast is like this. A view that baptism is only an ordinance to be obeyed tends to emphasise it as a human work. It spiritualises the faith proclaimed. It is individualistic rather than relational and plays down any suggestion that in the drama of baptism God has any part to play other than to call the real performers on stage.

By contrast, contributors to *Reflections on the Water* argued that baptism and the Lord's Supper are sacramental in that the God of creation and incarnation does use material means to mediate his saving action. To limit God's presence and work to the spiritual is reductionist. Baptism is one of the two God-appointed meeting places.[33] God encounters the candidate and the church in baptism such that while this is not necessary to salvation it is the case that God gives his grace in baptism. This is God acting in his freedom and is not *ex opere operato*.[34] The reason for baptised membership of the church is not because we have to be baptised, but because the God who calls us by the Spirit to the life in Christ offers his grace in baptism. As *Believing and Being Baptized* puts it, 'the obedience which belongs to discipleship is always to be set in the context of salvation, and salvation is to be seen as a process throughout the Christian pilgrimage rather than isolated within a single point. Baptism is a high point within the journey of salvation, a *rendezvous* that God has himself provided for the deepening relationship with him'.[35] Thus baptism is an act of God for the candidate and the church together.

What, on these arguments, would be an appropriate response by Baptists to one who comes to them having received infant baptism? The absolutist position that denies they have been baptised and therefore ought to be baptised is too blunt an instrument for pastoral care. But there is this important distinction to be drawn. Consider two different kinds of candidates. On the one hand, there are those who went through the rite as children and then received no serious Christian teaching or nurture, in no sense sharing the life of the church and, from a position of virtual paganism, have now come to faith in the Christ-like God by the work of the Holy Spirit. On the other hand, there are those baptised as infants who were taught and nurtured in the community of faith that received them, which helped them to respond to God in ways that were appropriate to their growth, who in maturity responded freely and reaffirmed for themselves the baptismal promises and confession,

---

33 G.R. Beasely-Murray spoke of baptism as the 'trysting place' of the sinner with the saviour in *Baptism in the New Testament* (London: Macmillan, 1963), p. 305.
34 Ellis, 'Baptism and the Sacramental Freedom of God', p. 30.
35 *Believing and Being Baptized*, p. 35.

receiving confirmation and continuing a journey of faithful discipleship with the church. The first group might well be candidates for baptism and most Baptists in Britain would baptise them because they are new Christians and believer's baptism is, of course, the baptism of Christians. With the others the practice would vary but some of us would refuse to baptise them as believers.[36] We would rather want to help them realise and affirm the work of God in their life, bringing them to faith and the fellowship of His people. The challenge is not to be baptised as a believer. He or she has been a believer for years. Their challenge is to live out the baptism. A public service of the renewal of baptismal vows could be held with the note of celebration that God too has his freedom and brings people to himself in ways beyond our controlling. Thus that the Spirit is at work in the individual's life is more important than the mode or rite of baptism. Yet I confess to a personal unease with this position, for the church and candidate's sake.

What is at issue here is the doctrine of God. Baptism (mis)understood as only an expression of commitment to Jesus, a personal act of witness and testimony, reflects an unhelpful christomonism. As such, baptism is almost being reduced to belonging to a Jesus cult. It is very different when faith is in God in Trinity. The baptismal confession that Jesus Christ is Lord remains a firm centre but, through Christ, baptism is into the life and mission of the triune God. Such a God touches not only the human will and soul but is fundamentally engaged with all that is. As Paul Fiddes argues:'in baptism a person becomes involved in a deeper and new way with the web of loving relationships that God weaves with His whole creation'.[37] The implications of a sacramental understanding of baptism are very wide, covering moral, political, social and spiritual issues.

In the baptismal narratives in the Synoptic Gospels, Jesus' identity as the beloved Son of the Father is declared, his solidarity in flesh and blood is expressed as he is immersed in the human lot, and the Spirit is actively present. He goes on in the power of the Spirit to proclaim, act and in all ways affirm the good news of the present and coming reign of God. British Baptists have been in danger of seriously reducing the meaning of baptism, of privatising and spiritualising salvation. That has shaped what we believe is the mission God calls us to share and, in consequence, we have sometimes focused that mission on church growth and the importance of personal relations. This is far from bad, but it is also far from our full calling in Christ. In *Reflections on the Water* some of us have affirmed not a polemical reaffirmation of a doctrinaire position, but an attempt to explore theologically more of the depth and height and

---

36   This is the line also proposed by G.R. Beasley-Murray, 'The Problem of Infant Baptism: An Exercise in Possibilities', in Faculty of the Baptist Theological Seminary, Rüschlikon (eds.), *Festschrift Günter Wagner* (Berne: Peter Lang, 1994), pp. 1-14.

37   Fiddes, 'Baptism and Creation', p. 59.

length and breadth of what it is to be baptised into the name of the Father, the Son and the Holy Spirit, to whom be praise and glory for ever and ever.

PART TWO

HISTORY

CHAPTER 9

Pure Clay and Time's Mud: Biography as History

Keith W. Clements

Most universities have a department of history but none, so far as I know, has a department of biography. This naive fact is eloquent testimony, if any were needed, that biography is generally accorded significance only as an attendant on historiography which is the 'real' science of the record of human affairs. Accounts of individual lives are valued only in the context of the larger chronicles of their times, as illustrative of what it meant to live amid the wider currents of social, political and cultural tendencies and, maybe, in certain cases, to acknowledge the specific contribution which a particular human being made to *those* features and tendencies. Where the real stuff of history is taken to be the interplay of trans-personal forces, be they political, ideological, economic or whatever, it is natural for biography to be viewed as mere embroidery on the underlying hard fabric of human affairs.

Yet biography remains immensely popular both to writers and readers and, judging by the contents of bookshelves in even the most academic libraries, is seen as somehow necessary to the study of history at large. This is especially true in the field of religious and church history. In each issue of the monthly *Expository Times*, for example, pride of place is given on the final page to a substantial editorial review of a recent biography. The purpose of this essay is to reflect briefly on the 'somehow necessary' nature of biography to historiography in the wider sense. I wish to argue that while biography does indeed make full sense only in relation to a history wider than the individual, that wider history in turn is dependent upon biography not only as a source of vital facets of information and insight, but as a means of preserving itself as a genuinely *human* science. This means that biography has an integrity and a discipline of its own to be observed as well as a relation to wider study. It should go without saying that, equally, this means eschewing exaggerated claims for biography over against history. 'There is properly no history; only biography', stated Ralph Waldo Emerson, echoing Benjamin Disraeli's dictum: 'Read no history: nothing but biography, for that is life without theory.'[1] Today we cannot speak so innocently, for we know it is barely possible either to write or read about a human life without some ingrained perspective, whether we call it theory or social conditioning or emotional prejudice.

I ought to make clear where some of my own perspectives hail from. Several years of teaching courses on modern church history to students who confessed to having little awareness of any kind of history of the nineteenth and twentieth centuries impressed on me the practical value of biographies of one or two key figures as ways into hitherto unfamiliar territory, both in terms of imparting information and giving a feel to what it was like, bliss or otherwise, to be alive in that dawn. Then, during the 1990s most of my own academic energies were consumed in writing a substantial biography of one of the formative personalities of the modern ecumenical movement, J.H. Oldham, in which I learned at first hand the daunting necessity of the biographer to try to be, at one and the same time, fact-gatherer, chronicler, detective, psychologist, portrait-painter and (yes) historian.[2] Finally, many of my theological and historical interests have focused on a figure of paramount interest in the twentieth century, Dietrich Bonhoeffer. This has involved, inevitably, much reflection on the variety of interpretations, both of his life-story and his theology, which have been generated by his impact over the half-century and more since his death. While aware that much else has been written on biographical purpose and method, I wish to speak primarily out of my own immediate experience and concerns.

Biography: A Short History

The most obvious riposte to the claim that there is 'no history, only biography' is that biography itself has a history: a history, moreover, which reveals an increasingly complex interplay between the biographer and the milieu in which he or she lives and writes. The *Parallel Lives* of Plutarch (c. AD 46–120) is generally taken in the West to be the earliest example of biography recognisable in the modern sense. For while his couplets of eminent Greeks and Romans are intended primarily to be illustrative of dominant virtues or vices manifested on the public stage, Plutarch also has an eye for the seemingly trivial detail of incident or

---

[1] Benjamin Disraeli, *Contarini Fleming* (4 vols; London: John Murray, 1832), I, p. 282.

[2] Keith Clements, *Faith on the Frontier: A life of J.H. Oldham* (Edinburgh: T. & T. Clark/Geneva: WCC, 1999).

behaviour as revelatory of character. Pericles is not only the great, restrained and noble oracle of democracy but the one who, having been dogged all day and all the way home by a foul-mouthed abusive character, 'stepping into his house, it by this time dark...ordered one of his servants to take a light, and to go along with the man and see him safe home.'[3] But the virtue–vice paradigm continued to predominate in whatever life-accounts were written during well over a thousand years or more of medieval Christendom, dominated as it was by a cosmography of clearly stated values. Fiction they may have been but in Chaucer's *Canterbury Tales*, which still delight us for their portraits of the travellers themselves at least as much as the stories they tell, we breathe a newer, dawning sense of interest in human individuality and character. It is no accident that in England it was the sixteenth century, the age which bred a Shakespeare, which also saw the first concerted attempts at biography of actual, public figures such as the anonymous *History of Richard the Third* found among Sir Thomas More's papers after his death, and the life of More himself written by his son-in-law William Roper. It was, however, the next century, curious as never before about human nature, which saw a real outpouring of accounts of lives and their shaping characteristics, seen perhaps above all in the work of Izaak Walton (1593–1683) and his lives of Donne, Hooker, Sanderson and Herbert. Women writers such as Margaret Lucas, duchess of Newcastle and Lucy Hutchinson made their mark. Autobiography, too, began to flourish, ranging from the egocentricity of *Life of Edward, Lord Herbert of Cherbury, Written by Himself*, to such intensely spiritual, confessional memoirs as John Bunyan's *Grace Abounding to the Chief of Sinners* and Richard Baxter's *Narrative of the Most Memorable Passages of His Life and Times*. Indeed, much of the biographical interest of that age of rationalism versus belief, of conformity versus nonconformity, centred in inward, spiritual struggle.

By the eighteenth century, what might be termed encyclopaedianism was in full swing: the desire to collect and assemble as much data and memorabilia about as many people as possible, seemingly as an end in itself. It was the age of the dictionary, which provides the occasion to remark that it was with Samuel Johnson that English biography reached one of its definitive peaks, he himself producing a noted biography of the poet and journalist Richard Savage, and being himself the subject of one of the greatest biographies of all time, James Boswell's *Life of Johnson*. It was Boswell who laid down the trademark of all subsequent biography of merit: a concentration upon what the subject *communicated* of himself, through letters and remembered conversation. To be interesting, of course, this requires that the subject generally has something worth saying. Johnson, seemingly, invariably did and his

---

3   *Plutarch's Lives* (Everyman edition; London: J.M. Dent, 1910), p. 230.

robust humanity always shines through (presumably Boswell did not include everything Johnson ever said and it might instructive to know some of the things he left out, consciously or otherwise). The Boswellian method continued to inspire much nineteenth-century biography, among the best being Robert Southey's lives of Lord Nelson and John Wesley, and Elizabeth Gaskell's *Life of Charlotte Bronte*. The Victorian era was the age of reading. It produced the public library, as education and a more leisured middle-class spread themselves abroad, with plenty of would-be biographers eager to fulfil their callings of supplying both moral uplift and entertainment. But much Victorian biography suffered on the one hand from a compulsive assemblage of data without judgment as to its relative significance, and on the other hand from an overweening sense of propriety and decorum. In even as notable a biography as A.P. Stanley's *Life and Correspondence of Thomas Arnold*, it has been remarked that the reader is left with an impression of moral stature rather than of vitality.

However, the Victorian age, posthumously, has never quite recovered from Lytton Strachey's *Eminent Victorians* (1918) which let in the draughts of irony and scepticism even—indeed especially—upon the good and the great. Subsequently, post-Marx and post-Freud, the biographer writes from within a culture of suspicion against all appearances and received opinions even if he or she may personally disavow the theoretical bases of such scepticism. The later twentieth-century biographer is characteristically a somewhat cautious figure, careful not to claim too much, circumspectly presenting the finished product as an 'intellectual' or 'political' or indeed 'theological' biography and implying that unqualified 'biography' is either inherently impossible or simply impracticable. By the start of the twenty-first century and the self-proclaimed virtues of the post-modernist, deconstructionist culture, not only is there suspicion as to the 'real' self lying behind reputation and appearance, even the concept of the 'self' as a distinct entity and moral agent is under attack. That might seem to be the end of the line for biography. Yet biography continues to be seriously written and avidly read.

The Nature and Purpose of Biography

The history of this particular literary species reveals a fairly clear picture of what biography is: a narrative of the speech, actions and personality of an individual life. It differs from history at large by focusing on an individual, yet the biographer shares (or should share) with the historian a rigorous concern with fact and actual chronology. Nor can the biographer work in isolation from still other disciplines. Edward Clerihew

Bentley's fourth-formish quip 'Geography is about maps/But biography is about Chaps' ignores the fact that not only are maps made by chaps (speaking inclusively) for particular human purposes, but most individual lives need setting in a map-context to be understood adequately. The biographer works on the uncertain borderland between the particular interest in his human subject, and all the sciences which attempt to define one aspect or another of living on this planet, from sociology to genetics, from the history of art to political science. But it is to art that biography has the most sensitive relationship. Biography differs from fiction by dealing with an individual who has actually lived, or is still living, yet the effective biographer shares with the novelist the desire to portray *character* and the emotional and moral texture of human decision-making and response to reality. The biographer is more than a chronicler. Perhaps even more than with the novelist, the analogy of the biographer is with the sculptor, for out of a—sometimes overwhelming—mass of factual detail and also at times a frustrating *lack* of suitable material the biographer has to *shape* a recognisably human life in all its individuality. Biography means a special combination of science and art, just as the Vatican *Laocoon* and Michelangelo's *Pietà* are exemplary fruits of both anatomical accuracy and compassionate psychological insight.

Not everyone is at ease with the artistic, quasi-novelistic (or -dramatic) element in biography, fearing that it is a specious leaven which corrupts the whole loaf. Abraham Lincoln famously dismissed most biographies as not only misleading but false, magnifying virtues and suppressing imperfections, but of course he was reacting to contemporary tendencies to panegyric and hagiography which political and religious interests have always generated. Not all biography, even predating Lytton Strachey, is such although earlier treatments of such Nonconformist heroes as William Carey, John Clifford and F.B. Meyer may now strike us as excruciating in their hagiographical tendencies. More searching is the view that biography, whether laudatory or critical of its subject, due to its inherently creative element can never vie in objectivity with strictly scientific history. The American novelist (and therefore friend of fiction) Bernard Malamud (1914–86) said: 'The past exudes legend: one can't make pure clay of time's mud. There is no life that can be recaptured wholly: as it was. Which is to say that all biography is ultimately fiction.'[4] But the 'ultimately' is a crucially important conditioning word here. For it might apply not only to biography, but to all attempts to comprehend, to shape into a coherent picture, not just an individual life but human life as a whole: in other words, history itself.

---

4   Bernard Malamud, *Dubin's Lives* (London: Chatto and Windus, 1979), p. 20.

History and Biography.

Historiography, it might be supposed, is a rigorous exercise in assembling the facts of what human beings have done, or have had done to them, in the realm of time and space, and uncovering the causal connections between these facts. It most certainly is concerned with events, dates and places. But the notion of causation as applied to human affairs is notoriously slippery and elusive. One can talk endlessly of social, economic and cultural forces and factors. Whether that can explain *why* precisely *this* event occurred at precisely *that* time and place is quite another matter. Historical theory attempts to distil the general principle out of particular events, but in history itself the general always awaits the particular. It was A.J.P. Taylor, that most fact-conscious but irreverent of modern British historians, who finally concluded that the reason why war broke out in August 1914 was simply that it happened, thanks to the decisions of Austrian Foreign Minister Berchtold and German Foreign Minister Bethmann-Hollweg and the carefully-laid plans of the German military strategist Schlieffen, however much they may also have been victims of circumstances.[5] Economic and imperial rivalries, national pride, socially-conditioned class perspectives, the technical requirements of mass mobilization may all have been *factors* but not at the end of the day the real *actors*, who were flesh-and-blood people with decisions to make. If one then asks how and why they made the decisions they took, one is into the realm of biography seen for example in Keith Robbins' almost hour-by-hour account of the life of Edward Grey, the British Foreign Secretary, during those days.[6]

The historian looks back on a past which in its happenedness is somehow complete, and is therefore driven to examine how the events bear upon each other in their interconnectedness, and are elements in wider and longer-term movements—often, it seems, with a momentum of their own. But in taking a cross-section of human affairs at a particular point in time, the historian has to come to terms with the fact that *then* it was by no means complete but on the edge of an unknown and unpredictable future. The historian would therefore do well to remember Soren Kierkegaard's remark that life can only be understood backwards but has to be lived forwards. Put naively, it has to be asked: 'What was it like to be alive just then, what were the perceived options for decision, and what were the felt attractions and repulsions of such options?' A good deal of moralizing cant imbued with the wisdom of hindsight would

---

   5   A.J.P. Taylor, 'The Outbreak of the First World War', in *Englishmen and Others* (London: Hamish Hamilton, 1956), p. ...
   6   Keith Robbins, *Sir Edward Grey: A Biography of Lord Grey of Fallodon* (London: Cassell, 1971).

be avoided if historians would seek to bear in mind the hindsight of the people in the age they are dealing with. No word today is more laden with moral opprobrium than 'appeasement'. The implication is that anyone who as late as Munich 1938 still wished to avoid war with Hitler's Germany was a moral coward as well as a political fool. But the example of a particular life such as that of George Bell, Bishop of Chichester,[7] shows that matters are not as simple as that. Bell was one who, earlier than most, had seen the depths of evil astir in Nazi Germany and was also actually better informed than most, thanks to his close contacts such as Dietrich Bonhoeffer. Equally Bell—at that time—could not but view the prospect of war as an utter disaster and unmitigated evil. The memory of 1914–18, in terms both of its overall colossal wastage of life and the particular grief brought by the loss of his brother, made that hindsight a crucial conditioning factor for such as him. What people of a particular time actually remembered, and therefore feared, is an elusive but vital factor in historical understanding. This is but one example of the rule that the historian has to come to terms with a peculiarly inward dimension of the subject, an inwardness to which his or her own consciousness provides crucial access. One stream of historiographical theory has long recognised this, beginning with Wilhelm Dilthey (1833–1911) who saw the method of the historian, in reconstructing past events from the evidence of documents, remains etc, as 'reliving' in one's own mind the events and experiences which gave rise to them.[8] In similar fashion R.G. Collingwood saw historical knowledge as knowledge of 'what mind has done in the past, and at the same time the reliving of this, the perpetuation of past acts in the present.' As historian, one thinks oneself into the 'inside' of an event, that which makes it a human action, as distinct from the 'outside', that which can be described in terms of space and time and movement.[9] Some historians may be averse to such ideas as inimical to their 'objectivity' but it is hard to avoid the impression that somewhere along the line, whether or not they admit it, this is what in practice they do if their work has the slightest human interest. It should not be surprising, then, that there is at least implicitly a biographical element in all historiography, and only someone who knows what it is to be a human being can write realistically about another human being. Such subjectivity can obviously lead to distortion, an excessive reading of one's own concerns or feelings or the issues of one's own context into the person or events being studied, but without it there can be no real

---

7 Cf. R.C.D. Jasper, *George Bell: Bishop of Chichester* (London: Oxford University Press, 1967).

8 For a selection of Dilthey's writings see H.A. Hodges, *Wilhelm Dilthey: An Introduction* (London: Kegan Paul, Trench and Trubner, 1944).

9 R.G. Collingwood, *The Idea of History* (London: Faber and Faber, 1943).

encounter with the event as human experience, and at the end of the day no real interest either.

The Discipline of Contemporary Biography

Biography is the most intense point of confluence of all historiography: the rigorous concern with facts as revealed by documents—letters, diaries, minutes of meetings, newspaper reports and so forth—and the reconstruction of the consciousness and motivations of the person or persons involved. Without the former, biography (or history) will be fictional. Without the latter, it will be sheer chronicle, and not a human story. The most challenging points in biography or historiography at large are those where certain outward facts are undeniable but the human motivations underlying them are, to say the least, ambiguous. (It also has to be recognized of course that even in the most fully documented lives obscure gaps and discontinuities in the facts themselves can appear, and it is a challenge to the biographer to resist the temptation of simply filling these in by conjecture or assumption.) In reconstructing the life of J.H. Oldham one of the most intriguing episodes concerned his behaviour in the year 1934 when, although secretary of the International Missionary Council (IMC) which he had effectively founded immediately after the 1914-18 War, he opted to became the organiser of the study programme for the conference of 'Life and Work' to be held at Oxford in 1937.[10] In effect he was jumping from one ecumenical boat to another, to the great consternation of some, especially John R. Mott, the chairman of the IMC. The received opinion in all ecumenical histories hitherto, was that Oldham's decision was prompted by his realisation that the Life and Work agenda emerging in 1934 offered the most promising way of fulfilling the concerns set out by the 1928 IMC World Missionary Conference in Jerusalem, especially in its identification of 'secularism', not other world religions, as the main enemy of Christianity. Oldham himself lent credence to this explanation by a letter to John Mott in the autumn of 1934 justifying his unwelcome decision, and by later remarks in interview to W.R. Hogg, the historian of the IMC. To challenge such views, emanating from the subject himself, might seem presumptuous. But the overall evidence just did not add up. At the time of the Jerusalem Conference itself Oldham was neither impressed by the event itself (he did not even attend it, despite being secretary of the IMC, choosing to participate in a British government commission to central Africa instead), nor particularly excited by the issue of secularism as set out by the American Quaker Rufus Jones. Moreover, his own approach to the issue

---

10 Clements, *Faith on the Frontier*, pp. 260-63.

of 'religion' and 'secularism' in the years between 1928 and 1934 was influenced far more by the neo-orthodox theologies of Karl Barth and Emil Brunner than by the western liberal sympathies towards 'religions' as a whole.

What then was going on in Oldham's mind in the summer of 1934, when he attended the council meeting of 'Life and Work' at Fanö, Denmark, which saw his election to take charge of the work for Oxford 1937? I came to the conclusion that Oldham had for some time seen that Life and Work was now offering more potential than the IMC for fulfilling his own agenda of a Christian-inspired vision of society, and that his letter of self-justification to Mott was a device which, couched in terms of the IMC agenda, offered an explanation with which Mott could hardly disagree in principle. This left open an even more intriguing possibility: that Oldham, despite his professions of surprise at suddenly being cornered at Fanö into taking up the responsibilities for Oxford, had all along being craftily manoeuvring himself into a position where he would be seen as the obvious candidate for the job. I have to admit that this is an intriguing *possibility*. His actions up to Fanö can be read equally well as either an ingenuous curiosity about Life and Work, or a clever camouflaging of his intentions which, if revealed too obviously or too soon, might well have provoked opposition from some influential quarters. But it is not without reason that Oldham was known to many of his contemporaries as 'a wily saint' or (as some preferred) 'that canny Scot.'

In all this, as biographer I was certainly seeking to 'relive' these events and, to a degree, to adopt Oldham's own role. It is often remarked that to know a human subject one must love him or her: or at any rate, to be able to empathize with that person. That is rather disconcerting to the biographer. One has to feel an interest, some degree of human affinity, with the subject. That leads some to question whether biography can proceed without admiration for the subject, and that the distorting tendency towards hagiography is always at least latent. I have not in fact found it an easy question to answer, posed by several people, whether I would have actually liked to have worked with Oldham. I have tended to fend off the enquiry with the qualified response, 'For most of his career, yes.' The points in his life-story which make me hesitate are probably as revelatory of me as a human being as of him, and no less than with an autobiography one cannot write an authentic biography without some degree of self-exposure, deliberate or unwitting. To relive the inner life and motivations of another may well require a recognition that the reshuffling of values and the hazy borderline between idealistic aspiration and self-seeking ambition, are familiar to oneself. But can one write a biography of someone whom one actually dislikes? Presumably one can, provided it is made clear why the dislike exists. Even a Hitler has a right to a biography.

However, the writing of religious, as of much political, biography also faces a challenge from a direction opposite to that of the personal involvement of the biographer. Often the subject being studied is significant because of his or her place in a movement, organisation or institution. It is then tempting for the biographer, in the cause of 'contextualizing' the life-story, simply to re-present the history of the community or organisation and to place the human subject as its figurehead without exploring the actual relationship between the person and the wider body. This is especially apt to happen in the interests of propaganda for the corporate cause. It is here that biography faces one of the severest challenges to its own integrity as the art and discipline of portraying a *life*. In writing on J.H. Oldham I was fortunate in that the archive of his letters and papers, assembled by the late Kathleen Bliss, contained more than enough evidence of the deeply critical attitude he often took towards the very ecumenical bodies, from the International Missionary Council to the World Council of Churches, which he himself had been instrumental in creating. He could no longer be simplistically and piously subsumed into the role of 'ecumenical leader.' The biographical problem in relation to very public figures is graphically illustrated by the recent, monumental biography of Pope John Paul II by George Weigel.[11] The earlier chapters are a vivid, compelling account of Karol Wojtyla's upbringing and life as priest and bishop in Poland. The account of his pontificate in Rome is no less engaging, but it is not at all clear just what it is that is being described: the life of the person himself or the outcome of the operations of the Vatican machinery. It is one thing to say, for example, that the encyclical *Ut Unum Sint* was 'issued' under the Pope's 'personal initiative',[12] but how did it actually come to be written, and by whom? How much was the Holy Father personally involved in its thinking and writing? To be true *biography*—and therefore the detail of the history—we need to know much more about the inner dynamics of the Vatican and the personal role of the Pope himself in them. Perhaps it is simply too soon to hope for that.

A Case-Study: Dietrich Bonhoeffer

No twentiethth-century Christian figure has attracted more attention than Dietrich Bonhoeffer (1906–45). Predictions repeated every few years of

---

11 George Weigel, *Witness to Hope: The Biography of Pope John Paul II* (London: HarperCollins, 1999).
12 Weigel, *Witness to Hope*, pp. 760-61.

the imminent demise of the 'Bonhoeffer industry' remain stubbornly unfulfilled, as new generations of doctoral students analyse a new facet of the complexity of his thought, as new historical research brings to light further material on the German resistance and its international and ecumenical ramifications and as, quite simply, at the more popular level more readers rediscover for themselves the fascination of a life of such daring integrity lived amidst evil and compromise with evil. Several biographies of Bonhoeffer have appeared. Towering over them all is the monumental and definitive work by Eberhard Bethge.[13] It is often said that for the biographer to have had a personal relationship with the subject gives the advantage of undeniable access to the character to be described, while at the same time it can inhibit a truly objective measure being taken. The best chemistry for biography would appear to be a personal acquaintance between writer and subject for *some* of the latter's life, sufficient indeed to know the character in some depth but not to tempt the writer to assume total comprehension—still leaving room for curiosity—combined with the largest possible usage of firsthand materials, letters, papers and so on. This worked brilliantly well with Boswell's treatment of Johnson. It also worked well for George Bell's biography of Archbishop Randall Davidson, of whom Bell was secretary during 1914-24.[14] It was also crucial for Bethge's treatment of Bonhoeffer. Bethge knew Bonhoeffer for the last ten years of his life. The acquaintance was peculiarly personal since Bonhoeffer chose Bethge, one of his first students in the illegal Confessing Church seminary at Finkenwalde, to be his own 'confessor' in the intensely communal life which he created there. Bethge became Bonhoeffer's closest friend, and towards the end of the saga was himself to be the recipient of most of the correspondence which has made Bonhoeffer so famous—his letters from prison.[15] Indeed, as a partner in dialogue with Bonhoeffer at this stage, Bethge (who died in 2000) may truly be said to have become part of the story himself. But while Bethge was so close to Bonhoeffer for a decade, and eventually became part of the Bonhoeffer family circle by marrying his niece, Bethge also had to a degree the relation of an outsider to the story which gave him a valuable perspective as an observer. Son of a country pastor, with no academic pretensions, Bethge came from a quite different world to the semi-aristocratic Bonhoeffer circle in Berlin where it was assumed that becoming (or marrying) a Herr Professor was the normal course of events. Much of the Bonhoeffer story, including its

---

13   Revised (and unabridged) English edition edited by Victoria Barnett, *Dietrich Bonhoeffer: A Biography* (Minneapolis: Fortress Press, 2000).

14   G.K.A. Bell, *Randall Davidson: Archbishop of Canterbury* (Oxford: Oxford University Press, 1935).

15   Cf. E. Bethge, *Friendship and Resistance: Essays on Dietrich Bonhoeffer* (Grand Rapids: Eerdmans/Geneva: WCC, 1995).

earlier theological elements, was quite new to Bethge for a long time. He had the privilege of ignorance combined with curiosity which, as Lytton Strachey observes, is the prerequisite of the biographer who wishes to shape the life under review. At the same time, Bethge made the most thorough and wide-ranging use of all Bonhoeffer's material, published and unpublished, and also set the story in the context of the German church and political struggles so well, but without an excess of 'contextualisation', so that the biography can equally well be read as a history of the church struggle. But through it all there is discernible a distinctly known character seeking a consistency of purpose in rapidly changing situations. Such a work deserves the supreme accolade of any biography or history: that while in the course of time much may be added to it, it can never actually be superceded and that all other 'lives' of Bonhoeffer will be dependent upon it.

The posthumous story of Bonhoeffer also, however, from two quite different directions shows the crucial necessity for biography to maintain itself as a discipline combining objective, factual historiography and the art of shaping the character and reliving the experience of the subject. On the one hand, there is the long-running intellectual interest in abstracting from such as Bonhoeffer some theological ideas quite divorced from their context. A tendency in interpretation of Bonhoeffer has always been to assume a certain kind of development or evolution of his thought, beginning with the intensely philosophical and theological dialogues with Hegel, Barth, Heidegger and company in his early *Sanctorum Communio* and *Act and Being*, through the biblically focused, christocentric works such as *The Cost of Discipleship* in the early years of the church struggle, then to the more 'worldly' orientated *Ethics* and so finally to the 'radical' prison writings in search of a 'religionless Christianity.' Depending on the interpreter's point of view, the 'development' from *The Cost of Discipleship* can then be seen as either a frontier-crossing breakthrough to a new maturity of thought, or a fall from (Barthian) grace to secular humanism. But all such interpretations are based on the assumption that Bonhoeffer's—or anyone else's for that matter—thought is a matter of *linear* development, with or without halts and breaks on the way. It is highly doubtful whether this is so with Bonhoeffer. What we see is rather a succession of attempts, in rapidly changing contexts, to reshape drastically a theology in order to address whatever seemed the most pressing need. In these reformulations, many of the same elements are present throughout: Christ, the world, concrete obedience, Bible, community and so on. The concept of 'development' is hardly adequate to the hermeneutical task here, and it should be the work of good biography to challenge such intellectualising generalisations and the values implicit in them.

From another direction has come the phenomenon of fictional and dramatising treatments of Bonhoeffer. It is perhaps simply inevitable that such a challenging and intriguing figure would attract the attention of novelists, playwrights and filmmakers, as others have done in modern times, from Martin Luther and Thomas More to Mozart, van Gogh and Eric Liddell. Equally inevitably, the old question arises again whether, given the artistic element in biography, there is any real boundary between biography and fiction. There is. The biographer does not include in the account material for which there is no evidence, though he or she may consciously speculate. Moreover, while the biographer is in some sense an artist in recreating or reliving events or experiences, it is not the dramatic effect which is being primarily aimed at, but the accurate account and its significance.

Is fictional biography, or a novel or play based on a real-life figure, legitimate? In principle it surely is. We should relish imagination, fantasy even, provoked by history as a way of knowledge of that history and knowledge of ourselves. The one condition is that artistic license should not violate either facts or known character for the sake of dramatic effect or propaganda interests. Bonhoeffer has suffered both responsible and less responsible treatment. On the one hand there is Mary Glazener's novel *The Cup of Wrath* which not only sensitively lives from inside the drama of Bonhoeffer's career and that of his associates, but actually involved ten years of painstaking research.[16] On the other hand there is Denise Giardina's *Saints and Villains* which was awarded a prize for fiction by the Boston Book Review.[17] This work has provoked much controversy in the USA, for while it seeks to introduce readers through 'imagination' to Bonhoeffer's 'spirit' it also introduces spurious fictional episodes into Bonhoeffer's story including a totally fabricated physical relationship with a (Jewish) woman. It is one thing for the novelist to say that the writer's job is to reintroduce 'mystery' into life, but the genuine mystery does not require such fabricated fantasy. The real mystery about human life already is here in the actual lives of real people. Where such real figures are involved, it is the task of the biographer to bring the mystery out in what actually happened, not that of the novelist to introduce it by spurious invention.

Finally, any notion that the biography as an art-form is rendered redundant by dramatisation on stage or screen is hardly supported by what has happened to Bonhoeffer in this regard. There have been a number of one-person 'talking heads' presentations of Bonhoeffer in the USA and UK, and several films, the most recent of which is the much

---

16   Mary Glazener, *The Cup of Wrath: The Story of Dietrich Bonhoeffer's Resistance to Hitler* (Macon: Smyth and Helwys, 1994).
17   Denise Giardina, *Saints and Villains: A Novel* (New York: W.W. Norton, 1998).

publicized *Agent of Grace*.[18] I have to confess that I have yet to see any dramatization of the Bonhoeffer story which is remotely satisfying. Indeed most of them are acutely embarrassing, What one finds painful about all such dramatizations is a difficulty inherent in the medium itself: the evident requirement, for dramatic effect, to focus on Bonhoeffer as an isolated individual thus making him a lone saint or hero struggling with his conscience or agonising over the future of the church or displaying a unique personal courage in abstraction from everyone and everything else around him. Such isolation is historically quite unreal and untrue, and in fact totally incompatible with the actual personal and intellectual spirit of Bonhoeffer. For Bonhoeffer *sociality* was central both in his thought and his life, even (perhaps especially in) prison. The fact that in *Agent of Grace* Eberhard Bethge never appears, nor is Bonhoeffer ever seen even writing a letter in prison, is grotesque (as incredible as the quaint portrayal of Bonhoeffer agonising over moral scruples about joining in the resistance, which in real life he never had). If that is an inevitable consequence of the dramatic requirements of the play or the film, then it is another way of saying that it is still only a *book* which can adequately deal with the full depth—and drama—of a life in which human relationships were crucial at every level, emotionally and intellectually.

Conclusion

Biography continues to play an essential role in historiography. It is not just that in biography much of the small but crucial detail appears. It is biography which guarantees that history remains a human science, attending to the role of human perception, emotion, decision, moral value and spiritual awareness in the wider story. And because even a single life-story is often full of ambiguity and paradox, hiddenness as well as overt character, it is biography which most effectively insists on keeping history open to new and fresh interpretation. But to do so it must preserve its own integrity as a discipline, being neither just chronicle on the one hand nor fiction on the other. It neither invents events nor just chronicles them. It seeks to understand what was going on inside them and between them in terms of an actual human life who carried out, suffered or in some way experienced them. Moreover, because it is one human life at a time which is being studied, for all the narrowness of focus which this might imply, it is biography which offers the best chance of preserving

---

18 *Bonhoeffer: Agent of Grace*, film presented 1999 by NFP Teleart GMBH and Co. and Norflicks Products Ltd in cooperation with Aid Association for Lutherans. Video distributed by Fortress Press.

what is at risk in study of the human scene today: the *wholeness* of our multifaceted life which may be capable of dissection into its various spheres as an academic exercise but as experienced by real people is one reality. Pure clay may not be possible out of time's mud, but who wants pure clay when it is in the very earthiness of temporal human life that the Word became flesh, and grace appears?

CHAPTER 10

Writing Local Church History

Haddon Willmer

John Briggs and I met as freshmen reading History at Cambridge nearly half a century ago. Now in our active retirements we have, besides our pensions, stores of experience to mull over. Perhaps we should give ourselves the leisure to do that—if mulling can be saved from being pointless self-indulgence. I think of a Baptist church founded a few years before we met. When I first knew it, it was in the innocence of youth— deciding its character, excited in doing things for the first time. Now it has settled habits and it has so much experience that it seeks relief from some of it in forgetfulness. Should this *church* have 'each sweet Ebenezer in review', along with the 'cisterns all broken'—even though it has lost the hymnody and the reading of the Authorized Version of the Bible which would make such expressions intelligible? Put the question in the plain secularised language which may be all the church now has left: should this local church write a history to mark its fifty years? Can it?

Why?

There are secular reasons for attempting it. A church is an idiosyncratic piece in the mosaic of local history and society. As face to face, participative local community has weakened, it may be useful to tell the story of any group such as a local church which has resisted, even bucked, the trend. Civil society is an empty ideological wish, unless there are, on the ground, intentional communities, with the courage to dissent and to take initiatives out of obedience to a transcendent call, not asking for the permission of the state or the support of the cultural mainstream—or even of bishops and the like.

In a society that sees itself increasingly as secular, so that it overlooks churches because it has ceased to have an eye for them, it is an issue of public health to tell the story of local churches, both as points where people are gathered in community and as bases for diasporic mission and service in society at large. In a society where religion has social salience mostly as it is intertwined with minority ethnicity, and where the white majority is judged to be secular and decisively dechristianised, media and administration assume too glibly that Christianity is dying, in contrast to other faiths which are lively and growing. A local church history might have a critical impact on these convenient but misleading simplicities of social managers and secular interpreters.

But the church has its own vital churchly reasons for taking on the hard work of writing a history. The local church professes to be a community of people called by God to be his friends, to share his life and mission. The church lives by confessed faith. It looks to God in prayer. The church is the steward and carrier of the gospel of grace. This gospel is not empty words, but the living word of God. The gospel therefore has a history in the church, if it has any truth; and the church's history is at heart the accounting for its standing or falling, which turns on its relation to the gospel. It is not consistent to confess faith in the history-making God of the Bible, Father, Son and Holy Spirit, making all things new and then to shy away from telling our own little histories within the horizons and priorities of the revelation and grace of God. A body claiming to be church is without integrity if it does not attempt to understand its history in wider categories than those of secular caution.

Church history is indeed to be written in modern fashion, evidence-based, critically open in interpretation, but it should be unhappy if there is little about the style and substance of what it writes to remind us of the Bible and to root us more deeply in the history-making love of God in Christ. The church is a community of faith only within the constant practice of critical reflection on its history. This reflection is not a way of leaving faith behind, but is an action of faith seeking understanding for fuller obedience. The church seeks to know itself by examining the way it has come to the present moment. The church takes responsibility for the way it is and, for that, it needs to understand its own history as the history of the gospel within the history of the world. Church history is a means of churchly self-monitoring, which helps it to navigate through the times given to it.

The Church Responsible in Time

The function of history in the church's service of God is not to root us in the past, but to help us to understand ourselves and our situation so that we may be faithful now to God's calling. The church is always in time, in situations where it must make decisions about its way. God does not have puppets or spare the church this responsibility. Church meetings, like councils and the papacy, not only may err, but do err and stray from God's ways (but not like lost sheep, rather as human beings who should know what they are doing). Nowhere in the church does God take away human freedom by the Spirit. Fallibility does not excuse the church from using every means to find the wisdom to make good decisions, which are simultaneously ambitious for the kingdom of God and modest in their reformability.

How then is *church* history to be written, if its centre is the history of the gospel in the church? In the church, all sorts of secular and religious elements, including theology, spirituality, church sociality, ethics, action and organisation intertwine: a history has to make the complexity intelligible, rather than denying it by simplification. Very easily church history slips into a kind of organisational history or cultural studies where the gospel is not the norm and inspiration of the enquiry. The slippage will not be prevented by imposing some doctrinal orthodoxy as the constant marker amidst the fluctuations of church life. Writing the history of doctrine, even of what we believe is essential and true doctrine, is not the same as writing the history of the gospel in the church. The historian needs to look for what I call 'operative theologies', which encompass the complexity of church existence, to discern what gospel the church really believes, embodies and communicates through the activities and relationships which make up the totality of its being. An operative theology of a church may be at variance, for better or worse, with the professed doctrine of the church. An operative *theology* is what the church is in relation to God, in the wholeness of its living. Operative theologies are useful heuristic instruments to get at the distinctive interrelating features of a local church, and at important changes it has worked through as a community of the gospel. A church may adhere without apparent change to an ancient doctrinal statement, while, as church seeking to be contextually faithful, it runs through a succession of operative theologies.

Why the History of the Last Fifty Years?

The most recent fifty years or so of any group's history is special, because that is virtually the whole of the period which is represented in the community today by persons still alive who shared in making and suffering the church's history. The church as an inclusive fellowship of responsible persons, who are called to grow up into truth in the love of Christ, has to be aware of and to incorporate what each of its living members bring to it. But this can only be done with those who are alive today.

Go back more than fifty years and we have to reckon seriously with the death of the past. Those who made history then are no longer alive now. They cannot explain, defend, prolong, apologise for, attempt to modify the outcomes of their action by doing something more. What they have done may be open to multiple interpretations and exploitations, but they no longer are the living, changing agents and foci of the process. The dead may be held in honour or execrated; they may illumine our life now, but only because *we* think about and make something of inert relics, their 'remains'. Those who now live have to pick up the pieces the dead have left as best they can. But they will not have them as fellow-workers in the flesh. Most of the dead are gone entirely into oblivion; we do not even know their names. Even those who have left evidence behind them have no voice to question what we make of it. (John: did you hear Saltmarsh in 1958, lecturing on archaeological sources for very early economic history, pathetically declaiming: 'But—the stones do not speak!'?) Though the old are on average nearer to the dead than the young, they are not to be treated as having already joined their company. Loving concern for senior people is proper to the church: listening to and respecting what the old have to say for themselves may save us on the day when the Son of Man comes: 'When did we see you old and overlooked you, as though you were already dead?' Many of the old are vigorously opinionated, loathe to yield interpretation and management to the young. So the history of the last fifty years is open to contestation in the whole community, in a way that earlier history is not.

Conversation and Congregational Edification

In the congregation of the living, the oldest sources are still part of the discussion about what the past means. Historical work on the last half-century is essentially conversational. It contributes very directly to answering questions like: Who are we today? What is this community? What has it been making of itself in the time in which we have been consciously active? What is its situation and condition? What are its possibilities for the future?

Because it is a *conversation* for the whole church, church history cannot be restricted to the faithful *recording* of the reminiscences of the old—that would be scissors-and-paste. It does not give an uncritical platform to the memories of the old: they are not fresh and reliable eyewitness accounts, for they have been spun and respun over the years in favour of the tellers. The old can insist on their accounts of the past or keep evidence locked up as their secret (too much for the young to bear, but we were tough, they say), so the conversation is truncated. As we get older, the lust for gerontocracy may grow (*Après moi, le déluge*) until we are saved only by forced terminal resignation. To get away from such control, the young may decide not to listen to the old any more. Thus, the one congregation is divided; but does the grace of God concede that 'crabbed age and youth' cannot live together? Rather, let us seek history writing as congregational edification.

This is not to claim that the old have more wisdom than the young—and therefore should be listened to with a view to going on just like our fathers did. The older people in the church should be modest in their claims. Individually, they have messed up and fallen short in various ways; taken together, we who are old today must admit how far we have failed to prevent or even come to terms with the massive decline of Christianity in this country in our lifetime. The elders are all fallen—though not more fallen than anyone else. They make a major contribution to church history by filling it out as a confession of sin and a record of sufferings. The natural man dies hard, lusting for unending celebration culminating in the one-sidedness of polite obituary; but the man in Christ grows into the truth: 'Nothing in my hand I bring, simply to thy Cross I cling'.

Practical Forgiving

Building up the congregation involves working with the people who are available. Though ministers and leaders sometimes sweep in like new brooms, and, deliberately or accidentally, purge the membership in order to renew the church, it is in the long run no way to build up the congregation. Eventually, even the perfect have to reconcile themselves, as God has done, to eating with publicans and sinners. It is in the table talk of Jesus, not by expulsions, that the church is sifted and reformed. What happens in meals where Jesus is present is decisive spiritual exposure of the detailed practices which are the building blocks of the history of the church: disciples disputing who is the greatest, or people despising a disreputable woman doing a good deed are made to think again and see themselves in a new way.

Older people, available to the church, are wrinkled by the struggles they have gone through—sometimes they load themselves with boasts built up over a lifetime which may cover unpacified insecurity; sometimes they are worn out by honest toil; sometimes they shrivel inside prisons of bitterness and disappointment. It requires spiritual discipline in the old to avoid writing church history so as to pass on their distortions and hurts in lament, complaint, accusation. Martyrology too easily interprets the death of the faithful to establish an overriding claim, a moral hold, over those who come after. More easily than we might suppose, Christian education can aim at loading the young with all the grievance and limitations of earlier generations, so that they do not have to wait until their own creative attempt to serve God brings them into their own share of suffering. Although Christianity has martyrs, its faith and ethics is not to be shaped by them. Jesus is not Lord through martyrdom in this sense: he died in a way that was forgiving, thus setting the future, and his disciples, free from any obligation to avenge him. As human and as Christian, we are called in Christ only to *liberating* remembrance, not to guiding and binding memory. And yet the losses, defeats, perplexities of life cannot be denied. Can the history of the church be written in freedom from the past's dead hands, the empty fingers still straining for satisfaction? Can this be done without a callous indifference to the dead which is incompatible with the hell-harrowing love of God? Can we review past conflicts and injustice, which cry out for revenge, in the spirit of the love of God for his enemies (which is the never to be forgotten foundation of the church)? Was it peace Christ made in the cross, or is that still the sign in which to conquer? Can those who are making new futures, aiming not to repeat the mistakes of the past and refusing to run complacently in the ruts of tradition, at the same time remember the past redemptively? History-writing will not redeem the past by excusing it, by gilding the cross or forgetting how the rulers of this age crucified the Lord of glory along with all their other victims, but only by learning from it, and by trying to live afresh from the reality to which the past has brought us. Resurrection means God begins again at the cross to which his love and the sin of the world has brought us all together. Each new day, to the end of life, invites old and young to try afresh in good hope. Simply because they probably have more years in front of them, younger people are significant—by younger people I mean not so much infants or teenagers, as everybody who is at least ten years younger than I am— because they are in a position to embark on *and finish* large projects for which I no longer have time. Such people *represent* the freedom of the future in the church, but they do not *possess* it, however great the virtue of their relative youth. The disappointed old are not to be left to seek empty comfort in stoic self-containment; being in church means they may trust God for resurrective redemption, earthed in the next generation's work. The young can truly help the old only if they strike out freely into new life, leaving father and mother. Of course if they leave as the prodigal did, to waste his father's substance in riotous living, they will bring the parents down to the grave in sorrow. But if they make a good attempt to live well, though differently from their parents, then the old will be blessed with signs of surprising redemption: they can depart in peace because they have seen the salvation of the Lord; they can accept the ending of their own life, although their own work was incomplete and faulty, because the work of God is being carried on in new ways responsive to new situations. The old are comforted not by seeing themselves prolonged in the young, but by sharing in Christ who is being formed in them too.

The old then do not demand or generate church history as celebratory vindication of their past. Nor is church history a record of the past detached from the future. Because it is a work of the inter-generational community, church history knows the past in the freedom and responsibility of the present which is called into the future. The church's historical work is transparent conversation between unrepeatable pasts and finite but open futures.

Friends

It is unlikely that a church, as a merely human company, will survive and grow so that it gets into a position to think of writing a fiftieth anniversary history, if it is unfriendly. The occurrence of friendship is an immense resource for the church. Little fruitful church history is made by friendless or unfriendly people. Certainly, the Baptist mode of church, as responsible covenanting congregation growing into Christ through truth and love, requires friendship as its medium. Since it is without coercive bonds, a voluntary association has to draw people into friendship if it is to hold them.

God as Trinity of love is the ground and source of the gospel as good news of a friendly God. God reaches to the ends of the earth, down to hell, making friends with enemies. The church has no life with integrity if it does not take the way of friendship. With all its limitations, 'as much as in it lies', it is to be at peace with all. Church is not merely a place where friendships happen, but where they are cultivated, disciplined, understood. Living in church should involve formal and informal training for friendship. In the context of its positive valuation of friendship, the church cannot but reckon with the shortfall in friendships—sometimes merely shallow, sometimes hurtfully broken by evil. Humanity in church is not unfallen, so friendship there needs to be criticised and redeemed in the gospel.

Friendships have histories and make histories. Charting the friendships in and around a church is a practicable way into the history of the gospel in the church. Friendship trees, like family trees, could be drawn up. Who has been friends with whom? How did they come together? What was the bond and inspiration of their friendship? Who have been the inspiring friendship-makers? Who the dependents of friendship made by others? Who the go-betweens and peace-makers? What strains did any friendship survive, what did it fall to—and how?

How did this friendship—or this circle of friends—relate to other circles in the church? Where were the centres of friend-circles, and where their peripheries? How were friend-circles related—by overlaps of their outlying members, or by links between their core members? How far did a friendship link friends in the church with friends outside? Who was excluded from this friendship—against whom was it a defence or a ploy? (Some friendships have negative inspirations and dynamics.)

How was the church built up or complicated by this or that friendship? Was the church aware of the importance of friendship? Did it do anything to foster friendships? Was there ever preaching and praying about it? What aspects of the church's life and organisation fostered or burdened this friendship?

Was this friendship grounded in a shared involvement in some part of the work of the church? Was it a friendship for the sake of the church? Some friendships are made through *working* as church together. Church is a common project in which people grow together through responding actively to a shared vision and loyalty. It is a journey, if not quite a contemporary *Canterbury Tales*, where people get to know one another. Focused by the gospel, friendship might have its centre in sharing in mission, serving something greater than themselves. Such friendship is then sustained by service—by 'office' rather than by merely personal attachments, to borrow the distinction Bonhoeffer used in his wedding sermon of 1943.[1]

Friendship oriented by churchwork may be distinguished from other friendships amongst church people, which can be more than semi-*detached* from the work of the church. Church can be a *place* where we meet other people and so find friends, but the joy of friendship is not integrated with the *joy of being* church. They are friendships which are untouched by church mission and responsibility. Such friendships may thus be part of the story of secularisation within the church, which is a topic not to be evaded in recent church history. Yet they are not on that account to be despised as worthless. The secular is also part of God's creation, not merely an occurrence within the space allowed by his permission, but a dimension of the human life God wills and delights in: the secular is the sacrament of human otherness, freedom and responsibility, and therefore it is also the sacrament of the will of God, who wants human partners not sacred puppets or dusty angels. The pietism which has marginalised uniformed youth organisations because they are not explicitly christian or 'keen' enough has too often relied on inadequate theology to defend its policy.

Sometimes friendship detached from the mission and management of church is all that keeps people in church. Church can be painful and

---

1 D. Bonhoeffer, *Letters and Papers from Prison* (ed. E. Bethge; New York: Collier, 1972), pp. 42-43.

dispiriting: the music distasteful, the preaching boring and yet complacent, the politics and organisation frustrating. Then people may take *refuge* in friendships. Sometimes they mourn together about what is going on in church—but they do it quietly in a trusted circle of friends, because otherwise they know the elders will preach against what they see as nothing but grumbling and a lack of submission, rather than as symptoms of malaise. Sometimes, people are too weary even to grumble: 'Tonight', they say, 'we will look after ourselves, keeping our friendships in repair, so we will talk about anything but church.' They may be one step away from leaving church altogether, as so many have in the last fifty years, on the verge of adding to that large crowd fixed outside the church by hurtful memories of why they left. But sometimes these mere friendships help people to get through periods of exasperation with church, so they stay long enough to give it another chance: people hesitate to make a final break with church where they have so many longstanding friends. It is not a sign of a wholly unchristian judgment if people decide that putting up with unsatisfactory church is a price worth paying for lively mature friendships. Churches would do better if their ardent leaders and people-managers had a better narrative awareness of how important this kind of calculation is for many people.

In all this, some of the strange and beautiful complications of life appear. For example, sometimes those who exercise power in ways which cause people to retire hurt from church, also make church attractive by the practical help they offer in genuine friendship. Sometimes people who make the public church hard to bear, by the religion they impose, show themselves in ordinary dealings to be considerate, humble and wise. The paradox of their humanity in church is comparable to the complexity of politicians, alienating by their ya-booing in debate, secretive under questioning, yet surprisingly thoughtful and open if ever they get into genuinely responsible conversation.

Friendship by itself is not enough to carry church in the full sense. Friendship, like music or caring for the fabric, or pastoral care, or even some sorts of evangelism as recruitment, can be an activity without intelligible connection with the profession of faith in God which is essential to church. But if friendship without confessed faith is not enough, it can at least hold people in the broad life of the church, within the hearing of the gospel; and without friendship, as James might say, faith is dead.

An enquiry into friendships would produce a much better historical picture than the notion of the church as a family. The family model is a fiction which has not helped the church in recent times. A history of friendship would also produce a better picture than the conventional structuring of historical narrative around the succession of ministers: friendship is a category which will include everyone, transcending any clericalist model. Discovering where ministers fit into friendship trees would tell us much about the history of ministry. Once ministers were told to avoid having friends in the church where they ministered lest they were seen to have favourites, failed to be equally available to all and got mired in church politics. That prohibition has faded, but there are still difficulties. Ministers are under stress, it seems, partly because they do not find supportive friendship in the church with the people who are constantly available to them.

Chasing the history of friendship will take us into the ordinary humanity of the church. That may be one reason why it is under-investigated in conventional historiography. Moreover, because it is mostly undocumented, it is not available to the historian working on documentary sources. But the living church in conversation is not so limited: the history of friendships is the systematising of its gossip. Friendships in one generation produce family connections as children marry. As friends talk, they recall and chew over experiences in church: without knowing it, they do church historical work. They build up the traditions, the jokes, as they put one layer of recall upon another, in response to new circumstance.

But the historian, or the church writing its own history, cannot expect the whole work to be done for them by the ordinary incessant chatter of friends. The care of friends for one another may well inhibit research into the history of friendship. Tact and respect for privacy rarely help the historian. Friendship tends to be patiently tolerant, uninterfering, un-inquisitive. To be a friend is to give the other space; we allow a friend to have his secrets, even guilty secrets—friendship does not want to know. Part of the goodness of friendship is that it is a loyalty to the person regardless of performance—it is looser than marriage or patriotism because it is less demanding—but it means friends shrug their shoulders where the historian starts digging. Friendship cools when one becomes suspicious of the other with an urgent need to know. Friends are for relaxing with.

Friends collude in developing stories and cultures which are like ideological armour shielding them from difficult truths about themselves. Their conversation, left to itself, has a built-in protection against the investigative historian. People who survive in church, as in life, develop stories selectively and purposefully. They want to put the best face they can on strife, sorrow, disappointment, boredom, unbelief, ineffectiveness and confusion in the church. How morale-boosting is the rhetoric of the Pharisee who went up to the Temple to pray—how friendly he was to himself. But the dismal service of the historian is in part to be the publican's voice and to get behind the best-face mask. History in the service of the gospel aims at a true confession of sin and a new life in the truth of forgiveness. The gospel is not hostile to friendship, but it requires friendship to transcend its easy natural forms.

Power

Friendship is not the only category we need to trace the history of the gospel in the church. No doubt there are many other themes of heuristic utility to be explored. In this discussion, we will consider one more, which has already appeared on the edges of friendship: *power*. The gospel is believed to be 'the power of God unto salvation'. Disciples receive power to be witnesses when the Holy Spirit comes upon them. The church is organised power. Nothing is without some kind of power intrinsic to its existence. All persons in themselves are power: the young have energy, innocence, time, capacity for growth; the old have proven experience, a repertoire of tricks, a fund of earned respect. Friendship is one sort of power—and unfriendliness is another.

Conventionally, histories of the contemporary church are as up-beat as possible, dwelling on what has been achieved and so on works of power of the sort that serve and realise gospel. The will to friendship, our desire not to damage the morale of fragile churches, and even our faith in God inhibit us from an unbounded exploration of power in church. We know enough about the church, without doing any research, to fear that to investigate power will open a can of worms—and, healthily, we have lost the taste for seeing ourselves as miserable worms. The church historian does not want to be like a muck-raking journalist. Nevertheless the discomfiting truth is that there cannot be church without power, and yet the powers at work in church often show themselves incompetent to build a plausible church has to be faced. This truth has to be worked through by the church, in the church, if it is not to be worked over by those outside the church, against the church. The church's mission is in trouble if the difference between the self-image it cultivates for internal consumption and the way outsiders see it cannot be bridged by honest intelligent conversation with those outside. The inadequacy of church power to match up to the tasks and standards set by the gospel unsettles us. In the church we will find examples of authoritarian, self-indulgent abuse of power by those who hold it, as well as their disillusioning incompetence. Where there is power, there will also be exclusion from power: in the church, there are mini-Machiavellis, whose frustrated obsession with power is rooted in the experience of not having it. Those who are spiritual and those who are friendly (two overlapping but not identical types) prefer the church to have an imagined life where there is no power but God's gentleness. There is damaging collusion between some spiritual people who want a higher life, friendly people who want a quiet life, and visionary people who are impatient for the true living church: they all try to have church without reckoning with the ambiguous realities of power. It is often held to be improper to look at ecumenical relations in terms of power, for the equality of churches is assumed, as though differences in size, wealth and political skills have no effect on their relationships. The resulting untruth breeds alienating scepticism about ecumenism. Some Baptists like to conceive church meetings theocratically, beyond being analysed realistically by analogies with democracy and constitutional politics, or with autocracy and management manipulation. Then they may be conducted without the ordinary decencies and concern for truth which has been painfully learned in some modern societies through centuries of struggle and experiment. The church is unwise to undervalue the gifts of such modernity.

Power goes astray in several directions. There is the *deliberate* abuse of excessive or unequally shared power in a community, power which can be tyrannical and manipulative. And there is *disillusioning* power, promising the enabling service necessary for humanity, but then proving incompetent to deliver the promise. Power is not always what it seems to be: it can be running for cover from its own insecurity. Then it seeks to escape accountability; it looks for freedom to act under cover of darkness. Secrecy expands power. Calling power to account is hard work; often ordinary church members, like ordinary citizens, have apparently better things to do—and so evil triumphs as good men do nothing. In church, these abuses are further corrupted by being spiritualised. Leaders are surrounded with divine aura ('Touch not the Lord's anointed') and the natural laziness and timidity of good people is justified by false teaching about submission as a virtue.

This incapacity to deal with power is common in the modern Baptist church where charismatic irrational ecstasy and mere administration have quenched the spirit of seventeenth-century rebellion and subsequent political creativity in the church. The spiritual flight from organisational formality has undermined church meetings. We have given up learning from worldly politics how to manage power; there is little transfer of practical learning between church and politics. Church often says it wants to be counter-cultural, prophetic, speaking truth to power, but it is ill-equipped to do so, since it cannot recognise or engage with the problems of power in itself. More ecumenical and historical literacy might help us to see that what the liberal Roman Catholic Lord Acton learned from studying the early modern papacy applies even to little Baptist churches now: all power tends to corrupt, and absolute power corrupts absolutely. Did you, John, like me, hear Walter Ullmann's lectures on medieval political thought? He schematised the conflictual history of cosmic and social order in the western medieval world in two 'theses' which it might be useful for the local church historian to reflect on still. According to the 'descending thesis' of government, all authority comes from God, flowing downwards through his representatives. So peasants look up to princes and lay people look up to priests. The 'ascending thesis' grew largely out of experience of the corruptions of the church. Those above did not oversee those beneath with reliable pastoral care, let alone humility and willingness to learn; instead they simply looked down on them. Faced with the demand for comprehensive reform 'in head and members' the 'heads', whether pope or king, or their successors, offered to reform members, while defending their own immunity from the reforming efforts of the members. Nevertheless, in some places, those below claimed authority. That involved more than force. They had to replace the apparently God-honouring thesis which put him at the apex from which all authority and power flowed. And that is difficult in churches that love to sing about enthronements. That authority could flow from below, from the people, has often been condemned as essentially secular, a democratic onslaught on the authority of God. But the ascending thesis is not necessarily godless: indeed it may put us on the track of the God who 'abhors not the Virgin's womb' making his dwelling with ordinary people. God creates all, speaks to all, calls all, asks service of all, seeks to bring all to glory. God's Spirit roves everywhere, freely. In the fellowship of God, his word does not only come from above, from the high-ups; a little child shall lead them and it is the still small voice they listen for. The ascending thesis was articulated within the later medieval Catholic Church, especially in the unhappily frustrated conciliar movement; Baptist churches should not forget their place in this development. It is odd when Baptist churches carry on as though they have no roots and no investment in the ascending thesis, and they need to work practically and theologically with the possibility it opens up, against all the oppressive, dumbing down power of the descending thesis.

Of course, the issue presents itself in a local church today in contemporary idioms. Power in church rests to a significant degree on personal relationships and allegiance, on friendship, fascination, crushes and personality-cults. The pulpit is easily exploited to build the church around the minister. It is doubtful whether this corruption has been prevented by moving to the guitar-laden platform, which has gone along with the switch from word to Spirit, from thought to feeling, from buttoned-up reticence to pop-culture self-projection, the last enhanced rather than disciplined by postmodern irony. Power in church tends to be personal rather than institutional; it is hidden in life's goings out and in, rather than made transparently accountable. Sermons and the conduct of worship bolster the power of leaders as they assume a significant, if mostly unconscious, personal identification with the gospel proclaimed. Such glorification is damaging enough for the fans, but even worse for the stars. An old ambassador came to Mussolini to report on an international conference about gas-warfare. 'Well', said the Duce, 'and what is the most dangerous gas?' *'Incense'*, the old man said. Ministers and leaders have often suffered from the admiration of people which they have preferred to the koinonia of critical conversation. While most other forms of monological speech-communication have declined, the sermon in Baptist churches would seem to have remained popular, or at least easily tolerated—in the church I know best sermons are probably longer than they were fifty years ago. It is therefore sad that institutionally there is virtually no accountability of the pulpit, no monitoring, or in-service training. It is easy for a preacher to promise well at the beginning, but to run to seed as his career progresses. The pulpit has an immunity which shields it from open discussion or shared preparation. Preaching, the preachers say, is a very personal matter: the preacher's responsibility is directly to God, in an unchurchly, individualistic, private fashion. Preachers are not wholly to blame for this situation. The church is unaware that preaching is a function not of the person in the pulpit, but of the whole church. Church meetings never discuss the quality of the preaching and how it could be improved.

The history of the last fifty years might show a decline, or at least, no increase in, the church's capacity to understand and manage power. But there is no freedom from power: if we fail to channel and discipline it with understanding, it will not evaporate, but rather to explode into destructive and baffling mayhem. Such preventable occurrences are not infrequently part of a local church's history. I confess that, having seen so much irresponsible and incompetent power in the church, I tend, in discussing how to write its history, to emphasise the need to *check* and *control* power. However, the validity of power comes logically before its control. We cannot check what is not there. Power is good before it is bad. The apparently spiritual temptation to honour God by eschewing power must be resisted. To attempt to live without power is ingratitude to the creator. It is to mistake the cross: that God's weakness is stronger than all other power does not make unqualified weakness or powerlessness a virtue. The history of the church, in the last fifty years, as in any other time, would not be made were it not for power of some sort. Despite and beyond all the church's sin and falling short of the glory of God, I believe there is still, and want to hear, a history of the gospel in the church by the abounding grace of God. It must be brought out into the open, not as though it is the only strand in the story, not as though it cancels the story of sin as though it never happened, but as a story of grace, love and hope as the gospel of God in humanity through Jesus Christ by the Spirit. The real church goes on existing only by being forgiven—and forgiving is always a particular use of power.

In a period when so many have been leaving church, or like the man who hid his talent in the earth, quietly filling up their place in the pew, but doing nothing else, church history must give prominence to telling the story of those who have displayed the power of an active faith, determined to oppose the cultural anti-Christian tide, not giving way to the deception that there can be Christian believing without belonging. The positive story of the gospel in the church is seen in those who give time and money, a bit of heart and even mind to the church, working hard to gather and hold groups for fellowship and teaching and service, and who have proved to be sacrificial (albeit undramatically) in making the most of every opportunity to share Christ. All this takes hard work which is not for the powerless. It involves taking up the cross in sorrow and care and love, in the struggle for health and hope in the confusions of people's lives. There are stories of power here. Influence is sought and won. Dangerous interventions in other people's affairs are taken, though not necessarily with violence or without consent. The power here is undeniable, however mysteriously human character and divine spirit may have mixed to make it what it is. And this power, which on the human side often does not understand itself, includes the capacity to take risks, to endure hardship, even to take Luther's advice to sin boldly. So the church in this half-century has accumulated an ambiguous history of faith, service and sin. Has it lost valuable habits and treasures, or has it been stripped of worn-out baggage? Has it progressed from one renewing movement to another, or has it passed through charismatic *renewal* to stifling charismatic *culture* and beyond that, to falling for divisive Toronto blessings? To its credit, it has never given up evangelism, from Billy Graham, through Lewis Misselbrook to Alpha. Taking risks for the gospel, it has gone into church planting and got tangled in building ecclesiastical empires which, like all empires, get out of hand and discredit themselves, show their feet of clay and collapse upon those who live within them. The history of the church, as of humanity, needs to be read and written within the perspective of the Christian gospel of forgiveness, not under the Gnostic wish that this world should never have happened because all its power is necessarily evil.

Is the Gospel Still There in Church for Us?

Considering power brings us into fundamental spiritual and theological crisis. The duty to be active in representing and following the gospel, seeking to be faithful to it in social form in the present (which is church-making) brings us face to face with impossible tasks and with profound discouragement—like Jeremiah, we did not ask to be chosen to do this work, and do not think it fair when we find we have been chosen only in order to be discredited by immersion in the mess of history-making.

When we feel like this about the church, even as the church, the critical question comes home: *is the gospel still there for us*? Can we take any comfort in the gospel if we discover it is preached only in unfriendliness and in the corruptions of power and ambition (Phil. 1.15-18)? The grace given to Paul enabled him to see that, whether out of false motives or true, *Christ was proclaimed*, and in that he could rejoice. Can we also rejoice? Sometimes it is not easy. There is incessant proclamation, but is *Christ* proclaimed? It is possible that sometimes the church blots out the sun, as Stephen Spender suggested was generally the case, the sins of the church making Christ invisible.[2] In view of the last fifty years, this is not an issue the church can brush aside, as simply ruled out by the faithfulness of God. Do we not have to do also with the God of the prophets, who dared in agony to tell the chosen people that God's faithfulness was not to be presumed on, that he could withdraw from them and let them be 'Not My People'? It is an interesting question which goes deep into the heart and mind of the church: how have local churches managed to go on in this time, after the Holocaust, in a century of terrors, rejoicing that despite all imperfections in its proclamation and service, the gospel is still proclaimed in the world? The history can be searched for answers. Can it be shown that the church has been aware of its precarious spiritual and evangelistic situation? Has it taken the measure of the difficulties of Christian communication in this time? Has it worked to discern and recover the gospel for itself—even before it preaches to anyone else—so that we can now write a history composed of the successive recoveries of the gospel, by which the church has been able to rejoice that somehow the *Gospel* has been, and will be, proclaimed? Does the history of the church have the same pattern as the story of the disciples in the gospel— God in Christ is not spared being obscured in darkness at the cross, nor the disciples their scattering, but then there follows, beyond expectation, resurrection to newness of life?

The gospel does not have a simple continuous history in the church. Old-time religion is always passing away, and most of it is probably is not to be regretted. If it was useful in its day, it did well enough. It is inhuman to ask for more. Only Jesus Christ is the same yesterday and today and forever—and 'same' here has a special mysterious sense. The Vincentian Canon is not a good guide: what has been 'believed everywhere, always and by everyone' is so minimal as to be a husk without a kernel of life. The church lives not by the continuity of its possession but by the recurrences of grace. God gives us to rejoice in one and then another contextual recovery and re-presentation of the gospel. Thus the gospel has to be appreciated historically, in its comings, goings,

---

2 S. Spender, 'The Landscape Near an Aerodrome', in *Collected Poems 1928-1985* (London: Faber & Faber, 1985), p. 42.

in its tarrying and its coming again. With modesty and fear, the church may go over its history in search of the gospel. Acquiring the skill of historical thinking may help it to hear what God is saying now.

CHAPTER 11

Attitudes Towards Erring Brothers and Sisters in Early Christianity as Reflected in the New Testament

John E. Morgan-Wynne

Such a theme seems appropriate in a volume *Ecumenism and History* and in a time when certain Christian churches still use some such phrase as erring brothers or sisters of other Christians. The attempt to survey the evidence of the New Testament in a single chapter runs the risk of superficiality, but there is perhaps value in an overview which gives the main outlines. There are, of course, a number of ways in which fellow believers may be considered to be erring or going astray. For the purposes of this essay, we have chosen five areas for examination,

Morally Unacceptable Behaviour

By morally unacceptable behaviour we mean, broadly speaking, breaches of the Ten Commandments, which were accepted and endorsed by Jesus and are reflected in the ethical exhortations of the letters of the New Testament.

Acts

From the early years of the church in Jerusalem comes the Ananias and Sapphira episode (Acts 5). The couple were not under an obligation to sell and hand over the total amount of their piece of property to the congregation. Their fault lay in lying to the Holy Spirit (represented by Peter, leader of a group who believed itself the recipients of the eschatological promise of the Holy Spirit in Joel 2.18-22). By that action, they had allowed the forces of evil (Satan) to invade the community and break its integrity and holiness (Acts 5.3). It should be noted that Peter does not actually pronounce judgment on either Ananias (vv. 3-4) or Sapphira (though he predicts her death v. 9). In the case of both of them there was opportunity of repentance and confession after Peter's questions to them (vv. 4, 8 and 9). The atmosphere in which the event takes place is reminiscent of Jesus' words: 'Every sin and blasphemy uttered by people will be forgiven them, but whoever blasphemes against the Holy Spirit will never be forgiven but is guilty of an eternal sin' (Mk 3.28-29). The community of the End Time, indwelt by God's Spirit, cannot tolerate such an offence against its holiness derived from the presence of the Holy Spirit.

Peter is also involved in a second episode relevant to our theme, this time in Samaria. Simon Magus, who had believed and been baptized by Philip (Acts 8.13), was deeply impressed by the fact that God's Spirit came on the Samaritan believers as a result of Peter's and John's laying hands on them (v. 17). He asks if he can buy the secret of this power. Peter says 'To hell with you and your money' and denies that Simon Magus can have any share in this ministry. His heart is not right with God. Despite the wish consigning Simon Magus to perdition, Peter urges him to repent and pray to the Lord to see if perhaps forgiveness might be granted to him (v. 23) and Simon Magus asks Peter to pray for him (v. 24).

Some scholars think that Simon Magus never truly became a Christian,[1] but it may be better to speak of a superficial faith with no transformation of his previous interest in power over people by extraordinary deeds (vv. 9-11), which reasserted itself when he saw the descent of the Spirit (vv. 16-18). H.-J. Klauck's view of Luke's aim is worth quoting: 'Luke's aim here is to make an appeal to his readers. Sadly it often happens that believers lapse in the way described above, and then a severe call to repentance is required. What happens next, depends not least on the behaviour of the sinner himself.'[2]

Common to both the episodes discussed is an offence against the Holy Spirit—lying to him (5.3), putting him to the test (5.9) and believing that humans had control over him (8.19).[3] The Spirit-filled Peter speaks to

---

1   E.g. B. Witherington III, *The Acts of the Apostles: A Socio-Rhetorical Commentary* (Grand Rapids, MI: Eerdmans/Carlisle: Paternoster, 1998), p. 288; cf. J.D.G. Dunn *Baptism in the Holy Spirit: A Re-examination of the New Testament Teaching on the Gift of the Spirit in relation to Pentecostalism today* (London: SCM Press, 1970), pp. 66-67.
2   H.-J. Klauck, *Magic and Paganism in Early Christianity* (Edinburgh: T. & T. Clark, 2000), p. 23.
3   G. Forkman, *The Limits of the Religious Community* (Lund: Gleerup, 1972), p. 174, believes that the two episodes of Ananias–Sapphira and Simon Magus answered the

the hearts of men and women and exposes the wrong attitudes lurking there. Where he actually pronounces judgment on Simon Magus, he can still urge repentance and possible forgiveness.[4]

Paul

From the writings of Paul we take first his handling of the case of a man cohabiting with his step-mother (1 Cor.5.1-13), an action obnoxious to Jews and non-Jews alike (5.1). Paul is deeply concerned that the church has taken no action (v. 2). He goes on to demand the expulsion of the offender: the clear statements of both v. 2 (the offender should be removed from their midst) and v. 13 ('Expel the wrongdoer from you') explain the demand 'to deliver this man to Satan' as also meaning expulsion from the congregation (however formally that was carried out and whether some illness was expected to befall such a person). This step is necessary to preserve the moral and spiritual integrity of the congregation (vv. 6-7). (The 'ethos' is similar to that of the Jerusalem church in Acts 5.8, except that here the text speaks of the presence of the risen Lord, there of the Spirit—in practice and experience, there is no difference.) At the same time Paul does have hope for the ultimate salvation of the offender: he is to be 'handed over to Satan for the destruction of the flesh that the spirit may be saved in the Day of the Lord' (v. 5). Exactly how Paul envisaged this happening[5] is beyond the scope of this essay. Suffice to say that Paul combines a concern for the spiritual state of the whole congregation and a concern for the ultimate salvation of the individual offender.

If Paul is categorical about what should be done in this case just discussed, he appears to be more lenient, and prepared to reason, with those who under the banner of Christian liberty ('All things are lawful for me', 1 Cor. 6.12; 10.23) actually defended having sex with

---

question what does it mean for a member of the community to blaspheme against the Holy Spirit.

4   Though he does not discuss these two episodes, E. Käsemann's essay 'Sentences of Holy Law in the New Testament', in E. Käsemann, *New Testament Questions for Today* (London: SCM Press, 1969), pp. 66-81, is useful for an explanation of assumptions lying behind these kinds of stories.

5   Käsemann, 'Sentences', p. 71, thinks of bodily death; Forkman, *Limits*, pp. 144-45, of illness and death, with death atoning for one's crime, but could Paul envisage something additional to Christ's death as atoning?; W. Schrage, *Der erste Brief an die Korinther* (EKKNT, 7.1; 3 vols; Neukirchen-Vluyn: Neukirchener Verlag, 1991–99), p. 377, contents himself with speaking of real consequences in the physical realm. C. Wolff, *Der erste Brief des Paulus an die Korinther* (THKNT, 7; Leipzig: Evangelische Verlagsanstalt, 1996), p. 103, makes the significant comment that this was not the first action of this type—otherwise Paul would have had to explain himself.

prostitutes (1 Cor.6.12-20: Corinth was full of 'sacred' prostitutes serving the goddess Aphrodite and her temple). Paul recoils from the idea that such behaviour is permissible and on a par with satisfying the need for food. The body is not for immorality, but for the Lord and the Lord for the body (v. 13). The body is the temple for the Holy Spirit to indwell (v. 19) and will be raised on the last day (v. 14; cf. 1 Cor. 15.35-37). We are members of Christ and united to him, so that to become one flesh with a prostitute would damage irrevocably that union with Christ (vv. 15-17). Paul concludes by pointing out that they have been bought with a price (an allusion to Christ's redemptive death on the cross) and so ought to glorify God in their bodies (v. 20).

Paul knew full well that the new creation in Christ was not something instant but that our ethical transformation is a process. Here in 1 Corinthians 6.12-20 he argues theologically and spiritually in a pastoral attempt to wean people from a false view of Christian liberty to a sounder ethically based life under the lordship of Christ. Perhaps this helps to explain why he adopts this approach in 1 Corinthians 6.12-20, while 'laying down' the law' authoritatively on an issue where he knew both Jewish and Gentile readers would agree with him.

In 2 Corinthians 12.20–13.5 Paul expresses a fear that when at last[6] he pays another visit, the Corinthians will not be in the spiritual and moral state which he hopes for. He lists what possible faults may still exist (quarrelling, jealousy, outbursts of anger, intrigues, slander, gossip, arrogance and disorder (12.20).[7] He may have to grieve over those who have not repented of 'impurity, sexual sin and debauchery which they have committed' (12.21). This may refer to the sins discussed in 1 Corinthians 6.12-20. Paul then quotes Deuteronomy 19.15, a passage which exercised a considerable influence in the early church. We need not here enter into the debate whether or not there is a one to one correspondence between Paul's visits and the words 'two or three' in the Deuteronomy quotation. Clearly, either way, the Corinthians have had ample warning.[8] If there is no repentance when Paul arrives, then he will not spare the offenders—those who had sinned earlier and all the others (13.2). He will give a proof of the Christ who speaks through him and the Corinthians will experience Christ's power (vv. 3b-4).

---

6   This would be his third visit (2 Cor. 13.1), postponed because of the painful second visit (1.23; 2.1).

7   C.K. Barrett, *The Second Epistle to the Corinthians* (London: A. & C. Black, 1973), p. 329, comments, 'these sins suggest the effect of a rival mission'.

8   Barrett, *Second Epistle to the Corinthians*, p. 333; and R.P. Martin, *2 Corinthians* (WBC, 40; Waco, TX: Word, 1986), p. 470.

What action is in mind? Something similar to 1 Corinthians 5.5, 13 would seem to be Paul's intention: either expulsion from the church[9] or, if the majority were not behind Paul (he seems to envisage this as a possibility when he acknowledges at 12.21 that God may humble him before them when he comes), then a handing over to Satan conceived as producing illness and/or death.[10]

Matthew

Matthew's Gospel (c. AD 100[11]) records the procedures to be followed if a fellow Christian sins (18.15—the phrase 'against you' is probably secondary, contrary to the NIV and NRSV, both of whom allow it). Given Matthew's concern for moral standards, there is a presupposition that primarily moral sins are in mind, not doctrinal error, while an offence against a fellow Christian is too restrictive. The rule (hardly offered by Jesus himself) envisages three warnings: a private remonstrance, a semi-private one and finally a rebuke from the whole congregation. If this final warning is ignored, the offender is to be expelled (18.15-17). The ensuing verses (vv. 18-20) support theologically the congregation's taking this step. Because the risen Lord is present with it, the congregation will admit or exclude correctly, and God will ratify its decisions. There breathes through these verses the conviction that the congregation is the messianic people of the risen Lord, who is himself the executor of the Father's purposes (cf. 28.18-20). The risen Lord will guide his people. Nevertheless, the material with which the evangelist has surrounded this rule of discipline is highly significant: vv. 10-14 inculcate going after the wandering sheep, which stands for the erring

---

9   So F.V. Filson, 'The Second Epistle to the Corinthians', *The Interpreter's Bible* (12 vols; Nashville: Abingdon, 1951–57), X, pp. 16-17; P.E. Hughes *Paul's Second Epistle to the Corinthians* (London: Marshall, Morgan and Scott, 1962), p. 472.

10   Barrett, *Second Epistle to the Corinthians*, p. 334; cf. C.K. Barrett, *The First Epistle to the Corinthians* (London: A. & C. Black, 1968), p. 126.

11   Among those placing Matthew's Gospel in the last decade of the first century are G.D. Kilpatrick, *The Origins of the Gospel according to St Matthew* (Oxford: Clarendon Press, 1946), p. 130; G. Strecker, *Der Weg der Gerechtigkeit* (Göttingen: Vandenhoeck & Ruprecht, 2nd edn, 1966), p. 36; F.W. Beare, *The Gospel according to Matthew* (Oxford: Blackwell, 1981), p. 8. R.E. Brown, *Introduction to the New Testament* (Anchor Bible Reference Library; New York: Doubleday, 1996), pp. 172 and 217, while himself favouring AD 80–90, wisely adds, 'but at least a decade in either direction must be allowed'. Those who prefer the AD 80s include P. Bonnard, *L'Évangile selon saint Matthieu* (Neuchatel: Delachaux & Niestlé, 1963), p. 10; D. Hill, *The Gospel of Matthew* (London: Oliphants, 1972), p. 50; E. Schweizer, *The Good News according to Matthew* (London: SPCK, 1976), p. 15.

church member[12] (it is not the heavenly Father's will that one of these 'little ones' should perish); while vv. 21-35 record Peter's question about forgiveness and the parable of the unmerciful servant which deals with forgiveness and mercy. The joint teaching of these two units is that of unlimited forgiveness of one's 'brother or sister' (vv. 22, 35).

This surrounding material cannot but reverberate on the rule of discipline and the way in which it is implemented. This rule was current in Matthew's church (that is, it was tradition) but, by framing it with the material on either side, the evangelist was seeking to advocate a more merciful and kindly approach to sinners in the congregation. Thus, while Matthew teaches that there will be an ultimate separation at the End, until then the congregation must be concerned for those who go spiritually and morally astray and must be ready to forgive and go on forgiving in the face of wrongs.[13]

Jude

The bulk of Jude (the date of which is difficult to pinpoint, but may be late first century[14]) comprises a denunciation of false teachers, who in Jude's view are guilty of antinomianism, distorting God's grace into licentious conduct (vv. 4, 8), and a recall of God's past judgments on sinners as an indication of what the false teachers can expect (vv. 5-19). While care must be exercised in handling polemic, which is not an objective description of an opponent's views, there is nothing inherently improbable in some misinterpreting the grace of God and using it to justify immoral behaviour (cf. Rom. 6.1-11; and the views of some at Corinth discussed above). The positive part of this short letter comes in vv. 20-23 which comprises a fourfold exhortation in vv. 20-21, followed by an encouragement to try and save those whom the false teachers have influenced. Unfortunately there are a number of textual variants in vv. 22-23, a fact which complicates the issue. The text preferred by the United Bible Society's third edition (twenty-sixth edition of the Nestle–

---

12   Among numerous scholars who hold this view, we mention only J. Jeremias, *The Parables of Jesus* (London: SCM Press, 1963), p. 39, and W.G. Thompson, *Matthew's Advice to a Divided Community* (Rome: Biblical Institute Press, 1970), p. 174.

13   Cf. Forkman, *Limits*, p. 130, who states that the stress is no longer on expulsion but on the attempt at rescue.

14   Cf. W.G. Kümmel, *Introduction to the New Testament* (London: SCM Press, 1966), pp. 301-02, and J.N.D. Kelly, *The Epistles of Peter and Jude* (London: A. & C. Black, 1969), p. 234. But R.J. Bauckham, *Jude, 2 Peter* (WBC, 50; Waco, TX: Word, 1983), p. 13, prefers a much earlier date in the 50s.

Aland text) accepts the 'longer' reading, which we shall follow here:[15] 'Have mercy on some who are wavering; save others by snatching them out of the fire; and have mercy on still others, with fear, hating even the clothing defiled by the flesh.'

On this reading there are three groups in mind. Some have been unsettled by the false teachers. Compassion to them is called for. Others may have gone further under the influence of the false teachers, but are still capable of being saved. There is yet a third group, to whom mercy should be shown, but this is coupled with a warning to be on their guard lest they themselves be polluted by this group's behaviour ('Hate the sins but love the sinner').

2 Peter

By contrast, 2 Peter, a pseudonymous writing[16] which incorporates a part of Jude, contains only harsh polemic (especially in ch. 2) and it lacks pastoral concern for those under the sway of the false teaching. The writer's concern is to ensure that his hearers/readers will be able to confirm their call and election, to avoid stumbling-off the Godward way (1.10) and to wait in purity of life for the coming of the Lord (3.14, 17-18).

Inadvisable Behaviour

There may be cases where a fellow Christian's behaviour is not, strictly speaking, immoral, but is regarded as inadvisable. It may be a case of an exaggerated or too one-sided emphasis, with the result that the brother or sister is regarded as 'in error'. Asceticism might be deemed one such type of behaviour.

---

15   For a defence, see B.M. Metzger, *A Textual Commentary on the Greek New Testament* (London: United Bible Socities, corrected edn, 1975), pp. 726-27. Bauckham, *Jude, 2 Peter*, pp. 108-11, prefers the short reading attested by P72.

16   A pseudonymous writing which utilises a part of Jude and incorporates it with alterations and which may be dated into the second century, perhaps as late as c.AD 130. Kümmel, *Introduction*, p. 305, places it in the second quarter of the second century. Bauckham, *Jude, 2 Peter*, p. 158, again dates much earlier, to the late first century. Recent defenders of Petrine authorship are M. Green, *2 Peter and Jude* (London: IVP, revised edn, 1987), pp. 13-39; and D. Guthrie, *New Testament Introduction* (Leicester: Apollos, revised edn, 1990), pp. 811-42.

Paul

Before we look at asceticism specifically, however, we shall look at 2 Thessalonians 3.6-15, where Paul lays down what should be done in the case of those who have given up working and in their idleness are acting like busybodies (v. 11). He commands the rest of the congregation to keep away from any such brother (v. 6). This is basically repeated later: 'Do not associate with him'—with the purpose of making him feel ashamed (v. 14). Then Paul adds: 'Do not consider him as an enemy but admonish him as a brother' (v. 15). How can one hold aloof from someone and not associate with them *and* warn them about their conduct? One solution is to take the command to keep away from them as meaning not to supply them with the provisions necessary for their existence, or, at any rate, exclude them from any communal meals.[17] This would still allow the possibility of pastoral admonition in gatherings for worship or prayer and does not appear to envisage total exclusion.[18] Paul's aim is that the partial withdrawal of fellowship should have remedial effect—it should shame those concerned and lead to repentance and hence restoration of fellowship.

Corinth

There appear to have been some at any rate among the married couples at Corinth who favoured an ascetical approach. I shall assume that 1 Corinthians 7.1b quotes the opinion of these particular church members:[19] 'It is best for a husband not to have sex with his wife' (the context is about conjugal relationships, not about any sex, though the proponents of this slogan would clearly not favour any sex either). Some Corinthians were assuming that they should live here and now as if they were already in the age to come (see 4.8) when the gender division will operate no longer. Paul sees this approach as unrealistic and potentially dangerous, for there will be the temptation to adultery. But he does not just brush aside the idea of abstinence totally. What he suggests is that

---

17   Forkman, *Limits*, pp. 135, 138; E. Best, *A Commentary on the First and Second Epistles to the Thessalonians* (London: A. & C. Black, 1972), pp. 333-34, 343; A.J. Malherbe, *The Letters to the Thessalonians* (New York: Doubleday, 2000), p. 460.

18   B. Rigaux, *Saint Paul: Les Épîtres aux Thessaloniciens* (Paris: Gabalda, 1956), pp. 704, 716; L. Morris, *The First and Second Epistles to the Thessalonians* (Grand Rapids, MI: Eerdmans, 1959), pp. 251, 258; W. Neil, *The Epistles of Paul to the Thessalonians* (London: Hodder and Stoughton, 1950), pp. 192, 195; Best, *First and Second Thessalonians*, p. 344.

19   See list of those who espouse this view, up to date of publication, in J.C. Hurd, *The Origin of 1 Corinthians* (London: SPCK, 1965), pp. 68, 163 n. 1. Subsequently Barrett, *First Corinthians*, p. 154, and Schrage, *Der erste Brief an die Korinther*, II, pp. 53-54, have supported this interpretation also.

there can be abstinence, but under certain conditions: by mutual consent; for a limited period; which is to be devoted to prayer. Then the couple should resume normal conjugal relationships. Paul does have a preference for the single state (see 7.7-8, 37, 38b, 40) and to that extent he agrees with the ascetics. But he also disagrees with them and seeks to qualify their extreme position. There is agreement and disagreement. Pastorally, he seeks to correct their position, while coming some way towards it.[20] He is also concerned for the whole congregation. For some, their charisma may express itself in abstinence from marriage, while others' charisma is worked out in marriage. Those who belong to the former should not impose it on others.[21]

Colossians

While the author of Colossians[22] rejoices in the good order and firmness of their faith in Christ and in how the word of truth, the gospel, is bearing fruit in them (Col. 2.5; 1.6), he is nonetheless concerned about them and the potential danger which they face from the teaching of one[23] who claims to have had visions induced by fasting and which involved seeing the worship offered by angels (2.18).[24] The danger may come from

---

20   Cf. H. Chadwick, 'All Things to All Men (1 Cor 9:22)', *New Testament Studies* 1 (1955), pp. 261-75.
21   Schrage, *Der erste Brief an die Korinther*, II, p. 72, makes the comment that celibacy cannot be commanded even by an apostle because it is something given by God and not decided by human decision or will power.
22   Accepting post-Pauline authorship with, e.g., E. Lohse, *Colossians and Philemon* (Hermeneia; Philadelphia: Fortress Press, 1971), pp. 84-91; J. Gnilka, *Der Kolosserbrief* (HTKNT 10/1; Freiburg: Herder, 1980), pp. 19-26; M. Kiley, *Colossians as Pseudepigraphy* (Sheffield: JSOT Press, 1989). E. Schweizer, *The Letter to the Colossians* (London: SPCK, 1976), pp. 23-24, attributes it to Timothy (during the Ephesian imprisonment) as does J.D.G. Dunn, *The Epistle to the Colossians and to Philemenon* (NIGTC; Grand Rapids, MI: Eerdmans/Carlisle: Paternoster, 1996), pp. 35-41 (but from Rome). Defenders of Pauline authorship include C.F.D. Moule, *The Epistles to the Colossians and Philemon* (Cambridge: Cambridge University Press, 1957), pp. 13-34; F.F. Bruce, *The Epistles to the Colossians, to Philemon and to the Ephesians* (Grand Rapids, MI: Eerdmans, 1984), pp. 3-33; M.J. Harris, *Colossians and Philemon* (Grand Rapids, MI: Eerdmans, 1991), pp. 3-4.
23   The indefinite pronoun used at 2.16 may indicate a particular leader of the opinions, someone known to the Colossians (so Dunn, *Colossians*, pp. 174, 176), or the possibility of someone presenting this sort of teaching, so Kiley, *Colossians*, pp. 63, 89.
24   This interpretation of *threskeia ton angelon* as worship offered by angels goes back to F.O. Francis, see F.O. Francis and W.A. Meeks (eds.), *Conflict at Colosse* (Missoula: Scholars Press, 1973), pp. 163-95, and has been espoused subsequently by many scholars, including T.J. Sappington, *Revelation and Redemption at Colosse*

some form of Jewish teaching outside the church but exercising some influence and attraction on it.[25] One of the elements of this teaching was fasting: 'Why do you obey regulations—"do not handle, do not taste, do not touch"?' (2.20-21). The author shows himself to be a true heir of Paul as a pastor–theologian. He argues the case against what he deems wrong teaching—it is merely human commands and instruction (2.22; cf. 2.8) and does not accord with Christ in whom are hid all the treasures of wisdom and knowledge (2.3). This teaching which advocates fasting and asceticism has the appearance of wisdom but all its style of worship and fasting do is to be severe on the body.[26] They have no lasting value since they promote satisfaction in external things (the flesh) (2.23). It is only union with Christ in his death and resurrection that can terminate the hold of evil upon us and produce the qualities of new life in us (3.17).

Pastoral Epistles

The third generation within the Pauline churches is represented by the Pastoral Epistles,[27] whose author was writing c. AD 100. Asceticism was characteristic of the false teaching which is the major problem facing the author of these letters. The false teachers forbid marriage and advocate the abstinence from certain foods (1 Tim. 4.3). Although the author tells 'Timothy' and 'Titus'—and through them, the ministers of his own day—not to get involved in disputes and verbal wrangles with these false teachers, he does himself attempt a theological rebuttal of the asceticism,

---

(JSNTSup, 53; Sheffield: Sheffield Academic Press, 1991), pp. 156-58; Dunn, *Colossians*, pp. 29, 180-84.

25   Dunn, *Colossians*, p. 34: 'we need look no further than one or more of the Jewish synagogues in Colossae for the source of whatever influences were thought to threaten the young church there'; cf. Kiley, *Colossians*, pp. 63-64, 104-105.

26   Col. 2.23 poses some extraordinarily difficult problems for the exegete (cf. the comment by Schweizer, *Colossians*, p. 168 'almost impossible to translate'). For the translation/paraphrase offered, see the lengthy discussion in Dunn, *Colossians*, pp. 194-98.

27   Accepting non-Pauline authorship with C.K. Barrett, *The Pastoral Epistles in the New English Bible* (Oxford: Clarendon, 1963); N. Brox *Die Pastoralbriefe* (RNT, 7; Regensburg: Pustet, 4th edn 1969); A.T. Hanson *The Pastoral Epistles* (London: Marshall, Morgan and Scott, 1983); L. Oberlinner, *Die Pastoralbriefe* (HTKNT 11.2; 3 vols; Freiburg-Basel-Wien, 1994–96). Pauline authorship is defended by C. Spicq, *Saint Paul: Les Épîtres Pastorales* (Paris: Gabalda, 1947); J. Jeremias, *Die Briefe an Timotheus und Titus* (NTD, 9; Göttingen: Vandenhoeck & Ruprecht, 1975); J.N.D. Kelly, *The Pastoral Epistles* (London: A. & C. Black, 1963); G. Fee, *The Letters to Timothy and Titus* (Grand Rapids, MI: Eerdmans, 1988). Some argue for genuine Pauline notes worked into letters by a Paulinist: P.N. Harrison *The Problem of the Pastoral Epistles* (Oxford: Oxford University Press, 1921); J.D. Miller, *The Pastoral Letters as Composite Documents* (Cambridge: Cambridge University Press, 1997).

albeit briefly.[28] Everything created by God is good (part of Christianity's heritage from the Old Testament) and we should, therefore, receive his gifts gratefully and with thanksgiving. Such prayer acts as a consecration (4.3-5). While physical exercise is of some value, the pursuit of godliness is far more important, and that on two scores: it holds a promise of life for the present and for the age to come (4.7-10). It is entirely in agreement with this position that the author wishes young widows to marry, have children and govern their households (5.14).

Thus, in handling the issue of asceticism, we have come across a fascinating trajectory through the Pauline churches during its first three generations. All three representatives have argued a theological case against asceticism.

Clash of Personalities

Disagreements may occur which are due to what we may term the 'clash of personalities'. No doctrinal disagreements cause the breach, but there may be a link with the issue of authority and leadership.

Paul

On Paul's 'painful' visit to Corinth, someone caused him pain (2 Cor. 2.1, 5). Two questions arise. First, what was the pain caused to Paul? Since Paul does not embark on any doctrinal discussion (as is the case with the rival missioners in chs 10–12), we may assume that it was a case of someone who flouted Paul's authority as the founding apostle. Temporarily, a majority of the church either sided with the unnamed person or at any rate did not rally round Paul. Second, who was this unnamed opponent? There are no solid grounds for identifying him with the offender of 1 Corinthians 5.1-13.[29] It is not likely that he was the leader of the rival mission, because, in view of what Paul says about these missioners (servants of Satan, etc.), he would hardly ask the Corinthians to prove their love towards this person (2.8). Perhaps this person was a

---

28 See L.R. Donelson, *Pseudepigraphy and Ethical Argument in the Pastoral Epistles* (HUT, 22; Tübingen: J.C.B. Mohr–Paul Siebeck, 1986), p. 83, for analysis of the structure of the argument and his comment: 'The contention that the author does not make coherent theological arguments when debating his opponents cannot be squared with passages such as this.'

29 So, convincingly, C.K. Barrett, *Essays on Paul* (London: SPCK, 1982), pp. 108-17; and against G.W.H. Lampe, 'Church Discipline and the Epistles to the Corinthians', in W.R. Farmer, C.F.D. Moule and R.R. Niebuhr (eds.), *Christian History and Interpretation* (Cambridge: Cambridge University Press, 1967), p. 353.

leader of one of the house churches of which the Corinthian church was made up.

As a result of the visit of Paul's emissary, Titus, the church rallied round Paul again and rounded on the offender so vehemently that there was a danger of his being so overwhelmed by remorse that he might drift from the church (2.6-7)[30] and this would further the designs of Satan who would gain an advantage if the offender was lost to Christ (v. 11). So Paul pleads with the congregation to forgive and encourage the offender to be part of the fellowship once more (v. 7). He affirms that whomsoever they forgive, he will also forgive (v. 10); indeed he has done so already before Christ (v. 10).

Paul's approach shows great pastoral concern and sensitivity. He is concerned that the individual should not be lost to Christ because of the attack by the church. He counsels forgiveness, reconciliation and restoration. He seeks to keep the individual within the body of Christ. He rises above the personal hurt to call for forgiveness. He is concerned that Satan should not gain a victory.

Philippians

Paul displays a similar spirit in the letter to the Philippians. Wherever Philippians was written from,[31] there were some local Christians who had been bolder in speaking God's word because of Paul's imprisonment. 'Some preach Christ on account of envy and selfish ambition; but others, out of good will. The latter do it out of love, knowing that I am appointed to defend the gospel, but the former from selfish ambition, not from pure motives, thinking to stir up trouble for me in my imprisonment' (1.15-17). It is not clear how people can preach God's word with more boldness to stir up trouble for Paul without stirring up trouble for themselves with the secular authorities. So perhaps the aim was somehow to lessen Paul's position in the eyes of the local Christians.[32] Paul is, however, not bothered about his own position. The main thing which counts is that Christ is being preached,[33] and he rejoices in that fact (1.18). Once more, he rises above the pettiness of jealousy and personal

---

30   Forkman, *Limits*, pp. 180, thinks of a temporary expulsion from the church.

31   Written around AD 58–62 and probably from Rome, though some place it in the Ephesian imprisonment.

32   B. Witherington III, *Friendship and Finances in Philippi* (Valley Forge, PA: Trinity Press International, 1994), p. 45: an attempt to make themselves prominent by displacing Paul in the eyes of other Christians; similarly M. Bockmuehl, *The Epistle to the Philippians* (London: A. & C. Black, 1999), pp. 78-80.

33   Witherington, *Friendship*, p. 46: 'What converts is the Word of God, not the messenger.'

dislikes. He, the slave or servant, is of no significance compared with the Lord whom he serves. He bears those who are envious of him no ill will.

The same letter gives us a glimpse of a disagreement between two women in the church at Philippi: Euodia and Syntyche. Since Paul describes them as having worked together with him in the service of the gospel, along with Clement and his other fellow-workers, we may legitimately surmise that these women had played a significant role in the life of the church. They could have been among the *episcopoi* to whom in part the letter is addressed.[34] The disagreement between Euodia and Syntyche is sufficiently serious for Paul to invoke the help of someone, unnamed but apparently recognisable to the Philippians, to mediate and effect reconciliation. No more is said, but Paul's view of the church as the body of Christ and the temple of the Spirit is such that a disagreement of this nature would seriously damage the fellowship of the church and hamper its ability to attract others from outside to Christ.[35]

Pastoral Epistles

Possibly we should place in this category the mention of certain personalities in the Pastorals. The historical worth of these notes has been much discussed.[36] We need not involve ourselves in that debate as we are here more concerned with the function which the mention of these names has in the letters. Two people, Phygelus and Hermogenes in 2 Timothy 1.15 are specified as among those who in the province of Asia deserted Paul, in contrast to Onesiphorus who 'refreshed' Paul and was not ashamed of Paul's chains (v. 16). Just prior to this, 'Timothy' has been exhorted not to be ashamed of the witness of the Lord or of Paul his prisoner (v. 8). Through 'Timothy', the Christian minister is warned not to be ashamed to stand by the gospel and the subject of that gospel, the

---

34 Cf. Witherington, *Friendship*, p. 108 'perhaps'.

35 Witherington, *Friendship*, p. 108: 'Paul wants them to stop quarrelling so that they may get on with their mission'. G.B. Caird's comment in 'Paul and Women's Liberty', *Bulletin of the John Rylands Library* 54 (1972), p. 281, that these two women were 'a couple of cantankerous old shrews' seems unnecessarily harsh and gratuitously insulting—and somehow uncharacteristic of Caird himself.

36 Conservative commentators like Spicq, *Épîtres Pastorales*, pp. cxix-cxxii; Jeremias, *Timotheus und Titus*, p. 8; Kelly, *Pastoral Epistles*, pp. 6-10; Fee, *Timothy and Titus*, pp. 3-5, defend their historicity; while others argue for genuine fragments incorporated by a Paulinist (see n. 27); while scholars like Donelson, *Pseudipigraphy*, pp. 56-57, 62, 101-106 and 125, and Oberlinner, *Erster Timotheusbriefe*, pp. xl, xlii-xlv, believe that these notes are part of the pseudepigraphical apparatus or framework.

Lord Jesus Christ. He should be like Onesiphorus and not Phygellus or Hermogenes.[37]

That said, it is true that in the Pastorals the gospel is above all Paul's witness to it and faithfulness to the former involves faithfulness to Paul too. So there could be an undertone that to desert Paul means veering over into heterodoxy (cf. 2 Tim. 4.10-11 where Demas is said to have deserted Paul because he is in love with this present world, whereas by contrast Luke remains faithfully with Paul).

3 John

In 3 John we have a clash between the elder and Diotrephes who is said to like to be first and does not 'receive' the elder, that is acknowledge the elder's authority. Although some scholars believe that Diotrephes had lapsed into 'heresy',[38] this is nowhere expressly stated and the letter is quite capable of satisfactory explanation without importing the false teaching into the discusssion.[39] We may say that the elder, a sufficiently well-known and authoritative figure not to have to mention his personal name, was probably a charismatic figure whose authority was recognised by churches over a certain area. The leader of one of these, Diotrephes— whether he was known by a title like *episcopos* or not—has resented what he deems to be the interference of the elder. He has clearly criticised the elder (in v. 10 he is accused of 'prating against me with evil words') and he not only refuses to welcome the itinerant evangelist–missionaries sent out by the elder but also tries to prevent those who want to welcome them and tries to put them out of the church (v. 10, taking the verbs as 'connatives': if this is correct, then Diotrephes' authority is not an absolute one and in such a step as excommunication the congregation as a whole could be involved as in Mt. 18.17). The dispute is a clash over authority and power—the authority of the supra–local charismatic figure, the elder, and the local leader of a congregation, Diotrephes. If Demetrius is a member of the congregation, he may be the most prominent of that group within it which wished to respect the elder's authority and keep the links with him. The situation in the letter reflects a stalemate, though the

---

37 The same technique of contrasting types of characters occurs at 1 Tim. 1.19-20; 2 Tim. 4.9-15. See the discussion in Donelson, *Pseudepigraphy*, pp. 90-108, esp. p. 107.

38 E.g. J.L. Houlden, *A Commentary on the Johannine Epistles* (London: A. & C. Black, 1973), pp. 8-9; S.S. Smalley, *1,2, 3 John* (WBC, 51; Waco, TX: Word, 1984), p. 356.

39 So R. Schnackenburg, *Die Johannesbriefe* (HTKNT, 13/3; Freiburg: Herder, 2nd edn, 1963), pp. 319-32, esp. 319 and 329; I.H. Marshall *The Johannine Epistles* (Grand Rapids, MI: Eerdmans, 1978), pp. 13-14.

elder believes that a personal visit will restore his authority (v. 10; cf 2 Cor. 13.1-5).

Apostasy

The most serious form of erring would be that of apostasy—an actual denial of faith in Jesus after someone had previously confessed him as Saviour and Lord and been baptised in his name (or the triune name as per Mt. 28.19).

The words found in Luke 12.8-9 (probably drawn from Q, see Mt. 10.32-33)—'And I tell you, everyone who confesses me before other people, the Son of Man will confess them before the angels of God; but whoever denies me before people will be denied before the angels of God'—and an adapted form found in Mark 8.38 were probably well known in the early church. They combine encouragement–promise and warning–threat in the Q form (the Marcan form is wholly warning–threat and uses the phrase being ashamed of Jesus and his words).

Hebrews

The author of the letter to the Hebrews believes that Jesus is God's last and ultimate word to us, the pioneer of our salvation, our eternal high priest, the mediator of the new covenant, the Son of God. For him, therefore, to renege on faith in this Jesus, to go back on one's confession of faith, to fall away, means inevitable judgment and condemnation. There is no other sacrifice for sins available. To refuse what Jesus has done for us is to put ourselves under the inevitable judgment of God: 'It is impossible to restore again to repentance those who have once been enlightened, who have tasted the heavenly gift and have become partakers of the Holy Spirit, and have tasted the goodness of God's word and the powers of the age to come, and then fall away, because they recrucify God's Son to themselves and expose him to ridicule' (6.4-6).

The fivefold description of a Christian, with its emphatic realised-eschatological standpoint, serves to offset more strongly the enormity of the act of apostasy. The author does not envisage any way back—he rules out the feasibility of a 'second repentance'. He assumes that the repudiation of faith is final.

A second passage speaks the same message (10.26-32). It concerns those who sin deliberately after having received the knowledge of the truth. This deliberate sin is then elaborated in a threefold description in v. 29 which leaves us in no doubt that apostasy is in mind: 'who has despised the Son of God; has considered cheap the blood of the covenant by which they were sanctified; and who has insulted the Spirit of grace'.

Such forceful language describes the disavowal of a faith once held. For such a person there awaits the vengeance of the God into whose hands 'it is a fearful thing to fall' (vv. 30-31). Later, in ch. 12, Esau is held out as a warning example of one who, having sold his birthright and then afterwards desperately sought to regain it, was rejected, 'for he found no opportunity to repent' (vv. 16-17). This warning comes after the exhortation to the congregation to exercise mutual pastoral care. They must take care that no one fails to obtain the grace of God. They must not allow any 'bitter root' to spring up and poison the atmosphere of the fellowship and taint others. They must see to it that none becomes sexually immoral or irreligious (vv. 15-16a).

A further warning comes in vv. 25-29 to the effect that since the Israelites incurred punishment when they disobeyed God when He spoke from the earthly Mount Sinai, Christians will not escape punishment if they refuse God who warns from heaven (cf. 2.1-4). God has warned that he intends to shake the whole cosmos and only eternal realities such as God's own kingdom can withstand such divine judgment.

We have no indication what formal measures the author envisaged a congregation taking when a person apostasised. He recognises that such cases occur and is convinced that they are—from a pastoral standpoint—'beyond redemption'.

We can only very briefly indicate here that while the recipients of this letter are in danger of drifting (2.1), probably back into Judaism—hence the appeal to go forth to Jesus outside the camp = Judaism, in 13.13—the author exegetes several Old Testament passages to show both that the Old Testament knew itself to be incomplete and was looking for something better, to complete itself, and that fulfilment and completion had in fact come in and through Jesus. In this way he hopes to stem the drift and keep them looking to Jesus and persevering along the pilgrim way to the heavenly city.

James

James brings up the case of a Christian who goes astray from the truth in 5.19-20. What meaning has 'the truth' here? In light of the reference to 'the word of truth' in 1.18, where it refers to the gospel[40] as having regenerative power, it is reasonable to assume that the same idea inheres in the reference to the truth in our passage.[41] That this then involves

---

40   J.B. Mayor *The Epistle of St. James* (London: MacMillan, 2nd edn, 1897), p. 60; P.H. Davids, *The Epistle of James* (NIGTC; Exeter: Paternoster, 1982), p. 89.

41   Against those who assume that only straying from the right way of living is in mind, S. Laws, *A Commentary on the Epistle of James* (London: A. & C. Black, 1980), p. 238; Davids, *James*, p. 89; L.T. Johnson *James* (AB, 37A; New York: Doubleday, 1995), p. 337; R. Bauckham, *James* (London: Routledge, 1999), p. 69.

moral implications is undoubtedly the case, but James could have expressed that point perfectly well without using the word 'truth' if only moral lapses were in mind.[42]

James by implication commends anyone who brings the erring Christian back. That person will be instrumental in restoring the backslider to a state of salvation ('will save him', that is, from death v. 20) and so obliterate the effects of the sinner's behaviour ('will cover a multitude of sins').

It would seem that if this interpretation is correct, James was much more optimistic about the possibility of saving an apostate than was the author of Hebrew.[43]

Doctrinal Disagreements

What happens when Christians disagree on interpreting Jesus, his teaching and his death-resurrection-ascension and their implications for living in the post-Easter era? Did Christians have any yardsticks by which they determined what was reasonable and what was unreasonable, unacceptable, erroneous interpretation?

Paul

In his discussion of whether there is a general resurrection (1 Cor. 15.12), Paul begins with a reminder of the terms in which he preached the gospel at Corinth. He quotes a confession of faith which he himself had received and which he had handed on to the Corinthians. This mentions Christ's death for our sins, his burial, resurrection and appearances. Referring to other apostles he states, 'whether then it was I or they, so we preach and so you believed' (15.11). From this we may conclude that Paul felt that there was a fundamental unity between his preaching and that of the apostles who were in Christ before him, and that unity lay in a common acceptance of Christ's atoning death and his resurrection from the dead, both grounded in God's eternal purpose revealed in the Old Testament

---

42   Even Laws, *James*, p. 238, admits that James is hardly likely to distinguish between ethical truth and the truth of the gospel as a whole. R.P. Martin, *James* (WBC, 48; Waco, TX: Word, 1988), pp. 217-18, speaks of the sin of apostasy ('rejection of the revealed will of God'), though he does also say that the overall stress in James is on orthopraxis rather than orthodoxy. Forkman, *Limits*, p. 185, seems to favour straying from the truth.

43   Laws, *James*, p. 241, says of James that 'he is optimistic; he does not consider the contingency of failure to convert a brother...or the possibility of sin so grave that reclamation may not be attempted (cf. Heb.vi.4-6; 1 Jn. v.16b; possibly also 1 Cor.v.2-5)'.

scriptures. We may surmise that in developing this confession and drawing out its implications, differences might arise.

Such was the case in connection with the Jewish–Christian missionaries who landed at Corinth (2 Cor. 11.22-23) and who clearly impressed some of the congregation. We need not enter the debate into the precise set of beliefs—interestingly, circumcision plays no part in Paul's discussion[44]—suffice it to say that Paul's theological evaluation of their beliefs is highly negative as is his opinion of their conduct—indeed he brands them as false apostles who disguise themselves as apostles of Christ (11.13), more than that—they are servants of Satan who disguise themselves as servants of righteousness (11.14-15).

Why is Paul so critical? He accuses the Corinthians of tolerating someone 'if he comes along and preaches another Jesus, whom we did not preach, or you receive another spirit, whom you did not (in the past) receive, or (preaches) another gospel which you did not (in the past) receive' (11.4). Unfortunately Paul does not elaborate on the details—he did not need to, the Corinthians would be conversant with the facts. What is clear, however, is that he disagrees strongly with the interpretation of Jesus and the gospel which his rivals offered and indeed their understanding of the Holy Spirit. Paul sees an unbridgeable gulf between what he believes and had taught and their version of the Christian message. He clearly believes that he was left with no option but to condemn outright. There could be no compromise. If their version was allowed to go unchecked, then the church would be deleteriously affected. These so-called apostles are letting Satan invade the 'space' of God's people.

Paul is equally dismissive of the Jewish Christian missionaries whom he attacks in Galatians. Here circumcision is prominent in the discussion[45]—another illustration that Jewish Christianity was not some monolithic entity.[46] He expresses amazement that the Galatians had so quickly moved away from God who called them on the basis solely of his grace, to another gospel (1.6). He immediately qualifies this by saying 'which is not another (gospel)' (v. 7a). Some wish to unsettle the Galatians and 'turn (them) away from the gospel of Christ' (v. 7). Then follow two

---

44   An indication that Jewish Christianity was not a monolithic entity, see J.D.G. Dunn, *Unity and Diversity in the New Testament: An Inquiry into the Character of Earliest Christianity* (London: SCM Press, 1977, p. 263: 'it was...a diverse phenomenon', italics his.

45   For the issues at stake, see especially the work of E.P. Sanders, *Paul and Palestinian Judaism* (London: SCM Press, 1977), and *Paul, the Law and the Jewish People* (London: SCM Press, 1983), and the various contributions of J.D.G. Dunn conveniently gathered together in *Jesus, Paul and the Law* (London: SPCK, 1990), chs 5–9. There has been a lively discussion sparked off by the debate between these scholars.

46   See n. 44 above.

sentences, each containing an anathema or curse on those people: 'But even if we or an angel from heaven preached a message contrary to what we preached to you, let them be accursed. As I have said before and now repeat, if anyone preaches to you what is contrary to what you received, let them be accursed' (vv. 8-9). At one level we could interpret this cynically as the intemperate outburst of someone who sees themselves as 'losing a battle' and their work being totally lost, and who seeks to bolster up their crumbling reputation by smearing their opponents with not preaching a true gospel. But, as the argument in Galatians unfolds, it is clear that something fundamental is at stake. There are two rival interpretations of the Christian faith. In a nutshell, did non-Jews have to become Jews in order to belong to the people of God? Paul knows what the gospel is and is not. He believes that what he has preached and is preaching is the gospel and that what these other preachers advocate is not 'gospel'. For him, their version of the Christian message goes beyond the parameters of the acceptable. Indeed, to accept it means to move away from God (1.6) and to be cut off from Christ and fall away from grace (5.4).

Paul also criticises some missionaries at Philippi whom he abusively describes as 'dogs, evil-workers, those who mutilate the flesh' (a fierce pun in the Greek on the word for circumcision), in Philippians 3.2. From Paul's stress on his Hebrew credentials and the ensuing antithesis between right standing before God based on doing what the Law required (circumcision, food laws and sabbath observance, which emphasised Jewishness) and right standing before God through faith in Christ, we may surmise some form of Jewish Christian mission (3.4-11).[47] Here in Philippians there seems to be an element of perfectionism in their teaching for Paul stresses that he has not yet obtained perfection but presses on towards the goal (3.12-16), hoping to attain the resurrection of the dead (v. 11) and looking for the coming of Christ (vv. 20-21). Then Paul urges the Philippians to mark those 'who live as enemies of the cross of Christ' (v. 18). This is clearly a theological verdict. While it could refer to non-Christian Jews, it could just as easily refer to Jewish Christians whose message, and lifestyle based on it, undervalued in Paul's eyes the cross of Christ and diminished the importance which it should have. If the rival mission stressed the Jewishness of Christianity and stressed that true perfection before God lay in observance of well known Jewish customs, this would mean for Paul nullifying the effects of Christ's death on the cross and would qualify its upholders for the description 'enemies of the cross of Christ'. Once more we have evidence

---

47   See J. Gnilka, *Der Philipperbrief* (HTKNT 10.3; Freiburg: Herder, 1968), pp. 211-18, and Witherington, *Friendship*, pp. 89-99, for useful discussions on these rival missionaries.

that Paul has clear criteria for assessing what is and is not true Christian faith: anything which threatened the primacy of God's grace in his dealings with us had to be rejected.

Deutero-Paul

While false teaching as such does not seem to be a specific problem in the church(es) to which the deutero–Pauline Ephesians is addressed, nonetheless a function of the gifts of ministry given by the ascended Christ to the church is to equip God's people ('the saints') for the work of ministry, for building up the body of Christ. The aim is for Christians to attain that unity inherent in the faith and knowledge of the Son of God, to grow up into the fullness of Christ: 'so that we may no longer be children, tossed to and fro and carried about by every wind of doctrine devised by the cunning of men, by their craftiness and deceitful wiles' (4.11-14). The author is well aware of the dangers of erroneous teaching and relies on the ministry so to preach and teach that members of the congregation will be mature enough and well grounded enough not to be seduced from the truth.

A somewhat similar approach is found in Acts, whose author also probably belonged to the Pauline stream of Christianity in the early church. Though Acts is primarily concerned with the taking of the gospel from Jerusalem in a north easterly arc on to Rome, one of the places where internal matters of Paul's churches is uppermost is the farewell speech to the Ephesians elders, which, while containing Pauline elements, was probably a Lucan composition.[48] In accordance with the form of a farewell speech, the person facing death looks ahead to conditions in the future: 'I know that after my departure fierce wolves will come among you. They will not spare the flock. Men from among your own ranks will come on the scene and speak perverted things in order to draw the disciples after them' (Acts 20.29-30). On this viewpoint, 'heresy' is a post-apostolic phenomenon. The congregations will be threatened both from outside and from within. Those from outside are called fierce wolves whose aim is to devour the flock. Those from within speak error— wrong, crooked or distorted teaching. While no detail is given, it is clear that for the author of Acts false teaching is around and there is no doubt in his mind that it can be recognised. He sees the ministry to whom the whole spectrum of Paul's teaching has been passed on (vv. 20, 27, 31) as a bulwark against this false teaching.

---

48   So also J. Dupont, *Le Discours de Milet* (Paris: Cerf, 1962), pp. 29-30; H.-J. Michel, *Die Abschiedsrede des Paulus an die Kirche Apg. 20.17-38* (Munchen: Kosel, 1973), pp. 15, 33; F. Prast, *Presbyter und Evangelium in nachapostolischer Zeit* (Stuttgart: Verlag Katholisches Bibelwerk, 1979), pp. 1-2, 28-38.

Trito-Paul

The main problem behind the Trito-Pauline Pastoral Epistles[49] is false teaching. The prediction of the Miletus speech has come true 'with a vengeance', and, as there, so in the Pastorals the ministry is a crucial weapon in the fight. As in the Miletus speech also, so in the Pastorals the ministry is in possession of Paul's teaching which is a 'deposit' to be guarded and passed on intact. It is the sound and true teaching which can offset the distortions introduced into the churches by false teachers—not that the appearance of false teachers should occasion surprise, because the Spirit forewarned of this as a phenomenon of the last times (1 Tim. 4.1-3).

The false teachers are said to be men of corrupt minds and they are as regards the faith 'disqualified'. In their resistance to the truth they are compared to Jannes and Jambres who opposed Moses (2 Tim. 3.8-9)— the reference is to a Jewish haggada elaborating Exodus 8.18-19. They are regarded as deceived deceivers (2 Tim. 3.13; Tit. 1.10). They profess to know God but deny Him by their deeds. They are detestable, disobedient, unfit for any good deed (Tit. 1.16). Their methods are condemned—they worm their way into households and make converts of gullible women (2 Tim. 3.6) and so upset families (Tit. 1.11). Donelson has described the author's tactic as putting the false teachers in the 'vice category' of a dualism of virtue and vice.[50] It is perhaps an indication of the rather loose organisation of church life at the time that such people are apparently still to some extent regarded as within the congregations.

So, how are the ministers, the sound and faithful men (2 Tim. 2.2), to react to these false teachers? A number of ways emerge in the Pastorals.

TEACHING

First, at all times ministers must teach sound doctrine in agreement with the Pauline legacy (e.g. 1 Tim. 4.6, 11-16; 2 Tim. 3.14; Tit. 1.9; 2.2, 7-8; 3.8, etc.).

REBUKE

Secondly, ministers must rebuke the false teachers (1 Tim. 1.3-4; 2 Tim. 2.25; Tit. 1.9-10, 13), while at the same time avoid getting entangled in

---

49   I had been using this phrase when I discovered that Oberlinner, *Erster Timotheusbriefe*, uses it on p. xlv and thereafter frequently in his three commentaries. Oberlinner mentions P. Trümmer, *Die Paulustradition der Pastoralbriefe* (BET, 8; Frankfurt am Main: Peter Lang, 1978), pp. 105, 208, and W. Schenk, 'Die Briefe an Timotheus I & II und an Titus (Pastoralbriefe) in der neueren Forshung (1945–85)', in H. Temporini and W. Haase (eds.), *Aufstieg und Niedergang der römischen Welt: Geschichte und Kultur Roms im Spiegel der neueren Forschung* (Berlin: Walter de Gruyter, 1972–), II.25.4, p. 3405, also as using this term before him.

50   Donelson, *Pseudepigraphy*, p. 127.

unprofitable disputes and verbal wrangling themselves, which promote division and unsettle people's faith (1.Tim. 4.7; 6.3-5, 20; 2 Tim. 2.16, 23; 3.5; Tit. 3.9). In addition, they must warn true believers against getting involved (2 Tim. 2.13).

The author sets the ministers no easy task to walk this tight rope, since rebuking could easily lead to getting embroiled in controversy. He assumes that the true and false teachings are well defined entities, distinguishable from one another. Holding to the truth and discussing with false teachers are irreconcilable. If the false teaching produces ungodliness (2 Tim. 2.16), then avoidance of it is justified. If it unsettles the faith of some and produces dissension in the congregation and subverts families, then avoidance of it is justified.

In some passages there is expressed a hope that the rebuke will be effective and bring about a change of mind. In 2 Timothy 'the Lord's slave' should not be quarrelsome, but kind to everyone, an apt teacher, forbearing, correcting his opponents with gentleness since perhaps God might grant them repentance which will lead them to a knowledge of the truth and to regain their senses and escape from the devil's snare after having been captured by him to do his will (2.24-26). The use of the optative mood, 'might grant', probably indicates uncertainty whether the wish will be granted, but still the idea is formulated (cf. too Tit. 1.13).

It might seem surprising that after such damning verdicts on these false teachers the author thought that they would respond to a rebuke and return to a sound belief (cf. the view expressed in 2 Tim. 4.3-4). Yet we should at the same time not forget that the Pastorals assert that God is the Creator and Saviour who wills the salvation of all and has provided a mediator for us, Jesus Christ, who gave himself a ransom for all (1 Tim. 2.4-5; cf. 4.10 where the statement that God is the Saviour of all men is repeated; see also Tit. 2.11). Furthermore, in 1 Timothy 1.12-16 Paul is depicted in his pre-Christian days in the darkest of colours—he was formerly a blasphemer, a persecutor and a violent man, v. 13—but he had been shown mercy (v. 13); Christ's grace had superabounded towards him (v. 14); Christ had exercised patience with Paul (v. 16). The inference is clear: if Paul could be saved, no one was possibly beyond the scope of grace. After all, Christ Jesus had come into this world to save sinners: if the chief of sinners could be saved, so could other people. Paul is thus a paradigm of conversion.[51]

---

51 Donelson, *Pseudepigraphy*, p. 101.

EXCOMMUNICATION.

A priori one would expect expulsion from the community would be the tactic to be adopted to stop the activity of the false teachers within the community. Here four passages call for comment.

1 Timothy 1.19b-20

Having mentioned that some people have shipwrecked their faith through failing to listen to their consciences, the author specifies two individuals by way of illustration—Hymenaeus and Alexander 'whom I have delivered to Satan that they might learn not to blaspheme'. Probably, in the light of 1 Corinthians 5.1-13, the handing over to Satan refers to excommunication.[52] Here Paul is depicted—apparently—as doing this himself, whereas in 1 Corinthians 5 Paul involved the whole congregation in the decision. The purpose of this step is remedial—it is to induce a 'learning experience', which will lead to reformation and a return to sound attitudes and beliefs (here encapsulated in the phrase 'not to blaspheme').[53] Compared with 1 Corinthians 5, the hoped-for effects seem to refer to the present rather than to 'the Day of the Lord'.

Titus 3

Ater exhorting Titus to avoid stupid controversies and disputes, because they are unprofitable and futile, the author goes on: '*paraitou* a man who is a *haeretikon* after a first and second admonition, knowing that such a person has become corrupted and is sinning, is (indeed) self-condemned' (v. 10). We notice that in this setting the step involved in *paraitou* is taken after two admonitions. Presumably an interval is allowed after the second admonition, and then, if this is ignored, action is taken. (By contrast three warnings are envisaged in Mt. 18.15-17; cf. 2 Cor. 13.1-2). What action is envisaged in the imperative *paraitou* ? The verb can bear a strong or weak sense: 'drive out' or 'keep away from, have nothing to do with'. While either sense could fit here, the strong sense is entirely fitting. It would agree with 1 Timothy 1.20; it fits the immediate context, namely the description of the person as corrupt, sinning and self-condemned, and also the broader context of strong polemic against false teachers; it makes sense tactically, as merely avoiding or refusing to meet the false teachers

---

52 Barrett, *Pastoral Epistles*, p. 48, goes for supernaturally inflicted bodily punishment; Kelly, *Pastoral Epistles*, p. 58, and Brox *Pastoralbriefe*, p. 120, combine some physical disaster and excommunication; Hanson, *Pastoral Epistles*, p. 66, and Oberlinner, *Erste Timotheusbrief*, p. 58, opt for excommunication, with Oberlinner adding 'at least for the time being'.

53 Oberlinner, *Erste Timotheusbrief*, p. 58, rightly sees more stress on an educative purpose here than in 1 Cor. 5.1-5.

would not serve to stop them. We opt for 'expel' or 'excommunicate' as the sense here.[54]

What meaning does *haeretikon* have here? Two senses are possible: 'factious' or 'heretical'. Given the overall concern with false teaching in the three letters, the example of 1 Timothy 1.20 and the fact that in the temporally not distant letters of Ignatius, the word is twice used in the sense of heretic,[55] we feel that the translation 'heretical' is justified.[56] Even if expulsion is envisaged, such a step is only taken after two prior warnings, so that it cannot be said that the procedure is rushed through.

2 Timothy 3.5

Scholars are divided as to whether at 2 Timothy 3.5 the command 'avoid' betokens a refusal of fellowship within the church or not. As stated above, mere avoidance of meeting such people would hardly curb their activity, so that on practical grounds some form of exclusion seems likely.[57]

Titus 1.11

A possible reference to excommunication occurs at Titus 1.11 where the office-holder (via Titus) is told 'to stop the mouths' of false teachers who are upsetting households. How can such teachers be silenced? Is 'skilful presentation of true doctrine'[58] or some 'sharp disciplinary action'[59] in mind? The former sounds too optimistic; if the latter, what form would it take? Could they be excluded from preaching and teaching[60] or would it have to be expulsion from the congregation?[61] In the light of the

---

54 So Barrett, *Patoral Epistles*, p. 146; Brox, *Pastoralbriefe*, p. 312; Hanson, *Pastoral Epistles*, p. 195; Oberlinner, *Titusbrief*, p187; I.H. Marshall, *The Pastoral Epistles* (ICC; Edinburgh: T. & T. Clark, 1999), pp. 337-39.

55 Ignatius, *Ephesians* 6.2; *Trallians* 6.1.

56 In agreement with Spicq, *Épîtres*, p. 299; Brox, *Pastoralbriefe*, p. 312, (or rigorous keeping at a distance); Hanson, *Pastoral Epistles*, p. 194; Oberlinner, *Titusbrief*, p. 187; and against Barrett, *Pastoral Epistles*, p. 146, and Kelly, *Pastoral Epistles*, p. 256.

57 In agreement with Jeremias, *Briefe*, p. 53, and Brox, *Pastoralbriefe*, p. 254. Hanson, *Pastoral Epistles*, p. 145, believes that no formal action is called for, and Oberlinner, *Zweite Timotheusbrief*, p. 125, denies that excommunication is in mind, while Barrett, *Pastoral Epistles*, p. 111, and Kelly, *Pastoral Epistles*, p. 195, opt for the sense of keeping clear of.

58 This is the view of D. Guthrie, *The Pastoral Epistles* (London: Tyndale, 1957), p. 187, and J.L. Houlden, *The Pastoral Epistles* (Harmondsworth: Penguin, 1976), p. 145, thinks of a public rebuttal at 1.13.

59 Barrett, *Pastoral Epistles*, p. 131, but he does not elaborate.

60 Oberlinner, *Titusbrief*, p. 36.

61 So Hanson, *Pastoral Epistles*, p. 175, and acknowledged as a possibility by Oberlinner, *Titusbrief*, p. 36.

command to 'reprove' in v. 13, we prefer a public warning, prior to the step of excommunication as in Titus 3.10.

1 and 2 John

1 and 2 John furnish us with the first known example of schism in the New Testament period—see 1 John 2.19; 4.1; 2 John 7 for references to people leaving the congregations and going out 'into the world'. The author calls them false prophets (1 Jn 4.10), deceivers (2 Jn 7), above all antichrists (1 Jn 2.18; 4.3; 2 Jn 7). They are indwelt by the spirit of error (1 Jn 4.6). Such demonising of the opponents is no worse than Paul's description of his opponents in 2 Corinthians 11. The elder argues that really they had never actually belonged in the Johannine congregations. Their exit from the congregations proved that all along they had not been 'of us'. This is a form of predestination. The exit from the congregations revealed that they were not of the elect, the true children of God. Indeed the exit was necessary to show them in their true colours and reveal that they were false members from the start (1 Jn 2.19). Eduard Schweizer has called this surrender in the face of the pastoral task of reclaiming erring members.[62] Certainly the letter reveals something of the gulf and the bitterness between the two sides.

The letter discloses two areas of disagreement between the elder and those who have left (although not all the details are clear, e.g., 1 Jn 5.6). We may call the first area of disagreement 'doctrinal'. In some way the opponents deny a true incarnation: 'coming in the flesh' is denied (see 1 Jn 4.2-3; 2 Jn 7); the opponents deny that the man Jesus is the Christ (1 Jn 2.22) and the Son of God (cf. 1 Jn 4.15; 5.5, 10-12), a position which in the eyes of the elder cuts one off from fellowship with God (1 Jn 2.23; cf. 4.15; 5.12). The second area of disagreement we may label 'ethical', as it concerns conduct. The true believer loves their brothers and sisters in the faith. Clearly the elder believed that those who had left did not love their fellow Christians (e.g. 1 Jn 2.9-11; 4.7-21; in typical semitic fashion, he speaks of those who hate their brother—i.e. anything less than total love is hate).

These two aspects are in fact like two sides of one coin. If one denies that the man Jesus is the Son of God fully incarnate, one denies a central foundation in the Christian belief that God is love (e.g. 1 Jn 4.9-10). The belief that God is love is in turn the foundation and basis for the command that we should love one another (e.g. 1 Jn 4.7-8).

From these letters we may infer that a 'battle' had gone on over the Johannine tradition. The elder in a sense claims to be the conserver of the

---

62   E. Schweizer, *Church Order in the New Testament* (London: SCM Press, 1959), p. 129.

Johannine tradition and accuses the secessionists of having 'advanced' beyond it: 'Anyone who goes ahead and does not abide in the doctrine of Christ does not have God; the one who abides in the doctrine has both the Father and the Son'(2 Jn 9). Hence, in the course of his letters, the elder claims to have reminded the readers of what had existed from the beginning in the Johannine congregations and which they had heard from the beginning (1 Jn 2.24; new/old command 1 Jn 2.7; 2 John 5-6; message 1 Jn 3.11).[63] As far as the elder is concerned, he remains true to the original Johannine teaching, whereas those who have now left the churches have in the development of their teaching moved beyond an acceptable interpretation of the original Johannine teaching (one might call it the Johannine 'deposit', borrowing a phrase from the Pastorals). The elder makes a judgment and deems the opponents' teaching false and unacceptable.

In 1 John the elder is pastorally concerned for those who are left after the schism, whose morale has been badly shaken, and seeks to reassure them (e.g. the stress in 2.20-28 that they all have an anointing from the Holy One and so all possess knowledge). He provides a series of 'tests' by which they can know that they are truly children of God. In 2 John he suggests two practical measures which the members of the congregations should adopt in order to check the spread of this false teaching (the opponents seem to be having some success according to 1 Jn 4.5): 'If anyone comes to you and does not bring this (the elder's) teaching, do not receive him into your home and do not greet him; for whoever greets him shares in his evil works' (v. 11). They are to refuse hospitality on which itinerant missionaries/teachers were dependent.[64] And they are not even to greet them—here we need to remember that the Hebrew greeting 'Shalom' was a religious greeting and charged with far greater significance than a secular 'Hello' and was in effect invoking God's blessing on the person addressed. Neither of these measures could of course stop the opponents trying to spread their version of Christianity, but the refusal of hospitality would not make life easy for them.

Finally, we may refer to the fact that the elder appears to forbid even praying for the opponents (5.16-17), on the assumption that when he mentions 'the sin which leads to death', he has in mind the false teaching.[65] This position is of course in agreement with his basic position

---

63   See H. Conzelmann, 'Was von Anfang', in W. Eltester (ed.), *Neu Testamentliche Studien für R. Bultmann* (Beihafte zur ZNW, 21; Berlin: Töpelmann, 1954), pp. 194-201.

64   See A.J. Malherbe, *Social Aspects of Early Christianity* (Philadelphia: Fortress Press, 2nd edn, 1983), pp. 92-110.

65   While R. Schnackenburg, *Die Johannesbriefe*, p. 278, is very cautious and believes that it is no longer possible to say precisely what the author was thinking of. Houlden, *Johannine Epistles*, p. 136, and R.E. Brown, *The Epistles of John* (AB, 30; Garden City, NY: Doubleday, 1982), pp. 617-19, are convinced that it is apostasy which

that those who had seceded never really belonged to the true children of God (1 Jn 2.19).

John of Patmos

In the congregations for which John of Patmos feels what I will call a 'prophetic pastoral concern' there are two where false teaching presents a problem: the content of this teaching is quite similar, though in the letter to Pergamum (Rev. 2.15) it is called the teaching of the Nicolaitans, while in the letter to Thyatira it is associated with a prophetess whom John calls Jezebel (2.20—presumably his nickname for her, based on the notorious queen of that name, consort of King Ahab and opponent of Elijah). John rebukes the church at Pergamum because they have some who advocate eating food sacrificed to idols and practise immorality. He compares them to Balaam hired by Balak, king of Moab, to cause the Israelites to stumble. The two issues were ones which Paul had had to deal with at Corinth (see 1 Cor. 6.11-20; 8-10; and indeed the former is handled in Rom. 14–15 and figures in the so-called apostolic decree of Acts 15.28-29). While some scholars take the verb *porneusai* metaphorically of spiritual infidelity, a literal sense is quite possible, as in some pagan worship orgiastic rites occurred. John summons these Nicolaitans to repent. If not, the risen Lord will come soon and wage war with the sword of his mouth against them (2.16). While Caird dissociated this coming from the parousia and took it as a conditional coming,[66] most scholars believe that John was thinking of the parousia:[67] for disobedient, unfaithful Christians that would mean judgment, whereas his coming would be salvation for the faithful. The church at Thyatira is rebuked for tolerating the woman whom he calls Jezebel and for allowing her to teach and entice members of the congregation to eat food sacrificed to idols

---

is in mind. Both Marshall *Johannine Epistles*, p. 247, and Smalley, *1, 2, 3 John*, p. 298, think more generally of sins incompatible with being a child of God, but which would include denying that Jesus is the Son of God.

66 G.B. Caird, *The Revelation of St. John the Divine* (London: A. & C. Black, 1966), p. 41. For Caird's views on eschatology and the use of eschatological language, see his *The Language and Imagery of the Bible* (London: Duckworth, 1980), pp. 243-71.

67 E.g. T. Holz, *Die Christologie der Apokalypse des Johannes* (TU, 85; Berlin: Akademie-Verlag, 1962), pp. 166-173, esp. 171, 206-208; E. Schüssler Fiorenza, *The Book of Revelation: Justice and Judgment* (Philadelphia: Fortress, 1985), p. 49; F.D. Mazzaferri, *The Genre of the Book of Revelation from a Source-Critical Perspective* (Berlin and New York: Walter de Gruyter, 1989), pp. 233, 236-37, 243 and 287; J. Webb Mealy, *After the Thousand Years* (JSNTSup, 70; Sheffield: Sheffield Academic Press, 1992), p. 222; R. Bauckham, *The Climax of Prophecy* (Edinburgh: T. & T. Clark, 1993), e.g. pp. 12, 30 and 34; P.R. Carrell, *Jesus and the Angels* (SNTSMS, 95; Cambridge: Cambridge University Press, 1997), pp. 116-17.

and to practise immorality. Both she and her adherents will incur a dire fate at the hands of the Lord of the church when he comes (2.20-23).

Perhaps surprisingly, John of Patmos does not call for the immediate expulsion of these false teachers and their adherents.[68] If John expected the imminent end of the world, such a measure might seem ludicrously 'puny' in comparison with Christ's judgment. Additionally, he probably sat loose to church 'structures'. In none of the seven letters does he make specific mention of the leaders of the congregations (the roughly contemporary Pastoral Epistles envisage bishops/elders and deacons, possibly bishop, elders and deacons, in the same area—Asia Minor). John of Patmos may well have been a charismatic, prophetic figure who exercised an itinerant ministry and felt a concern for the churches in Asia Minor in the light of the impending church–state struggle as the prelude to the end of all things and the establishment of the kingdom of God and of Christ.

Conclusion

We chose five areas which might offer insights into the attitude of New Testament writers to erring brothers and sisters. Our survey showed what would be true of many themes and topics—that we cannot speak of the New Testament approach; rather, there is a fair amount of diversity. Of the five subjects, the first four could figure within a congregation of any modern denomination, while the fifth subject touches on inter-denominational discussions today.

As to moral failure, there is diversity, even within an author, for Paul condemns the man who was cohabiting with his stepmother, while reasoning with those consorting with prostitutes. Even here Paul hopes for the ultimate salvation of the former, while it looks as if his patience may have run out as regards the latter if our interpretation of 2 Corinthians 12.21 is correct. Paul holds together a concern for the church and its reputation with outsiders and a concern for the individual and their reclamation. Matthew and Jude both advocate attempts to reclaim offenders, but 2 Peter is content to condemn. We might say that in differing ways Paul, Matthew and Jude are grappling with the issue of holding together grace and judgment, pardon and condemnation, no easy task as any 'pastor' knows.

Concerning inadvisable behaviour, the evidence of Paul and Colossians suggests a willingness to argue and reason in an effort to draw the persons concerned back to a healthier approach (e.g. from a too rigorist

---

68   Forkman, *Limits*, p. 162, also noted this.

asceticism). Even the Pastoral Epistles too give a brief argumentation on this theme.

Paul displays a breadth of outlook when it comes to coping with clashes of personality which may or may not be related to 'power struggles' for leadership. He rises above the temptation to be indignant for himself and displays a concern for both the other individual(s) and the well-being of the church or for the proclamation of the gospel. By contrast, the elder of 3 John is far less tolerant of opposition.

We found also a contrast on the issue of those who abandoned their faith. The author of the letter to the Hebrews adopted a rigorist or uncompromising attitude. For him there was no way back for the apostate—it was a sheer impossibility to renew again to repentance a person who had taken such a step. On the other hand, James envisaged the possibility that such a person could be won back to faith again: there is hope for the backslider.

Our final category, that of true or false doctrine, revealed a remarkable degree of agreement in the Pauline and Johannine streams of Christianity. While we need to be cautious here—some scholars will remind us that we have only the writings of 'the winners'—nevertheless whether it is Paul in the fifties or the elder at the beginning of the second century, there is an awareness of limits in the interpretation of Jesus and his saving work, beyond which it is illegitimate to go. Long before the Nicene Creed and the Chalcedonian definition, long before even Irenaeus' conviction that there was broadly a rule of faith to which the churches everywhere subscribed in the second century, nascent Christianity appears to have had a good idea of what was acceptable in ways of expounding the work and words of Jesus the Messiah, the Son of God, as God's appointed Saviour for all humanity. This unanimity in respect of the importance of correct interpretations of the gospel and Christian teaching has an important 'word' to the churches today, when so much stress is laid on experience and not on doctrine.

CHAPTER 12

The Sociology of Hymns in Western Christianity

Marjorie Reeves

An article in the *Independent on Sunday* for 7 May 2000 announced in a prominent headline: 'Church casts out Golden Oldie Hymns'. The Church of Scotland was ditching two hundred hymns from its revised hymnbook. Worshippers were urged to cast aside 'sentimental' attachments to the old favourites and focus their hymns on such 'modern' themes as 'ecology, healing and unity with people round the world'.[1] Should hymns change with changing cultures? What does the history of hymns tell us about the social purposes of hymn–singing? Such questions are raised by a noticeable renewed interest in hymns at the beginning of this new millennium.

It would seem that the singing of ritual songs as a binding activity in early communities goes back far into the history of societies. For the Christians it emerges from the mists in Jewish rituals of both family and rabbinical worship. Our Book of Psalms is, of course, the great legacy of Judaism to Christianity, albeit modified by successive translations. Introduced by the Magnificat itself, the canticles of our worship descend to us directly from the Hebrew culture of Christ's day and the evidence of the Pauline Epistles reveals the infant church worshipping in 'psalms and hymns and spiritual songs'.[2] So from the very beginning the Christian church as a young society nurtured its sense of identity and strengthened the faith of its members through song. In this short essay I want to look briefly at three cultural aspects of Christian hymn-singing: pagan images in early Christian themes; the rise of lay participation in worship; and the question of what qualities have allowed some hymns to survive vast cultural changes whilst others become dated and unacceptable.

---

1   *The Independent on Sunday*, 7 May 2000, p. 11.
2   Colossians 3.16.

I

On the subject of pagan images in Christian hymns there is only space here for three early examples. The universal symbol of Light is movingly embodied in *Phos Hilaron*, a hymn which comes to us from a Greek text dated before the fourth century. It is associated with a candle-lighting ceremony of the early evening in the catacombs. When we recreate the scene in imagination its verses strike notes both of pathos and triumph: a fearful Christian minority stealing secretly out of a pagan society to reaffirm faith in the Eternal Light. We have the hymn in Robert Bridges translations: 'O gladsome light, O grace / Of God the Father's face / The eternal splendour wearing'.[3] At the same time, with astonishing boldness, they claim to sing for the whole world: 'Thee, therefore, O Most High / the world doth glorify / And shall exalt forever.'

My second example shows the educated Roman gentleman bringing his poetic learning to the celebration of the advent of the Christ. Aurelius Clemens Prudentius (348–c. 410)[4] was a civil servant in Rome when the last struggle of paganism against the new religion was in progress. When, in middle life, he embraced Christianity he retired to transmute the imagery and rhythms of his classical poetry into Christian themes. We see the interaction of the two cultures subtlety revealed in a famous poem, the *Psychomachia*, on the battle for the soul between the Virtues and Vices, where the contrast is not always between repulsive vices and shining virtues but also between two kinds of beauty, earthly and spiritual. In his great Advent hymn, *Corde natus ex parentis*, 'Of the Father's Heart begotten', it is the Cosmic Christ for whom he claims all the realms of the natural world, all the meaning of history, all the symbols of time. We are swept from the Alpha and Omega, the Creating Word, to the fulfilment of pagan history: 'This is he whom seer and Sibyl Sang in ages long gone by' and on to the acclamation of the universe: 'Every tongue his name confessing / Countless voices answering / Evermore and evermore.' It is a stunning vision, which has come down to us from a still half-pagan world.

The setting of my third example stands in sharp contrast. It is the barbarian world of the Frankish Kingdom of the sixth century. Into the court of Sigebert, the Frankish King, wandered the north Italian poet

---

3   Unless otherwise indicated, all hymns cited in this essay can be found in the current edition of the *New English Hymnal* (Norwich: Canterbury Press, 1988) and other main hymn collections.
4   On Prudentius, see Helen Waddell, *The Wandering Scholars* (London: Constable, 1927, pp. 17-18, and Appendix A, p. 223. See also F.L. Cross and E.A. Livingstone (eds.), *The Oxford Dictionary of the Christian Church* (Oxford: Oxford University Press, 3rd edn, 1997), *sub.nom.* and bibliography.

Venantius Fortunatus (c. 530–608).[5] He too carried the training of classical education, but the influence of the tribal culture now bore strongly upon him. He could still write a classical *epithalamion* (wedding ode) for the wedding of Sigebert to Brunhilde of Spain and elegant posies of verse for his patron, the Lady Radegunde, but when he turned to celebrate the Christian season of Passion, he drew his images from barbarian rituals, though he wrote in Latin. So the first line of the well-known hymn 'The royal banners forward go' in Latin runs: 'Vexilla Regis prodeunt'. The *vexilla regis* are transmuted from the tribal banners carried in the royal chariot when the tribe went to war with another tribe into the insignia of a different type of ruler. They were sacred symbols to be defended to the last drop of blood and here they meet us baptised into the service of another prince and another sacrificial warfare. In another hymn for Good Friday, Venantius uses an ancient image from northern mythology. The tree is drawn from the great forests of northern Europe. Woden hung for nine days and nights on the sacred tree Yggdrasill seeking to solve the riddle of the world. As Fortunatus baptises it into the Christian faith, he understands it as an animate creature accepting its tragic destiny from God and itself covered with strange glory:

> Faithful Cross! Above all other,
> One and only noble tree!
> None in foliage; none in blossom,
> None in fruit thy peer maybe;
> Sweetest wood and sweetest iron,
> Sweetest weight is hung on thee.

II

Hymn singing as a Christian activity at once raises the question: Who participates? The Pauline reference implies that the whole congregation sang, no doubt in their appropriate language. But what happened among the newly converted peoples of the barbarian West? All the surviving early hymns are in Latin, many of them translated from Greek. St Ambrose (c. 339–97) is credited with the encouragement of hymn singing in the western church but there is no suggestion of vernacular hymns. There is perhaps a clue as to the part played by lay people in the development of processional hymns. Fortunatus' hymn, *Vexilla Regis*, was written for a great ceremony when relics of St Martin of Tours were

---

5   On Venantius Fortunatus, see Waddell, *Wandering Scholars*, pp. 23-27, and her *Medieval Latin Lyrics* (London: Constable, 4th edn, 1929), pp. 59-67, 300-302. See also Cross and Livingstone (eds.), *Oxford Dictionary of the Christian Church*, sub.nom. and bibliography.

translated to Poitiers. This was part of the church's liturgy in which lay people would join enthusiastically, venerating the relics as the procession passed. In the eighth and ninth century St Theodulph of Orleans[6] wrote the processional hymn for Palm Sunday, which passed into common western usage and is still heard yearly in its English version. 'All glory, laud and honour' provided a chorus which could be repeated by a laity with little Latin.

In the Celtic and Anglo–Saxon world, however, lay people seem to have played a less passive part. Both Bede and Caedmon speak of vernacular hymns, while in Ireland we have the great eighth-century invocation of St Patrick's Breastplate drawing deeply on tribal mythology. Elsewhere, however, the church's liturgy becomes centred largely in early monastic communities where 'office hymns' were regularly chanted in Latin.

We do not, however, have to wait for the Reformation for a lay challenge to the dominance of Latin-educated clergy. As merchant trade and city economies develop in western Europe, so a middle class begins to emerge, expressing itself in a new individualism and a more personalised religious devotion. This finds expression in the cult of the Virgin Mary and the widespread use of the *Ave Maria*. Although still within the framework of the religious orders, it is significant that the devotional hymn translated as 'Jesus the very thought of thee / with sweetness fills my heart' (*Jesus dulcis memoria*), once ascribed to St Bernard of Clairvaux, is now thought to be by a twelfth-century nun. By the end of the twelfth century lay people, now becoming better educated, were seeking the right to create religious devotions of their own. Peter Waldo,[7] a merchant of Lyons, appealed to the Pope for permission to read and expound the scriptures with the group he had gathered. The clash between early Waldenses and ecclesiastical authorities turned on this right to interpret the Bible for themselves.[8] In the prospering cities of Lombardy a more docile group, the Humiliati were actually permitted in the early thirteenth century to form a lay fraternity with its own Rule and devotional practices, an alternative to monastic orders.[9] These and other early experiments paved the way for the thirteenth-century arrival of Friar orders in which, while first and second orders of men and women

---

6   See Cross and Livingstone (eds.), *Oxford Dictionary of the Christian Church*, *sub.nom.* and bibliography.

7   On Peter Waldo and the Waldenses, see Cross and Livingstone (eds.), *Oxford Dictionary of the Christian Church*, *sub.nom.* and bibliography: M. Lambert, *Medieval Heresy: Popular Movements from Bogomil to Hus* (London: Edward Arnold, 1977), pp. 67-91.

8   See letter of Pope Innocent III to the faithful of Metz in 1199, J.-P. Migne (ed.), *Patrologia Latina* (221 vols; Paris: Vives, 1844–64), CCXIV, cols. 695-99.

9   Lambert, *Medieval Heresy*, pp. 70-71, 96.

took full vows, third orders of lay people rapidly developed. It was St Francis and his followers in particular who took their vocation to the city people and therefore it is no surprise that their third order proliferated into many active lay groups—some in Provence and Catalonia, for instance, were driven into heresy.[10] Religious literature in the vernacular begins to appear and it is surely no accident that St Francis himself was inspired near his death in 1226 to compose our most famous medieval vernacular hymn, *The Canticum Fratis Solis vel laudes Creaturarum* ('The canticle of Brother Sun and praises of all creatures'). Thomas of Celano, writing in 1226, recorded it along with the story of its composition.[11]

This was a season of revivalist outbursts in Italian cities. The Franciscan chronicler Salimbene gives us a moving description of the 'Year of the Great Alleluia' in 1233 when Parma and other cities were swept by spontaneous fervour which brought all classes on to the streets singing holy *laude*. Every parish, says Salimbene, wanted its own procession.[12] What were these *laude*? We deduce that they were spiritual songs outside the liturgical traditions of the monastic 'office' hymn. A *lauda* seems to have been a personal type of religious song, mostly in the vernacular. There survives an early thirteenth-century text called 'The Prose of the Ass', written in the vernacular for a procession commemorating the Flight into Egypt in which a *lauda* was sung to a folk tune now known as *Orientis Partibus* (Eastern Parts). In 1260 and the following years western Europe was swept by processions of the Flagellants. Starting in Italian cities these penitents moved from place to place beating themselves and chanting songs of judgement. It is possible that the movement was sparked off by a prophecy attributed to Joachim of Fiore which associated the year 1260 with the advent of Antichrist and the end of the *saeculum* (age).[13]

The terror and passionate emotions associated with this movement are encapsulated in the famous hymn:

Dies irae, dies illa
Solvet saeclum in favilla
Teste David cum Sibylla

---

10   M. Reeves, *The Influence of Prophecy in the Later Middle Ages* (Oxford: Oxford University Press, 1969; Notre Dame: University of Notre Dame Press, rev. edn. 1993 [1969]), pp. 194-207, 219-25.
11   This is the view of Fr Patrick Colbourne, Ordo Minorum Capuchin. See also K. Esser, OM, *Gli Scritti di S. Francesco D'Assisi* (Padova, 1952), pp. 157-58.
12   Salimbene, OM, *Cronica, Monumenta Germaniae Historica Scriptores*, xxxii, pp. 22-24.
13   Reeves, *Influence of Prophecy*, pp. 49-50.

(Day of anger, day of terror,
All shall crumble into ashes,
Witness David and the Sibyl.)

Reaching its final form in the mid-thirteenth century, this poem in the 'vulgar' rhymed Latin becoming common at this period is surely a marching song of the people:

Tuba, mirum spargens sonum
Per sepulchra regionum
Coget omnes ante Thronum

(Sounds the trump with awful note,
Through the tombs of [deathly] regions,
Summoning all before the throne.)

Rex tremendae majestatis
Qui salvandos salvas gratis
Salva me, fons pietatis![14]

(King of glorious majesty
Saving those who need salvation
Save me also, fount of pity.) (Free translation to keep the rhythm.)

By the early fourteenth century there is evidence of cross fertilisation between popular folk music and church worship. A popular marching song, *L'homme arme* (The armed man), was used in many settings of the Mass, including two by Josquin des Pres. At Cortina and Urbino songbooks survive. One of the masters of the *lauda* was the third order Franciscan, Jacopone di Todi (c. 1230–1306),[15] whose religious visions were poured out in vernacular poems. For one, *O Christi omnipotente* (All powerful Chirst), music has survived, while his long series of poems on the Virgin, '*Donna del Paradiso*' (Lady of Paradise), was almost certainly used by groups devoted to the cult of Mary. In the fifteenth century, Bianco of Siena (c. 1434), a member of the lay order known as the *Gesuati*, was writing vernacular *laude*.[16] We have inherited one of these which, even in R.F. Littledale's translation, still carries its lyrical

---

14   F. Ermini, 'Il "Dies Irae"', *Biblioteca dell'Archivum Romanieum*, ser. i, x-xii (1928–29), pp. 1-158.
15   G. Peck, *The Fool of God: Jacopone da Todi* (Alabama: University of Alabama Press, 1980), see especially ch. 5.
16   Information kindly supplied by Prof. Roberto Rusconi. See also *Dizionario Bibliografico degli italiani* (10 vols; Roma: Istituto della Enciclopedia italiana, 1960–73), X, pp. 220-23.

quality. 'Come down / O, Love divine'. Finally, it is, of course, in the late Middle Ages, that the townspeople, led by the guilds, captured the dramas of Christian faith, drawing them out of the churches into the high streets in the vernacular mystery plays and the carols which accompanied them. The carol, originally a dance, becomes a song often arranged as stanza and chorus for use in procession (the leader could get his breath in the chorus line).[17]

So the stage is set for the great outburst of hymnology which was the gift of the Reformation to the western Church. It is no surprise to find that the early sixteenth-century followers of Jan Huss in Bohemia compiled the first congregational hymnbook while Martin Luther produced his chorale songbook in 1524. For centuries in the latin church Christian worship had been focused on the main act of the Mass. In its new Protestant interpretations this remained true in the main. But liturgy was now coloured by national forms of piety. In Germany this took the shape of the famous chorale hymn, a full congregational expression of collective religious emotion. In Geneva, however, Calvinist worship turned rather to psalm-singing, which was carried back by Protestant refugees to England and Scotland.[18] Plain song Gregorian chant gives way to metrical hymn versions, pioneered by Thomas Sternhold and John Hopkins and popularised in the psalters of 1562 in England and 1564 in Scotland. Thus the tremendous range of human experience—from anguish to hope, from guilt to confidence—which had been enshrined in Hebrew worship was recaptured for the people. It is fascinating to compare the lyrical devotion of German hymns and tunes with the rugged scriptural psalm-chanting of Scottish Calvinists.

In the newly established Church of England the Prayer Book orders of service did not allow for the singing of anything but psalms. Indeed, hymn-singing had no official place in Anglican prayer-book worship until the early nineteenth century. It was in the newly-freed Dissenting churches of the later seventeenth and early eighteenth centuries that the first of our great English hymn writers found their inspiration. We should remember that, though poets such as George Herbert have given us beautiful hymns,[19] they were not written as such, whereas Isaac Watts (1674–1748) deliberately set out to give a tongue to the worship of ordinary congregations: 'I would neither indulge in any bold metaphors nor admit of hard words, nor tempt the ignorant worshipper to sing above

---

17   See Erik Routley, *The English Carol* (London: Herbert Jenkins, 1958).

18   P.A. Scholes, *Oxford Companion to Music* (ed. J. Owen Ward; Oxford: Oxford University Press, 10th edn, 1970), p. 493.

19   The well known Herbert hymns are poems which first appeared in a collection entitled *The Temple* in 1633. He had sent his collection to his friend Nicholas Ferrar.

his understanding.'[20] He was followed by prolific hymn writers, such as Philip Doddridge and Thomas Kelly. In 1735 John and Charles Wesley, on their mission to Georgia, found themselves singing hymns with a group of Moravians in the hold of their ship crossing the Atlantic. It was perhaps this experience which sparked off the creative impulse in the Wesley family to write and collect hymns and set them to music. John was convinced of the vital role of congregational singing in meeting the spiritual needs of simple people while acting as a powerful binding force in the congregation.

This socialising aspect of hymn-singing was seized upon by John Newton, slave-trading sailor turned Anglican priest (1725–1807). He focused much of his evangelising effort in the weekday prayer meetings at Olney where he worked for seventeen years. There were no strictures on hymn-singing in these informal gatherings and for them he produced in 1779 the Olney hymn-book for which he himself wrote 280 hymns besides those contributed by William Cowper. The impact which these shared, uplifting experiences had on society did not go unnoticed among Anglicans. In 1802 John Venn, the evangelical rector of Clapham wrote: 'I am persuaded that the singing has been a great instrument in the Dissenters hands of drawing away people from the Church and why should we not take that instrument out of their hands?'[21] The removal of constrictions on introducing hymns into the Anglican liturgy, following a judgement in the York Consistory Court in 1819, opened the way to the great period of Anglican hymn-writing, translating and tune composing. It was not only evangelicals who grasped the psychological power of community singing. High churchmen searched medieval sources for office hymns, which they brought out of their monastic settings and translated for the people. Chief among these translators was J.M. Neale. With a different emphasis Robert Bridges in his *Yattendon Hymnal* (1895–99) brought both ancient and German hymns into modern English worship. The movement is seen spreading to the Roman Catholic Church in the Westminster hymnbook of 1905. Thus in the history of hymns, their composers and translators, we can trace the recovery by lay people of their own distinctive part in Christian worship.

---

20   Quoted by George Wakefield (ed.), *Dictionary of Christian Spirituality* (London: SCM Press, 1997), *sub.nom.*.
21   Quoted Ian Bradley, *Abide with me: The World of Victorian Hymns* (London: SCM Press, 1997), p.15.

III

My third point concerns the question of why many hymns seem to be indestructible while others quickly pass out of date. When one reflects on the vast cultural changes since Christians sang in the catacombs, the survival of great hymns seems remarkable. But, of course, what this really brings out is the unchanging nature of the Christian gospel, founded on the particular memory of a particular historical moment in time. The once-for-all revelation of the Creator God in the Word is for all time. Repeating the story of the Incarnate Word in hymns touches fundamental human emotions, experiences, expectations which do not change with changing cultures. The ancient formulations of our faith, even the metaphors and images of past ages, form a rich heritage for Christians today. Yet beside this stands a desire of new generations to reaffirm the gospel in contemporary idiom. There is no case for throwing out the grand old hymns: worship today can embrace both categories.

There is, however, a different kind of problem with some hymns. The nineteenth and twentieth centuries witnessed a widening of Christian concern for worldwide mission and the uplift of society, which inspired hymns of 'outreach'. From the heroic labours of missionaries in far countries came hymns which painted the world in black and white, as in Bishop Heber's famous hymn 'From Greenland's icy mountains': 'The heathen in his blindness / bows down to wood and stone' and 'Where every prospect pleases / and only man is vile'. A culture of religious colonialism is simply not acceptable today. In the global village even the multicoloured 'Hills of the North rejoice' cannot be sung in its original version. In the latest edition of the *English Hymnal* it appears in an emasculated form. Similarly, some national hymns are questioned. When Kipling wrote his Recessional for Queen Victoria's Diamond Jubilee in 1897 it gave national utterance to a sense of achievement with responsibility in British imperialism. It could still be sung when the *English Hymnal* of 1906 appeared but has vanished since. Here 'political correctness' has been too hasty in its judgement, for Kipling's hymn was a plea for penitence as well as a celebration. We certainly still need a hymn today to voice repentance for all our blundering arrogance in the Third World. Again, many people find difficulty in singing the first verse of Cecil Spring-Rice's hymn: 'I vow to thee, my country', although 'the love that asks no question' of this verse is balanced by the vision of a higher loyalty in the second verse.

Characteristic of an increasing social concern from the nineteenth century onwards are the hymns which call for social justice and evoke a vision of a new society. James Russell Lowell's anti-slavery hymn 'Once to every man and nation' (1844) leads the way. In England Henry Scott Holland, with the Anglo–Catholic Charles Gore, founded the Christian

Social Union in 1889 and it was in the society's organ, *The Commonwealth*, that his hymn 'Judge eternal, throned in splendour' first appeared. There is an enduring quality here, as in Lowell's words: 'By the light of burning martyrs / Christ thy bleeding feet we track / Toiling up new Calvaries ever / With the Cross that turns not back.' But in hymns of aspiration for the future of society, we meet two trends, which are now dated. G.K. Chesterton's hymn (which also appeared in *The Commonwealth* in 1906), 'O God of earth and altar', makes an eloquent plea for a society adrift but culminates in a nostalgic vision which takes us back to the Middle Ages: 'Tie in a living tether / The prince and priest and thrall'. Few would want to live in such a society today. On the other hand there is a trend towards an optimistic vision of the future which twentieth-century experience has now killed. When the American Unitarian Samuel Johnson wrote 'City of God, how broad and far / outspread thy walls sublime' in 1864, he committed the singer to the words: 'How grandly hath thine empire grown / Of freedom, love and truth'. Again, Frederick Hosmer's hymn 'Thy Kingdom come! On bended knee / The passing ages pray' is unwavering in its expectation of the day, 'When knowledge hand in hand with peace / Shall walk the earth abroad / the day of perfect righteousness / The promised day of God.' It was, however, John Addington Symonds (1840–93) who went over the top in picturing the Utopia of later Victorianism:[22]

> These things shall be! A loftier race
> Than e'er the world hath known, shall rise
> With flame of freedom in their souls
> And light of science in their eyes. —And so on

This was much sung by students in the first half of the twentieth century but not since. Scientific progress does not seem to lead automatically to increasing wisdom.

Finally, children's hymns of the Irish Cecil Frances Alexander (1818–95) have come under censure both for her aristocratic social picture of 'The rich man in his castle / the poor man at his gate', and for her model of a meek Christchild: 'Christian children all must be / Mild, obedient, good as he', which is hardly attractive to rumbustious children of today. In both cases later hymn collections have modified the text. In his great hymn Lowell wrote:

---

22   The verses included in *Songs of Praise* in 1931 were selected from a poem entitled 'A Vista', with fifteen verses, first published in J.A. Symonds' *New and Old: A Volume of Verse* (London: Smith Elder, 1880).

New occasions teach new duties;
Time makes ancient good uncouth;
They must upward still and onward
Who would keep abreast of truth.

We need new social hymns for a changing culture to give voice to our continuing search for truth in society.

In the long history of the Christian church the truly wonderful gift of God has been the capacity to embody eternal verities in the life of ever-changing and ever-renewed societies. For a range of reasons, religious and social, hymn-singing as a collective activity of worship has been a continuous thread in this history. Today it forms a striking example of ecumenism. Many great hymns were written originally for a specific type of theology or church worship. But today we all sing each other's hymns.

CHAPTER 13

The Democratization of British Christianity: The Baptist Case, 1770-1870

D.W. Bebbington

The thesis of Nathan Hatch that between 1780 and 1830 American Christianity underwent a process of democratization has received widespread and deserved acceptance.[1] Hatch argues that in this shaping era of the new republic the flow of religion was diverted from traditional courses into populist channels. The development involved a number of trends, one being a spirited anti-elitism. There was an assertive challenge to the Congregational establishment of New England and its equivalents elsewhere such as the Anglican dominance of Virginia. The inherited authority of the clergy to supervise religious practice was dismissed in favour of the right of laypeople to work out their own salvation. Another dimension was the spread of enthusiasm. Popular expressions of spirituality such as dreams and trances became acceptable; vigorous new hymns were sung with gusto; and fresh ideas circulated rapidly through increasing use of the printing press. And a further characteristic of these years was the rise of untrained outsiders to leadership in movements that they often created for themselves. Alexander Campbell of the Churches of Christ, Joseph Smith of the Mormons and (less originally because of his commissioning by John Wesley) Francis Asbury of Methodism spread new versions of the faith across the land. Although they often displayed an authoritarian streak, such men remained identified with the common people. In these various ways popular pressure transformed the practice of Christianity. The period included the so-called Second Great Awakening, an upsurge of eagerness for propagating the gospel, but, as the mention of the Mormons illustrates, the mobilisation was not confined

---

1   N.O. Hatch, *The Democratization of American Christianity* (New Haven, CT: Yale University Press, 1989).

to the ranks of orthodox Evangelicals. A broader impulse, Hatch argues, was at work: the impact of the secular context on Christianity in the new world. The ideal of democratic initiative, introduced by the American Revolution, was carried over into the religious sphere. The old principle of establishment, still operating in Massachusetts down to as late as 1833, was excluded from the competence of the federal government, so allowing experimentation by new men. The result was the populism that has marked American religion ever since, extending down to the televangelists of the late twentieth century and beyond.

A feature of the Hatch thesis is the contrast the author draws between the United States and Great Britain. Whereas in America revival was yoked with liberty, in Britain religion was bound up with deference, paternalism and gentility. The Church of England was a bastion of the conservative order against social disruption while British Methodism under Jabez Bunting was turned into another agent of control.[2] The democratization of Christianity, on this reading, was a distinctively American phenomenon. British religion, on the other hand, continued to be an elite phenomenon that avoided adaptation to the tastes of the many. How just is this contrast? We can ask whether America was unique in embracing a populist style or whether, on the contrary, there was a process of democratization in Britain as well. It may be admitted that the Church of England and Wesleyan Methodism under Bunting were both organized so as to restrict opportunities for rabble rousing, but the net should be cast wider. Breakaway Methodists, for instance, showed many of the characteristics of the American backwoods. The New Connexion under Alexander Kilham, inspired by the democratic ideology of the French Revolution, asserted the rights of laypeople in religious organizations; the Primitive Methodists were a strange group in their early years, associating with the Magic Methodists who specialized in dreams and being deeply influenced by Lorenzo Dow, one of the idiosyncratic American preachers about whom Hatch writes; and Wesleyan Reformers successfully combined revivalism with a passion for liberty.[3] All these groups fit the model of the democratization thesis. There were other bodies outside Methodism that bore the same stamp. The Peculiar People of Essex, founded by the farm labourer James Banyard, went in for divine healing; and the Society of Dependants of Sussex, established by John Sirgood, produced a mass of their own hymnody, organized co-operative stores under church auspices and

---

2   Hatch, *Democratization*, pp. 7-8, 218-19.
3   David Hempton, *Methdism and Politics in British Society, 1750–1850* (London: Hutchinson, 1984), pp. 67-73; J.S. Werner, *The Primitive Methodist Connexion: Its Background and Early History* (Madison, WI: University of Wisconsin Press, 1984), pp. 69-70, 45-47; D.A. Gowland, *Methodist Secessions: The Origins of Free Methodism in three Lancashire Towns* (Manchester: Chetham Society, 1979).

discouraged marriage as an inferior state of life.[4] Beyond the bounds of orthodoxy there were the followers of Joanna Southcott, the daughter of a Devon farmer who claimed to be about to bear a spiritual son, Shiloh, and died in 1814, leaving a box of secret documents to be opened by the bishops; the Freethinking Christians set up in London in 1798 by Samuel Thompson, who had seceded from the Universalists, to advocate a radical blend of reason and religion; the adherents of Joseph Barker, a West Riding wool-spinner who was expelled from the Methodist New Connexion in 1841 and set up his own grouping of rationalist chapels before eventually finding his way back to the Primitive Methodists; and many more.[5] Britain generated a variety of sects led by people from humble circumstances that show all the vibrancy and capacity for innovation of their American equivalents. The same processes were at work on both sides of the Atlantic.

The issue addressed here is how far British Baptists match the democratization thesis. The period covered is the century after 1770, a longer period than the one examined by Nathan Hatch so as to illustrate more symptoms of what was taking place. The starting point is the year of the foundation of the New Connexion of General Baptists, which will call for careful scrutiny in this context; the terminal point of 1870 is the end of a decade of fervent evangelism that flowed from high expectations of revival. It might be supposed that democratization could hardly take place because already, before that century, the Baptists were democratic in spirit. During the seventeenth century they had popular leaders of lowly origins, they were associated with Fifth Monarchy Men in revolutionary schemes and they possessed a democratic form of church government. It is clear, however, that during the eighteenth century there emerged an influential elite, at least among the Particular Baptists. The Baptist Board of London ministers played a major part in shaping the denomination's life. The board contained country representatives, but the meetings were dominated by the metropolitan men who could attend regularly. Advice was sought from the board by provincial churches about building a meeting house or disciplining an errant member.[6] The

---

4   Mark Sorrell, *The Peculiar People* (Exeter: Paternoster Press, 1979); Peter Jerrome, *The Story of the Loxwood Dependants: John Sirgood's Way* (Petworth, West Sussex: Window Press, 1998).

5   J.K. Hopkins, *A Woman to Deliver her People: Joanna Southcott and English Millenarianism in an Era of Revolution* (Austin, TX: University of Texas Press, 1982); Iain McCalman, *Radical Underworld: Prophets, Revolutionaries and Pornographers in London, 1795–1840* (Cambridge: Cambridge University Press, 1988), pp. 73-75; O.A. Beckerlegge, 'Joseph Barker', in D.M. Lewis, *The Blackwell Dictionary of Evangelical Biography* (2 vols, Oxford: Blackwell, 1995), I, p. 60.

6   Raymond Brown, *The English Baptists of the Eighteenth Century* (A History of the English Baptists, 2; London: Baptist Historical Society, 1986), p. 41.

ministers on the board, with laymen from their churches, administered the Particular Baptist Fund, and so exercised the power of the purse over developments elsewhere. Some such as Joseph Stennett, minister of Little Wild Street (1736–58), were of significant social standing, mixing with the Speaker of the House of Commons and the Bishop of London.[7] It was the London ministers who were primarily responsible for sustaining the regularity of church order that Michael Walker found existing at the start of the nineteenth century.[8] Even if in the remoter parts of the country there were churches during the eighteenth century that went their own way, there existed a Baptist elite, chiefly clerical and mainly metropolitan. There was scope for subsequent democratization in the life of the denomination.

One grouping that emerged during the late eighteenth and early nineteenth centuries clearly stood apart from the London ministers and yet would be hard to characterize as populist in the sense that Hatch gives to the term. The Scotch Baptists, founded in Edinburgh in 1765, were, it is true, largely the creation of a single man, Archibald McLean, whose writings fostered the whole movement. There was also a distinct spirit of self-reliance among the elders leading the churches who pursued their own callings, their plurality in each congregation being the most obvious feature differentiating the Scotch Baptists from their Particular Baptist contemporaries. They were not, however, marked by an enthusiastic spirituality. On the contrary, their theology, Andrew Fuller complained, was Sandemanian. They supposed that faith was simply a matter of bare assent to propositions, so that they revealed the impress of the age of reason. The group, furthermore, often shared in elite status. The Dundee congregation included a lawyer, some manufacturers and several merchants; the mother church in Edinburgh contained some of the higher professionals of the capital city of Scotland.[9] For these men the aim was the reproduction of the New Testament model of church life in all its purity rather than the propagation of the faith to a mass audience. Although other Scotch Baptist churches drew largely working-class support, the denomination does not fit the democratization theory very closely. It is true that the attempt to revive the primitive pattern of the church was similar to Campbellite restorationism and that many Scotch Baptist churches went over to the Churches of Christ, but the willingness

---

7   L.G. Champion, 'The Social Status of Some Eighteenth Century Baptist Ministers', *Baptist Quarterly* 25.1 (January, 1973), pp. 10-14.
8   Michael J. Walker, *Baptists at the Table: The Theology of the Lord's Supper among English Baptists in the Nineteenth Century* (Didcot: Baptist Historical Society, 1992), pp. 121-22.
9   Derek Murray, 'The Seventeenth and Eighteenth Centuries', in D.W. Bebbington (ed.), *The Baptists in Scotland: A History* (Glasgow: Baptist Union of Scotland, 1988), p. 19.

of the McLeanites to back the Baptist Missionary Society drew them into wider denominational circles. Perhaps it is not surprising that a dimension of Baptist life should prove to be ambiguous, not firmly pointing one way or the other in relation to the applicability of the American hypothesis to Britain.

There is, however, a great deal of evidence suggesting that democratization was operating among the Particular Baptists. One indication was the Serampore controversy in the Baptist Missionary Society (BMS). This dispute was not just an issue dividing the missionaries around William Carey from their home organization, for it was also a question that revealed tensions between the provinces and London. Early support for the BMS was based in the Northamptonshire Association, but embraced a broad provincial network sustained by Andrew Fuller, its secretary, through personal visits and correspondence. During his life-time, from the foundation of the society in 1792 down to 1815, Fuller insisted on keeping the seat of the organization in Northamptonshire, where he served at Kettering, rather than in the capital, as some wanted. He explained that he was opposed to holding public meetings where persons of rank would take the chair and where there would be long speeches savouring of ostentation. He was evidently suspicious of the flunkeyism of the capital. In 1810, of the BMS committee of seventeen, only one man was from London. This was William Burls, a City merchant at 56 Lothbury, whom Fuller trusted sufficiently to let him transact much of the society's business. In 1812 the committee was enlarged to incorporate three of the leading metropolitan ministers, F.A. Cox, Joseph Ivimey and William Newman, together with a number of others. Directly after Fuller's death, early in 1816, a committee meeting was held at 56 Lothbury. Of the six present, five were from London, the sixth being the new secretary, James Hinton from Oxford. This meeting raised the question whether additional trustees were necessary for BMS property in India, thus igniting the missionary controversy. The Londoners were questioning the capacity of Carey and his colleagues to look after their own buildings responsibly. In 1818, when the committee sent the expostulatory letter to the Serampore trio that caused most offence, one of the three Scots present, probably Christopher Anderson, deplored the quarrel with the missionaries. It was a sign of continuing provincial restiveness with metropolitan policy. In 1819 there was a *coup d'état* in the society when a new management structure was introduced despite objections from John Ryland of Bristol. A central committee of seventeen was to meet monthly in London. Now only five members were from the provinces, the twelve from the capital including Joseph Gutteridge, a wealthy layman who was the keenest on what he called 'systematic management'.[10] It was this 'junto in London', as an opponent called it, that kept up the controversy with the missionaries in India. By contrast the trustees chosen by the Serampore trio for their property included, apart from men in India and the BMS secretary, Christopher Anderson in Edinburgh, a Glasgow layman, another from Liverpool and an American.[11] The take-over of the BMS was an effort by the London elite to seize authority back from the provincial rank and file. Fuller's early network of support for the BMS, on the other hand, represented part of a democratization process. The traditional London leadership of the denomination resented what had happened and, in the name of business efficiency, terminated the experiment.

The provincial spirit shown in the BMS had its counterpart in attitudes to the Baptist Union (BU). This body, first founded in 1812, was promoted by the London elite: again Cox, Ivimey and Newman were among them. The story of the BU is often told as a one of gradual progress, substantially a success story. That approach reflects the chief source, *The Baptist Magazine*, which was enthusiastically favourable towards the new organization, not least because one of the purposes of the BU was to encourage subscriptions to the magazine.[12] There is therefore not a trace in its pages during the years 1812–14 of any opposition to the centralization represented by the Union. But opposition there was: Ernest Payne notes in his history of the Union that there was no representative from the north of England or from Wales at the inaugural gathering.[13] Again after the refoundation of the BU on a broader basis in 1832, growth was very slow. After five years, of the roughly 1,200 Baptist churches in existence, only 329 had affiliated to the Union. Some of the reasons for the reluctance to join can be inferred from an extremely defensive account of its annual session in 1837: 'Strictly a voluntary society, without having even the desire of ecclesiastical power, and only anxious for combined effort, for the sake of increased efficiency, the Baptist Union invites the full investigation of its proceedings, assured that the results can only be good.'[14] Critics were

---

10   Joseph Ivimey, *Letters on the Serampore Controversy* (London: for the author, 1831), pp. 16-30. *Baptist Magazine* [hereafter *BM*], June 1850, p. 334.

11   An Old Subscriber to the Baptist Mission, *Two Letters to a Member of the Committee of the Baptist Missionary Society on their Disputes with the Serampore Brethren; With Addenda* (London: Parbury, Allen and Co, 1829), pp. 7, 11 (quoting letters by R. Nichols).

12   *BM*, August 1813, p. 352.

13   E.A. Payne, *The Baptist Union: A Short History* (London: Carey Kingsgate Press, 1959), pp. 20-21.

14   *Account of the Proceedings of the Twenty-Fifth Annual Session of the Baptist Union* (London: G. Wightman, n.d. [1837]), pp. 10, 9.

evidently claiming that there was a secretive cabal seeking power over the churches to the destruction of Baptist independency. Popular resistance still existed in the 1860s. In 1863, when it was still the case that fewer than half the churches of the denomination had joined the Union, J.H. Hinton, who as joint secretary had good reason to know, explained from the chair that Baptists, though one in name, were in fact many and could be called legion. The BU had been useful, he contended, 'but its existence has been a continual struggle, and even by those who learn only by experience, it must be expected to be so still'.[15] A sturdy independency was deeply rooted. In 1832 more than half the Particular Baptist churches had not even affiliated to a regional association; in 1863 the proportion was still only a third.[16] Part of the explanation must lie in a feeling no stronger than apathy. Yet there was also a powerful sense of localism, often theologically grounded, that was highly suspicious of apparent moves to exert outside control over an individual church. In America the same temper among Baptists, expressed for example in the anti-missionary movement from the second decade of the nineteenth century, has been recognized by Hatch as a symptom of the democratic spirit.[17] The British resistance to the BU must be seen as fitting the democratization thesis.

The separation of the Strict Baptists from the denominational mainstream is another indication that there were similarities with what was happening in America. Many Baptists who maintained the traditional teaching that the bread and wine at communion should be for none but baptized believers continued to associate with the growing number of churches that followed Robert Hall in holding that the Lord's Supper should be open to all Christians. Others, however, identified with the magazines that arose to argue for the older practice: *The Gospel Standard*, *The Earthen Vessel* and *The Gospel Herald*. These churches diverged steadily from those coming together in the Baptist Union. They would make no concession to the novel pragmatism of the age that drew on the wisdom of the Enlightenment to contend for allowing any sincere believer to participate in the Lord's Supper. The strong-minded saw no reason to compromise in a way that seemed to betray the convictions of their ancestors in the faith. They continued, like their seventeenth-century predecessors, to insist on the details of church polity. Likewise they retained a piety of the seventeenth-century type, nourished by Puritan texts, highly introspective and often melancholy. They championed a high Calvinism that clung to double predestination, resisting the

---

15 Payne, *Baptist Union*, p. 87.
16 J.H.Y. Briggs, *The English Baptists of the Nineteenth Century* (A History of the English Baptists, 3; Didcot: Baptist Historical Society, 1994), p. 256. Payne, *Baptist Union*, p. 86.
17 Hatch, *Democratization*, p. 101.

theological innovations of Andrew Fuller. They stood for the ability of the common man to interpret scripture without the aid of modern learning. These traditionalists were commonly, though not consistently, in less populated rural areas, especially in East Anglia and parts of southern England.[18] They included many of the humbler folk in their ranks. Their most prominent minister in the early nineteenth century, William Gadsby of Manchester, paraded his identification with the poor, even on political platforms. The Strict and Particular Baptists were often less demonstrative than their spiritual cousins who adopted the novelties of the Evangelical Revival, but in other ways they formed the equivalent of many of Hatch's populist American movements. They were in fact identical in ethos to the Primitive Baptists of the American South. They form another illustration that among Baptists the democratic spirit was not confined to the United States.

Admiration for the Americans among British Baptists helped to foster their common values. During the Revolutionary War, Dissent generally favoured the cause of the Americans. When John Wesley denounced the colonists, Caleb Evans of Bristol Academy took up the cudgels on their behalf.[19] These sympathies became rooted. In 1846, David Douglas, the historian of the Baptists in the north of England, wrote of the late eighteenth century: 'The children of the Puritans had just terminated a war which laid the foundation of an empire, on principles somewhat similar to those their fathers had attempted in England; but on a field of far mightier range.'[20] The American experiment was the Puritan Commonwealth writ large. Baptists emigrated in large numbers to the United States; ministers came and went across the Atlantic; and correspondence was freely exchanged. There were specially close relations between the Baptists of Wales and their co-religionists in Pennsylvania.[21] By the 1840s the Voluntary movement that seized the imagination of many Baptist ministers such as J.H. Hinton and Thomas Price was a self-conscious effort to Americanize British society by putting religion on a voluntary basis, as it was in the United States.[22] Their public

---

18   Kenneth Dix, 'Varieties of High Calvinism among Nineteenth-Century Particular Baptists', *Baptist Quarterly* 38.2 (April, 1999), pp. 56-69.

19   J.E. Bradley, *Religion, Revolution and English Radicalism: Nonconformity in Eighteenth-Century Politics and Society* (Cambridge: Cambridge University Press, 1990), p. 149.

20   David Douglas, *History of the Baptist Churches of the North of England, from 1648 to 1845* (London: Houlston and Stoneman, 1846), pp. 247-48.

21   H.M. Davies, *Transatlantic Brethren: Rev. Samuel Jones (1735–1814) and his Friends: Baptists in Wales, Pennsylvania and Beyond* (Bethlehem, PA: Lehigh University Press, 1995).

22   Timothy Larsen, *Friends of Religious Equality: Nonconformist Politics in Mid-Victorian England* (Woodbridge: Boydell Press, 1999), pp. 88-93.

philosophy was distinctly American in content. In one respect, in fact, radical British Baptists were more 'democratic' than their white American counterparts. Roused by the campaign to end slavery in British dominions that triumphed in 1833, they adopted a firm stance against the continuing practice in America. Hostility to racial prejudice became part of the standard attitudes to public affairs professed by British Baptists. A black preacher from Philadelphia was welcomed when he went round raising money to pay off his chapel debt. Yorkshire Baptists were horrified by his tales of being kept at a social distance by his white co-religionists. In 1850 they sent a letter to the Baptists of the northern United States urging them to free themselves from 'a species of pride so irrational, so vulgar, and so *unChristian*, as that of pride in difference of colour!'[23] In this instance the Baptists of an English county were pursuing the democratic principle more rigorously than their American contemporaries.

Voluntaryism was not just a public philosophy, for it also represented a deliberate act of separation from the established church by many individual believers. It was often a costly experience to break with an institution so bound up with national and local identity. Dissenters were still outsiders. Particular instances demonstrate the social reality of the times. Joseph Green, for example, was born in 1752 near Sutton Coldfield, where he attended the parish church until he was twenty-three. Then he was converted through hearing a Baptist minister. 'Educated in the doctrines and discipline of the church of England', explained his obituarist in *The Baptist Magazine*, 'Mr. Green's mind was strongly prejudiced, as the minds of the great majority of our fellow-countrymen are, against the instructive and useful doctrine of Believer's Baptism.'[24] At first he warmly resisted the idea of being baptized, but then, convinced by the scriptures, he submitted to the rite and joined the local Baptist church in 1776, later serving as a General Baptist minister. For Green the act of baptism was clearly a bold one, separating him sharply from his previous associations. Likewise John Paddon, converted in the 1790s at about fourteen, was baptized two years later, joining the church at Bovey Tracy in Devon. His relatives and friends were alarmed. 'They', reported *The Baptist Magazine*, 'being warmly attached to the established church, could not approve of the young man's becoming a dissenter'. Paddon, however, was independent-minded. 'He knew Religion to be a personal concern, and that he must be accountable to God for himself; therefore, however he might be obliged to differ from his friends, in matters of religion, he saw Christ to be his only master, and that it was his duty and

---

23   *BM*, April 1850, p. 228.
24   *BM*, July 1809, p. 284.

honour to be obedient to his commands.'[25] Such obedience could entail social ostracism, the loss of employment and even, in villages with hostile landlords, eviction from home. To become a Dissenter was to reject the existing social order; to become a Baptist was to mark the rejection by a public ceremony. For many in the century before 1870 believer's baptism was in itself a democratic gesture.

The element of enthusiastic spirituality in the Hatch thesis was very much present in Britain as well as in America. There was fervour among the itinerant preachers, many of them Baptists, who from the 1790s carried the gospel round the country. It was even more apparent in the revivalism that was imported from the United States from the 1820s. This was the variety associated with Charles Finney, who argued that there was a science of revivals. If certain conditions were fulfilled, mass conversions would follow. He therefore advocated techniques such as the 'anxious seat', in which an enquirer was isolated from the congregation to be prayed through to salvation. Finney's *Lectures on Revivals* (1835) proved extremely popular in Britain. His methods were adopted by the Baptist Home Missionary Society in the 1830s.[26] Thus the most advanced religious views canvassed among the Americans were grafted into Baptist life. Although revivalism receded during the 1840s, it was again in vogue after 1859, when it was copied from the American 'businessman's revival' of 1857–58. Baptists participated fully in the wave of enthusiastic religion that swept into the country through Ulster, new congregations often springing up in these years. There were two spectacular leaps in English Baptist membership at this time: in the year 1859–60 some 25,000 individuals (over 25% of existing membership) were added to the chapels and in 1865–66 another 20,000.[27] Revivalism derived from America played a significant part in the denomination.

Hatch stresses the role of self-educated leaders from lowly social origins in the development of American Christianity. His examples can be matched from British Baptist life. Two examples may suffice. One was Sinclair Thomson, 'The Shetland Apostle'. He was born in the islands in 1784 into a family of the upper peasant type, possessing its own boat but no social pretensions. He received less than three months' formal schooling before setting off to Greenland on a whaling ship, taking up liquor smuggling and becoming a fiddler in great demand for island festivities. Because of his musical abilities, he acted as precentor in the parish church of Dunrossness. At the age of thirty he was converted through a tract handed to him by a woman belonging to the Independent denomination. At first he tried to preach within the Church of Scotland,

---

25 *BM*, July 1809, pp. 277-78.
26 Richard Carwardine, *Transatlantic Revivalism: Popular Evangelicalism in Britain and America, 1790–1865* Westport, CT: Greenwood Press, 1978), chs 2 and 3.
27 Briggs, *English Baptists*, p. 262.

but his efforts were thwarted and he was dismissed as precentor. For a while he worked with the Independents, but then, it is said, without knowing of the existence of Baptists, he reached baptistic views through personal Bible study. He was baptized by a visiting Edinburgh Baptist in 1815. In the following year he formed Dunrossness Baptist Church, and by his subsequent efforts founded five further causes in the Shetlands. No fresh Baptist church was to be formed on the islands between his death in 1864 and the 1990s. Thomson sustained himself by fishing and small scale farming while he co-ordinated a Methodist-style preaching circuit. Here was a man who was prepared to experiment with new methods of church organization while dominating his religious body.[28] Thomson is a classic case of a figure who trained himself on the job, created a substantial movement and yet remained close to the people. He fits the typology of Hatch's 'democratic' religious leaders precisely.

Charles Whitfield, Baptist minister at Hamsterley in County Durham, is another. Born in 1748, Whitfield was apprenticed in Newcastle, where he was converted when Wesley visited the city and joined the Methodists. While still an apprentice, he devoted five hours a day to study. Becoming a Calvinist, he was baptized at Tuthill Stairs Baptist Church and then, in 1771, called to the ministry of the remote cause at Hamsterley. He cultivated the land to support himself, and, with his 'manly and portly appearance', seems to have been a jolly farmer who got on well with his neighbours. He also kept a school to bring in income, gaining a reputation for his learning. He became one of the leading Hebrew scholars of the denomination, though his dependence on personally acquired knowledge sometimes showed when he gave mistaken advice on legal questions. Warmly attached to his own village—he remarked that 'Hamsterley' would be found engraved on his heart—he nevertheless set up churches in Bedale, Sunderland, Stockton-on-Tees and Wolsingham and joined in establishing others. It was typical that when, in 1809, the Stockton church was newly revived, Whitfield arranged for a minister to come and bought a house for the man himself. Twice Whitfield refounded the Northern Baptist Association and in 1798 he became president of the newly formed Northern Evangelical Society that united Baptists and Independents in itinerant gospel work. He wrote *The Form and Order of a Gospel Church* (1775), defining Baptist identity, and created a library at his meeting house in Hamsterley to spread sound views. He was a masterful personality, 'warm in his temper', according to his successor, 'and, sometimes, rather overbearing in his manner'. Down to 1819, when, two years before his death, he suffered paralysis, Whitfield was the pivotal figure among Baptists in the northernmost counties of

---

28   J.A. Smith, *Sinclair Thomson: Or The Shetland Apostle* (Lerwick: Shetland Times, 1969).

England.[29] He was the same type of confident autodidact who moulded the religious bodies across the Atlantic.

Ministers of the period were generally, like Whitfield, men of the people. Ken Brown has suggested that humble origins were normal in the early nineteenth century.[30] A couple of ministers from Suffolk are representative. One, Isaac Double, began as an illiterate agricultural labourer. He enjoyed unusual strength, being able to load a wagon with sacks of wheat, each weighing over 250 pounds, without help. Having been taught to read by a small boy, he became a lay preacher and then settled at Chelmondiston. He nevertheless continued labouring in the fields because the chapel was too poor to pay him. 'To follow the plough all day', he remarked, 'was light work in comparison with preaching.' Another was Samuel Collins, formerly a draper's apprentice, who served as pastor at Grundisburgh from 1826. His sermons were said to be like old Suffolk farmhouses, rambling structures but with great oak beams in every room. Weighty sentences gave solidity to his not too orderly addresses.[31] Double's continuation of his secular work while in pastoral charge was very common. *The Baptist Magazine*, with its urban and urbane perspective, deplored bivocationalism. 'As a tradesman', it observed in 1812, 'a minister must associate with tradesmen; and it is vain to expect that such should in general be those who are pious and likely to promote the piety of the minister.'[32] As the nineteenth century wore on, the twin forces of rising prosperity and growing respectability decreased the frequency of ministers obtaining outside work to sustain themselves. A higher standard of education was required and so college-trained men were preferred. By 1870, the Monmouth Association decided to recognize only stated ministers or academic students.[33] Yet in the following year still only 58% of Baptist ministers in England had received a formal training.[34] There remained little sense of a uniformly separated ministry. In large centres of population, ministers might be grandees of their profession; but in the countryside the pastors represented the common people. The 'democratic' patterns persisted among the Particular Baptists of Great Britain almost as much as amongst those of the United States.

---

29   Douglas, *Baptist Churches of the North*, pp. 199-267, quoted at pp. 229, 266.

30   K.D. Brown, *A Social History of the Nonconformist Ministry in England and Wales, 1800–1930* (Oxford: Clarendon Press, 1988), p. 29.

31   A.J. Klaiber, *The Story of the Suffolk Baptists* (London: Kingsgate Press, 1931), pp. 77-81, quoted at p. 79.

32   *BM*, June 1812, p. 232.

33   B.P. Jones, *Sowing beside All Waters: The Baptist Heritage of Gwent* (Cwmbran: Gwent Baptist Association, 1985), p. 193.

34   Briggs, *English Baptists*, p. 89.

Some of the most striking evidence of the existence of democratization in Britain, however, comes from the General Baptists. In the late eighteenth and early nineteenth centuries the New Connexion of General Baptists arose as a popular Evangelical movement with its heartlands in the East Midlands. Its future leader, Dan Taylor, who was born in 1738 at Northowram in the West Riding of Yorkshire, went to work with his father down a coal mine from the age of four. He initially educated himself through reading in his parents' home. Only later after he had become first a Methodist and then a Baptist by conviction, did he study more formally, under the guidance of John Fawcett, minister of Wainsgate near Hebden Bridge in the West Riding. Although Fawcett was a Calvinist, Taylor remained an Arminian. In 1763 he formed the Birchcliffe Church at Hebden Bridge, the only General Baptist church in the north. Since Taylor was a man of great dynamism, the church prospered. Dissatisfied with the low christology of the old General Baptists, he set up the New Connexion in 1770 to co-ordinate those in the denomination who adopted the faith of the Evangelical Revival. There were to have been two conferences of the connexion, south and north. The southern conference, lacking a co-ordinator, collapsed; the northern one under Taylor flourished. Having transferred in 1783 to the large town of Halifax, two years later he moved to Whitechapel, where he remained until his death in 1816, providing the leadership required in the south.

Taylor generated his own theology. Despite his zeal for orthodox christology, he was content to be imprecise over the Trinity. He recognized that God is one and that he is represented by the names of Father, Son and Holy Ghost. 'But', he told the Whitechapel church on his arrival, 'I cannot find, that any man has yet learned to describe from scripture how these three are united in one Godhead; nor the exact modes of their distinction... As I do not find them called in Scripture, three Persons, I do not chuse to call them so myself; but, I neither wish to condemn nor to contend with those who think it proper to use this manner of speech.'[35] Accordingly the New Connexion catechism drawn up by Taylor has nothing to say about the Trinity.[36] Doctrine, Taylor assumed, has to be forged from the Bible alone by each person individually. His views prevailed as much in matters of organization as on questions of theology. He often presided or preached at the New Connexion annual association, he wrote many of its circular letters and he edited its first periodical, *The General Baptist Magazine*. It was Taylor who masterminded New Connexion experiments in polity. He insisted that the traditional General Baptist usage of laying hands on the newly

---

35 Adam Taylor, *The History of the English General Baptists* (2 vols, London: for the author, 1818), II, pp. 471-72.

36 Dan Taylor, *A Catechism: Or Instructions for Children and Youth in the Fundamental Doctrines of Christianity* (London: for the author, 6th edn, 1805).

baptized was non-essential. He set the example of holding frequent and regular church meetings and encouraging members to attend, a pattern subsequently endorsed by the association. And whereas the early association meetings, much like Wesley's annual conferences, consisted of only ministers and elders, it was Taylor who steered them into becoming assemblies of church delegates.[37] At both local and national levels he promoted democratic authority in his movement. Dan Taylor was a man who rose from obscurity to create an organization with popular appeal that upheld his own views of doctrine and practice.

Yet it has to be admitted that even the New Connexion shows elements of ambiguity. Taylor carried through his resolve to move from the provincial West Riding to metropolitan Whitechapel notwithstanding the opposition of his church at Halifax and the hesitation of several others that were consulted. He was evidently determined to be a minister in the capital. There one of his closest friends was Abraham Booth, once a General Baptist but now minister of the premier Particular Baptist cause in London at Little Prescot Street. Another was Henry Foster, an Anglican clergyman who had read with Fawcett at the same time as Taylor. Foster was a member of the Eclectic Society, the discussion group of the leading Evangelicals in the Church of England.[38] Through his two friends Taylor was associated with the London elite of the Particular Baptists and even of the established church. His attitudes were coloured by the circles in which he moved. He commended the work of the London Board of Protestant Dissenting Ministers, of which the Baptist Board formed a part. He argued that the ministry should receive a liberal education so that 'the General Baptist interest may be rendered more respectable'. And he deplored the deliberate omission of the laying on of hands at the setting apart of a pastor at another London General Baptist church. The statement then made that the ministers did not come together to ordain the new pastor but merely to recognize his status was, according to Taylor, a mistake, since '*ordination* is not the work of the people, but of ministers'.[39] There was to be no populist laxity in matters of church order. Even in the Baptist movement most obviously democratic in ethos, the decorum of the capital exercised a certain sway.

An overall evaluation of the extent to which the Baptists of Britain fit the Hatch thesis must take into account the continuing elite influence. It

---

37   Taylor, *General Baptists*, II, pp. 320, 211n, 328. *Minutes of an Association of General Baptists* (n.p, n.d), 1787, p. 10; 1788, p. 14.

38   Adam Taylor, *Memoirs of the Rev. Dan Taylor* (London: for the author, 1820), pp. 189, 32. J.H. Pratt, *The Thought of the Evangelical Leaders: Notes of the Discussions of The Eclectic Society, London, during the Years 1798–1814* (Edinburgh: Banner of Truth Trust, 1978), p. 2.

39   *General Baptist Magazine*, June 1798, p. 253; February 1798, pp. 65, 78. All these items appear to come from the pen of the editor.

is illustrated by the BMS *coup d'état* after Fuller's death, transferring power in the organisation to the capital. It is also evident in Dan Taylor's stance as a metropolitan leader. London was the centre of prestige, prosperity and power in British society, the equivalent of Boston, New York and Washington, DC, rolled into one. As in other aspects of life, it exerted a potent force in British religion, encouraging the values of deference, efficiency and order. Baptists were by no means exempt from its magnetism. The evidence reviewed here suggests that there was a difference between Britain and America, with the British Baptists more susceptible to anti-democratic pressures than religious groups across the Atlantic. When that has been appreciated, however, it is also plain that there was a tendency for Baptists to be affected by the same process that Hatch analyzes for the United States. There was resistance to centralization and to theological innovation; there were deliberate separation from the established church and active participation in revivalism; there were self-educated leaders of new movements and ordinary ministers identified with the mass of the people. There was even conscious imitation of the United States. In Britain, however, the chief factor at work was not the American Revolution with its consequences. The new trends were being felt, for example in the foundation of the New Connexion, before the revolution began, and in Britain the impact on religious practice of American independence was relatively marginal. The process of democratization among British Baptists cannot have the explanation that Hatch gives for the American experience.

There were other factors that were far more significant among the Baptists of Britain. In the religious sphere, the Evangelical Revival created a new imperative to spread the gospel. Both Whitfield and Taylor came to faith among the Methodists, whose pattern of organization was followed by Thomson in the Shetlands. The Evangelical currents flowing so powerfully in the century after 1770 stirred many a Christian initiative by the people for the people. The cultural context created by the Enlightenment was also crucial. It fostered a pragmatism that made people willing to abandon accustomed methods. The experimental technique associated with Enlightenment thought was liberally applied to religion in this era. In the social and political field the collapse of the establishment of religion for most practical purposes opened doors for the spread of expressions of Evangelical faith such as that promoted by the Baptists. In large towns and even most villages there was no parish discipline to restrain the advance of popular religion. The decay of religious establishments was by no means a solely American phenomenon. Likewise the Evangelical Revival and the impact of the Enlightenment were common features in the two lands. Consequently there was a large dimension of British Christianity that paralleled the trajectory of its American counterpart. It was an English General Baptist, though it could have been an American, who declared in 1798 that it was 'the indispensable duty of every man to inquire for himself, to assert his rights, and to act with a manly boldness, in every thing wherein religion is concerned'.[40] A democratic temper was almost as prominent among the Baptists of Britain as it was among the Christians of America.

---

40   *General Baptist Magazine*, April 1798, p. 157 (J. D[eacon].).

CHAPTER 14

'Every Apostolic Church a Mission Society': European Baptist Origins and Identity

Ian M. Randall

One of the significant contributions that John Briggs has made to Baptist life has been his commitment to the larger Baptist family. His involvement in international Baptist affairs through the Baptist World Alliance has been an embodiment of that commitment. This study explores one part of the world Baptist story—aspects of European Baptist beginnings. The nineteenth century saw remarkable Baptist advance in mainland Europe, the leading figure in this advance being Johann Oncken (1800–84), an outstandingly gifted pastor in Hamburg who has been seen as the father of continental Baptists.[1] The powerful contribution of Oncken and of the German Baptist movement that emerged in the 1830s was only part of the mainland European Baptist story. In many places Baptists grew out of existing renewal groups which had no contact with Germany.[2] Also, as we will see, the channelling of Baptist life through German contacts across Europe meant that in a number of places other language groups were to some extent marginalised. Nonetheless, the role of Johann Oncken and his associates is pivotal. One of Oncken's most famous statements was that 'we consider every member a missionary' (the motto became *Jeder Baptist ein Missionar*) and he also viewed every church as a mission society. Prior to 1834, the year in which Oncken was baptised, organised Baptist life was virtually non-existent on the continent of Europe, whereas by 1900 there were about 220,000 members in Baptist churches. The

---

1 J.H. Rushbrooke, *The Baptist Movement in the Continent of Europe* (London: Kingsgate Press, 1923), p. 76.
2 See I.M. Randall, '"Pious Wishes": Baptists and wider renewal movements in nineteenth-century Europe', *Baptist Quarterly* 38.7 (July, 2000), pp. 316-31. In this study I am dealing only with some important regions where there were Germanic influences on Baptist life. The study is not comprehensive: for example it does not cover the Czech lands, Slovakia and countries in the former Yugoslavia.

contribution of the German Baptists to this process, and the questions it raised for Baptist identity, are the subjects to be examined in this study.

The First German Baptist Church

Johann Oncken was born in Oldenburg, Germany, but at the age of thirteen was sent to Scotland, and it was during the years he spent in Scotland and then in England that he experienced evangelical influences.[3] His conversion took place in a Methodist chapel in London. He considered that a dramatic change took place in his life.[4] As the outworking of his experience of evangelical conversion, Oncken was keen to involve himself in evangelism, and in 1823, at the age of twenty-three, he was accepted by the interdenominational Continental Society as a colporteur in Hamburg, Germany. At this stage Oncken was content to work in conjunction with the English Reformed church in Hamburg, but by 1826 he was beginning to have questions about infant baptism. He and several others, who were meeting as a small Bible study group in Hamburg, came to believer's baptist convictions in 1829, especially through the study of the New Testament, but they had to wait five years until someone was able to baptise them. On 22 April 1834, Oncken and six other candidates, one of whom was his wife, were baptised in the river Elbe by a visiting American, Barnas Sears, a professor from Hamilton College, Rhode Island, USA. A Baptist church was constituted with Oncken as pastor.[5] The story of Baptist church life in Germany had begun.

The names of the founder members of the Hamburg church, together with their occupations in most cases, were listed by Johann Oncken as Sarah Oncken, Henriette Lange (wife of the following), Diedrich Lang (shoemaker), Heinrich Kruger (shoemaker), Ernst Buckendahl (mirror frame maker) and Johannes Gusdorff (linen dealer, a Jewish convert).[6] Strong opposition to the Baptists from the city authorities, especially

---

3   Oncken's father had fled to England after being involved in an attempt to overthrow the Napoleonic regime. He died in England. On Oncken and his role in Baptist expansion in Germany, eastern Europe and Russia, see Richard V. Pierard, 'Germany and Baptist Expansion in Nineteenth-Century Europe', in D. Bebbington (ed.), *The Gospel in the World: International Baptist Studies* (Studies in Baptist History and Thought, 1; Carlisle: Paternoster, 2002), pp. 189-208.

4   H. Luckey, *Gerhard Oncken und die Anfang des Deutschen Baptismus* (Kassel: J.G. Oncken Verlag, 1934), p. 42.

5   Rushbrooke, *Baptist Movement*, p. 76.

6   Unpublished conference paper delivered by G. Balders at the Baptist World Alliance History and Heritage Commission in Dresden, Germany, 'Johann Gerhard Oncken—Aspects of his Life and Work' (1999), p. 7.

Senator Nikolaus Binder, and from Lutheran Church leaders, soon followed, and Oncken was imprisoned at one point. This reaction was in part because of the strongly evangelistic nature of the church's activity. In 1837 it was reported that twenty church workers were distributing tracts and scriptures, with 100,000 tracts distributed in one year.[7] This kind of endeavour was to be a feature of most German-speaking Baptist churches. By 1842 the Hamburg church needed larger premises and in that year a granary with three floors was obtained. The same week as the move to the new building was made the Great Fire in Hamburg broke out. The effects on the city were devastating, with thousands left homeless. Oncken immediately offered the new meeting place as accommodation. This offer was accepted, and eighty people found food and shelter for eight months. The authorities, including Binder, became much more favourable to Baptists. When a mob attacked the church shortly afterwards the police were protective.[8] Baptists began to root themselves in the German context.

Rapid numerical growth was experienced following 1842. In the following two years the numbers baptised in the Hamburg church were 322 and 380 respectively. Who were the converts? Local residents were among those baptised, but many were from other parts of Europe. During the reconstruction of Hamburg after the fire, 'travelling' men, who moved around to different towns for work, came from German-speaking communities across Europe to engage in the rebuilding. Some of these were unskilled, although others were craftsmen. This influx of itinerant workers created a missionary opportunity that the church was ready to grasp. Many who came to Hamburg without contacts—knowing no local residents or having no accommodation—were befriended by members of the Hamburg Baptist congregation. The strength of the church lay in its adaptability to local situations and its willingness to adopt diverse methods. To a large extent the Baptist movement was accessible to ordinary German people, which was a crucial factor contributing to its steady growth.[9]

The total number of members in the Hamburg church at the end of 1865 was 719 people. In the decade 1854 to 1864 the records show 476 baptisms. To assist Oncken two others, Julius Köbner (1806–84), who was Jewish and was brought to evangelical Christian faith under Onken's

---

7   *American Baptist Missionary Magazine* 16 (1836), p. 135; 19 (1838), p. 145, cited by D.R. Kirkwood (ed.), *European Baptists: A Magnificent Minority* (Valley Forge, PA: n.p., 1981), pp. 52-3.

8   For books on Oncken in German and English see G. Balders, *Theurer Bruder Oncken* (Wuppertal und Kassel: Oncken Verlag, 1984); J.H. Cooke, *Johann Gerhard Oncken* (London: Partridge & Co, 1908).

9   For an analysis of growth see W.L. Wagner, *New Move Forward in Europe* (South Pasadena, CA: William Carey Library, 1978), pp. 15-17.

ministry, and Carl Schauffler, were chosen as preachers by the church. Oncken was keen to train younger pastors and students first came to Hamburg for training during the winter of 1849–50. For some years, courses lasting six months were held. Congregational expansion necessitated a larger building and a chapel was opened in 1867, with C.H. Spurgeon, from the Metropolitan Tabernacle in London, preaching at the opening services. There was, however, a period of tension in the church in the 1870s, which began with a dispute about the authority of the pastor over the deacons. Oncken considered that the deacons were not undertaking enough house visits, so he brought their ministry to an end. The position of Oncken was one of enormous authority and this in itself was an issue of Baptist identity. The Hamburg church split, and a second congregation, the Hamburg Altona Baptist Church was formed. Julius Köbner worked hard to achieve reconciliation, writing a famous letter to Oncken in 1877.[10] Right up until Oncken's death the original Hamburg church, with its commitment to every member being a missionary, continued to shape Baptist identity in Germany and elsewhere in Europe.

Wider Mission in Germany

From the Hamburg base, wider Baptist mission and church planting in Germany took place. Oncken's most respected ministerial colleagues in Germany were Julius Köbner and Gottfried W. Lehmann (1799–1882), from Berlin, who came to embrace Baptist beliefs through Oncken. It was Köbner who helped to establish a theological seminary in Hamburg, which from 1859 provided formation training for pastors and evangelists. A three-year seminary programme operated from 1880. This training was crucial in creating cohesion among the churches. Julius Köbner also played a major role in his native Denmark. He saw himself as an ally at Oncken's side.[11] Lehmann and his wife, along with four others, were baptised by Oncken just outside Berlin in 1836 and formed a Baptist church with Lehmann as pastor.[12] Berlin became another centre of Baptist life. Lehmann travelled widely, helping to form churches. In 1848 there were twenty-six German Baptist churches, and round each were preaching stations, some later becoming churches. Towns such as Breslau, Bremen, Elbing, Kassel, Marburg and Oldenburg were supplied with pastors and became centres for mission. After 1848, with new religious

---

10 Balders, *Theurer Bruder Oncken*, pp. 147-48.

11 I. Barnes, *Truth is Immortal: The Story of Baptists in Europe* (London: Carey Kingsgate Press, 1955), p. 24. The role of the Hamburg seminary would require a separate study.

12 H.L. McBeth, *The Baptist Heritage: Four Centuries of Baptist Life* (Nashville, TN: Broadman Press, 1987), p. 473.

freedoms in Germany, there was rapid expansion. By 1856 there were forty-four German Baptist churches, with 4,398 members and sixty-six pastors, helpers and missionaries. A decade later, Baptist membership was 11,326.[13]

In July 1848, Lehmann summoned representatives from Baptist churches in Prussia to meet in Berlin where they formed an association, or 'corporation', a move which was to be the precursor to a wider Baptist Union structure. The association set up a fund for mission and it was decided that two-thirds of the total contributions to the fund should be devoted to work in Germany, with one-third for foreign mission. The emphasis on growth through active outreach at home and abroad was evident. The association also appointed Wilhelm Weist as the first travelling home missionary for the eastern part of Europe. The wider German union was, inevitably, formed in Hamburg. Fifty-six representatives met in Hamburg in 1849 and organised what was called the Union of Associated Churches of Baptised Christians in Germany and Denmark. The reason given by Oncken for the creation of the Union was both biblical and pragmatic: 'Every apostolic Christian church must be a Mission Society...but the mission work must be furthered by the joining together of more churches'.[14] The German union had four associations (*Vereinigungen*), with centres in Berlin, Hamburg, Eimbeck and Copenhagen. Through these structures, through common commitments and through annual union meetings an identity was forged.

The purposes of the structures, as defined by the representatives at the 1849 union meeting, included confessing the Baptist faith, encouraging and strengthening Baptist fellowship, promoting Baptist missionary activity and gathering statistical data.[15] The faith that was confessed was a Calvinistic one, although Lehmann was influenced by the spirituality of the Moravian community at Herrnhut and he utilised Moravian elements such as love feasts. German Baptists also sang Herrnhut hymns, as well as Lutheran chorales and new songs. Köbner, known as the songful theologian, edited a hymnbook.[16] The mission dimension was, however, paramount. As well as engaging in evangelism, German Baptists began to establish outward-directed Baptist organisations, such as the deaconess movement. This ministry was led by Eduard Scheve in the 1880s. *Haus Bethel* was established as a focus for deaconess work. Baptists developed nursing, social work, care for orphans—often in the homes of Baptist

---

13   Wagner, *New Move Forward in Europe*, pp. 16, 36.
14   Wagner, *New Move Forward in Europe*, p. 13, from the Union 'Protokol' of 1849.
15   *The American Baptist Missionary Magazine* 29 (1849), p. 37, cited by Kirkwood (ed.), *European Baptists*, p. 99.
16   G. Balders, 'Germany', in A.W. Wardin (ed.), *Baptists Around the World* (Nashville, TN: Broadman and Holman, 1995), p. 199.

members—and larger homes for the aged. This mirrored the work of F.B. Meyer, a socially-orientated English Baptist leader, and the deaconess movement among English Baptists.[17] Joseph Lehmann, son of G.W., was a Baptist leader whose work included ministry to younger people. The union also appointed evangelists who contributed to church growth. German Baptists were bound together by their beliefs, liturgy and, above all, common commitment to active Christian service.

Nonetheless, there were challenges from outside and also from within the movement. In the 1860s the Baptists were seen by Lutheran evangelicals who supported the German Evangelical Alliance—and who were therefore sympathetic to many Baptist beliefs—as adopting a regrettably hostile position towards Lutheran pastors. This was considered by Lutherans such as F.W. Krummacher, the court preacher in Berlin, to be endangering the cause of German evangelical unity and advance.[18] Later, however, renewal movements in the Lutheran Church began to adopt some of the evangelistic ideas promoted by the German Baptists. During the time of internal German Baptist struggle in the 1870s—the 'Hamburg Argument' (*Hamburger Streit*)—the growth that had been experienced by Baptist churches in Germany was arrested. This setback was only temporary and the conflict led to constructive results. Local congregations acquired greater independence and had to take more responsibility for missions. Boards of elders began to provide leadership.[19] Baptist unity was also maintained. At the time of his death Oncken was able to leave behind a united German movement amounting to 15,967 members in ninety-six Baptist churches, and in the year of his death there were 2,341 baptisms.[20] Oncken also played a major part, as we will see, in helping to establish many other Baptist churches outside Germany.

German Baptists and their Protestant Neighbours

The first Baptist church in Scandinavia was formed in Copenhagen in 1839 when Köbner and Oncken baptised eleven people who had already become convinced, while still members of the Lutheran Church and involved in group Bible study, about believer's baptism. Peder Mönster, a skilled goldsmith and engraver, took on leadership. As in Germany, there was a reaction against this unauthorised ecclesiastical group. In 1844

---

17 I.M. Randall, 'Mere Denominationalism: F.B. Meyer and Baptist Life', *Baptist Quarterly* 35.1 (January, 1993), pp. 19-34.
18 G. Carlyle (ed.), *Proceedings of the Geneva Conference of the Evangelical Alliance* (London: Hamilton, Adams & Co, 1862), p. 13.
19 Balders, 'Germany', p. 199.
20 Wagner, *New Move Forward in Europe*, p. 19.

Oncken wrote to the American Baptist Missionary Board about the Danish situation. 'In Denmark', he reported, 'the pastor [Mönster] of the church at Copenhagen has undergone a fifth imprisonment; but abides faithful. The church is steadfast; and has lately received seventeen members by baptism.'[21] Mönster was determined to press for religious toleration for non-Lutherans, and in part as a result of his efforts this was granted by the government in 1849.[22] In the 1850s the Copenhagen church declined, but Julius Köbner moved to Copenhagen in 1865 to become pastor and the congregation began to grow again. When Köbner left Denmark in 1879 there was a need for fresh leadership. This was provided by Marius Larsen, described as the ablest preacher Danish Baptists have produced.[23] In 1886 the Danish Baptists left the German union and looked increasingly for inspiration to Baptist immigrants in the USA. Together with indigenous movements in Denmark, however, German contributions were crucial to Baptist beginnings and growth.

In Sweden the first Baptist group also had links with Oncken and the German Baptists. Frederick O. Nilsson, a Swedish seaman who was converted in the USA, returned to Sweden in 1839 as an evangelist. His study of the Bible and the influence of Gustavus Schroeder, a Swedish sea captain who had been baptised at the Baptist Mariners' Church in New York, resulted in Nilsson's acceptance of Baptist views. Nilsson described how 'after a long and sore conflict with myself, I have at last been obliged to submit to and receive the truth. I was baptized in July, 1847, by the Rev. Mr. Oncken, in Hamburg; and on the 9th of September, this year, my wife and four others were baptized by a Danish brother by the name of Foster [Forster], a missionary by the Baptists in England. Thus the Lord has been pleased to commence a Church on New Testament principles even here in Sweden.'[24] In 1850 Frederick Nilsson was banished from Sweden, but freedom for Baptists followed and in 1852 Nilsson baptised Anders Wiberg, who emerged as a powerful leader of Baptist life in Sweden. Wiberg had left the Lutheran ministry because he

---

21 *The American Baptist Missionary Society* 25 (1845), p. 169, cited by Kirkwood (ed.), *European Baptists*, pp. 54-55.

22 I am indebted to Bent Hylleberg from Denmark for his help with this section. See also N.B. Nielsen, 'Development of Religious Liberty in Denmark in the First Half of the Nineteenth Century, with Special Reference to Baptists' (BD thesis, International Baptist Theological Seminary, Rüschlikon, 1964).

23 F.W. Herrmann, 'The Movement in Denmark, Holland, Switzerland, Austria', in J.H. Rushbrooke (ed.), *Baptist Movement in the Continent of Europe* (London: Carey Kingsgate Press, 1915), p. 39.

24 T. Armitage, *A History of the Baptists* (New York: Bryan, Taylor & Co, 1887), p. 831.

was unhappy about indiscriminate access to communion.[25] He later met Oncken and Köbner in Hamburg and as a result of discussions with them his views changed and he wrote an influential book defending the Baptist view of baptism. Swedish Baptists, however, unlike Danish Baptists, did not join the German union, preferring to have their own structures.

The 1840s saw Baptist life emerge in Holland and again German Baptists were involved. Johannes Elias Feisser, a theologically acute minister in the Dutch Reformed Church, came to the point in the early 1840s where he rejected infant baptism. His own study and experiences led him to the conclusion that only believers should be baptised and he was removed from the Dutch Reformed Church ministry in 1843. The news of this dramatic event reached Hamburg and Oncken sent Köbner to meet Feisser. Although he had in effect already arrived at Baptist convictions, Feisser had never heard of Baptists. It is often said that this new movement was thoroughly Dutch in its origins: 'The Dutch Baptist Movement is a plant of our own soil.'[26] But it was also through his conversations with Köbner and through the contacts that followed that Feisser was persuaded that he should be baptised. Accordingly, Feisser and six others were baptised by Köbner in May 1845 and formed a church with Feisser as pastor. This first Dutch Baptist church moved from Gasselternijveen to Stadskanaal in Groningen, which became a significant Baptist centre. From there other preaching points were established. Mennonite influences, too, were present. A former Mennonite, E. Gerdes, came to Stadskanaal and later became pastor.[27]

German Baptist influence was also seen in the second Dutch Baptist church, in Zutphen, in the province of Gelderland. A church was formed in the later part of 1845 through contacts between Feisser and Köbner and a group led by a Mennonite, Jan de Liefde. This group did not, however, last long. Oncken reported in 1845 that Köbner was excited by Dutch developments and that as well as congregations emerging in Gasselte, Zutphen and Haren, a foundation had been laid in Amsterdam.[28] The church in Amsterdam was formed in 1847, four people from a prayer and Bible study group having already been baptised by Feisser and Köbner. By contrast with Feisser's developing thinking, which questioned Calvinism, the Amsterdam church was Calvinistic. This issue was to create tensions. Two Reformed ministers in

---

25 M. Lindvall, 'Anders Wiberg: Swedish Revivalist and Baptist Leader', *Baptist Quarterly* 32.4 (October, 1987), p. 174.
26 J.A. Brandsma, 'Johannes Elias Feisser and the Rise of the Netherlands Baptists', *Baptist Quarterly* 16.1 (January, 1955), pp. 10-21; J. Reiling, 'Baptists in the Netherlands', *Baptist Quarterly* 28.2 (April, 1979), pp. 62-68.
27 Herrmann, 'Denmark, Holland, Switzerland, Austria', p. 44.
28 *The American Baptist Missionary Society Magazine* 25 (1845), p. 43, and 26 (1846), p. 42, cited by Kirkwood (ed.), *European Baptists*, p. 56.

north-western Holland, one from Franeker, wrote a book in the 1860s on infant baptism, and H. Willms of the Ihren Baptist church in Germany replied stating that infant baptism was 'contrary to the commandment of the Lord'. Some Reformed church members in Franeker were convinced by Willms, and the Ihren church sent them an evangelist trained by Oncken, Peter Johannes de Neui, who spread German Baptist thinking. A Baptist congregation was formed and others were planted in neighbouring towns. These churches did not, however, join the Dutch Baptist Union and adhered to the German Baptist Calvinistic confession of faith.[29] Dutch Baptists struggled to forge their own identity.

In the same year in which the Amsterdam Baptist church was formed, 1847, Oncken undertook a preaching tour of Switzerland. There he contacted a number of home fellowship groups. In one such group, at Hochwart, Oncken found twelve people who had already been baptised by immersion, and this group became a Baptist church. Oncken commissioned Friederich Maier, a colporteur in southern Germany, together with I. Harnisch, to promote missionary work in Switzerland. Maier baptised eight people in Zurich and a Baptist church was founded there in 1849. This church grew rapidly and functioned as the leading centre of Swiss Baptist life.[30] A revised political constitution in 1848 for the Swiss Confederation provided religious freedom for 'recognised Christian confessions'. In 1865 the federal council in Berne stipulated that there should be freedom of worship, but a year later Anton Haag, a gifted blind Baptist pastor, and Harnisch, were expelled by the council. In the 1860s preaching stations in eastern Switzerland became churches, according to the German model. Later evangelical groups in St Gallen, Bulach, Basel and Buchli became Baptist churches. The Baptist presence in German-speaking Switzerland, however, remained small, with Baptists looking for their identity to German thinking. The Swiss churches joined the German Baptist Union in 1870 and did not become an independent body until 1948.

Mission in the Catholic Context

German Baptists were committed to reaching not only into Protestant regions but also into traditionally Roman Catholic areas such as Poland. A serious complicating factor in Polish Baptist endeavour was that some of the earliest Baptist witness in Poland, in the country's western districts, was undertaken by Baptist preachers who did not communicate in Polish

---

29 Rushbrooke, *Baptist Movement*, p. 57.
30 Wagner, *New Move Forward in Europe*, p. 19; J.D. Franks, *European Baptists Today* (Rüschlikon–Zurich: Baublatt, AG, 1952), p. 81. There is debate about whether Hochwart or Zurich was the first Baptist congregation.

but directed their energies to people who spoke German. During the later years of Prussian domination of areas of Poland there was a policy of 'Germanisation' and for Baptist preachers to be linked in any way with that policy meant that their impact was likely to be limited. Nonetheless, the *American Baptist Missionary Magazine* for 1858 stated: 'An awakening has occurred on the Polish frontiers. A German brother having business in that region distributed tracts, one of which, falling into the hands of an aged lady, led to the holding of an evening meeting, at which sixty souls were present. The tidings quickly spread to the neighboring village, and much inquiry for the truth and an earnest desire to have regular meetings is the result.'[31] The role of lay missionaries was typical of German Baptist mission.

The first Baptist church in Poland was formed three years later in the village of Adamow, near Warsaw, in the Russian part of Poland. A teacher, Gottfried Alf, who was a German and a cantor in the Lutheran Church, was baptised on 28 November 1858 as part of a group of nine people who were converted and then were baptised by Wilheim Weist, the German Baptist home missionary. Alf himself had been conducting a home Bible study and had, on his own, begun to arrive at Baptist convictions. On the day after the initial baptisms, seventeen more people were baptised. The Baptist church in Adamow was founded in 1861 and in the next ten years Baptist membership in Poland grew to about 1,000. As in other countries, those who were baptised were often marked out for harassment. It was not unusual for Russian police to observe an outdoor baptismal service and then march the entire Baptist community from the river bank to prison.[32] Inevitably, as the leading Baptist figure, Alf himself had a number of periods of imprisonment, but he remained undaunted and his work spread within Poland and by migration into Volhynia in Russia.[33]

Gottfried Alf was not only an evangelist, he was also concerned that there should be proper biblical knowledge in the new churches. His own training was received in Hamburg under Oncken and the need for adequate leadership and biblical teaching in Poland was underlined during his period of absence when some of the Adamow congregation became involved in disputes. After his return there was what J.H. Rushbrooke called 'an outbreak of disorderly and even riotous fanaticism, of a type too familiar in eastern lands'.[34] Soon after the founding of the church in Adamow a second church developed at Kicin

---

31   *The American Baptist Missionary Magazine* 38 (1858), pp. 267-68, cited by Kirkwood (ed.), *European Baptists*, p. 65.
32   M.S. Lesik, 'The Baptists in Poland', *Baptist Quarterly* 7 (1934–35), p. 81.
33   See D.N. Miller, *In the Midst of Wolves* (Portland, OR: Multnomah Printing, 2000).
34   Rushbrooke, *Baptist Movement*, p. 189.

as a result of Alf visiting the area. He was initially welcomed by a Mennonite leader. Preaching was carried on in a barn and the church that was established became influential in Poland. Seeing its potential, Alf moved there himself. A congregation formed in 1872 in the village of Zelow, near Lodz, is seen as the mother church of Poland's Slavic Baptists, but of the 4,162 Baptists in Poland in 1900 only 200 were Slavs. Most of those who had accepted the preaching of the gospel from Baptists were those who spoke German or Russian. On the whole they had little interest in Polish traditions. Added to this there was challenge for Baptists of the powerful loyalty of Poles to the Catholic Church. Poles who became Baptists often felt that they were out of place and significant numbers either lapsed or emigrated to the USA.

Travellers in Central Europe

After the fire in Hamburg in 1842 many craftsmen and their families temporarily left Austria to find work in Hamburg. Several of them came into contact with Baptists. In 1846 two families who returned to Austria as Baptists held meetings and distributed tracts. A year later the first couple were baptised as believers. In the following year Oncken visited Austria and also travelled in Hungary. There was very little freedom for Baptists and growth was slow. In the period 1849 to 1851 one pastor in Vienna, J.L. Hinrichs, was expelled and in a police raid nine men and eight women were arrested.[35] Four leaders of the Baptists congregation were imprisoned in 1851 and those not born in Vienna were expelled. Also in 1851, the British and Foreign Bible Society appointed Edward Millard, a Baptist from England, as its agent in Vienna. Although he was forced to leave in 1852 he returned eleven years later. He held home meetings for Bible study to which increasing numbers were attracted and December 1869 saw the formation of a church with twenty members. A colporteur who had been baptised in Hamburg, Karl Rauch, was a founding member. Austrian Baptists had a continuing link with German Baptists. Although Millard was English, his ministry as a Baptist was in Germany and Austria. By 1884 the church in Vienna had 125 members, but a significant proportion lived outside Vienna, especially in the Czech lands (when a Baptist church was founded in Prague in 1885 eighteen of the Vienna members were transferred to it) and Steyermark.[36] In 1885 an Austrian–Hungarian association was founded.

Travelling Hungarian construction workers had also gone to Hamburg in 1842, then part of the Austro–Hungarian empire, and had encountered

---

35 Wardin (ed.), *Baptists Around the World*, p. 195.
36 Wagner, *New Move Forward in Europe*, pp. 90-94.

Baptists. As C.T. Byford put it, 'the Baptists in Hungary trace their spiritual pedigree to the modern apostle, J.G. Oncken'.[37] In 1845 several Hungarian carpenters working in Hamburg were converted, baptised and joined the Hamburg Baptist church. The initial contact was through a Hamburg church member with whom one of the carpenters, Johann Rottmayer, was lodging. Rottmayer encouraged the others. Joseph Lehmann later said that five converted Hungarians had formed a Tract Society to which eight families had contributed.[38] The Hamburg church's Young Men's and Women's Unions decided to send out 'worthy young men' in mission and in 1846 Rottmayer, together with Karl Scharschmidt and Johann Voyka (part of the original group of carpenters) were sent back to Hungary. Meetings were held in Rottmayer's house in Budapest and in 1848 Oncken baptised a number of candidates. The church that was formed was the first Baptist cause in Hungary, but it did not survive. The obstacles to the ministry are seen in the fact that no further baptisms took place until 1865 when G.W. Lehmann, the pastor in Berlin, made a preaching tour of Hungary, baptising six people, including Rottmayer's eldest son, in the Danube.[39]

Hungarian Baptist work ultimately took root through the ministry of Heinrich Meyer, who was baptised in Hamburg and become a member of the Hamburg church in 1862. Meyer became involved in youth ministry and in church planting in Germany and Russia. At the age of thirty-one, Meyer, supported by the British and Foreign Bible Society, settled in Budapest and in the following year he baptised four people and established a Baptist church. Through Anton Novak, a friend of Johann Rottmayer's who had become a Baptist and who had come to Hungary from Vienna with the Bible Society, Meyer heard about a group meeting in Salonta and in August 1875 he baptised eight people. This represented a move beyond the boundaries of the German-speaking community to Hungarian-speaking people. Among the candidates was Mihály Kornya, who together with Mihály Toth, became committed to Meyer's work. Meyer never learned the Hungarian language and it was Kornya and Toth who had the greatest success in evangelism and church planting. They became known as the 'peasant prophets' of the Hungarian Baptist mission—although Kornya had a house and land and Toth was a rich farmer. Toth worked not only among Hungarians but also among Slovacs and Slovenes. He is reckoned to have baptised around 5,000 people. The outreach by Kornya was mainly among Hungarians in

---

37 C.T. Byford, 'The Movement in Hungary: Progress and Difficulties', in Rushbrooke (ed.), *Baptist Movement in the Continent of Europe*, p. 100.
38 *The American Baptist Missionary Society Magazine* 46 (1866), p. 302, cited by Kirkwood (ed.), *European Baptists*, p. 61.
39 I. Gergely, 'Hungarian Baptist Beginnings: The Struggle for Identity', *Journal of European Baptist Studies*, 1.1 (September, 2000), p. 20.

Hungary and Transylvania. He baptised over 11,000 people during his thirty years of ministry. About 90% of the churches he planted were Hungarian, but he also learned Romanian. This was a powerful indigenous movement.

During the first decade or more of organised Hungarian Baptist life, most of the churches in the Budapest area were regarded as outposts of the Budapest congregation and under the direct care of Meyer, who saw himself as the teacher of all the churches. In 1883 there were 499 members registered in fifty centres. By 1893 membership was 3,200. Most of the worship in the churches started by Meyer was conducted in German and the Hungarian Baptist churches were part of the wider German Baptist fellowship. Indeed when a new church was built in Wesselényi Street in Budapest Meyer put under the foundational corner stone a paper which said that the only language that could be used in the church was German.[40] But when two young Magyars, Lajos Balogh and András Udvarnoki, returned from four years of training at the Hamburg seminary in 1892 tensions became evident, since the younger leaders did not accept that Meyer should direct them about how and where their ministry should be undertaken. Division emerged, partly over Meyer's autocratic leadership and partly over questions of identity—whether the churches were German or Hungarian. Mission stations that Meyer had controlled were soon organised by the Hungarians into separate churches. In the region as a whole Baptist churches were to be divided until 1920 into a Hungarian and Slovak Union and a German and Romanian Union.[41] Questions of identity had provoked division.

German Outreach in Romania and Bulgaria

Romanian Baptist life traces its origins back to more than one source. Various ethnic groups made contributions, notably German, Hungarian and Romanian. The first known Baptist evangelist to enter what is now called Romania, Karl Johann Scharschmidt, was closely identified with the German stream of Baptist outreach. Scharschmidt, who as we have seen was one member of the group of carpenters baptised by Oncken in Hamburg in 1845, came to Romania in 1856 with his wife, Augusta. Within a few years other German Baptists, and one English woman, Elizabeth Peacock Clarke, found themselves in Romania and began to meet. Scharschmidt baptised enough converts to plant a church among the German-speaking population of Bucharest. This was the first Baptist church in Romania and it became an important base. In 1863 Oncken

---

40 Gergely, 'Hungarian Baptist Beginnings', pp. 27-28.
41 Wardin (ed.), *Baptists Around the World*, p. 262.

sent August Liebig, one of his associates in Hamburg and a teacher at the Hamburg seminary, as pastor, and Oncken himself visited the church in 1869. In the 1860s Johann Rottmayer extended his activity beyond Hungary and was working among Romanian people as a colporteur. He learned Romanian and as a Bible Society colporteur he had considerable success. In one year, in Cluj, he was able to sell more than 10,000 Bibles.[42]

Evangelical German–Russians from Ukraine who had been exiled and had migrated in the direction of Romania provided another source of Baptist witness in the region. The delta of the Danube, where many of them settled, was then Turkish territory. By the mid-1860s, some of these Ukrainian migrants, with help from Liebig (who was working in the area), took steps towards forming a Baptist church. The first Baptist church was formed in a German colony, Cataloi, in the Dobruja, between the Black Sea and the Danube, an area that in 1878 became part of Romania. In 1869, on a visit to the area, Oncken established a German–Russian church. In Bessarabia, which today is within the scope of the conflicting political interests of Moldova, Ukraine, the Russian Federation and Romania, there was a pietistic revival among the German Lutheran colonists and a Baptist church was formed in 1870 in Chichma.[43] Liebig moved from Bucharest to travel elsewhere and the Bucharest church was left without a pastor for a number of years, but through Edward Millard in Vienna a pastor named Daniel Schwegler took up the leadership in 1878. The work was German-speaking until the early twentieth century when Constantin Adorian, who had studied in Hamburg, became minister of a Romanian-speaking Baptist church in Bucharest.

The needs of mission in Bulgaria were brought to the attention of Baptists in the West through an article, 'The Macedonian Cry Re-Echoed from Macedonia Itself', which appeared in commonly-read German Baptist publications in 1880. Within the article was a letter from Grigor B. Druminkov from Kazanlak in central Bulgaria. He was writing on behalf of a group of Congregationists who had been drawn to Baptist convictions by the visit in 1875 of a colporteur, probably Stefan Kucdov, who was of German extraction and who had heard the Christian gospel from Armenian believers in Constantinople in 1867.[44] The appeal of the

---

42 I. Bunaciu, *Istoria Raspandirii Credintei Baptiste in Romania* (Bucharest: Edituria Universitati, 1995), p. 86, cited by Gergely, 'Hungarian Baptist Beginnings', p. 21.

43 Unpublished conference paper by S. Sannikov, 'Over Barriers, Maintaining Unity: Baptists in Bessarabia under Romanian domination (1918–1940)', delivered at the second International Conference on Baptist Studies, Wake Forest University, 2000.

44 I am indebted to help from Dr Parush Parushev of the International Baptist Theological Seminary, Prague, and research by Dobrinka Dader. See *Vitania*, May/June

group in Kazanlak was for someone to come as Baptist pastor. There were in fact Baptist missionaries in Bulgaria, since two colporteurs from the Baptist church in Cataloi—Martin Heringer and Jacob Klundt—moved to Bulgaria. From 1871 Heringer served as a colporteur with the British and Foreign Bible Society, first from Lom and then in Ruse. In 1872 Klundt began work with the society, based in Skopje in Macedonia, and in 1880 he moved to Lom. At one point he was arrested and condemned to death, but he was saved by the intervention of the British consul.[45] Because, however, neither Heringer nor Klundt were pastors, they did not baptise or establish churches.

Help in forming a Bulgarian Baptist church in Kazanlak was to come from another source—and this source, too, had Germanic links. Although the group in Kazanlak did not know it when they made their appeal in 1880, Ivan G. Kargel, who had received his theological education in Germany and was in St Petersburg in the late 1870s, was to be part of the answer to their needs. Kergel was encouraged by Colonel Pashkov, an evangelical leader in St Petersburg, to move to Bulgaria, and he settled in Ruse. On 19 September 1880 Kargel immersed five people from the Kazanlak group in the Tundzha River. The small number baptised was due to strict examination of the candidates and the countervailing influence of the Congregational minister.[46] The Turkish rule in the region, which had been so oppressive, had come to an end in 1878, and Kargel took advantage of the new situation to build up Baptist work in Ruse as well as Kazanlak. In 1884 the Ruse congregation became an independent Baptist church and Kargel chose to make it the centre of his work, with Kazanlak as a station. Baptists in Kazanlak resented this development.[47] Kargel returned to Russia and his place as pastor was eventually taken by Vasil Marcheff, who had studied in Hamburg. Further difficulties were in store for the Baptist witness. From 1888 a Baptist Association operated, but it was German-speaking, and three of the churches in Bulgaria appealed to the American Baptist Missionary Union for help as they felt alienated. In the early twentieth century American Baptists supported P.E. Petrick, a German, as a missionary in Bulgaria, and he achieved greater recognition for Bulgarian Baptists.[48] The German connection continued.

1997, pp. 7-11. There is some doubt about the name of the colporteur who arrived in 1875. In other accounts his name is Herboldt.
    45   Rushbrooke, *Baptist Movement*, p. 168.
    46   A.W. Wardin, 'The Baptists in Bulgaria', *Baptist Quarterly*, 34.4 (October, 1991), p. 149.
    47   Wardin (ed.), *Baptists Around the World*, p. 259.
    48   Wardin, 'Baptists in Bulgaria', pp. 148-59.

Germans and Russian Baptist Beginnings

The Russian Baptist movement was also indebted to a number of streams of influence, one of these being German Baptist outreach.[49] Martin Kalweit, a German who settled in Tiflis (now Tbilisi, in Georgia) in 1862, had been born into a Lutheran family in Lithuania, had been baptised as a believer in 1858 in a German Baptist congregation in East Prussia, and held worship in his home. Other Germans attended. Through Jakov Delyakov, a Bible colporteur who was not a Baptist, Kalweit met a Nikita Voronin, a Russian merchant. Voronin belonged to the Molokans ('milk-drinkers'—probably a name that referred to their rejection of the Orthodox Church fasts or possibly their desire for the 'pure milk' of the Word), a reform movement that emphasised the authority of scripture and sought to recover the practices of the early church. They thought in terms of a 'spiritual' baptism, but many became deeply interested in Baptist views.[50] After some discussion, Voronin was convinced that what he heard from Kalweit about the baptism of believers was correct, although at odds with Molokan beliefs. Under cover of darkness, on 20 August 1867, Kalweit baptised Voronin in a mill creek on the Kura River in the Caucasus of southern Russia, near Tiflis.[51] The baptism of Voronin is celebrated as the first Baptist immersion of a Russian in Tsarist Russia, although some Russians were baptised before 1867. The significance of the event lies in the way a Baptist community was subsequently built up.[52] Voronin encouraged other Molokans to be baptised.

The group of Baptists around Tiflis slowly grew, with services being held in German and Russian. After four years there were still only about a dozen people, reflecting the reluctance of the population to accept this

---

49   Albert Wardin has full bibliographic material on Baptists in the Russian Empire in *Evangelical Sectarianism in the Russian Empire and the USSR: A Bibliographic Guide* (Metuchen, NJ: Scarecrow Press, 1995). I am indebted to Marina Sergeyevna Karetnikova from St Petersburg for her help in this section. See also M. Dowling, 'Baptists in the Twentieth-Century Tsarist Empire and the Soveit Union', in Bebbington (ed.), *Gospel in the World*, pp. 209-32.

50   McBeth, *Baptist Heritage*, p. 491; A.I. Klibanov, *History of Religious Sectarianism in Russia, 1860s–1917* (trans. E. Dunn; New York and Oxford: Pergamon Press, 1982). Klibanov, pp. 224-25, speaks of the 'Baptization of the Molokans' and suggests that by 1900 almost half of the Baptists in Russia were former Molokans.

51   W. Sawatsky, *Soviet Evangelicals Since World War II* (Kitchener, ON/Scottdale, PA: Herald Press, 1981), pp. 27-33.

52   *Bratskii vestnik* 3 (1957), p. 4, cited by P.D. Steeves, 'The Russian Baptist Union, 1917–1935: Evangelical Awakening in Russia' (PhD thesis, University of Kansas, 1976), p. 3. See also P. Belkov, 'Unity and Leadership in the Evangelical–Baptist Movement in Russia through the mid-1920s' (BD thesis, International Baptist Theological Seminary, Prague, 1998), p. 12.

new teaching, but three of these early Russian Baptists were to be crucial figures in Baptist advance. Ivan Kargel joined the group in 1869. Kargel's later ministry (as we have seen) took him to Bulgaria and subsequently he became a significant figure among evangelicals in Russia. Another crucial figure was Vasilii G. Pavlov, a sixteen year-old who was baptised by Voronin in 1871 and joined the Tiflis church. The third person to join the Tiflis church was Vasilii V. Ivanov-Klyshnikov, who heard about believer's baptism in 1866 and began to write to Protestants in different parts of Europe. In 1870 he met the Baptist group in Tiflis and he then became involved in the spreading of Baptist beliefs, going on to organise the second congregation of Baptists in the Caucasus.[53] The Tiflis church sent Vasilii Pavlov to study at Hamburg, and upon his return he evangelised widely. Oncken ordained Pavlov as a Baptist evangelist. Pavlov and the Tiflis church thus represented the more specifically Baptist wing of the south Russia movement and owed significant aspects of their identity to German Baptist thinking.

There was also Baptist work among the non-Slavs found in Russia. Some German-speaking churches were formed in the Ukraine in the mid-1860s. The Russian government, seeing what was happening, tried hard to restrict Baptist commitment to German settlers. It was this pressure that meant that some German–Russian Baptists left the Ukraine, several playing a part, as we have seen, in the emergence of Baptist churches in Romania and Bulgaria. In 1879 a Russian imperial decree was issued which allowed liberty of worship for Baptists. Within five years a Russian Baptist Union was formed, which included Baptists in the Ukraine and in the Caucasus. Count Sievers, however, the Russian Minister of the Interior, made it clear to Oncken that no conversion from the Orthodox Church would be allowed.[54] In response, Oncken did emphasise Baptist distinctives. He told Count Sievers that Baptists wished to 'win souls to Christ' and preached a message about Christ and his death 'among the millions throughout Europe, who have rejected all revealed truth and who form a most dangerous element to all good governments'.[55] On rare occasions Oncken could be reticent about Baptist identity.

In spite of the difficulties, German Baptist teaching began to spread among Russian Orthodox peasants in the Ukraine.[56] Germans who had

---

53 N.V. Odintsov, 'Obrazets dlia vernykh', *Baptist* 2 (1929), p. 10, cited by Steeves, 'The Russian Baptist Union', p. 5.

54 C.T. Byford, 'The Movement in Russia', in Rushbrooke (ed.), *Baptist Movement in the Continent of Europe*, p. 74.

55 J. H. Cooke, *Johann Gerhard Oncken* (London: Partridge & Co, 1908), pp. 146-48.

56 See S.J. Nesdoly, 'Evangelical Sectarianism in Russia: A Study of the Stundists, Baptists, Pashkovites, and Evangelical Christians, 1855–1917 (PhD thesis, Queen's University, 1971).

colonised in the south of Ukraine, some of whom were Mennonites, were a vital link for Baptist growth. Paul Steeves, in his thesis on the Russian Baptist Union, talks about them rejecting the 'pedobaptist teachings of their tradition in favour of the doctrine of believer's baptism'.[57] In fact Mennonites practised believer's baptism, but not by immersion. Many Russians became curious about Baptists. In 1869, following a visit by Oncken in which he spoke to some Mennonites, Efim Tsymbal, who belonged to the German–Russian 'Stundist' (from *stunden*—hours) prayer and Bible study movement, was baptised by a Mennonite Brethren leader. In the same period Mikhail Ratushnyi, a harvest labourer in Osnova, in Kherson Province, began to read the Bible and to talk to a German Baptist farmer. By 1870 about one hundred people were attending meetings led by Ratushnyi. A blacksmith, Ivan G. Riobashapka, who worked for a German Baptist, drew together a similar group. He wished to be baptised, but the Germans he approached refused to baptise him because of the law against converting Orthodox believers. Tsymbal, however, baptised Riaboshapka who in turn baptised Ratushnyi. Vasilii Pavlov met Ratuschny, which resulted in a stronger connection between German Baptist thinking and Baptist witness in Transcaucasia and Kherson.

Baptists in the Baltic

A final example of German Baptist mission reaching across national boundaries is the Baptist growth that took place in the Baltic countries. A German Baptist congregation was established in Memel (today Klaipeda), in East Prussia, as early as 1841. This church was on the border of Lithuania (and Memel was taken by Lithuania in 1923) and it attracted a number of Lithuanians. One service per month was in the Lithuanian language. The first baptism of a German–Lithuanian, Karl Albrecht, took place in 1851. Under the gifted leadership of Albrecht, who was supported by the German Baptists to work among his own people, efforts were made to extend the Baptist witness. Lithuanian tracts and a hymnbook were produced.[58] Mission points were established and then six churches, four of them Lithuanian, were formed. There was also progress among the Latvians living in Lithuania and three churches were formed. A German-speaking church was formed in Kaunas (formerly Kovno). From here mission work was also carried out in the Russian language. The limitation in the early period was the lack of Baptist preachers who could communicate with Lithuanians in their own language.

---

57 Steeves, 'The Russian Baptist Union', p. 6.
58 Wardin (ed.), *Baptists Around the World*, p. 246.

The German Baptist Memel church was crucial to mission in Latvia, the middle Baltic state. Most of the Latvian people were members of the Lutheran Church and in the 1840s there were groups of people within the Lutheran Church, in Libau and its neighbourhood, who gathered for prayer and Bible reading without the official blessing of the Lutheran Church leaders. During the Crimean War, 1853–56, unemployment forced some of these Latvians to Memel. Among the emigrants was a young ship's carpenter named Frizis Jekabsons, who came into contact with the Baptist church in Memel and was baptised there in 1855. Later he settled in Libau, as did other Memel church members. There were fourteen Latvians in the Memel church in 1859. At Windau a group meeting for prayer and Bible study came to Baptist beliefs, and Adam Gertners, his wife (both Germans) and nine others (Latvians) were baptised in Memel in 1860. This is celebrated as the beginning of organised Latvian Baptist church life.[59] The first baptisms on Latvian soil occurred in early September 1861 when Gertners baptised seventy-two believers.[60] The Memel church building became a model for Baptist buildings, but more importantly the German model of central organisation, mediated through the Memel church, was employed as a vehicle for growth.

The 1860s also saw, however, considerable opposition against Baptists and this contributed to Baptist re-thinking about ecclesiastical strategy. People who came to Memel to be baptised were often arrested.[61] The centralised operation was in some respects unhelpful. In 1875, the Memel church had 2,780 church members in the central church and its mission stations (most of them were in Latvia, with six being in Lithuania). From 1876 onwards Memel began to give independent church status to the mission points, beginning with Riga. In 1876 a remarkable 1,242 Memel members were transferred to newly-established churches. 1,315 were transferred in the period 1878–80.[62] In 1879 the Prussian Association of the German Baptist Union gave the Latvian Baptists the right to form the Baltic Baptist Association. In 1881 the association had 3,944 members. A split took place in the mid-1880s, however, within this association. Latvian Baptists had been unhappy about their subordination to the German Baptist Union and this division led to the formation of the Baltic Association of Latvian Baptists Churches in Russia, with about 2,500

---

59 I am indebted to Janis Tervits from Latvia and to his book *Latvijas Baptistu Vesture* (Riga: Latvijas Baptistu Draudzu Savieniba, 1999), a part of which he has translated into English.
60 Wardin (ed.), *Baptists Around the World*, p. 244.
61 Kirkwood (ed.), *European Baptists*, p. 37.
62 O. Ekelmann, *Gnadenwunder Komissionsverlag: Verlagshaus der deutschen Baptisten* (Kassel: GMBH, 1928), p. 234. I am indebted to Linas Andronovas from Lithuania for his help with this section.

members and with Jekabs Rumbergs as its leading figure. Rumbergs established his own publishing house, editing a magazine entitled *Ewangelists* and also publishing a hymnal. In 1889 the earlier Baptist Association joined the predominantly German Union of Baptist Churches in Russia, but in 1891 the Latvian unions came together.

Estonia, the northernmost Baltic state, has an affinity linguistically and racially with Finland, but missionary work in Estonia came through Germany. As early as 1865, as Toivo Pilli describes, an Estonian named Johannes Schwan, who had been baptised by immersion in St Petersburg by Johann Oncken, was preaching and teaching on the Estonian Island of Saaremaa. However, it took almost two decades for the first Baptist church to be founded.[63] There was a preparatory period, as Rushbrooke notes, when the believers knew nothing of Baptists, 'but the reading of the scriptures had led them to reject infant baptism'.[64] The Estonians approached Adam Reinhold Schiewe, a German Baptist pastor in St Petersburg, who on a cold winter night on 24 February 1884 baptised seventeen people by immersion in the river Ungru, near Haapsalu. An opening had to be made in the ice to allow the baptisms to take place. In the same year other Baptist churches were also established—in Pärnu, Tallinn, and Kärdla. In Pärnu, Julius Herrmann, a German Baptist pastor from Riga, helped to organise the church. Estonian Baptist churches were considered mission stations of the St Petersburg or Riga German Baptist churches, another instance of German Baptist mission crossing over into other language groups and creating, to some degree, a conflict of identity.

Conclusion

This study has traced the way in which Baptist church life took root in Germany from the 1830s and how churches were planted in other countries. This did not take place without outside help. American Baptists gave considerable assistance to Johann Oncken and in England there was a finance office for the German Baptist Union. But to a large extent the Baptist churches that were planted in the countries across Europe that we have examined were the product of Oncken's vision rather than deriving their identity from outside mainland Europe. Most evangelistic success was evident in countries that shared Germany's Protestantism. In Scandinavia, for example, Baptists drew from existing renewal movements in the Lutheran Church. The impact of German mission was less in

---

63　T. Pilli, 'Baptists in Estonia, 1884–1940', *Baptist Quarterly*, 39.1 (January, 2001), p. 27.
64　Rushbrooke, *Baptist Movement*, p. 121.

traditionally Roman Catholic or Orthodox countries, in part because the German language and networks were alien. Despite this, Baptists grew significantly in Russian-speaking regions, where many within the Orthodox Church were searching for spiritual reality. Tensions over national issues emerged in some places in the later nineteenth century. Because of the strong links between German-speaking communities across Europe it was difficult for German-speaking Baptists to move beyond those communities and foster indigenous churches. Nonetheless, Baptist life in Germany continued to be an inspiration, and German Baptist ideas were translated into other contexts. German Baptists, with their vision of every apostolic church as a mission society and of these churches acting jointly, were crucial in the process of forming a European Baptist identity in mainland Europe.

CHAPTER 15

Businessmen as Preachers among Methodists in the Early Twentieth Century

David J. Jeremy

Preaching invites public exposure and appraisal.[1] As employers of labour, business heads underwent a measure of public scrutiny during the week and might therefore be forgiven for preferring a lower profile on Sundays. Despite the drawback of heightened public gaze many men (few women) in business, both in divided Methodism and since union in 1932, have taken preaching appointments. What do we know about their numbers, their backgrounds, their motives, the pulpits they occupied, their sermon preparation and sources of thought, their theology, their preaching styles, their length of service, their other roles related to preaching, and how they reconciled tensions between religion and business? In these respects were they any different from other lay preachers in Methodism? Given the tens of thousands of local preachers and the thousands who have been business people, relatively little evidence is available to answer these questions. The following impressions pertain chiefly to Methodist businessmen preachers in late-Victorian and Edwardian England, when churchgoing was at its twentieth-century height.

Historical Context

In contrast to a hundred years earlier, in the 1890s Methodist preaching was a largely respectable activity. Village green preaching and open-air

---

1   I should like to thank the Leverhulme Trust for awarding me a Research Fellowship in support of my work on boardroom culture and governance in the UK, 1900–1980s, to which this essay contributes. I am also grateful to the Business School at The Manchester Metropolitan University, for releasing me in 2000–2001 to take up this Fellowship.

camp meetings, like city street-corner preaching, were the exception rather than the norm. Hearers gathered in chapels whose buildings, if not their congregations, stood between their jubilees and their centenaries. The seven Methodist groupings then found in England were mostly on their way from sect to denomination in their development.[2] Their members at the end of the nineteenth century could frequently claim to be second- or third-generation Methodists, though membership was still predicated on the personal conversion experience. Earlier conflicts between professional ministers and leading laymen in local congregations or the wider sect, though sometimes still a cause of tension, were being resolved, in part by a more careful attention to the education of ministers and, with less effectiveness, to the training of lay preachers. By the 1890s over 13% of Wesleyan ministers held degrees, compared to under 2% among the Primitive Methodists.[3] In society at large, doubts abounded about the existence of hell, of original sin, of miracles, of God. Churchgoing was in decline. Leisure activities were widening. Aristocratic and capitalist paternalisms were being challenged.[4]

Crucial roles in the organizational and economic development of all the Methodist groups were played by rich laymen, invariably men in business. They built and endowed chapels and mission rooms. They organized church finances. They built Sunday Schools. They helped set up national church headquarters. They funded colleges for the training of professional ministers. Many of them taught in Sunday School. And many of them occupied the pulpit on a Sunday.

As preachers, rich laymen had served the Methodist movement since Wesley's day.[5] For example, in the North East of England, for which Geoffrey Milburn has compiled a valuable biographical listing, Michael Longridge (1757–1815), a prosperous draper and mercer of Sunderland, William Smith (1736–1824), a wealthy Newcastle corn merchant, and Thomas Thompson (1753–1828), a banker in Hull, all served as preachers in their localities, supplementing the full-time travelling preachers appointed by Wesley. Frequently they undertook other forms of church work, as did Longridge who not only preached but also organised Sunday Schools and led a Class Meeting.

2   David Martin, *A Sociology of English Religion* (London: Heinemann, 1967), p. 79.
3   Kenneth D. Brown, *A Social History of the Nonconformist Ministry in England and Wales, 1800–1930* (Oxford: Clarendon Press, 1988), p. 83.
4   Hugh McLeod, *Religion and Society in England, 1850–1914* (London: Macmillan, 1996), pp. 169-220.
5   See the essays by Margaret Batty, 'Origins: The Age of Wesley', and John Munsey Turner, 'Years of Tension and Conflict, 1796–1850', in Geoffrey Milburn and Margaret Batty (eds.), *Workaday Preachers: The Story of Methodist Local Preaching* (London: Methodist Publishing House, 1995), pp. 11-34 and 35-56 respectively.

Businessmen figured among the local preachers in the various divisions of Methodism throughout the nineteenth century. Thus, to cite the North-East again, local preachers among the Wesleyans included Thomas Hudson Bainbridge (1842–1912), a wealthy draper of Newcastle, John Bramwell (1794–1882), a Durham solicitor, Sir Alfred Gelder (1855–1941), a Hull architect, Walter Runciman (1847–1937), 1st Baron Runciman, a South Shields shipowner, and Sir William Haswell Stephenson (1836–1918), a multiple company director on Tyneside. Among Primitive Methodists, who drew on social classes lower than the Wesleyans, businessmen preachers included George Coward (1805–77), a Durham stationer, Robert Huison (b. 1821), a Sunderland stationer and shipowner, and George Race (1810–86), a Weardale grocer and draper.[6]

Numbers

At the turn of the century some 36,000 'local preachers' (as opposed to 'itinerant' or 'travelling' preachers, the equivalent of ministers) served the Methodist denominations. The Primitive Methodists relied on their local preachers more than the Wesleyans (see Table 1). Nothing is known of their occupational composition: such data, inimical to the religious egalitarianism that flowed from the Reformation doctrine of the priesthood of all believers, were never officially collected. No biographical directory of Methodist local preachers, recording occupations, was published until 1934. By this time reportedly 40,000 (35,000 is more accurate[7]) lay and voluntary preachers were preaching two thirds of the sermons in 15,000–16,000 Methodist chapels up and down the land.[8] Nothing like the 1934 directory has appeared since.

Backgrounds

As Thomas Bainbridge observed, 'Methodism is largely dependent upon lay help. The bulk of our pulpits every Sunday are supplied by lay

---

6   Geoffrey E. Milburn, 'Piety, Profit and Paternalism: Methodists in Business in the North-East of England, c.1760–1920', *Proceedings of the Wesley Historical Society* 44.3 (December, 1983), pp. 45-92, 'Biographical Appendix', pp. 70-92.

7   Robert Currie, Alan Gilbert and Lee Horsley, *Churches and Churchgoers: Patterns of Church Growth in the British Isles since 1700* (Oxford: Clarendon Press, 1977), p. 206.

8   These figures were quoted by Sir Robert Perks, a former railway company lawyer and director, and vice-president of the first (1932) Methodist Conference (but not a local preacher) in his *The Aim of the Methodist Church: An Address to the Uniting Conference of the Methodist Church of Great Britain* (London: Epworth Press, 1933) p. 10.

preachers. Hence the necessity of ensuring a supply of the right class of men.' He specified 'men of education and good social standing' as desirable candidates for local preaching and though he did not mention businessmen, they invariably had good social standing, often supported by skills in communication.[9]

This seems to have occurred. Clive Field's sampling of the 1934 Methodist directory of local preachers shows a predominance of farmers, dealers, retailers and accountants among people in business.[10] In contrast, national lay leaders undertaking preaching in twentieth-century Methodism hailed from somewhat different backgrounds. Before the First World War those in the Wesleyan denomination who came from business were more likely to be in manufacturing and the professions than in farming or services. By the 1930s, services (distribution and finance) and the professions provided more than half the lay leaders from business. By the 1950s, manufacturers were a rarity among Methodist lay leaders (see Appendices 1 and 2).

These concentrations of business activity among the lay leaders did not always supply preachers in proportion to their relative strengths. As Appendix 2 shows, among national lay leaders some industrial backgrounds provided more preachers than others. Among Wesleyans c. 1907, a fifth of the 'workhorse' preachers were from the textile industries (no doubt reflecting the strength of the Methodists among Nonconformists in the North West of England[11]) and half that proportion were in the non-business professions (education and medicine). By the 1930s, Methodist lay leaders in distribution and finance most frequently engaged in preaching. By the 1950s, those in the professions predominated, but absolute numbers were tiny.

Motives

Businessmen were no different from other men or women in their motivations for entering the pulpit. They did so because they had come to faith in Christ and felt called to share their faith through conducting public worship and engaging in preaching. As noted at the outset, people in business might well have strong, if not always commendable, reasons for resisting the preaching opportunity. For those who obeyed the call, the dominant motive was apostolic: to obey the command of Christ to

---

9   Thomas H. Bainbridge, *Reminiscences* (ed. Gerald France; London: Charles H. Kelly, 1913), pp. 155-56.
10   Clive D. Field, 'The Methodist Local Preacher: An Occupational Analysis', in Milburn and Batty (eds.), *Workaday Preachers*, p. 240.
11   See Peter F. Clarke, *Lancashire and the New Liberalism* (Cambridge: Cambridge University Press, 1971) ch. 3.

'go into all the world and preach the good news to all creation' (Mark 16.15 NIV). Sir William Stephenson, on Tyneside, boldly asserted that 'if he did not think he was as much called to preach as the Archbishop of Canterbury, he would never get into a pulpit again'. Local preachers, he declared, were a 'band of men animated by one common purpose—to present a life of devotion and labour to the Master, determined to bring into contribution their utmost talents and influence, all that they had and all that they were, for the highest, grandest, and most important occupation to which one could be sent—the salvation of the world'.[12] Sir William Smith, the Nottinghamshire merchant miller, declined to stand for Parliament on the grounds that 'he could serve God and Methodism better as a local preacher'.[13] To Moses Bourne, that fourth-generation pillar of Primitive Methodism and a colliery company secretary at Church Gresley, south Derbyshire, 'preaching is a supreme delight. He preaches because he must preach.'[14] Looking back, Thomas Bainbridge identified 'the strongest and most influential motive in my life has been a sense of responsibility and stewardship...[which]...led me to become a local preacher and class-leader'.[15]

These were the highest motives. Doubtless, less worthy ones at times intruded but were rarely admitted.

Pulpits

Like other local preachers, businessmen in the pulpit frequently found themselves planned to preach at the small village chapels serving rural Methodism. Thus, Alderman Stephen Hilton, Leicester shoe retailer and Primitive Methodist, 'was one of the most conscientious local preachers, as willing, even more willing, to serve the small village churches than the town church'.[16] Of Sir James Duckworth, self-made founder of a northern retail empire, it was reported, 'As a local preacher he was known and welcomed throughout the denomination. He was as ready to go to the assistance of a small, struggling church as to a large and prosperous one, and there are few pulpits in United Methodism he had not occupied.'[17] It was recalled of Sir William Stephenson, chairman of the Tyne Improvement Commissioners and thus holder of the 'premier commercial position on Tyneside',[18] that 'he went cheerfully to his

---

12   *Wesleyan Magazine*, 1907, p. 732.
13   *Wesleyan Magazine*, 1916, p. 700.
14   *Aldersgate Magazine*, 1912, p. 551.
15   Bainbridge, *Reminiscences*, p. 173.
16   *Aldersgate Magazine*, 1914, p. 415.
17   *Rochdale Observer*, 2 January 1915.
18   *Methodist Recorder*, 9 May 1918

duties Sunday by Sunday, never selecting his appointments, but doing the task assigned to him, however lowly, as though it were the best'.[19]

Sometimes local preachers had special callings. Following missionary and sectarian precedents, some preached outdoors. For example, Norman Thomas Carr Sargant, a London metal broker and another Wesleyan, specialised in open air preaching on a busy metropolitan corner near Archway Chapel, London.[20] On the other hand, a popular and powerful preacher like Moses Bourne of the Primitive Methodists had a denominational reach: 'It is no uncommon thing for him to preach on thirteen Sundays per quarter; and during the winter months he has taken evangelistic services for weeks together in churches near home. When men and women are being converted Moses lives in a heaven of delight. Of this joy he has had a large share. Though his services are in great demand in regions far beyond his own Circuit, nine Sundays per quarter are reserved for places within easy reach of his home, and four are given to more distinct fields. His Sunday morning Bible Class, consisting of fifty young men, lies near his heart, and to its interests he gives of his best. His preaching parish includes places so far away as Newcastle-on-Tyne, Manchester, Hull, Sheffield, and Grimsby, and he not infrequently travels all Sunday night so as to be at business on Monday morning.'[21] James Duckworth, as Vice-President of the United Methodist Free Churches in 1894, had a similar national audience: 'it is said that in the twelve months he delivered 296 sermons and addresses, wrote 1,130 letters on connexional matters, and travelled 17,102 miles (at a cost to himself of £250). All this was outside the customary routine of connexional work.'[22]

Training and Preparation for Preaching

As ministerial colleges improved the level of clerical education in the main Methodist denominations, so congregations expected better sermons from their lay preachers. The Wesleyans led the way, in their aspirations if not their realizations at the beginning of the twentieth century. Their new local preachers, listed on their quarterly plans detailing who would be taking which services at which chapels, were supposed officially to advance from 'On Note' to 'On Trial' to 'On Full Plan' by means of a careful practical and educational sifting. This started by accompanying an accredited preacher and later preaching a trial sermon in front of the circuit's body of local preachers. Early on, the

---

19 *Wesleyan Magazine*, 1907, p. 512.
20 *Methodist Recorder*, 27 July 1905
21 *Aldersgate Magazine*, 1912, pp. 551-52.
22 *Rochdale Observer*, 2 January 1915.

novice local preacher was urged to sit and pass examinations. However, very few apparently did so in any of the Methodist denominations, until the formation of the Methodist Church in 1932.[23]

The Wesleyan syllabus for local preachers' examinations is nevertheless instructive. The choice of set texts changed year by year. In 1906, the Elementary level examination textbooks were (chapters from) Robertson's *Teachings of Our Lord*, and Moulton's *Short Introduction to the Literature of the Bible* while the books for examination for 1908 were Boyd-Carpenter's *Introduction to the Bible* and Stewart's *Evidences*. The Advanced level examination textbooks were (chapters from) Westcott's *Historic Faith* and Davidson's *Christian Ethics* while the books for examination for 1908 were Laidlaw's *Foundation Truths* and Paterson's *Apostles' Teaching*. In 1907 the distinction between Elementary and Advanced levels was dropped. The majority of these texts, it may be noted, were not by Wesleyan authors and were a mixture of the theologically conservative (John Laidlaw) and up-to-date (B.F. Westcott). The books were available to local preachers at a third of their published price.[24] Foundational of course was the Bible, use of which was aided by Cruden's *Concordance* (an invaluable Bible 'search-engine'), and, for Methodists, Wesley's *Sermons* and *Notes on the New Testament*. In the 1890s copies of these could be purchased from the Rev. Thomas Champness's Joyful News Book Depot at Rochdale. In addition there were magazines and handbooks available to local preachers able to afford them.[25] Sermons by great preachers were published in the weekly *Methodist Times*.[26]

Preaching involves preparation. As Dr Frederic Greeves said to his son, 'You must have trouble either in the pulpit or in your study. You can choose which.' Recalling this advice, Thomas Bainbridge added, 'Some local preachers unfortunately choose the pulpit!'[27] No doubt this was one reason why busy people in business declined to become local preachers. Those who did had to spend time in study, praying and thinking about what they would say, how they would expound a passage or text of Scripture. Invariably this meant writing out headings, key thoughts, even the whole sermon. Bainbridge himself, his editor recalled, left at his death in 1912 'two large boxes...filled with his own carefully-prepared and

---

23   Geoffrey Milburn, 'Role, Status and Training in Divided Methodism, 1850–1932', in Milburn and Batty (eds.), *Workaday Preachers*, pp. 76-82.

24   Wesleyan Methodist Church, *Minutes of Conference, 1906*, p. 90.

25   Geoffrey Milburn, 'Role, Status and Training in Divided Methodism, 1850–1932', in Milburn and Batty (eds.), *Workaday Preachers*, pp. 75-79.

26   See the advertisement sections of the Wesleyan Methodist Church, *Minutes of Conference, 1906*.

27   Bainbridge, *Reminiscences*, pp. 156-57.

wonderfully neatly-written notes of sermons'.[28] Sermon content was not the only aspect of preaching that required preparation. The delivery of the sermon had to be practised. In Bainbridge's day the weekly Class Meeting was 'the nursery for Christian service. There people learn to speak and pray in public.'[29]

Theology

At a time when the work of German theologians was sowing deep doubt about the reliability of scripture, and a 'New Theology' was being discussed in scholarly journals, it was not surprising that anxieties arose in the hearts and minds of local preachers in the Methodist churches. Businessmen in the pulpit were imaginably torn between their reflex attitudes favouring the novel and innovative and, on the other hand, their loyalty to the faith of their fathers. Whichever direction they felt more strongly pulled, as men of business they were used to defending their corner with vigour. An episode which threatened to derail the annual Conference of the Primitive Methodist Church in 1907 illustrated what some businessmen preachers thought about the 'New Theology'.

The Conference was held at Leicester and on its first evening, on Wednesday 12 June 1907, an annual Conference lecture, the eleventh in the series, was given in the Belgrave Gate Primitive Methodist Church.[30] In the minds of the ministers and laity present there was a heightened buzz of interest because that year they were celebrating the centenary of the birth of Primitive Methodism at Mow Cop. Imaginably, the thoughts of the audience centred on three figures: the benefactor of the lecture series, the lecturer and the chairman.

The benefactor was sixty-one year old William Pickles Hartley, Aintree jam manufacturer, munificent patron of Primitive Methodism, and the connexion's leading laymen. The connexion was indebted to him for organising their Chapel Aid Association, to fund chapel building (1886–89);[31] for serving many years as treasurer of the Primitive Methodist Missionary Society; for raising the standard of ministerial training by funding a college at Manchester; and for recruiting to it from Oxford Arthur Samuel Peake (1892), the connexion's leading biblical scholar (in 1904 appointed the first Rylands Professor of Biblical Criticism and Exegesis in the University of Manchester). As an aside, it may be recalled

---

28   Bainbridge, *Reminiscences*, p. 154.
29   Bainbridge, *Reminiscences*, p. 176.
30   *Primitive Methodist Leader*, 20 June 1907; *Methodist Recorder*, 20 June 1907.
31   In 1905 proceeding at the rate of 48 chapels a year at a cost of £76,000, of which just under half was debt. See *Minutes [of the]...Eighty-Seventh Annual Conference of the Primitive Methodist Connexion* (London, 1906), p. 125.

that one of the few Nonconformist women in big business was then playing a key role in supporting the cause of theological scholarship at Manchester. This was Mrs Enriqueta Augustina Rylands, the widow of John Rylands (Manchester's greatest nineteenth-century cotton manufacturer and a Congregationalist) who poured a fortune into the foundation of the John Rylands Library, opened on Deansgate, Manchester in 1904, and took advice from Peake about purchasing the most recent German books on theology.[32] Unlike his protégé Peake, Hartley was never a local preacher: at his mother's bidding he learned to play the harmonium and was thereafter enlisted as organist at the Colne chapel where he worshipped as a young man.[33] Perhaps that was one reason why he made no reported intervention over the lecture he had sponsored. Certainly he was a 'modern' man who read Alfred Russel Wallace's *Man's Place in the Universe: A Study of the Results of Scientific Research in Relation to the Unity or Plurality of Worlds* (1903) 'with thrilling interest'.[34] Peake's presence at the Conference was signalled by an inspiring and challenging address to local preachers.[35] Most likely, both men were in the Hartley Lecture audience.

The lecturer was the Reverend John Day Thompson, senior minister among the Primitive Methodists. A third generation Primitive Methodist, with a son in the ministry, Geordie-born, fifty-eight year old Thompson was then superintendent of the Blackpool circuit, with over thirty years in the ministry behind him. In the connexion he was Vice-Secretary of the General Committee which had oversight of 1,150 ministers, 16,200 local preachers, and 210,000 members.[36] He was known for preaching without notes and for being a 'master of ideas'.[37] Before spending six years in Adelaide, Australia, he had preceded Peake as literature review editor of

---

32   Douglas A. Farnie, 'Enriqueta Augustina Rylands (1843–1908), Founder of the John Rylands Library', *Bulletin of the John Rylands University Library of Manchester* 71.2 (Summer, 1989), pp. 1-38; idem, *John Rylands of Manchester* (Manchester: John Rylands University Library of Manchester, 1993); Leslie S. Peake, *Arthur Samuel Peake: A Memoir* (London: Hodder & Stoughton, 1930), pp. 147-51.

33   Arthur S. Peake, *The Life of Sir William Hartley* (London: Hodder & Stoughton, 1926), p. 34.

34   Hartley to Peake, 14 December 1903, Peake MSS IV, no. 640, John Rylands University Library of Manchester.

35   *Primitive Methodist Leader*, 20 June 1907, pp. 401-402.

36   *Minutes [of the]...Eighty-Seventh Annual Conference of the Primitive Methodist Connexion*, pp. 20, 57, 60.

37   For Thompson's biography see *Primitive Methodist Leader* 20 June 1907, p. 403; *Primitive Methodist Magazine* 1919, pp. 480-81; *Minutes [of the]...Eighty-Seventh Annual Conference of the Primitive Methodist Connexion*, p.244; *The Methodist Who's Who 1910* (London: Robert Culley, 1910). In June 1914 he unveiled a portrait of Peake at Hartley College, Manchester. Peake, *Arthur Samuel Peake*, p. 124.

the *Primitive Methodist Quarterly Review* (later the *Holborn Review*).[38] Widely read and travelled, he was familiar with recent intellectual trends and aspects of the new theological scholarship. However, he could not read Hebrew and his writings on Old Testament questions were 'entirely from the standpoint of an English reader and on broad literary, historical and theological lines'.[39] The subject of his lecture, for which he received ten guineas (the equivalent of an eighth of his salary[40]), was 'The doctrine of immortality and its present day aspects'. His inspiration was undoubtedly the ideas of the Rev. R.J. Campbell, minister of the City Temple, London, the most prestigious Congregational pulpit in the kingdom, whose unorthodox views, earlier reported in the *Daily Mail*, were troubling thoughtful Nonconformists.[41]

The lecturer's chairman was Councillor George Green, JP, of Glasgow. In secular life Councillor Green was a powerful figure in a powerful business. He was the dynamic and tenacious Inspector for Scotland of the Prudential Assurance Company. The Pru then had well over 20,000 employees, most of them agents collecting door-to-door the weekly premiums on life insurance policies taken out by hosts of late-Victorian and Edwardian working class families.[42] A Lanarkshire County Councillor, a Lanarkshire magistrate and recently elected chairman of the Liberal Association of Scotland, Green was approaching the summit of his career. Then aged sixty-four, he was born in Stockport, the son of a powerloom weaver. When only eight, he followed his father into the mill but left in his twenties after the American Civil War brought cotton famine to Lancashire. Green joined the Prudential where his 'big, breezy personality...volcanic energy...tenacity of purpose...initiative and "go" and business faculty, as well as the tact and authority of the born ruler' took him up the corporate hierarchy of a rapidly expanding business, culminating in his appointment to Glasgow in 1891 to take charge of the Prudential's business in the whole of Scotland. While still in the cotton mill he had been converted and joined the Methodist New Connexion but work-related moves took him beyond New Connexion territory and he joined the Primitive Methodists at Bedford. Chesterfield, Birkenhead, Clapham, Edinburgh, Glasgow, Birmingham: all those places where he

---

38   John T. Wilkinson, *Arthur Samuel Peake: A Biography* (London: Epworth Press, 1971), p. 134.
39   Thompson to Peake, from N. Adelaide, 9 January 1893, Peake MSS IV, no. 1716.
40   Brown, *Social History of the Nonconformist Ministry*, pp. 148-49; *Garlick's Methodist Registry, 1983* (London: Edsall, 1983), Appendix.
41   Keith W. Clements, *Lovers of Discord: Twentieth-Century Theological Controversies in England* (London: SPCK, 1988), ch. 2.
42   Laurie Dennett, *A Sense of Security: 150 Years of Prudential* (Cambridge: Granta Editions, 1998), pp. 131, 155.

worked for the Prudential saw him serve the Primitive Methodists, as local preacher, Sunday School superindent, or church founder. In 1904 he was elected Vice-President of the Primitive Methodist Connexion.[43]

As Thompson's lecture unfolded, George Green the chairman, and others, liked what they heard less and less. In the words of the Wesleyans' *Methodist Recorder*, the lecture's 'teaching seemed to be so out of harmony with Methodist standards of belief [the Primitive Methodists had eleven articles of faith, as well as Wesley's *Notes and Sermons*, as their Doctrinal Standards[44]] that during its delivery it was apparent that the audience was not prepared to endorse it, and some of the connexional leaders sat looking grave as Mr Thompson advanced and advocated his theories, and especially was this so when he began to describe the Second Coming, the literal Day of Judgement, and the raising of the physical body, whether of Jesus or of the believer, as non-essentials. Aside from this, it was a brilliant effort'.[45]

The reaction to Thompson's lecture was consternation.[46] With its 'basal principle' that 'the great, simple seminal intuitions of religion, in relation in especial to Immortality, have been held everywhere, always, and by all, and that these take form and body according to the intellectual climate—the culture, civilization, and general conditions—of any given time; the core abiding, the cover ever changing',[47] Thompson's lecture echoed the Kantian idealism of R.J. Campbell's New Theology.[48]

The following afternoon the Hartley Lecture was debated in Conference session. The President of Conference declared he had no wish to fetter minds, and thought the lecture, of book-length, could be published as an expression of the author's own convictions and conclusions. Councillor Green declared that 'Personally he did not associate himself with Mr Thompson's views. He had consented to be

---

43   *The Methodist Who's Who, 1910*; *Primitive Methodist Magazine*, 1913, pp. 113-18; 1916, pp. 712-13.

44   Peake did not like these Doctrinal Standards and wanted to get rid of them, later welcoming the prospect of their abandonment with the coming of Methodist church union. Peake, *Arthur Samuel Peake*, pp. 168-69.

45   *Methodist Recorder*, 20 June 1907, p. 7.

46   The *Methodist Recorder* later described it as 'what threatened to be the creator of disorder and confusion in the Conference'. *Methodist Recorder*, 20 June 1907, p. 7.

47   John Day Thompson, *The Doctrine of Immortality: Its Essence, Relativity and Present-Day Aspects: The Hartley Lecture Delivered to the Primitive Methodist Conference, Leicester, June 12, 1907* (London: Primitive Methodist Publishing House, 1908), Preface.

48   For the broad context of Campbellism see David W. Bebbington, *Evangelicalism in Modern Britain: A History from the 1730s to the 1980s* (London: Routledge, 1989), pp. 198-202; and more specifically, Clements, *Lovers of Discord*, pp. 19-48.

chairman without thought of hearing such teaching. What they heard last night might be New Theology or the Coming theology, but he did not want it. If it were to be taken as the "official" view on the subject, he dissented from it.' Thompson replied that 'He did not want Mr Green to endorse his findings, nor did he ask anyone else in the Conference to do so.' He suggested that they let him publish the lecture with Conference's general congratulatory resolution printed 'as a fly-leaf'. His emotional appeal to the fathers and brethren of the church brought loud applause.[49]

The matter of publication was referred to the Hartley Lecture Committee, but not before the Connexional Editor (the Reverend John Ritson) confessed that 'through somebody's blunder he had not seen the Book until he came to Conference'; and the Connexional Book Steward (the Reverend Edwin Dalton) was immediately and permanently added to the Hartley Committee.[50]

On the Saturday the report of the Hartley Lecture Committee was considered by Conference. Their motion that Thompson's lecture should not be published by Conference was seconded by Councillor Green and the matter was left to the January meeting of the connexional Book Committee. The Reverend Arthur T. Guttery, Vice-Secretary of the General Missionary Committee, sought to halt further discussion of the issue and Stephen Hilton, one-time mayor of Leicester, proprietor of six Leicester shoe shops, former Vice-President of the Primitive Methodist Conference (the previous year), freemason and local preacher, advised that 'it would be well if the subject was not referred to in speeches made at public meetings'.[51] To preclude a similar problem in future, Conference passed a resolution that 'after this year the manuscript of the Hartley Lecture shall be the property of the Conference, whether it be published or not.'[52]

Evidently more wrangling followed. The lecture was published, but without the congratulatory Conference resolution Thompson would have liked. It was reviewed in the *Holborn Quarterly,* by the Reverend W. Jones Davies, Vice-Principal of Hartley College, Manchester, a choice of reviewer in which Peake must have been involved. Davies gave 'this belated volume' a long review and a warm welcome, concluding that he would have been grateful if 'the lecture had not been removed from the Connexional *Index expurgatorius'*.[53] Presumably this was in line with Peake's views. Unfortunately, Peake's correspondence with both Hartley and Thompson does not cover the years 1906 and 1907.

---

49   *Primitive Methodist Leader* 20 June 1907, p. 403.
50   The membership of this committee is not recorded in *Minutes [of the]...Eighty-Seventh Annual Conference of the Primitive Methodist Connexion, 1907.*
51   *Primitive Methodist Leader,* 20 June 1907, p. 406.
52   *Primitive Methodist Leader,* 20 June 1907, p. 409.
53   *Primitive Methodist Quarterly Review,* April 1909, pp. 193-207.

The centenary excitement of the 1907 Primitive Methodist Conference, threatened by the Hartley Lecture fracas, was retrieved by William Hartley. On the following Saturday evening, he and his wife and family hosted a 'brilliant' reception for conference delegates in the King's Hall of the Grand Hotel, Leicester. Earlier in the week Conference had inaugurated a £250,000 Centenary Thanksgiving Fund. At the Grand Hotel reception news of the Fund's progress was announced. The Reverend George Armstrong reported that 154 laymen had promised over £8,000, or an average of £50 each, and a larger number of ministers an average of £12 each (at a time when the annual average income of a skilled worker was £100[54]). Then Hartley came forward. He 'played around with the matter of his own gift without actually stating what it would be for a considerable time. There was a sort of breathless anxiety, and it was delightful to notice how cleverly he kept close to the point without actually touching it. At last, however, the figure came. The connexion must raise £100,000 for connexional purposes and he will add £15,000 to it.' Hartley also promised to add 15% to whatever the Connexion raised.[55]

Soon after, he purchased Holborn Town Hall, London, refurbished it, and sold it back to the Primitive Methodist Connexion at two-thirds the cost price for use as its denominational headquarters (1909–10). The Connexion elected him to it highest offices of Vice-President (1892) and President (1909). He became the only layman ever to hold the latter. Hartley was knighted in 1908 and died a millionaire in 1922.[56] George Green too was knighted, for social and political services in 1911. He died five years later in his seventies. As for the Reverend John Day Thompson, he was shortly after stationed to north London and later Cambridge. In 1916 he was elected President of the Primitive Methodist Conference and a couple of years later became editor of the *Holborn Review*, the church's quarterly journal. When he died in 1919, his obituarist observed that 'he penetrated where few of his generation had ventured, and what he gained for himself he told faithfully and fearlessly. The charge of heterodoxy was bound to come.'[57]

The whole episode is instructive for understanding the strength and roles of the business laity within Nonconformity, as well as reaction to the new scholarship of biblical criticism. Unlike the Wesleyans, the Primitive Methodists had no separate Conference sessions for clergy.

---

54   John Burnett, *A History of the Cost of Living* (Harmondsworth: Penguin, 1969), p. 253, citing the Wage Census of 1906.
55   *Primitive Methodist Leader*, 20 June 1907, p. 402.
56   Peake, *Sir William Hartley*; David J. Jeremy, 'Sir William Pickles Hartley', in David J. Jeremy and Christine Shaw (eds.), *Dictionary of Business Biography* (6 vols; London: Butterworths, 1984–86), III, pp. 96-99.
57   *Primitive Methodist Magazine*, 1919, pp. 480-81.

Consequently, ministers were open to lay appraisal, dissent, rebuke. Lay criticism encompassed theology as much as any other aspect of church teaching and behaviour. The line between lay 'local preachers' (stationed by circuit ministers) and professional 'travelling preachers' (the ministers, stationed by Conference), was as narrow as it could be in Primitive Methodism. At another level, the dispute was of course about the age-old tension betweeen simple faith and scholarly insight (here influenced by German theologians and philosophers). At a further level, the episode suggests growing denominational maturity, with the more educated and speculative ministerial brethren expressing independent views. Significantly perhaps, neither Hartley nor Peake, a director of the *Primitive Methodist Leader*, was reported as participating in the controversy.

Among the Wesleyan Methodists, one pulpit defender of the traditional faith was Sir William Smith (1843–1916), merchant miller of Langley Mill, Nottinghamshire. Having conducted his first service at the age of seventeen, his obituarist recalled, William Smith 'was very jealous for the safety of the ark. If at times he appeared angry at the work of the Higher Critic, we know well that he was grieved beyond all words at what he believed to be the attempts to undermine faith in the Scriptures as the very word of God, and in the proper Godhead of the Lord and Saviour Jesus Christ.'[58] Another was Thomas Bainbridge. In the 1900s, again, he regretted that preaching 'is not nearly so heart searching or so analytical of the soul's struggle as it used to be. The great cardinal truths are not preached nearly so constantly as formerly; the fact of sin—its guilt, its enthralling power, its destructive power; the work of the Holy Spirit—His enlightening and striving—His being grieved or quenched. Christ as an atoning Saviour is not "lifted up" so frequently as of old, and the fact that at each service there may be some one seeking Him secretly is not recognised by an invitation to trust him now.'[59]

Preaching Styles

Sometimes the pulpit styles of these businessmen preachers were characterised in profiles of Conference delegates or in obituaries. James Calvert Coates, a London varnish manufacturer and Wesleyan, it was reported in 1907, 'has an inexhaustible stock of amusing stories, and except in bed is never seen without a flower in his button-hole'.[60] In a few cases we know rather more. Of Moses Bourne it was claimed, 'As

---

58 *Wesleyan Magazine*, 1916, p. 700.
59 Bainbridge, *Reminiscences*, pp. 161-62.
60 *Methodist Recorder*, 18 July 1907.

preacher and platform speaker he ranks with our best. He possesses a gentlemanly presence, a well-stored mind, a good memory, a musical voice, great facility of expression and a stout, warm heart. His voice has been heard at the Metropolitan Missionary Meeting, at the last great Centenary Camp Meeting on Mow Cop, and in many of our largest churches. The preaching passion is dominant. The books which crowd his study shelves are a standing witness to the fact. All reading and observation are subservient to the ministry of the word, and all texts lead to the Cross. He has read widely and well, in history, poetry, biography and theology, but he clings tenaciously to the evangelical gospel. Sin and salvation are to him tremendous facts, and he preaches them in season and out of season.'[61] Thomas Bainbridge's style was eulogised at his funeral thus: 'His addresses were straight, strong, convinced, and convincing; full of the warmth of earnestness and the glow of love.'[62] Bainbridge believed that it was essential to hold the attention of the congregation and therefore, in this 'age of pictures', each part of the service should be 'crisp and bright'. There should be two prayers of not more than four or five minutes each, hymns should not be too long and sermons no more than 20–25 minutes on Sunday mornings, 25–30 minutes on Sunday evenings. 'Then we should have more illustrative preaching. Our Lord's example in this respect should be followed. The fields of history, biography, natural history, and our daily life are all full of illustrations. Each good illustration is like a window that lets in the light, or like a nail fastening the truth on the minds of the hearers. If preachers ignore illustrations because they are discreditable to an intellectual preacher, their motive is itself a discreditable one.'[63]

Length of Service

On the lengths of time served by local preachers there seems to be only individual and anecdotal evidence. Once having put their hand to the plough, it was assumed that they followed a lifetime calling. Fall-out rates are unknown. Traces of great longevity were frequently reported, however. At Rochdale, for example, the United Methodist Church in 1914 honoured five men who had each completed fifty years as a local preacher. They included Sir James Duckworth and William Cunliffe, chairman of the innovative Lancashire textile machine makers, Tweedales & Smalley.[64]

---

61 *Aldersgate Magazine*, 1912, p. 552.
62 Bainbridge, *Reminiscences*, p. 209.
63 Bainbridge, *Reminiscences*, pp. 159, 161.
64 *Rochdale Observer*, 2 January 1915.

Preaching-Related Roles

In at least two directions these articulate businessmen preachers advanced the cause of local preaching outside the pulpit in Methodism. One was by supporting institutions designed to promote the cause of lay preaching. The other, more modestly perhaps, was through publishing helpful books and pamphlets.

Among the institutions two stood out: the Local Preachers' Mutual Aid Association (LPMAA)[65] and Cliff College.[66] The former was established in 1849 to 'provide for relief in sickness, old age, and at death' for Wesleyan Methodist local preachers.[67] Among the presidents of the LPMAA, businessmen preachers were prominent. Sir William Stephenson, director of numerous companies on Tyneside, four times mayor of Newcastle-upon-Tyne, well-known local philanthropist, and a Wesleyan Methodist local preacher from the age of twenty-three, was twice elected LPMAA president.[68] Moses Atkinson, a linen manufacturer of Leeds, retired from the family business in 1883 at the age of thirty-five, served as LPMAA president in 1886 and for more than a decade worked for the extension of the LPMAA overseas, especially in the USA.[69] Charles Heap, head of a large bleaching, dyeing and finishing business at Rochdale, was LPMAA treasurer between 1896 and 1922.[70] The other mainspring of the LPMAA who worked closely with Atkinson in an effort to improve the qualifications and status of local preachers was Sir John Bamford-Slack (1857–1909), a London solicitor and Liberal MP. Bamford-Slack was LPMAA president in 1894–95 and honorary secretary in 1902–04. For many years the LPMAA General Committee held its December meetings at his home, 10 Woburn Square.[71] Yet another was Sir Thomas Rowbotham (1851–1939), seventy-one years a local preacher and LPMAA president in 1909–10. Starting work in a cotton mill near Stockport at the age of eleven, he was apprenticed to a village blacksmith and served '19 years at the anvil', later founding his own engineering

---

65 See F. Harold Buss and R. G. Burnett, *A Goodly Fellowship: A History of the Hundred Years of the Methodist Local Preachers' Mutual Aid Association, 1849–1949* (London: Epworth Press, 1949). Also C. Alan Parker, 'Self Help among the Local Preachers', in Milburn and Batty (eds.), *Workaday Preachers*, pp. 201-22.

66 See David W. Lambert, *What Hath God Wrought : The Story of Cliff College, 1904–1954* (Calver: Cliff College, 1954).

67 Buss and Burnett, *Goodly Fellowship*, p. 27.

68 *Wesleyan Magazine*, 1907, pp. 730-33; 1918, pp. 510-12; *Methodist Recorder*, 9 May 1918.

69 *Methodist Recorder*, 22 July 1897; *Methodist Who's Who, 1910*.

70 *Rochdale Observer*, 25 July 1923.

71 *Methodist Recorder*, 18 February 1909.

firm and serving as mayor of Stockport, 1916–19.[72] It would be interesting to know how much these businessmen preachers contributed financially to the work of the LPMAA.

The other institution in late nineteenth-century Methodism dedicated to the cause of local preaching was Cliff College, set up in the Peak District in Derbyshire for the purpose of improving lay witness and leadership. Thomas Bainbridge recorded, 'I am inclined to think that English Methodism has not at present any institution that is of such usefulness and importance as that of Cliff College.'[73] Again it would be interesting to know how far businessmen financially supported this the prime vehicle for developing lay leadership.

As for publications, a check of the British Library *Catalogue of Printed Books* indicates something of late nineteenth-century activity among Wesleyan lay leaders. Of the twenty-five local preachers and businessmen among the seventy-six lay leaders in 1907 (see Appendix I) one, Henry Arthur Smith, a barrister, published a volume of sermons;[74] one, Thomas Bainbridge, published a small volume on the leadership of Class Meetings;[75] and two, Bainbridge and William John Davey a professional engineer, wrote works of an autobiographical nature.[76] Clearly men busy in industry and commerce had limited opportunity to write and publish. Unlisted in that *Catalogue*, Bainbridge's *Counsels to Young Christians* (c. 1875) apparently sold 250,000 and his *Conscience and System in the Stewardship of Money* 100,000 copies.[77]

Reconciling Tensions between Preaching and Business

The main tensions between preaching and business were those related to time, to wealth, to authority and to ethical behaviour. The issue of time has been noted earlier. Here it may be remarked that some of the most distinguished laymen in Methodism declined to be local preachers. Conspicuous by their absence from the ranks of the preachers were men like Sir William Hartley, among the Primitives; Sir Robert Perks, Joseph and J. Arthur Rank, Josiah Stamp, 1st Baron Stamp, all Wesleyans. None of these men were recluses, though J. Arthur Rank was not one who liked

---

72 *Stockport Advertiser*, 13 October 1939.
73 Bainbridge, *Reminiscences*, p. 156.
74 Henry Arthur Smith, *Things New and Old and Other Sermons for the Times* (London: Charles H. Kelly, 1894).
75 Thomas Hudson Bainbridge and the Revd E. I. Page (eds.), *Thoughts for Class Leaders* (London: Charles H. Kelly 1895).
76 Bainbridge, *Reminiscences*; William John Davey, *Recollections, 1849–1936* (privately printed, 1936).
77 Bainbridge, *Reminiscences*, pp. 181-82.

the limelight. On the contrary, Hartley, Perks and Stamp were major public figures, not infrequently heard on national or regional platforms and well beyond Methodism between the 1900s and the 1920s.[78] In some cases it can only be assumed that the demands on their time, from matters of business and public affairs, prevented them undertaking regular commitments on the preaching plan. Others, like Joseph Rank, preferred to superintend the Sunday School, or like Hartley, to play the organ, perhaps slightly less demanding on weekend time and nerves.

The use of their wealth exercised pious rich men in England in the mid-nineteenth century, as Jane Garnett has shown.[79] The evangelical resolution of the dilemma was systematic and proportionate giving, that is, the regular distribution of fixed proportions of gross income to religious, charitable and philanthropic causes. Among the local preachers strongly and publicly advocating this practice was Thomas Bainbridge who wrote a book on the subject (see above). Sir Thomas Rowbotham gave away at least £50,000 including £10,000 to a fund for training Wesleyan ministers (in 1930).[80]

On the question of authority, of how far congregations containing employees were able to respect their employer in the chapel setting, there is all too little evidence. Clearly that question could be bound up with the ethical aspect: the requirement that the preacher's word and life should broadly agree. The most powerful endorsement of gospel proclamation lay in the direction of works of visitation, mercy and charity. For these many a Methodist local preacher became well known in his or her locality. Among the businessmen preachers, Thomas Bainbridge found time to visit the sick and dying.[81] Others, like Sir Thomas Rowbotham at Stockport, [82] or William McNeill at Crewe,[83] or Sir James Duckworth and Charles Heap at Rochdale,[84] immersed themselves in civic offices by

---

78   See the references in David J. Jeremy, *Capitalists and Christians: Business Leaders and the Churches in Britain, 1900–1960* (Oxford: Clarendon Press, 1990).

79   Jane Garnett, '"Gold and the Gospel": Systematic Beneficence in Mid-Nineteenth Century England', in W.J. Sheils and Diana Wood (eds), *The Church and Wealth* (Oxford: Blackwell, 1987), pp. 347-58; idem, 'Evangelicalism and Business in Mid-Victorian Britain', in John Wolffe (ed.), *Evangelical Faith and Public Zeal: Evangelicals and Society in Britain, 1780-1980* (London: SPCK, 1995), pp. 59-80.

80   *Stockport Advertiser*, 13 October 1939.

81   Bainbridge, *Reminiscences*, pp. 198-203.

82   Rowbotham made a great impact on Stockport, its local government, magistrates' bench, hospital, schools, police, recreational facilities, all memorialised in an obituary running to nine newspaper columns.

83   McNeill, a travelling draper and a Primitive Methodist, held all church offices possible and was five times mayor of Crewe: *Aldersgate Magazine*, 1912, pp. 19-22.

84   On whom I am writing a fuller contextual analysis as part of my study of 'Culture and Governance in British Boardrooms, 1900–1980s'.

which they served the whole community in practical ways and thereby supported their claims to credibility as preachers.

Conclusion

In conclusion, it may be said that the majority of Methodist business people decided that occupational demands on their time and energy precluded a commitment to the preaching plan. However, a surprising proportion did take on this office with its requirements of worship and sermon preparation and exposure to public scrutiny. So far as can be discovered, businessmen preachers differed from other local preachers with respect to their advantages (perhaps encumbrances) of worldly wealth and status. Together with individual talents and religious commitment, these economic assets allowed them to play leadership roles in their congregations and connexions and among their fellow local preachers. Reconciliation between a Sunday pulpit ministry and weekday commercial activity was most effectively achieved through personal integrity, a careful stewardship of riches and personal service in the community.

Table 1
Local preachers, ministers, members, churches of the major Methodist denominations, 1890–1914

	Wesleyan Methodists	Primitive Methodists	United Methodists
1890			
local preachers	16,038	16,317	
ministers	2,004	859	311
members	387,847	181,124	121,367*
churches	n/a	n/a	n/a
lps: members	24.2	11.1	
ministers: members	193.5	210.9	
1907			
local preachers	19,672	16,007	n/a
ministers	2,445	1,088	833***
members	446,368	206,445	148,988
churches	8,520**	5,214	2,421*
lps: members	22.7	12.9	
churches: lps	2.3	3.1	
ministers: members	182.6	189.7	
ministers: churches	3.5	4.8	
1914			
local preachers	19,463	15,718	
ministers	2,513	1,092	825
members	432,370	204,033	143,096
churches	8,479	4,907	3,038
lps: members	22.2	13.0	
churches: lps	2.3	3.2	
ministers: members	172.1	186.8	
ministers: churches	3.4	4.5	

Notes

* This figure is reached by adding the figures for the Methodist New Connexion, the United Methodist Free Churches and the Bible Christians, who merged in 1907.

** Figure for Great Britain.

*** Figure for 1908.

Sources

Robert Currie, Alan Gilbert and Lee Horsley, *Churches and Churchgoers: Patterns of Church Growth in the British Isles since 1700* (Oxford: Clarendon Press, 1977), pp. 142-43, 205; Wesleyan Methodist Church, *Minutes of Conference, 1907*, p. 553, and *1914*, p. 650.

Appendix 1

Data relating to the busiest lay people in Methodism in the years 1907, 1935 and 1955 have been assembled and analysed.[85] These show that among them preaching was undertaken by a goodly proportion but not by a majority. Of seventy-six national 'workhorses' (i.e. those sitting on five or more connexional committees) in Wesleyan Methodism in 1907, sixty-five were men in business (in the case of three, occupation was unknown: see Appendix 2) and of these twenty-five, or just over 38%, were local preachers. In other words a very high proportion of the Wesleyan denomination's lay leadership were businessmen and of these well over a third expressed their faith and their leadership qualities in the pulpit.

Two of the other Methodist denominations exhibited a similar strong support of local preaching among their leading laymen from the business world.[86] Among the Primitive Methodists in 1907 there were thirteen men who held five or more national offices and, of these, ten (including a solicitor) were in business (for two of the thirteen occupation is unknown). Of these ten, six were local preachers. Among the United Methodist Free Churches eight multiple office holders at a national level were all in business (again a solicitor is included) and half of them were local preachers. Least involved in local preaching among Methodists in 1907 were the lay leaders in the two smallest of the Methodist denominations: the Methodist New Connexion and the Bible Christians (who had only about 30,000 members each, compared to the Wesleyans' 446,000, the Primitives' 206,000 and the UMFC's 80,000). In the New Connexion all nine lay leaders were in business but only one was a local preacher (though no church career information was available for one of the nine). The three multiple office holders among the Bible Christians included one in business and one of unknown occupation; none was memorialised as a local preacher.

By 1935, and now in the recently-united Methodist Church, forty-three lay persons held five or more national committee posts. Of these, thirty-five were, or had been, in business and three were of unknown occupation. Of the thirty-five some fourteen were listed as local preachers in the *Methodist Local Preachers' Who's Who, 1934*. As 32% of the

---

85   Jeremy, *Capitalists and Christians*, pp. 295-352; idem, 'Late-Victorian and Edwardian Methodist Businessmen and Wealth', in David J. Jeremy (ed.), *Religion, Business and Wealth in Modern Britain* (London: Routledge, 1998), pp. 71-85.

86   For numbers of businessmen among non-Wesleyan Methodist lay leaders in 1907, see Jeremy, *Capitalists and Christians*, p. 324.

denomination's lay leaders, this proportion suggests that local preaching was still an honoured mark of lay leadership in the denomination.

By 1955 the number of connexional lay 'workhorses' was down to twenty-three; of these fourteen had business backgrounds (including professional people, some of whom worked at Methodist headquarters).[87] Among the fourteen, at least six were local preachers.[88] So, at mid-twentieth century local preaching was still relatively well supported by national lay leaders with business backgrounds.

---

87 The difference between these figures and those in Table 8.10 of my *Capitalists and Christians* is explained by the present extension of the definition of business to include people in agriculture and professionals (excluding medical and educational professionals).

88 See Jeremy, *Capitalists and Christians*, p. 338 for 1935 and 1955, figures which have been marginally updated. My identification of local preachers among the 1955 lay leaders has been made from *The Methodist Local Preachers' Who's Who, 1934* (London: Shaw Publishing Co., 1934); *Whos's Who in Methodism, 1933* (London: Methodist Times and Leader, 1933); and *Who's Who in the Free Churches, 1951* (London: Shaw Publishing Co., 1951).

Appendix 2
Businessmen as preachers among Wesleyan and Methodist 'workhorses' 1907, 1935 and 1955

Sector	1907 Workhorses No. %	1907 Preachers No. %	1935 Workhorses No. %	1935 Preachers No. %	1955 Workhorses No. %	1955 Preachers No. %
Agriculture	1 1.3%					
Mining	2 2.6%					
Manufacturing						
food	1 1.3%		3 7.0%		1 4.3%	1 16.7%
petroleum	1 1.3%					
chemicals	4 5.3%	1 3.1%	1 2.3%			
metals	4 5.3%	2 6.3%	2 4.7%	1 7.1%	1 4.3%	1 16.7%
engineering	1 1.3%		1 2.3%	1 7.1%		
textiles	11 14.5%	7 21.9%	2 4.7%		1 4.3%	
leather	3 3.9%	2 6.3%	1 2.3%			
glass	1 1.3%					
timber	1 1.3%	1 3.1%				
paper	1 1.3%		1 2.3%			
other	1 1.3%					
Construction	2 2.6%	1 3.1%	2 4.7%			
Transport			1 2.3%	1 7.1%		
shipping	3 3.9%					
railways	2 2.6%	1 3.1%			1 4.3%	1 16.7%
Distribution						
wholesale	4 5.3%	2 6.3%	7 16.3%	4 28.6%		
retail	4 5.3%	2 6.3%	1 2.3%	1 7.1%		
Finance	6 7.9%	1 3.1%	10 23.3%	5 35.7%	5 21.7%	1 16.7%
Professions						
group 1	12 15.8%	5 15.6%	3 7.0%	1 7.1%	5 21.7%	2 33.3%
group 2	5 6.6%	4 12.5%	4 9.3%		4 17.4%	
(medics & educators)						
Public administration	2 2.6%	2 6.3%	1 2.3%		1 4.3%	
Trade unions	1 1.3%	1 3.1%				
Housewife					4 17.4%	
Unknown	3 3.9%		3 7.0%			
TOTALS	76 100%	32 100%	43 100%	14 100%	23 100%	6 100%

Preachers among workhorses (%)	42%	33%	26%
Businessmen among workhorses	65 86%	35 81%	14 61%
Businessmen preachers among workhorses	25 33%	14 33%	6 26%

CHAPTER 16

Britain, World History, Christianity and the Millennium

Keith G. Robbins

I

In his 1971 Rede Lecture at Cambridge University, given towards the close of his career as a historian, Herbert Butterfield wondered about the transmission of wisdom in human affairs. Instancing a variety of episodes, he noted how one generation reversed the assumptions of its predecessor, sometimes in a salutary, sometimes in a harmful manner. His reflections on 'The Discontinuities between the Generations' particularly focused on the transmission of political experience but are more generally applicable.[1] He recognized the difficulties in defining the span of a 'generation', but nevertheless believed there had been clear instances in the past where the 'spirit of the age' discernibly shifted, as one set of men (and it usually was *men*) of a particular cohort yielded 'hegemony' to another. A new generation might well not be uniform in its beliefs and actions but its members often felt that the experiences through which they passed, the influences which played upon them, and the events to which they reacted, gave individuals a sense of proprietorship over 'Our Generation'.[2] 'In time', however, fresh faces appeared and a new generation made its mark.

It seems particularly pertinent, therefore, to pursue the passage of time in an essay composed at the millennium, when the significance of time present and time past has received at least some attention. It also seems

---

1   Herbert Butterfield, *The Discontinuities between the Generations in History: Their Effect on the Transmission of Political Experience* (Cambridge: Cambridge University Press, 1972).

2   Noel Annan, *Our Age* (London: Weidenfeld & Nicolson, 1990), is a classic piece of such 'generational' writing.

appropriate as a contribution to a *Festschrift*, itself a genre which pays tribute to a scholarly life when it reaches a particular maturity. It is also, in this instance, a scholarly life which has been balanced by activity, in various ecclesiastical contexts, which has been local, national and global. This essay, therefore, seeks to explore some of the 'discontinuities between the generations' in half a century of British history. It is, of course, an exploration in contemporary history and cannot therefore escape a certain autobiographical element. John Briggs and this author do belong to the same generation and our paths have crossed unpredictably over four decades in various contexts. Despite many 'overlaps' in our careers, however, no exact correspondence in opinion or involvement should be assumed. It would be surprising, however, if this assessment of 'reception' and 'transmission' struck no chord with him.

I was conceived in a Britain at peace and born in a Britain at war. My arrival, on the day Hitler invaded Norway, and with the fall of France a mere month away, showed a certain maternal sense of timing. To be born on 9 April 1940 was indeed to be brought into a world 'between the times'. Life frequently spent nocturnally in an air raid shelter in an English city—Bristol—was not naturally conducive to infant speculation on the nature of Christian civilization and the prospects for its survival.[3] The generation that ran the British world war, however, was not that of my Baptist parents, and even my Baptist grandparents were all younger than the two war-time British Prime Ministers. Insofar as the concept of 'Christian civilization' could be politically prayed in aid of the British war effort, it was one which struck a chord with that generation which had come to maturity at the height of the British Empire. It is likely that the Christian denunciation of the degradation or savagery of extra-European societies, commonplace throughout the nineteenth century, had buttressed and justified 'the imperial mission'.[4] Although Mr Churchill was never exposed to Sunday School, and formed his imperial impressions at first hand, his sense that he had not become the King's First Minister to preside over the liquidation of the British Empire fitted

---

3   Keith Robbins, 'Britain, 1940 and "Christian Civilization"', in Derek Beales and Geoffrey Best (eds.), *History, Society and the Churches: Essays in Honour of Owen Chadwick* (Cambridge: Cambridge University Press, 1985), pp. 279-300; Malcolm Smith, *Britain and 1940: History, Myth and Popular Memory* (London: Routledge, 2000); David Reynolds, '1940: Fulcrum of the 20th century', *International Affairs* 66 (1990), pp. 325-50.

4   Andrew Porter, 'Religion and Empire', in Andrew Porter (ed.), *The Oxford History of the British Empire: The Nineteenth Century* (Oxford: Oxford University Press, 1999), p. 240.

neatly with his public commitment to the survival of Christian civilization.[5]

The tangled strands of Churchill's thinking and the adoption of 'Christian civilization' caused some problems for the churches in the Second World War. On the one hand, there was little or no desire to break the unity of the nation. If war was ever justified—and only a small but articulate minority thought that, from a Christian perspective, it could never be justified—this war was justified. On the other hand, the generation of men in positions of church leadership had long repented of the exuberant nationalism to which they had succumbed in their youth or which they accused their parents of having succumbed to.

In October 1939, in an article in *Theology*, William Temple recognized that the war would be likely to intensify a sense of divergence between older and younger theologians, and he sought to occupy a mediating position: 'We are not fighting for Christianity', he wrote, 'that must always be both wrong and futile. But we are fighting to maintain an order of society which gives free course to the Christian gospel and offers a hope of advance towards a truly Christian civilization.'[6] There was much that was admirable in the British Empire but it was quite wrong to speak of some parts of the earth as 'belonging to' Great Britain. The British Government had a solemn obligation to train the indigenous peoples towards self-government as members of the family of civilized peoples. He held to the view, however, as he wrote elsewhere at this time, that 'We are Christians, we are also Englishmen; and both by God's appointment. By creation and Providence we are citizens of a nation with its own history and traditions.' Christians had to act as citizens of this nation and take a share in all that it did.[7] Nonconformists were not quite sure that they as fully shared in that nation as Temple felt he did, and this time they did not have a kind of Baptist to lead it, but the archbishop's general stance was well-received by them. It was an outlook, however which could only have emerged, in its developed form, from the global vision which had captured many of his generation over the previous two decades. As J.H. Oldham put it in his 1935 preparatory booklet for the Oxford conference to be held two years later, the relationships between church,

---

5   It was in India that Churchill read Winwood Reade's *The Martyrdom of Man* (1872) and came to the conclusion that when the great laws of Nature had been fully understood Christianity could be dispensed with. For the moment, however, 'religious toys' could be tolerated. He let his former Harrow headmaster, who had become Bishop of Calcutta, know that Christian missions were a bad thing. Keith Robbins, *Churchill* (London: Longman, 1992), pp. 17-18. See also Maurice Cowling, *Religion and Public Doctrine in Modern England* (Cambridge: Cambridge University Press, 1980), p. 312.

6   William Temple, *The Hope of a New World* (London: Macmillan, 1940), pp. 87-88.

7   William Temple, *Thoughts in War-Time* (London: SCM Press, 1940), p. 8.

community and state was 'a world issue'.[8] And, looking back on that conference in 1940, he believed that in the consciousness of Christians there was a real unity and, moreover, that unity was world-wide: the church was indeed a universal fellowship.[9]

The Provisional Committee of the World Council of Churches assembled at Geneva in February 1946 for its first meeting after the World War. Now that 'peace' of a kind had returned, it was time to take stock and plan afresh.[10] Temple himself had not lived long enough to see how far that universality to which he aspired had been realized. Enthusiasm was reinforced by the belief, as some council members had expressed it in 1942, that it had been 'possible in the midst of this world war not merely to continue our ecumenical work, but even in many respects to broaden and intensify it'.[11] In the Cathedral in Geneva on 20 February, therefore, Bishop Berggrav (Norway) and Pastor Martin Niemöller (Germany) celebrated the miracle of their meeting and declared that the *Una Sancta* was no mere luxury but would form for the future an indispensable part of their faith.

There had been preparatory meetings in New York and London in the spring of 1945 but at that time it had not been possible to be certain whether what Visser't Hooft referred to as 'a truly representative meeting' would prove possible. There had been no such meeting since 1940. It had only been in various geographical clusters—the USA, Britain and Europe (Geneva)—that members of the Provisional Committee had managed to meet. A certain amount of cohesion had been maintained during the war but it could scarcely be claimed that it had been a 'world council' in effective operation. So, it was by no means easy to decide what a 'representative meeting' of a body with aspirations to universality might actually be in 1945–46. To judge by its composition, the 'world' of the Provisional Committee of the World

---

8 J.H. Oldham, *Church, Community and State: A World Issue* (London, SCM Press, 1935).

9 Temple, *Thoughts in War-Time*, pp. 46-50.

10 The sketch by W.A. Visser't Hooft in Ruth Rouse and Stephen Neill (eds.), *A History of the Ecumenical Movement 1517–1948* (London: SPCK, 1954), pp. 708-13, is still a useful summary, though a great deal more material is now available: P.W. Ludlow, 'The International Protestant Community in the Second World War', *Journal of Ecclesiastical History* 29.3 (1978), pp. 311-62; Keith Robbins, 'Protestant Churches and the Question of Peace', in M.Vaïsse, (ed.), *Le Pacifisme en Europe des années 1920 aux années 1950* (Brussels: Bruylant, 1993), pp. 223-35; and the entry on 'Religion', which I contributed, with others, in I.C.B. Dear, (ed.), *The Oxford Companion to the Second World War* (Oxford: Oxford University Press, 1995), pp. 937-44.

11 The comment is reported by W.A. Visser't Hooft, who had been General Secretary of the 'World Council of Churches (in process of formation)' since 1938, in his introduction to W.A. Visser't Hooft (ed.), *The World Council of Churches, its Process of Formation* (Geneva: World Council of Churches, 1946), pp. 11-12.

Council was in practice a small one. There were five Presidents—a Frenchman (M. Boegner), a Swede (Archbishop Eidem), an Englishman (Archbishop Fisher) a London-based Greek (Archbishop Germanos) and an American (J.R. Mott). Just over half of the members came from the English-speaking world (nine Americans, eight Britons, two Canadians) together with one Norwegian, one Dutchman, one Swede, one Greek, one French-based Russian, one Dane, one Hungarian, one Yugoslav, one Frenchman, one Swiss and two Germans. Such a pattern of membership was scarcely surprising. It was very similar to the composition of the various meetings of 'Life and Work' and 'Faith and Order' in the inter-war period out of which the World Council sprang. Eurocentricity was obvious, though the 1938 Tambaram international missionary conference in India had offered a rather different perspective.[12]

Even so, in 1946, it was perhaps a somewhat narrow base from which to address 'the world' after the war. There was indeed recognition that a new world order was emerging, but few grasped the speed with which it would come into being and the extent to which, in turn, that new order would disturb the 'world' of the Euro–Americans who formed the World Council. The intellectual climate, understandably, was set by the formidable minds whose preoccupations stemmed from the political, cultural and theological crises of Euro–America up to and through the war—such names as Karl Barth, Emil Brunner, Jacques Ellul, Reinhold Niebuhr, Paul Tillich and others. Already, however, particularly for British members, the global signs of the times were evident. For example, Sir Stafford Cripps, earlier in his career a pillar of the World Alliance for International Friendship through the Churches but now a Labour government minister, was in India again in 1946 seeking a settlement on the basis of which the *Raj* would come to an end.[13] He failed, but a year later it did come to an end. Some European powers might still seek to reassert themselves in South-East Asia—France in Indo-China and the Netherlands in the East Indies—but if so they would have a fight on their hands.

There was some debate as to whether it was a sensible thing to send a message to 'the world'. At one point, it looked as though the members of the drafting committee had only reached one clear decision, namely to decide neither for nor against speaking to the world. The Archbishop of

---

12 Darril Hudson, *The Ecumenical Movement and World Affairs* (London: Weidenfeld & Nicolson, 1969), pp. 162-65.

13 Simon Burgess, *Stafford Cripps: A Political Life* (London: Victor Gollancz, 1999), pp. 36-41 and 206-15. I have an assessment of Cripps forthcoming in Kevin Jefferys (ed.) *Labour Leaders* (London: I.B.Tauris, 2002). Reinhold Niebuhr was on close terms with Cripps, as he was with Wedgwood Benn and his Oxford undergraduate son Anthony. Ursula M. Niebuhr, (ed.), *Remembering Reinhold Niebuhr: Letters of Reinhold & Ursula M. Niebuhr* (San Francisco: HarperCollins, 1991), pp. 192 and 229-30.

Canterbury sensed that this was not an adequate position to adopt, though he was adamant that the council should in no way pretend to be 'the voice of the church'. Representatives could not commit the churches to which they individually belonged. A statement from the World Council would merely have such authority as the weight of what was said conferred upon it. Dr Hendrik Kraemer, however, argued strongly that people in the church and outside were looking for a strong lead. In the end, on 23 February 1946, a 'message' was adopted. It expressed the view that the world stood poised between life and death. A lasting peace, it argued, could only be built on true spiritual foundations. The Five Great Powers were called upon to unite their whole strength in promoting the development of 'a world community of free peoples'. For their part, the churches had to help the nations choose the way of life. Christians were called to a ministry of reconciliation.[14]

It was avowedly a prophetic statement rather than a political programme. Apart from an endorsement of the United Nations, no specific proposals for international order were endorsed. A Commission on International Affairs would subsequently address ways in which world order might be strengthened. It was further resolved that the First Assembly of the World Council would meet in 1948, probably in the Netherlands. Themes for future discussion were identified and they were gathered together under the title *Man's Disorder and God's Design* when the assembly did meet which, in the event, it did in Amsterdam in August–September 1948.[15] There was then to be a bitter irony in the fact that in the months that followed the Dutch massed their forces in the East Indies for what was intended as a decisive blow against Indonesian republicans.

Four weighty volumes, contributed to by forty men and two women, all of whom were Euro–Americans with the exception of three Indians, were prepared for the Amsterdam conference. The tone of the tomes was set by Henry P. van Dusen when he wrote in his general introduction that 'The World Council of Churches has come into being at a moment of peril for all mankind which is without precedent in the whole of human history.' Frustration and fear, he observed, had gripped the minds of men and women.[16] The 1946 message had indicated that the time for a change of direction was short. Man's triumph in the release of atomic energy

---

14 Visser't Hooft (ed.), *World Council of Churches, its Process of Formation*, pp. 46-48 and 70-73.

15 Niebuhr was very conscious of the difference in the accents of Anglo–Saxon and continental religious thought, differences which could 'hardly be bridged', Niebuhr, (ed.), *Remembering*, p. 262.

16 H.P. van Dusen (ed.), *The Church and the Disorder of Society: An Ecumenical Study prepared under the Auspices of the World Council of Churches* (London: SCM Press, 1948), p. 9.

threatened his destruction. World history might well come to an end. There was also a recognition, however, that the churches had little to be smug about. It was not sufficient to pontificate on the need to build 'on true spiritual foundations' if the churches themselves could not, in some fashion, be reconciled with each other and offer this illustration to the world. There were indeed signs of penitence, hope and reconciliation. Visser't Hooft had long recognized that the restoration of Christian fellowship with Germany would be a key test for the nascent World Council. After 1918 it had taken some years before steps could be taken; that should not happen again. Deep issues of guilt and responsibility had to be wrestled with in an atmosphere of mingled suspicion and goodwill. The World Council had sent a strong delegation which participated in the 'Stuttgart Declaration' of the Evangelical Church in Germany in October 1945. In consequence, as John Conway puts it, German Protestantism was 'launched on a new path of ecumenical encounter and international involvement'.[17]

Ten years after the Amsterdam assembly, as an eighteen year old Baptist impending Oxford historian undergraduate, I made my first foreign foray on a long train journey through northern Germany to Berlin to attend a substantial conference of the European Baptist Federation at which one of the speakers was Martin Niemöller. I was not aware at the time that this was in itself something of an act of reconciliation. I moved on to Zeist in the Netherlands. At the conference centre where I stayed—itself the scene of earlier ecumenical gatherings—I found and dipped into the substantial volumes prepared in connection with the 1937 Oxford conference on Church, Community and State. Two summers later, somewhat to my amazement, I found myself in possession of a full set of these volumes, together with other material, given to me by the President of my college (Magdalen), the art historian T.S.R. Boase, who, to my surprise, had acted as conference secretary at the above conference. He had learnt that I was attending the July 1960 Ecumenical Youth Assembly in Europe held in Lausanne. It was a gathering addressed by some of the 'senior' ecumenical figures, such as Visser't Hooft whom I had hitherto only read about in books.

The mood, however, was somewhat different from that of the immediate post-war years—though the generation represented at the conference was scarcely aware of the extent to which the decade that was to follow would be so iconoclastic.[18] 'There is no future for the Church which is just the "spiritual aroma" of a traditionally Christian civilization', Visser't Hooft declared. One suddenly became aware of

---

17 John Conway, 'How Shall the Nations Repent? The Stuttgart Declaration of Guilt, October 1945', *Journal of Ecclesiastical History* 38.4 (1987), p. 619.

18 A. Marwick, *The Sixties: Cultural Transformation in Britain, France, Italy and the United States 1958–74* (Oxford: Oxford University Press, 1999).

one's age (twenty) and that one was probably present at a turning point. A new generation would have new and different challenges and opportunities: it was a new world which was opening up before us. In a sense, until the early sixties, the debates of 1933-45 about 'Church, Community and State' were being continued, often with the same participants, though this time in the context of the Cold War. Substitute 'Communism' for 'National Socialism' and many of the arguments of the earlier period were reiterated. Was there a 'Third Way', a system which was neither communist nor capitalist? What was totalitarianism? And, given the existence of the 'Iron Curtain' through the heart of Europe, it was inevitable that the 'Christian agenda' in the modern world should still focus so sharply on Europe. 'Christian democracy' in its various manifestations had come to Western Europe.[19] 'Christian civilization' and 'Christian Europe' were terms falling frequently from papal lips. Was 'Christian-Communist dialogue really possible? Did Christianity require religious freedom as an absolute? Some contemporaries pointed to the dangers in identifying the fate of Christianity with the success of American foreign policy. Others pointed to the perils if Christians allowed themselves to become 'fronts' for Soviet policy objectives in Europe.[20] All these issues were present in young minds in Lausanne (particularly when they were addressed on these matters by Tom Driberg, MP, no less), but, even so, a shift of attention could be detected. The Indian, M.M. Thomas, told us that Europe and the European churches had to adjust themselves to the diminished place that they would have in the world. Europe as the home of Christendom was dead. That was a fitting prelude to the New Delhi conference which was to be held in 1961. As one scholar remarks: 'European ecumenism became global in the 1960s, even if it was shaped still by the continuing Cold War between the Soviet Union with its allies and the West.'[21]

---

19 M.P. Fogarty, *Christian Democracy in Western Europe 1820-1953* (London: Routledge and Kegan Paul, 1957), is an account written close to the period and itself reveals something about the mood of the period.

20 These issues are discussed, in an Anglo-American context, by D. Kirby, 'Divinely Sanctioned: The Anglo-American Cold War Alliance and the Defence of Western Civilization and Christianity, 1945-48', *Journal of Contemporary History* 35.3 (July, 2000), pp. 385-412, and D. Kirby, *Church, State and Propaganda: The Archbishop of York and International Relations: A Political Study of Cyril Forster Garbett, 1942-55* (Hull: Hull University Press, 1999). The major new volume by Gerhard Besier, Armin Boyens and Gerhard Lindemann, *Nationaler Protestantismus und Ökumenische Bewegung: Kirchliches Handeln im Kalten Krieg (1945-1990)* (Berlin: Duncker & Humblot, 1999), throws valuable light on controversial issues.

21 Nicholas Hope 'The Iron Curtain and its Repercussions for the Churches in Europe', *Kirchliche Zeitgeschichte* (Heft 2/1999), pp. 426-40.

II

Forty years on, celebrating the millennium in Britain, it is very evident that the 'world' that has just been outlined, in which John Briggs and this author were raised, has indeed 'passed on'. Church historians writing around this time struggled to begin the process of historiographical adjustment, to try to think 'globally' about Christianity. It remains difficult, however, to escape from an Eurocentric perspective which thinks first of that continent and then, and still somewhat peripherally, moves on to consider 'expansion' elsewhere.[22] It remains an enormous task to try to achieve a satisfying account of what Adrian Hastings referred to as 'the most specifically international dimensions of modern Christian history'. He states what he regards as a 'primary truth', namely, 'that the writing of Christian history needs to escape imprisonment within a Europe-centred story in order not only to serve the needs of the many hundred of millions of Christians who live elsewhere but also to provide an objectively balanced account of a straightforward historical kind of something which has for long been seen in too Eurocentric a way'.[23]

It is, of course, a revaluation not only made necessary by what the world has become but also by what 'Britain' has become over the decades since the 1960s, decades which, at the millennium, have raised questions about Christianity and British identity in ways that would scarcely have been conceivable even in 1945.[24] On the one hand, it is argued that 'secularization' should be seen as something that has become rampant since the 1960s rather than a process that has been going on for a much longer period of time, an argument which, if it is accepted, gives recent decades a distinctive characteristic.[25] On the other, while the global

---

22 In the writings, for example, of Stephen Neill, Kenneth Scott Latourette and Jaroslav Pelikan. Short assessments and relevant bibliographies of their work and that of others can be found in Michael Baumann and Martin Klauber (eds.), *Historians of the Christian Tradition: Their Methodology and Influence on Western Thought* (Nashville, TN: Broadman & Holman, 1995), by Richard V. Pierard pp. 531-49, Richard W. Pointer pp. 411-30, and W. David Buschart pp. 551-77 respectively. It was anxiety on the score of 'Eurocentricity' in relation to the *Oxford Illustrated History of Christianity* which led the South African Oxonian Peter Hinchliff to embark on a volume, edited after his death by Adrian Hastings, which appeared under the title *A World History of Christianity* (London: Cassell, 1999).

23 Hastings (ed.), *A World History of Christianity*, p. 5.

24 Keith Robbins, *The World since 1945: A Concise History* (Oxford: Oxford University Press, 1998), and *Great Britain: Identities, Institutions and the Idea of Britishness* (London: Longman, 1998) pp. 334-36.

25 Callum Brown, *The Secularization of Britain* (London: Routledge, 2000); J.Wolffe, *God and Greater Britain: Religion and National Life in Britain and Ireland 1843–1945* (London: Routledge, 1994), pp. 262-64, speculates briefly on the extent to

nature of Christianity has become ever more apparent, so 'world religions' have come to Britain.[26]

It is the combination of all these factors that has rendered the recognition of the millennium in contemporary Britain so problematic. It is an event that relates very specifically and very directly to Christianity. As such, therefore, one might think that it should only engage the attention of Christians (though one must admit that Christians have themselves have had some difficulty with calendars!). Indeed, the churches did mark the millennium (leaving aside the question of whether they jumped the gun) 'in their own domain' in various ways. They did contrive to have more exposure on television and radio in relation to the millennium than is now customarily allocated to them. Somewhat surprisingly, the Archbishop of Canterbury's millennial message was brought before its readers by the *News of the World*. The millennium 'Resolution' was broadcast at ten minutes to midnight as the New Year approached.

However, Christians did not 'celebrate' on their own—though whatever it was that non-Christians were celebrating might be thought problematic. Very many bodies in one way or another 'observed' the millennium and made it the occasion for some form of event, project or entertainment— 'the Dome' being the most conspicuous example. The *national* attention to the millennium is perhaps explicable in that it coincides with a period of uncertainty and anxiety about 'Britain'. Paradoxically the national use of the millennium has been to demonstrate the inclusiveness of 'multi-faith' Britain rather than an opportunity to emphasize 'Christian Britain'.[27] This also reflects the fact that the millennium has even been

---

which the loss of the imperial framework for British unity opened the door to more secular and more uncompromising expressions of nationhood. Peter Smith, 'Anglo-American religion and hegemonic change in the world system c.1870–1980', *British Journal of Sociology* 37.1 (1987), pp. 94-105, speculates, from a sociological perspective, on the way in which a sense of national dominance (or decline) coincides with or is reinforced by 'religious florescence' (or collapse).

26   See the two volumes edited by Gerald Parsons, *The Growth of Religious Diversity: Britain from 1945* (2 vols; London: Routledge, 1994). The contributors to John L. Esposito and Michael Watson (eds.), *Religion and Global Order* (Cardiff: University of Wales Press, 2000), explore religious transnationalism from a variety of perspectives.

27   The 'Millennium Section' of *The Times*, 1 January 2000 contained, amongst its many contributions, nothing which reflected on the religious significance or insignificance of what was being celebrated. Elsewhere in the paper its religious correspondent, Ruth Gledhill, carried a report (p. 3) on events up and down the country under the banner 'Blairs join Royal Family in prayers for a new era'. She noted that the Prince of Wales was strategically located in St Giles' Cathedral, Edinburgh, and remarked that 'Even some non-Christian religious communities marked the date change', though

seen as a commercial opportunity in countries which have little Christian past or present but which have felt obliged to produce items for the 'millennium global market'. In this sense, the second millennium, in a way that was certainly not true of the first, has become a 'world history date'. The remainder of this essay will explore some aspects of the British millennium celebrations in the light of these considerations.

III

At one level, it may be merely the fact of the passage of a thousand years which has excited the public. The desire to mark the passage of time, and the ability to do this in a variety of ways, appears to be universal. Arguably, therefore, what has been primarily present in the British public mind is simply the fact that a thousand years have passed. That in turn has caused a certain reflection on the nature of time. Archbishop Ussher in his *Annales Veteris et Novi Testamenti* (1650–54) famously produced his chronology of scripture. He fixed the date of creation, with agreeable precision, at 4004 BC. In such a perspective, of course, a span of a thousand years is significant. If, however, we suppose that it was about 100,000 years ago that scattered packs of modern kinds of man were to be found in Africa and perhaps Asia as well, one thousand years is less significant. The notion of 'one thousand years' appears to have an almost irresistible appeal to politicians. It was in 1962 that the Labour leader, Hugh Gaitskell, declared that for Britain membership of the 'Common Market' would mean 'the end of Britain as an independent nation-state, the end of a thousand years of history'. In 1996 John Major told the Conservative party conference that Labour's constitutional plans, by which he meant devolution, 'would vandalise nearly 1,000 years of British history'. Whether 'Britain' has even existed for one thousand years as a nation-state might be a reasonable question to ask. Certainly, in the event, there was very little disposition to celebrate 'one thousand years of the British state' in the year 2000.

A millennium, one might think, primarily offers various possibilities within a Christian framework. The main body of Christian tradition has not endorsed millenarianism, but that perspective has had its advocates from the earliest Christian centuries. Some have anticipated a thousand-year reign of the saints before the return of Christ, some have anticipated it immediately after. It was the French revolution which made premillennial Adventism much less tenable in British evangelical circles. Millenarian enthusiasms have often been supposed to have arisen in

---

only gave as an instance the participation of a Liberal Jewish Rabbi in a hospital service alongside an Anglican clergyman and a Roman Catholic priest.

periods of great social change or crisis—and to have an appeal to marginal or excluded social groups. That view, however, is only a generalization. It was a wealthy banker, Henry Drummond, who expressed the view in his *Dialogues on Prophecy* (1828) that the existing Christian dispensation would not pass 'insensibly into the millennial state by gradual increase of the preaching of the Gospel' but would be terminated by what he called 'judgements' which would culminate in the destruction of the visible church and its polity. He believed that the judgements would fall principally, if not exclusively, upon 'Christendom'. They would be succeeded by a period of universal blessedness to all mankind. During the time that the judgements were falling, the Jews would be restored to their own land.[28] There were, not surprisingly, some groups who had expectation of high cosmic activity at the 1999–2000 millennium but, in contrast to previous dates when millenarian expectations have been high, the millennium does not appear to have stimulated very strong millenarian expectations.

Leaving millenarianism aside, however, the relationship of Christianity to time, and to particular events in time, has arguably been problematic throughout its history. Over the last two centuries, to summarize boldly, there have been many attempts both to write a 'Life of Jesus', on the one hand, and to deny that such a thing is either possible or desirable, on the other. For some theologians, Christianity, as they interpret it, does not rest upon 'the historical Jesus'. Paul Tillich, for example, took the view that Christology was entirely independent of the problems of historical enquiry. For others, however, it is the extent to which Christianity is 'a historical religion', rooted in the picture presented in the Gospel narratives, which gives it its distinctive character. Events occurring at a particular point in time have fundamental significance.[29]

This central, but unresolved, issue in the understanding of Christianity, too simply though it has been stated above, naturally has a deep bearing on the significance attached to 1,000 years of 'British Christian history'. On one analysis, now the predominant one, what has happened over the past 1,000 years is the transformation of a 'Christian society' into a secular one. If so, it hardly seems appropriate to be 'celebrating'—one might be thought to be present at a wake. A.N. Wilson is not the only writer to have forecast that by the middle of the twenty-first century Christianity in Britain will be close to extinction, if not already extinct. An interpretation that paints a picture of a transition from 'Christian society' to 'secular society' certainly cannot be dismissed out of hand.

---

28   C.G. Flegg, *'Gathered under Apostles': A Study of the Catholic Apostolic Church* (Oxford: Oxford University Press, 1992), pp. 38-39.

29   Margaret F. Brearley, 'Jewish and Christian Concepts of Time and Modern Anti-Judaism: Ousting the God of Time', in Diana Wood (ed.), *Christianity and Judaism* (Studies in Church History, 29; Oxford: Blackwell, 1992), pp. 481-93.

Yet there are various reasons why that presentation seems too simple to be an altogether convincing interpretation. Do we really move in linear fashion from 'Christian Saxons' in AD 1000 to the 'non-Christian British' in AD 2000? In present circumstances, it is perhaps not surprising that there has been renewed interest in what Peter Brown called in his 1992 Raleigh Lecture before the British Academy, 'The Problem of Christianization'.[30] His concern in that lecture was to go more deeply into the process of conversion and examine what was entailed in the 'end of paganism'—something that is generally supposed to have taken place in the relatively short period from the conversion of Constantine in 312 to the death of Theodosius II in 450. He is very interested in the passionate monotheism of Augustine of Hippo. Brown writes that we are most likely inclined to suppose that christianization must have been 'a slow, heroic struggle on earth against the unyielding, protean weight of an unconverted ancient world', fourth- and fifth-century Christians might have seen conversion as a stunning and supernatural victory over pagan gods. And, to take the story forward, he suggests that an ancient pagan past lay close to the heart of medieval Christendom.[31] The French historian Jean Delumeau will not use the term 'Christendom' and goes so far as to suggest that the attempt to make medieval society 'Christian' was a failure. It has also been suggested, in similar vein, that the supposed 'Christendom' of 1500 was in fact more akin to 'mission country'. Paganism may have been forced back between the sixteenth and eighteenth centuries—but even then far from completely. Delumeau comes to the conclusion that the antithesis between a past when 'the God of the Christians' was alive and the present when that God is dead is unconvincing.[32] The 'conversion' of Europe, Richard Fletcher has recently argued, must be seen as a multi-faceted affair in which 'Calculation and hesitation, diplomatic nicety, considerations of Realpolitik, greed, self-promotion, the hard-nosed search for political advantage' must all be taken into account. He concedes, however, that an impious age may be particularly attracted to the presence of these factors in 'conversion'. The general point, however, is that 'the Christian centuries' in Europe amply displayed an indifference and/or ignorance of 'Christian truth'. Fletcher cites, to give but one example, a parochial visitation in Saxony in 1584 which found the parishioners 'completely ignorant...they drink brandy all day long on Sundays and are unmoved

---

30 J.N. Hillgarth (ed.), *Christianity and Paganism 350–750: The Conversion of Western Europe* (Philadelphia: University of Pennsylvania Press, 1986).
31 P.R.L. Brown, 'The Problem of Christianization', *Proceedings of the British Academy* 82 (1993), pp. 89-106.
32 J. Delumeau, *Christianisme va-t-il mourir?* (Paris: Hachette, 1977), pp. 26 and 84. See also A. Wessels, *Europe: Was it Ever Really Christian?* (London: SCM Press, 1994).

by warnings and punishments'.[33] And this was well before the advent of television.

The issues raised by these scholars lead us to grapple again with 'the essence of Christianity'. How much can be assimilated? What must be rejected? Is there an orthodoxy? For some, it scarcely needs to be said, 'Christianity' entails a clear body of belief, thought and practice and can be so identified from its very beginnings. Such a Christianity can be clearly defined and authoritatively interpreted—and its 'rise' or 'fall' can be objectively measured. For others, however, there is not, and never has been, 'the Christian tradition' but rather a variety of Christian traditions. The issue of how much 'unity' requires 'uniformity' has been perennial and the staple of ecumenical encounter.[34] One distinguished liturgical scholar has recently argued, and he is of course not alone, that primitive Christianity was essentially diverse in character. In relation to the eucharist, for example, he argues that only gradually over time and then never completely, did standardization of practice and understanding develop.[35] If, however, we are at all persuaded that Christianity is always in evolution, its capacity to change, even in relation to matters sometimes thought to be 'unchangeable', may yet surprise. In other words, any understanding of global Christianity must be intrinsically ecumenical but also inescapably diverse as it both penetrates and is penetrated by the societies and cultures in which it exists. Viewed from this perspective, the millennium is only a tedious date in a sequence of other dates. It is neither the end of an era nor the beginning of another. We might put the implications of this contention in certain propositions.

First, there has never been a time when Christianity has been dominant throughout the world, though it has come to be more globally present than any other religious faith. Its adherents, however they are defined, have sometimes been in a majority within some societies and some cultures but in others have always been minorities. Its intertwining with the history of Britain has been fundamental but it has also been exceptional. That dominance has now come to an end even though it remains the case that in two of the territories of the present United Kingdom the state still gives to two of the many Christian churches a degree of 'established' recognition. It is arguably still too early to judge what will be the impact of these changes on the self-definition of both

---

33   R. Fletcher, *The Conversion of Europe: From Paganism to Christianity 371–1386 AD* (London: HarperCollins, 1997), pp. 509 and 521.

34   D.M. Thompson, 'The Unity of the Church in Twentieth-Century England: Pleasing Dream or Common Calling?', in R.N. Swanson (ed.), *Unity and Diversity in the Church* (Studies in Church History, 32; Oxford: Blackwell, 1996), pp. 507-31.

35   P.F. Bradshaw, 'Early Christian Eucharistic Practice', in R.N. Swanson (ed.), *Continuity and Change in Christian Worship* (Studies in Church History, 35; Woodbridge: Boydell & Brewer, 1999), p. 17.

Britons and Christians. Butterfield in his Riddell Lectures on *Christianity in European History*, delivered half a century ago, thought that it was the case then that the people of England were still living more than they knew on 'old capital', on what were in fact concealed Christian assumptions.[36] That may still be the case, but if so, taking society as a whole, it may not last much longer. From Butterfield's perspective, however, their minority position, and perhaps increasing distance from positions of power, should not cause Christians much despondency. 'Christian principles' had been as much abused as honoured when Christians had been in power in church and state and had exercised dominion over their fellow human beings. Christianity, he believed, should seek to achieve human solidarity in a world of free personalities by a voluntary love which carried personality to a still higher power.

Second, in Britain itself, whatever may be Christianity's future, it is evident that it can no longer be the only religious voice in a secular society. It is a commonplace to remark that there are more Moslems in Britain than Methodists. A contributor writing on 'The New Millennium through Muslim Eyes' thought that Christianity could no longer provide the religious dynamic which modern Britain required. In his view, it was enshrined 'in the canons of the long bygone Roman empire' and would lose its foundation when trying to adapt to modern times. Islam did not have the problem of a priesthood elite.[37] The relationship between Christianity and Islam in Britain in the twenty-first century is likely to be of critical importance. One can see circumstances in which 'the three monotheistic faiths'—Christianity, Islam and Judaism—can come together in mutual respect and make common cause against some of the dominant forces in contemporary British society (to put it negatively). It is, however, not possible to be altogether sanguine in this regard and it is not inconceivable that tensions evident in Egypt, Indonesia or the Philippines may even appear in Britain. The place of Islam in the life of a country which has a Christian heritage raises complex and unresolved issues.[38]

Third, if active Christians constitute a minority in British society, a society which is generally religiously indifferent but one which contains powerful opponents of all religion, the new millennium appears likely to be very different from the one which has now passed. What 'core values' a state can seek to enshrine in legislation or encourage within its funded institutions becomes highly problematic. The continuity of a millennium of 'British Christian history' may have little guidance to offer. It

---

36 H. Butterfield, *Christianity in European History* (London: Collins, 1952), p. 61.
37 *Q News: The Muslim Magazine* (December, 1999), pp. 24-25.
38 Keith Ward, *Religion and Community* (Oxford: Oxford University Press, 2000); Will Kymlicka, *Multicultural Citizenship* (Oxford: Oxford University Press, 1995).

becomes increasingly pertinent to study the history of other societies hitherto thought alien for a greater understanding of the process of accommodation and differentiation in 'secular' but 'plural' societies.

Finally, the new millennium appears likely to be one in which the centre of gravity in Christianity shifts away from the European-centred traditions in which it has been encased. The historical centres of European ecclesiastical traditions—Rome, Geneva, Canterbury—look likely to have a diminishing real weight even if formal power and control can still to an extent be exercised. It scarcely needs to be said that however formative Christianity has been in the shaping of European history, it was not European in its roots. Its first two millennia may, therefore, be but prelude to a very different future. Andrew Porter has also noted, in relation to the nineteenth century, that for missionaries 'experimentation and adaptation to local conditions were inevitable, in language, liturgy, and church organization. As they occurred, the extent to which a 'British' metropolitan religious culture was being exported, let alone imposed, became increasingly attenuated'.[39] In the twenty-first century, it may become necessary, indeed may become unavoidable, for Christians in Britain to distance themselves from the Christian heritage and ecclesiastical landscape which still exists as an aspect of 'Britishness' and to see themselves, rather, in a possibly uncomfortable and unpalatable way, as the local embodiments of a truly global and ecumenical faith—and one in which, for a time at least, dynamism lies elsewhere. Although it has often been so used, religion should not be the bond of a tribe or a nation.[40]

---

39 Porter, *British Empire*, p. 245.
40 Hans Küng and Helmut Schmidt (eds.), *A Global Ethic and Global Responsibilities* (London: SCM Press, 1998).

Select Publications of John H.Y. Briggs

1969
'Image and Appearance: Some Sources for the History of Nineteenth Century Nonconformity', *Baptist Quarterly* 23.1 (January) and 23.2 (February), pp. 14-31 and 59-72

'The Nature of Explanation in History', *Faith and Thought: The Journal of the Victoria Institute* 97.3, pp. 37-50

Biographical entries in E. Lousse and J. de Launay (eds.), *Dictionnaire d'Histoire Contemporaine* (Lausanne: Editions Recontre), pp. 182-83, 297, 392, 455-56

1970
'Church, Clergy and Society in Victorian Britain', *Baptist Quarterly* 23.5 (January), pp. 223-33

'Recent Contributions to Free Church History', *Baptist Quarterly* 33.6 (April), pp. 283-84

'Religious Education: The Victorian Controversy', *Spectrum* 2.2, p. 58

1972
A Hundred Years and More: Baptists in Newcastle-under-Lyme (Newcastle-under-Lyme: Newcastle-under-Lyme Baptist Church)

1973
Editor and contributor, *Newcastle-under-Lyme, 1173–1973* (Newcastle-under-Lyme: Newcastle Borough Council, 2nd edn, 1979)

With I. Sellars, *Victorian Nonconformity* (Documents of Modern History; London: Edward Arnold)

'Captain John Garland, James Cokayne and the Staffordshire Baptists: A Note', *Baptist Quarterly* 25.4 (October), pp. 164-66

1974

'The Burning of the Meeting House, July 1715: Dissent and Faction in Late Stuart Newcastle', *North Staffordshire Journal of Field Studies* 14, pp. 61-79

'Consolidated in the Faith', *The Fraternal* 171 (September), pp. 6-12

1977

Consultant editor with D.F. Wright and R.D. Linder, and contributor, *The History of Christianity* (Tring: Lion Publishing, 2nd edn 1991)

1978

Freedom: A Baptist View (London: Baptist Publications)

St George's, Newcastle: A Parish History (Newcastle-under-Lyme: St George's Parish Church Council)

1979

'From Christendom to Pluralism', in D.F. Wright (ed.), *Essays in Evangelical Social Ethics* (Exeter: Paternoster), pp. 59-81

'Self-Help and Social Discipline in Victorian England', *Hungarian Studies in English* (January)

1982

A History of Longton: Volume I. The Birth of a Community (Keele: University of Keele Adult Education Department, 2nd edn 1983, republished by Three Counties Publishing, 1999)

1984

'Vancouver Experience', *The Fraternal* 206 (January), pp. 3-9

1985

Editor *et al, Christianity: A World Faith* (Oxford: Lion Publishing, reissued as *The Quiet Revolution*, 1989)

'William Edward Harrison (1875–1937), colliery owner', 'Sir Alfred Seale Haslam (1844–1927), manufacturer of refrigeration equipment', Robert Heath II (1816–1893) coal and iron master', 'Robert Heath III (1851–1932), Sir James Heath (1852–1942) and Arthur H. Heath (1856–1930), colliery owners and ironmasters', in D.J. Jeremy and C. Shaw (eds.), *Dictionary of Business Biography* (6 vols; London: Butterworths, 1984-86), III, pp. 87-89, 105-109, 142-45, 145-48

Extended Review, J. Cox, *The English Churches in Secular Society*, and D.W. Bebbington, *The Nonconformist Conscience*, in *Victorian Studies* 28.3, pp. 546-48

1986
'Charles Haddon Spurgeon and the Baptist Denomination in Nineteenth Century Britain', *Baptist Quarterly* 31.5 (January), pp. 218-40

'She-Preachers, Widows and Other Women. The Feminine Dimension in Baptist Life Since 1600', *Baptist Quarterly* 31.7 (July), pp. 337-52

1987
Editor, *Faith, Heritage and Witness: A Supplement to the Baptist Quarterly Published in Honour of Dr. W.M.S. West, President, Bristol Baptist College, 1871-1987* (London: Baptist Historical Society), including 'Double Affirmations: Baptists since 1945', pp. 60-64

'The Revd. B. Vale, A Staffordshire Clergyman', in P. Morgan (ed.), *Staffordshire Studies: Essays Presented to Denis Stuart* (Keele: Keele University, Department of Adult Education), pp. 140-53

1988
'The Radical Saints of Shelton: The Ridgway Family, Methodist Pottery Manufacturers', in D.J. Jeremy (ed.), *Business and Religion in Britain* (Business History Seres, 5; Aldershot: Gower, pp. 47-71

The Radical Saints of Shelton: The Ridgway Family, Methodist Pottery Manufacturers (Keele: the Author) [expanded version of previous entry]

'The Baptists', 'Pottery and Pottery Workers', 'The Religious Press', 'Ragged Schools', 'Social Darwinism', 'Sunday Schools' and 'Theology', in S. Mitchell (ed.), *Victorian Britain: An Encyclopaedia* (Garland Reference Library of Social Science, 438; New York: Garland), pp. 66-67, 621-23, 632-33, 661-62, 729-30, 772-73 and 801-803

1989
With G.F. Nuttall, *Dissent in Birmingham, 1689-1989* (Birmingham: Resource Centre Productions, Carrs Lane Church Centre, 1989), including 'The Last Hundred Years: Whither Dissent', pp. 9-21

'Chapel-Goers, Chapels and Local Community', *Baptist Quarterly* 33.2 (April), pp. 53-62

1990
'Baptists and Higher Education in England' and 'Towards a Baptist Identity', in W.H. Brackney and R.J. Burke (eds.), *Faith, Life, and Witness: The Papers of the Study and Research Division of the Baptist World Alliance—1986-1990* (Birmingham, AL: Samford University Press), pp. 92-115 and 146-49

'The Visit of a Potter to Salendine Nook in 1723', *Baptist Quarterly* 33.6 (April), pp. 286-88

1991
'Evangelical Ecumenism: The Amalgamation of General and Particular Baptists in 1891', *Baptist Quarterly* 34.3 (July) and 34.4 (October), pp. 99-115 and 160-79

1993
'The Development of Industrial Specialization' and 'Urban Institutions and Administration', in A.D.M. Phillips (ed.), *The Potteries: Continuity and Change in a Staffordshire Conurbation* (Stroud: Alan Sutton), pp. 94-106 and 130-44

Contributor to F. Gumley and Brian Redhead, *Protestors for Paradise: The Story of Christian Reformers from the Thirteenth to the Twenty-First Centuries* (BBC Publications), pp. 98-118 [publication of interviews for two broadcasts]

1994
The English Baptists of the Nineteenth Century (A History of the English Baptists, 3: Didcot: Baptist Historical Society)

1995
'A. British Isles', in A. Wardin (ed.), *Baptists Around the World: A Comprehensive Handbook* (Nashville, TN: Broadman & Holman), pp. 181-86 [member of Editorial Board and Editor of Part III 'Europe and Eurasia', pp. 177-285]

'English Baptists and Their Hymnody: An Introduction', in W.H. Brackney and L.A. Cupit (eds.), *Baptist Faith and Witness: The Papers of the Study Division of the Baptist World Alliance 1990-1995* (Birmingham, AL: Samford University Press), pp. 152-59

'Orthodox and Evangelicals', *One World* 209, pp. 12-14

185 biographical entries to D.M. Lewis (ed.), *The Blackwell Dictionary of Evangelical Biography 1730-1860* (2 vols; Oxford: Blackwell)

1996
With C.J. Harrison, A.J.D. MacInnes and D.M. Vincent, *Crime and Punishment in England: An Introductory History* (London: University College of London Press)

'Local Church and Global Citizenship', in C. Deweese (ed.), *Defining Baptist Convictions: Guidelines for the Twenty-First Century* (Franklin, TN: Providence House), pp. 214-21

'Elite and Proletariat amongst Birmingham Nonconformity', in A.P.F. Sell (ed.), *Protestant Nonconformists, 'Strangers' and the West Midlands of England* (Keele: Keele University Press), pp. 71-98

1997
'Message of the Consultation' and 'A Lot In Common: Orthodox and Evangelicals Compare Notes', in H. van Beek and G. Lemopoulos (eds.), *Proclaiming Christ Today: Orthodox–Evangelical Consultation, Alexandria, July 1995* (Geneva and Syndesmos: WCC Books), pp. 11-15 and 44-48

1998
'Beyond Membership', *The Ecumenical Review* 50.3, pp. 315-20

1999
Editor with W.H. Brackney and P.S. Fiddes, *Pilgrim Pathways: Essays in Baptist History in Honour of B.R. White* (Macon, GA: Mercer University Press), including '"Active, Busy, Zealous": The Reverend Dr. Cox of Hackney', pp. 223-41

'Politics and the Pulpit: Robert Hall and the "Signs of the Times"', in A. Kreider and J. Shaw (eds.), *Culture and the Nonconformist Tradition* (Cardiff: University of Wales Press), pp. 63-94

2000
Editor with F. Bowers, *Baptists Together: Papers Published in Memory of W.M.S. West, JP, MA, DTheol, Hon LLD 1922-1999* (Didcot: Baptist Historical Society), including with F. Bowers, 'Introduction', p. 1

'F.A. Cox of Hackney: Nineteenth-Century Baptist Theologian, Historian, Controversialist, and Apologist', *Baptist Quarterly* 38.8 (October), pp. 392-411

'Accra Conference (1957–58)', 'Bankok Conference (1973)', 'Commission on World Mission and Evangelism', 'Europe', 'Jerusalem Conference (1928)', 'Melbourne Conference (1980)', 'Mexico City Conference (1963)', 'San Antonio Conference (1989)', 'Tambaram Conference (1938)', 'United Kingdom' and 'World Council of Churches Conferences', in A.S. Moreau *et al* (eds.), *Evangelical Dictionary of World Missions* (Grand Rapids: Baker Books), pp. 32-33, 108, 212-13, 330-32, 516, 614, 619-20, 851, 928-29, 984-85 and 1026-27

2001
Entries in M.J. Walsh (ed.), *Dictionary of Christian Biography* (London: Continuum)

2001
'Differences between Evangelicalism and the Orthodox Church' [uncredited], in *Evangelicalism and the Orthodox Church* (Carlisle: Paternoster) [responsible for the original text]

Forthcoming

'Samuel Drew', 'John Howard Hinton', 'William Medley' and 'T. Vincent Tymms', in W.J. Mander and A.P.F. Sell (eds.), *Dictionary of Nineteenth-Century British Philosophers* (2 vols; Bristol: Thoemmes Press, 2002)

'Nonconformists and the Pottery Industry', in D.W. Bebbington and T. Larsen (eds.), *Modern Christianity and Cultural Aspirations* (Sheffield: Sheffield Academic Press, 2003)

'John Clifford (1836–1923)', 'Alexander McLaren [or Maclaren] (1826–1910)', 'Baptist Wriothesley Noel (1798–1873' and 'John Ryland (1753–1825)', in T. Larsen (ed.), *Biographical Dictionary of Evangelicals* (Leicester: IVP, 2003)

Editor with G. Tsetsis and M. Odoyoye, *History of the Ecumenical Movement. Volume 3* (Geneva: WCC Publications, 2003) author of final chapter

Contributing a chapter to R.V. Pierard (ed.), *History of the Baptist World Alliance* (2005)

With D. Thompson and J. Munsey Turner, *Twentieth-Century Volume of Nonconformist Texts* (Edinburgh: Edinburgh University Press)

With C. Scouteris, drafting the 'Report of the Special Commission on Relations of the World Council of Churches with the Orthodox'

Professor Briggs has written extensively in weeklies and monthlies, broadcasted, contributed various entries and revised numerous entries for the *Dictionary of National Biography*, written many book reviews and editorials, the latter particularly in the *Baptist Quarterly* since he took up its editorship in 1985.

Index

Acton, Lord 219
Adorian, Constantin 294
Advisory Committee on Church Relations 12
Advisory Council on Missionary Strategy 106-107
African Instituted (or Independent) Churches 118
Ah Sou, L.T. 94
Albrecht, Karl 298
Alexander, Cecil Frances 263
Alf, Gottfried 290, 291
Alleine, Richard 63
Ambrose 256
American (Northern) Baptists 149-74
American Baptist Churches in the USA 170, 171, 173
American Baptist Convention 165, 170
American Baptist Foreign Mission Society 93, 99, 165,
American Baptist Historical Society 157, 158, 159, 166
American Baptist Home Mission Society 151, 160, 161
American Baptist Missionary Board 287
American Baptist Missionary Union 295
American Baptists 36, 93, 94
American Protestantism 149, 153, 155
American Revolution 266, 272, 279
Amey, Basil 11
Anabaptists 31, 179,
Anderson, Christopher 269, 270
Androutsos, Christos 128
Anglican communion 114
Anglican Consultative Council 107
Anglicanism 61
Anglicans 62, 63, 117, 278
Anglo–Catholics 90, 97, 98, 99
anti-sacramentalism 187
antinomianism 57, 64, 230
apostasy 239-41,
Apostolic Fathers 62, 120
Aquinas, Thomas 179
Arminianism 55

Arminians 277
Armstrong, George 314
Asbury, Francis 265
asceticism 231, 232, 234, 235
Athanasius 123
Atkinson, Moses 317
atonement 134, 140
Augustine 143, 338
Austrian Baptists 291
Azariah, Anbu 101, 102
Azariah, V.S. 78, 87, 91, 95, 100, 101

Bainbridge, Thomas Hudson 304, 306, 308, 309, 315, 316, 318, 319
Balogh, Lajos 292
Baltic Baptist Association 299
Baltic Baptists 298
Bamford-Slack, John 317
Banyard, James 266
baptism 23-49, 52, 115, 120, 123, 124, 132, 138, 141, 142, 148, 175-89, 271, 273, 275, 282, 283, 286, 290, 292, 295, 296, 297, 298, 299, 300
baptism in the Holy Spirit 180-81, 296
Baptism, Eucharist and Ministry 23, 29, 30, 31, 32, 33, 46, 179, 180
Baptist Board, The 267, 278
Baptist confessions 32, 41, 121, 122, 126, 127, 134, 135, 141, 145, 146, 150, 183, 187, 289
Baptist Historical Society xxi, 5, 8, 12, 17
Baptist Home Missionary Society 274
Baptist Men's Movement 11
Baptist Missionary Society 93, 99, 269, 270, 279
Baptist Quarterly xxi, 7, 12
Baptist Students' Federation 3
Baptist Union of Great Britain xxi, 11, 12, 14, 26, 28, 48, 136, 178, 270, 271
Baptist World Alliance Heritage Commission xxi, 13, 14
Baptist World Alliance xxi, 3, 7, 12, 13, 14, 18, 107, 109, 111, 281

Baptist World Congress 33
Baptists xi, xxi, 2, 3, 5, 7, 10, 11, 14, 17, 24, 28, 29, 30, 31, 32, 33, 34, 36, 41, 42, 47, 48, 91, 93, 94, 120, 121, 122, 149-74, 175, 176, 178, 182, 184, 185, 188, 208, 214, 219, 220, 221, 267, 268, 272, 273, 274, 275, 277, 278, 279, 280, 281-301, 327, 328
Barbour, Thomas 99
Barde, Edouard 77
Barker, Joseph 267
Barth, Karl 143, 201, 204, 330
Baxter, Richard 63, 195
Beach, Bert 116
Beasley-Murray, George R. 48
Bebbington, David 5, 6, 8
Bede 257
Bell, George 199, 203
Bentley, Edward Clerihew 196
Bentley, Eljee 13, 14, 18
Berggrav, Bishop 329
Bernard of Clairvaux 257
Berridge, John 66
Bethge, Eberhard 203, 204, 206
Beveridge, William 63
Bianco of Siena 259
Bible Christians 322, 323
Bible Training Institute, Glasgow 92
Binder Nikolaus 283
Binfield, Clyde 3, 4, 6, 9, 16
biography 193-207
Bitton, W. Nelson 91, 92, 94, 95, 99
Black, Don 14
Bliss, Kathleen 202
Boase, T.S.R. 332
Boegner, M. 330
Böhler, Peter 56
Bonhoeffer, Dietrich 194, 199, 202-206, 215
Bonomelli, Geremia 90
Booth, Abraham 278
Boswell, James 195-96, 203
Bottoms, Ruth 31
Bourignon, Antoinette 62
Bourne, Moses 306, 307, 315
Bowers, Faith 13, 18
Boyd, Mrs William (Corabel Tarr) 83
Bramwell, John 304
Brethren 32
Bridges, Robert 255, 261

Briggs, John H.Y. xi-xix, xxi, 1-20, 23, 29, 121, 149, 208, 281, 327, 334
Briggs, Joyce 3, 4, 17
Bristol Academy (Bristol Baptist College) 272
British and Foreign Bible Society 291, 292, 295
British Council of Churches xxi
Brown, Arthur 92
Brown, Ken 276
Brown, Peter 338
Brown, Raymond 2, 3
Brunhilde of Spain 256
Brunner, Emil 201, 330
Buckendahl, Ernst 282
Bulgarian Baptists 294, 295
Bunting, Jabez 266
Bunyan, John 142, 183, 195
Burls, William 269
Busfield, Carolyn 4, 5, 6, 20
Butterfield, Herbert 326, 340
Byford, C.T. 292

Cabasilas, Nicholas 132
Caedmon 257
Calamy, Edmund 63
Calvin, John 70, 120, 141, 143, 146
Calvinism 34, 55, 64, 65, 126, 127, 134, 145, 260, 288
Calvinistic Methodists 55
Calvinists 53, 54, 260, 275, 277
Cambridge Inter-Collegiate Christian Union 2
Campbell, Alexander 149, 153, 158, 161, 172, 265
Campbell, R.J. 311, 312
Campbell, Thomas 150, 151
Campbellites 268
Campbell–Stone movement 157
Camphor, Alexander 91
Carey, William 36, 89, 197, 269
catechesis 36, 37, 41
catechumenate 185
Catholic mysticism 63, 64
Cave, William 63
Celestino, Pedro 71
Cennick, John 56
Centre for the Study of Baptist History and Heritage xxi
Champness, Thomas 308
charismatic renewal 222
Chatsworth Baptist Church 1

Index 353

Chaucer, Geoffrey 195
Chesterton, G.K. 263
Chiba, Yugoru 94
children and the church 178, 185, 186, 187
China Inland Mission 99
Ching-yi, Ch'eng (Cheng Jingyi) 92, 93, 94
Chiu, Moses 92
Christ Church Congregational Church, London 1
Christian Conference of Asia 113
Christian perfection 57, 59, 60
Christian Social Union 262-63
Christian World Communions 117
Christianity 326-41
christology 37, 40, 48, 53, 119, 122, 123, 124, 125, 128, 132, 239, 249, 253, 277
Chrysostom, John 139
Church Missionary Society 93
Church of Christ in China 92
Church of England 24, 30, 63, 66, 67, 97, 98, 260, 261, 266, 278
Church of Scotland 154, 274
Church of the Brethren 116
church membership 47, 182, 183, 186, 187
Church, Community and State conference 332, 333
Churches Together in England xxi, 16, 30
Churchill, Winston 327, 328
Clarke, Elizabeth Peacock 293
Clement of Rome 61, 62
Clements, Keith W. 33, 35, 36
Cliff College 317, 318
Clifford, John 197
Coates, James Calvert 315
Coffey, David 29
Coleman, Siôr 11
Collingwood, R.G. 199
Collins, Samuel 276
Commission for Inter-Church Aid, Refugees, and World Service 116
Commission of the Churches on International Affairs 116
Commission on World Mission and Evangelism 116
common baptism 26, 30, 46, 178, 182
Conference of Secretaries of Christian World Communions 113, 117, 118, 119

Confessing Church 203
confirmation 26, 187-88
Congregationalism 265,
Congregationalists 5, 101, 104, 295, 311
Constantine 338
Continental Society, The 282
conversion 43, 44, 45, 54, 142, 148, 181, 183, 282
Conway, John 332
Cook, Gaines 169
Cook, Jean-Paul 76
Cook, Thomas 78
Council of Churches for Britain and Ireand 12
covenant 24, 42, 122, 126, 127, 128, 129, 145, 146, 147, 148, 213
Cowper, William 261
Cox, F.A. 269, 270
credobaptists 32
creeds 32, 33, 34, 35, 36, 37, 38, 39, 40, 41, 42, 47, 48, 53, 55, 116, 253
Cripps, Stafford 330
Crusade for a Christian World [Order] 166, 168
Cunliffe, William 316
Cyprian 38
Cyril of Alexandria 123
Czech Baptists 291

Dahl, Nils A. 40
Dahlberg, Edwin 165
damnation 58
Danish Baptists 284, 285, 287, 288
Datta, S.K. 79, 87
Davey, William John 318
Davidson, Randall 203
Davies, W. Jones 313
de Liefde, Jan 288
de Molinos, Miguel 62, 63
de Neui, Peter Johannes 289
Decade of Decision 166, 169
Degroot, Alfred T. 156
deification 123, 124, 130, 132, 136, 138, 139, 140, 143, 144, 148
Delumeau, Jean 338
Delyakov, Jakov 296
democratization 265-80
DePuy, Norman R. 170
des Pres, Josquin 259
di Todi, Jacopone 259
Dilthey, Wilhelm 199

Disciples Ecumenical Consultative Council of the Christian Church–Disciples of Christ 107, 111
Disciples of Christ (Churches of Christ) 32, 265, 268, 149-74
Disciples of Christ Historical Society 157
discipleship 184, 185, 186, 187, 188
Disraeli, Benjamin 194
Dissent 272
Dissenters 54, 146, 260, 261, 273, 274
doctrinal disagreements 241-52
Doddridge, Philip 261
Double, Isaac 276
Douglas, David 272
Dow, Lorenzo 266
Downing, George 66
Driberg, Tom 333
Druminkov, Grigor B. 294
Drummond, Henry 337
Duckworth, James 306, 307, 316, 319
Dunant, Henry 76
Dunn, James D.G. 40, 43, 180, 181, 182, 183, 186
Dunnavant, Anthony 172
Dutch Baptists 288
Dutch Reformed Church 288

early church 35, 36
East Asian Christian Conference 113, 114
ecclesiality 150, 164-69
ecclesiology xviii, 24-29, 30, 42-43, 45, 46, 47, 48, 75, 120-48, 175, 176, 177, 178, 179, 183, 184, 185
Eclectic Society 278
Ecumenical Methodist Conferences 107
ecumenical pragmatism 35, 47
ecumenism xi-xviii, xxi, 5, 10, 12, 15, 16, 23-49, 50, 69-88, 90, 106-19, 122, 131, 133, 175, 176, 178, 179, 180, 182, 194, 252, 329, 332
Eddy, G. Sherwood 78, 101, 102
Eggington, Peter 4
Eidem, Archbishop 330
eighteenth-century revival 52, 55
election 52, 58
Eliou, Prof. 84
Ellis, Christopher J. 45
Ellul, Jacques 330
Emerson, Ralph Waldo 194
encyclopaeadianism 195

enthusiasm 265,
Ephrem the Syrian 139
Episcopalians 158
episcopacy 29
establishment 266
Estonian Baptists 300
eucharist 23, 24, 25, 26, 27, 29, 31, 45, 46, 47, 115, 123, 125, 129, 130, 131, 140, 148, 182
European Baptist Federation 332
Evangelical Alliance 74, 76
Evangelical Church in Germany 332
Evangelical Revival 272, 277, 279
evangelicalism xiv-xvi, 50, 53, 55, 75, 76, 84, 121, 279, 336
evangelicals xi, xiv-xvi, xxi, 48, 60, 67, 89, 97, 119, 266, 289
evangelism 103, 285
Evans, Caleb 272
excommunication 247-49

Faith and Order 23, 24, 29, 32, 115, 116, 118, 330
faith 184, 188
Fawcett, John 277
Federal Council of Churches of Christ 154
Feisser, Johannes Elias 288
Fermaud, Charles 78
Fetter Lane Society 52, 57
Fey, Harold 107
Fiddes, Paul S. 26, 188
Field, Clive 305
Fiers, A. Dale 169, 172
Fifth Monarchy Men 267
final perseverence 58
Findlay, W.H. 95
Finney, Charles 274
Fisher, Archbishop Geoffrey 330
Flagellants 258
Flavel, John 63
Fletcher, Richard 338
Florovsky, Georges 120
Foreign Mission Committee of the Church of Scotland 93
Foreign Mission Committee of the United Free Church of Scotland 93
Fortunatus, Venantius 256
Foster, Henry 278
Francis of Assisi 258
Free (will) Baptists 154
Free Church Council 16
Free Churches Group xxi, 16

Index

Free Churches xxi, 7, 16
freedom of God 176-77, 186
Freethinking Christians, The 267
French Revolution 266
Friends World Committee for Consultation 107, 111
Fries, Karl 80, 81, 86, 87
Fuller, Andrew 89, 145, 268, 269, 270, 272, 279

Gadsby, William 272
Gairdner, Temple 91, 94, 101
Gaitskell, Hugh 336
Garfield, James A. 158, 163
Garnett, Jane 319
Garrison, J.H. 153
Garrison, Winfred E. 156
Gaskell, Elizabeth 196
Gelder, Alfred 304
General Baptists 32, 78, 122, 127, 134, 145, 277, 278, 279
General Conference of Seventh-day Adventists 106, 116
Gerdes, E. 288
German Baptist Union 289
German Baptists 281, 282, 283, 284, 285, 286, 287, 288, 289, 290, 291, 296, 297, 298, 299, 300, 301
German Evangelical Alliance 286
Germanos, Archbishop 330
Gertners, Adam 299
Gesuati 259
Ghose, S. 93
Giardini, Denise 205
Gladstone, J.H. 87
Glazener, Mary 205
Gnosticism 39
Gomme, Andor 3, 4, 5
Goodwin, Thomas 63
Gore, Charles 90, 97, 262
grace 53, 58, 132, 138, 142, 144, 147, 148, 177, 179, 182, 184, 185, 186
Graham, Billy 222
Greek Catholic Church 84
Greek Orthodox Church 116
Green, George 311, 312, 313, 314
Green, Joseph 273
Greeves, Frederic 308
Gregory of Nazianzus 143,
Gregory of Nyssa 62, 123, 144
Grey, Edward 198
Gusdorff, Jahannes 282
Gutteridge, Joseph 269

Guttery, Arthur T. 313
Guyon, Madame 63

Haag, Anton 289
Hall, Robert 271
Hamburg Baptist Seminary 284, 293, 294, 295, 297
Handy, Robert T. 151
Harnisch, I. 289
Harris, Howell 58, 59, 60
Hartley College, Manchester 313
Hartley, William Pickles 309, 310, 314, 315, 318, 319
Hastings, Adrian 334
Hatch, Nathan 265, 266, 267, 268, 271, 272, 274, 275, 278, 279
Heap, Charles 317, 319
Heber, Bishop 262
Hegel, G.W.F. 204
Heidegger, Martin 204
hell 65
Herbert of Cherbury, Edward, Lord 195
Herbert, George 260
heresy 244,
Heringer, Martin 295
Herrmann, Julius 300
high Calvinism 53, 64, 271
Highgate Baptist Church, Birmingham 11
Hill, Richard 62
Hilton, Stephen 306, 313
Hinchcliff, Peter 334
Hinrichs, J.L. 291
Hinson, E. Glenn 35, 41, 42
Hinton, J.H. 271, 272
Hinton, James 269
Hippolytus 38
history 193-207
history, local church 208-24
Hodge, J.Z. 102
Hoekendijk, J.C. 103
Hogg, W.R. 200
holiness 53, 63, 64, 66, 67
Holland, Henry Scott 262
Holy Spirit 26, 38, 44, 45, 46, 125-26, 142, 143, 145, 177, 179, 180, 181, 184, 186, 187, 188, 225, 226, 227, 228, 242, 315
Hopkins, John 260
Horneck, Antony 55
Hosmer, Frederick 263
Howe, John 63
Huison, Robert 304

Humiliati 257
Hungarian Baptists 292
Huss, Jan 260
Hutchinson, Lucy 195
Hutton, James 57
hymns 254-64, 265, 285

Ignatius 62
immersion 38, 289, 296, 298, 300
immoral behaviour 225-31
inadvisable behaviour 231-35
incarnation 53,
independency 271
independent churches xiv, xvi
Independents 275
Indian Decennial Missionary Conference, Madras, 1902 96
individualism 177, 187
indulgences 62
infant baptism 26, 30, 31, 35, 179, 180, 185, 186, 187, 282, 288, 289, 298, 300
infant presentation 30
initiation 31, 37, 43, 44, 181, 184
Inter-Varsity Fellowship 4, 5
International Baptist Theological Seminary, Prague 13
International Congregational Council 106, 111
International Convention of the Disciples of Christ 156
International Missionary Council 200, 201, 202
International Old Catholic Bishops' Conference 116
Irenaeus 38
irresistable grace 58
Islam 340
Ivanov-Klyshnikov, Vasilii V. 297
Ives, Eric 2, 4, 6, 12, 16
Ivimey, Joseph 269, 270

James Stokes Society 71
Japanese Baptists 94
Jekabsens, Frizis 299
Jesus Christ xiii, 26, 27, 40, 72, 126, 127, 128, 132, 133, 140, 147, 177, 182, 188, 212
Joachim di Fiore 258
John of Patmos 251-52
John Paul II, Pope (Karol Wojtyla) 202
Johnson, Lyndon B. 158
Johnson, Samuel 195, 196, 203, 263

Jones, Keith 13, 17
Jones, Rufus 200
Joseph Rank Benevolent Trusts 71
Judaism 340
Jude 230-31, 252
justification by faith 53, 54, 59, 66, 67, 140, 141, 143
Justin Martyr 38

Kalweit, Martin 296
Kargel, Ivan G. 295, 297
Keach, Benjamin 145, 146, 147, 148
Kelly, J.N.D. 40, 46
Kelly, Thomas 261
Ken, Thomas 63
Kerr, George W. 152
Khomiakov, Alexis 122, 131, 132, 145
Kierkegaard, Soren 198
Kilham, Alexander 266
King, Martin Luther 87
kingdom of God 104
Kinnaird, Lord 99
Kipling, Rudyard 262
Klauck, H.-J. 226
Klundt, Jacob 295
Köbner, Julius 283, 284, 285, 287, 288
Kornya, Mihály 292-93
Kraemer, Hendrik 331
Kruger, Heinrich 282
Krummacher, F.W. 286
Kucdov, Stefan 294

Laget, Emile 84, 86
Laidlaw, John 308
Lambeth Appeal 48
Lambeth Conference 106
landmarkism 150
Lang, Diedrich 282
Langdon, William Chauncy 76
Lange, Henriette 282
Larsen, Marius 287
latitudinarianism 52
Latourette, Kenneth Scott 334
Latvian Baptists 299, 300
Lausanne Committee xv
laying on of hands 277-78
Lehmann, Gottfried W. 284, 285, 286, 292
Lehmann, Joseph 286, 292
Lenwood, Frank 104
liberty 266

Liebig, August 294
Life and Work Movement 80, 201, 330
Limbert, Paul 73, 74, 87
Lincoln, Abraham 197
Lithuanian Baptists 298
Littledale, R.F. 259
Local Preachers' Mutual Aid Association 317, 318
London Board of Protestant Dissenting Ministers 278
London Missionary Society 91, 92, 93, 94, 104
Long, R.A. 167
Longridge, Michael 303
Lord's Supper 36, 187, 271
Lossky, Vladimir 121, 123, 124, 125, 126, 138, 139, 143, 144, 145
Louisville Plan 152, 153, 155, 162
Lowell, James Russell 262
Lucas, Margaret 195
Luke, St 226, 238
Lund Principle 25
Lund-Quist, Carl E. 111
Luther, Martin 179, 205, 222, 260
Lutheran Church 24, 286, 290, 299, 300
Lutheran World Federation 107, 108, 109, 111, 114
Lutheranism 57, 140
Lutherans 108, 283, 286, 294, 296

Macarius of Egypt 62, 144
MacDonald, James Ramsey 87
Mackay, Donald 101
Mackay, John A. 109, 110
Mackay, Tomas 13
Maclaren, Alexander 33
Maclennan, Kenneth 95
Madsen, Roy 165
Magic Methodists 266
Maier, Friedrich 289
Major, John 336
Malamud, Bernard 197
Malcolm, Howard 158,
Marcheff, Vasil 295
Martin of Tours 256
martyrology 212-23
maryolatry 62
Mass 260
Mathes, James 152
Matthew, St 229-30, 252
Maximus the Confessor 124, 144
Mays, Benjamin Elijah 87

McBee, Silas 90
McConaughy Jr, David 85, 86
McLean, Archibald 268
McLeannites 269
McNeill, William 319
Mead, Sidney 154
Men and Millions Movement 166, 167, 168
Mennonite World Conference 107, 116
Mennonites 32, 288, 291, 298
Methodism 52, 60, 265, 266, 302, 304, 305, 317, 318, 319, 323
Methodist Church 24, 30, 308, 323
Methodist New Connexion 266, 267, 311, 312, 322, 323
Methodist Societies 50, 54
Methodists 7, 55-56, 58, 60, 67, 76, 158, 275, 277, 279, 282, 303, 305, 307, 308, 309, 323, 324, 340
Metropolitan Tabernacle 1, 284
Meyendorff, John 38, 39
Meyer, F.B. 197, 286
Meyer, Harding 113
Meyer, Heinrich 292
Milburn, Geoffrey 303
Millard, Edward 291, 294
millenarianism 336, 337
millennium 254, 326, 334, 335, 336, 337, 339, 340
Mills, W.H. 86
ministry 23, 25, 26, 45, 46, 47, 115, 178, 182, 184
Misselbrook, Lewis 222
mission 35, 36, 37, 103, 113, 178, 218, 281-301
missionary societies 90
Miyoshi, Taizo 79
Molokons (milk-drinkers) 296
Molther, Philip 57
Moltmann, Jürgen 104, 175
monastic orders 257, 258
Mönster, Peder 286, 287
Montgomery, H.H. 97
Moore, William T. 152
Moravians 52, 54, 56, 57, 58, 67, 261, 285
More, Thomas 195, 205
Morehouse, Henry L. 151
Mormons 265
Morse, Richard C. 80
Moslems 340
Mott, John R. 70, 71, 80, 81, 84, 85, 87, 92, 94, 95, 98, 102, 200, 330

Neale, J.M. 261
Neill, Stephen 334
Nelson, Reuben E. 165
New Connexion of General Baptists 267, 277, 278, 279
New Theology 309, 313
Newman, William 269, 270
Newton, John 66, 261
Niebuhr, Reinhold 330
Niebuhr, Richard 154
Niemöller, Martin 329, 332
Nilsson, Frederick O. 287
Nonconformists 310, 328
Nonconformity 314
Northamptonshire Baptist Association 269
Northern Baptist Association 275
Northern Baptist Convention 151, 161, 165
Northern Evangelical Society 275
Novak, Anton 292

Oldham, J.H. 78, 79, 87, 91, 92, 93, 94, 95, 97, 98, 99, 194, 200, 201, 202, 328
Oldham, Mary 95
Oncken, Augusta 293
Oncken, J.G. 281, 282, 283, 284, 285, 286, 287, 288, 289, 291, 292, 293, 294, 297, 300
Oncken, Sarah 282
open membership 30
open membership churches 183
ordinance 187
Oriental Orthodox Church 116
Origen 38
original sin 51, 53, 54, 66, 67
Orthodox Church xvi, xxi, 15, 24, 82, 84, 90, 98, 111, 117, 120, 132, 148, 296, 297, 301
Orthodoxy xiii, xv, xvi, xvii, 121, 122, 123, 126, 128, 130, 131, 132, 135, 136, 137, 138, 139, 140, 141, 143, 144, 145, 148
Osborn, Ronald 172
Owen, John 64

Paddon, John 273
Palamas, Gregory 123
papal infalliblity 62
Particular Baptist Fund 268
Particular Baptists 122, 127, 142, 145, 183, 267, 268, 269, 271, 276, 278

Pashkov, Colonel 295
Patrick, Simon 63
Patrick, St 257
Paul, St 48, 54, 133, 181, 223, 227-29, 232-33, 234, 235-37, 238, 241-44, 246, 252, 253
Pavlov, Vasilii G. 297, 298
Payne, Ernest A. 270
Peake, Arthur Samuel 309, 310, 312, 313, 315
Peck, John Mason 158
Peculiar People of Essex, The 266
Pelikan, Jaroslav 39, 334
penal substitution 141,
Pentecostal churches 182,
Pentecostal World Conference 107
Pentecostalism xiv, xv, xvi
Pentecostals 24, 32, 116
Pericles 195
Perks, Robert 318, 319
personality clashes 235-39
Peter, St 27, 225, 226
Petrick, P.E. 295
Phillips, Thomas W. 157
Pilli, Toivo 300
Plutarch 194
Polish Baptists 289, 290, 291
Polycarp 62
Pontifical Secretariat (Council) for Promoting Christian Unity 116
Pope, The 25, 27, 116, 202, 257
Porter, Andrew 341
preaching 302-25
predestination 52, 55, 56, 59, 60
premillennial Adventism 336
Presbyterian Board of Foreign Missions 92
Presbyterians 158
Price, Thomas 272
priesthood of all believers 304
Priestley, Jack 16
Primitive Baptists 272
Primitive Methodist Missionary Society 309
Primitive Methodists 266, 267, 303, 304, 306, 309, 310, 311, 312, 313, 314, 315, 318, 319, 321, 323
Princeton Theological Seminary 109
proselytism 99
Protestant missions 99
Protestantism xvi, xvii, 75, 76, 77, 103, 121, 141, 260, 289, 300
Protestants 41, 47, 54, 65, 66, 70, 297

Prudentius, Aurelius Clemens 255
purgatory 62
Puritan Commonwealth 272
Puritanism 271
Puritans 62, 63, 64, 272

Race, George 304
Radegrunde, Lady 256
Radical Reformation 32, 121
Rangiah, John 91, 93
Rank, J. Arthur 318
Rank, Joseph 318, 319
Ratushnyi, Mikhail 298
Ratzinger, Joseph 25, 27, 29, 31, 32
Rauch, Karl 291
Reay, Lord 101
rebaptism 30, 31, 179
reconciliation 140, 141
redemption 54
Reformation, The 257, 260
Reformed Church in the USA 73
Reformed churches 282
Reformed Ecumenical Council 107, 116
Reformed tradition 41
Regent's Park College, Oxford xxi, 7, 12, 17
religious liberty 116
reprobation 64
restorationists 24, 32
revival 266
revivalism 266, 274
righteousness 57, 141
Riobashapka, Ivan G. 298
Ritson, John 313
Robbins, Keith G. 198
Robert Hall Society 2, 3
Robson, George 95
Rockerfeller, John D. 151
Rogerson, Barry 15
Romaine, William 66
Roman Catholic Church 24, 25, 26, 27, 28, 32, 63, 71, 84, 90, 111, 112, 116, 132, 261
Roman Catholicism 103, 121, 289, 291, 301
Roman Catholics 41, 47, 48, 53, 54, 62, 64, 65, 66, 70, 98, 99, 158
Romanian Baptists 293, 294
Roncalli, Angelo (Pope John XXIII) 90
Roper, William 195
Rosman, Doreen 4, 9, 11, 17, 18
Rothwell, David 18
Rottmayer, Johann 292, 294

Rouse, Ruth 82
Rousseau, J.-J. 70
Rowbotham, Thomas 317, 319
rules of faith 37, 38
Rumbergs, Jekabs 300
Runciman, Walter 304
Rushbrooke, J.H. 290, 300
Russell, David S. 11, 31
Russian Baptists 294, 296-98
Russian Orthodox 116
Ryland, John 269
Rylands, John 310
Rylands, Mrs Enriqueta Augustina 310

sacramentalism 176, 177, 181, 187, 188
sacraments 24, 33, 35, 44, 72, 123, 128, 130, 139, 142, 144, 176, 177, 186
Salimbene 258
Salvation Army 24, 32, 107, 116, 182,
salvation 27, 38, 51, 55, 72, 120-48, 165, 175, 177, 186, 187
Samartha, Stanley 103, 104
sanctification 51-52, 57, 63, 141, 143
Sandemanianism 268
Sargant, Norman Thomas Carr 307
Savage, Richard 195
Scandinavian Baptists 286
Schaff, Philip 39
Scharschmidt, Karl Johann 292, 293
Schauffler, Carl 284
Scheve, Eduard 285
Schiewe, Adam Reinhold 300
schism 249-51
Schroeder, Gustavus 287
Schwan, Johannes 300
Schwegler, Daniel 294
Schweizer, Eduard 249
Scialabba, Raul 13
Scotch Baptists 268
scripture 33
Sears, Barnas 282
Second Great Awakening 265
Selly Oak Federation 15, 16
Serampore Controversy 269-71
Seraphim of Sarov 144
Seventh-day Adventists 116
Shaftesbury, Lord 87
Shanghai Missionary Conference, 1907 96
Shaw, Henry 163,
Sherman, Charles Dunbar 87

Shirley, Walter 66
Sibbes, Richard 63
Sievers, Count 297
Sigebert 255, 256
Simms, Florence 83
Simon, Walter 5
Sirgood, John 266
slavery 273
Slovak Baptists 292
Smith, Henry Arthur 318
Smith, Joseph 265
Smith, Luther W. 165
Smith, William 303, 306, 315
Smyth, John 127, 134, 137, 147
sobornicity 125
Society for the Propagation of the Gospel 90, 93, 97
Society of Dependents, The 266
Society of Friends 24, 32, 54, 182
Socinianism 53,
Söderblom, Nathan 80, 87
Soper, Meg 3, 6
Sorabji, R.K. 93
Southcott, Joanna 267
Southern Baptist Convention 24
Southern Baptists 35, 36, 151
Southey, Robert 196
Spangenberg, August 58
Spender, Stephen 223
spiritual gifts 60, 125
spirituality 265
Spring-Rice, Cecil 262
Spurgeon's College 2, 5
Spurgeon, C.H. 1, 3, 284
St Andrews Street Baptist Church, Cambridge 2
Stamp, Josiah 318, 319
Staniloae, Dumitru 121, 125, 126, 129, 131, 132, 133, 138, 140, 141, 144, 148
Stanley, A.P. 196
Steeves, Paul 298
Stennett, Joseph 268
Stephenson, William Haswell 304, 306, 317
Sternhold, Thomas 260
Strachey, Lytton 196, 197, 204
Strict and Particular Baptists 272
Strict Baptists 271-72
Student Christian Movement 3, 69, 97
Study Commission on Denominational Structures 170, 171

Study Commission on Relationships 171
Study of Administrative Areas and Relationships 171
Stundists 298
Stuttgart Declaration 332
supplementary membership 30
Swedish Baptists 287, 288
Swiss Baptists 289
Symongs, John Addington 263

Talbot, E.S. 90
Talbot, Edward 97
Tatlow, Tissington 97
Taylor, A.J.P. 198
Taylor, Dan 277, 278, 279
Taylor, Jeremy 63
Taylor, John 53, 54
Teegarden, Kenneth L. 172
Telegu Baptist Home Missionary Society 93
Temple, William 328, 329
Tertullian 38
Thangkhan 94
Theodosius II 338
Theodulph of Orleans 257
Thomas of Celano 258
Thomas, M.M. 333
Thompson, John Day 310, 312, 314
Thompson, Philip E. 41
Thompson, Ralph Wardlaw 92, 93, 99
Thompson, Samuel 267
Thompson, Thomas 303
Thomson, Sinclair 274, 279
Tillich, Paul 330, 337
Tillotson, John 63
Toplady, Augustus 62
Torbet, Robert G. 155
Toth, Mihály 292
Tractarians 187
transubstantiation 62
Trinity 37, 38, 39, 40, 41, 42, 43, 45, 46, 47, 48, 53, 122, 123, 124, 125, 137, 140, 142, 146, 147, 177, 178, 186, 188, 189, 213, 277
Tsing-en, Tong 94
Tsymbal, Efim 298

Udvarnoki, András 292
Ullmann, Walter 219,
unconditional election 58

Index

Union of Associated Churches of Baptised Christians in Germany and Denmark 285
Unitarians 263
United Bible Societies 117
United Christian Missionary Society 156
United Methodist Church 316, 321
United Methodist Free Churches 307, 322, 323
United Reformed Church 7, 30
United Societies 55
Universalists 267
University of Birmingham 15
University of Birmingham, Westhill (formerly Westhill College) xxi, 15-16
University of Cambridge 2
University of Keele xxi, 3, 4, 5, 6, 7, 8, 9, 10, 14, 18
Upton Baptist Church, Lambeth 1
Ussher, Archbishop James 336

van der Bent, Ans J. 106
van Dusen, Henry P. 331
Vatican II 25, 27, 28
Venn, Henry 66
Venn, John 261
Vidler, Alec 89
Virgin Mary 257, 259
Vischer, Lukas 116
Visser't Hooft, W.A. 108, 111, 112, 116, 329, 332
Voltaire, F.-M.A. 70
voluntarism 34-35, 184, 213, 273
von Balthasar, Hans Urs 137
Voronin, Nikita 296, 297
Voyka, Johann 292

Waldenses 257
Waldo, Peter 257
Walker, Michael J. 268
Wallace, Alfred Russel 310
Walton, Izaak 195
Wang, C.C. 91
Ware, Kallistos 133, 141, 143, 144
Watts, Isaac 260
Wayland, Francis 150
Weigel, George 202
Weist, Wilhelm 285, 290
Wesley, Charles 52, 56, 58, 59, 60, 261

Wesley, John 50-67, 179, 196, 261, 265, 272, 275, 278, 303, 308, 312
Wesleyan Methodism 266
Wesleyan Methodist Missionary Society 93, 99
Wesleyan Methodists 55, 266, 303, 304, 305, 307, 308, 312, 314, 315, 317, 318, 319, 321, 323
Wesleyan Societies 57, 61
West, W.M.S. 33, 34, 47
Westcott, B.F. 308
Westminster Confession 127
Whitefield, George 52, 55, 56, 58, 59, 60, 66
Whitehead, Isabel 95, 101
Whitfield, Charles 275, 276, 279
Whyte, Mrs Alexander 95
Wiberg, Anders 287
Wickizer, Willard 163, 169
William Knibb Society 3
Willmer, Haddon 2, 6, 9, 11, 17, 19
Willms, H. 289
Wilson, A.N. 337
Wishard, Luther D. 80, 81, 85
World Alliance of Reformed Churches (Presbyterian and Congregational) 106
World Confessional Bodies 112
World Confessional Church Groups 112
World Confessional Families 112, 115, 117
World Confessional Groups 112
World Convention of the Churches of Christ 107, 116
World Council of Churches xi-xviii, xxi, 7, 11, 12, 15, 24, 28, 31, 47, 80, 106, 108, 109, 110, 111, 112, 113, 114, 115, 116, 117, 118, 121, 178, 202, 329-30, 331, 332
World Evangelical Alliance 116-17
World Evangelical Fellowship xv
World Methodist Council 107, 111, 114
World Missionary Conference, Edinburgh 1910 85, 89-105,
World Presbyterian Alliance 106, 109, 111
World Student Christian Federation 69, 70, 72, 80, 82, 83, 84, 85, 86, 87, 95
Worrall, B.G. 89

Yorkshire Baptist Association 11
Young Men's Christian Association 69, 70, 71, 72, 73, 74, 76, 77, 78, 79, 80, 81, 82, 83, 85, 86, 87, 95, 101
Young Women's Christian Association 69, 70, 71, 72, 82, 83, 84, 85, 86, 87

Zinzendorf, Count 56-57
Zion Baptist Church, Cambridge 2
Zizioulas, John 121, 124, 125, 126, 129, 138, 139
Zwingli, Huldrych 129